The Golden Lion

Pamela Haines was born in Yorkshire, like so many of the characters in *The Golden Lion*. Knaresborough, Leeds and Harrogate have all played a part in her family background. She was educated at a convent school in the Midlands, and then read English at Cambridge.

As a child she wrote non-stop, but around seventeen real life caught up with her and she did not write again until her late thirties, by which time she was married to a doctor and had five children. In 1971 she won the *Spectator* New Writing Prize with a short story and in 1973 completed her first novel, *Tea at Gunter's*. Acclaimed by the critics, it was joint winner of the first Yorkshire Arts Association Award for Young Writers. It was followed by *A Kind of War* in 1976, *Men on White Horses* in 1978, *The Kissing Gate* in 1981 and *The Diamond Waterfall* in 1984.

PAMELA HAINES

The Golden Lion

FONTANA/Collins

First published by William Collins Sons & Co. Ltd 1986
First issued in Fontana Paperbacks 1987

Copyright © Bluestar Productions Ltd 1986

Made and printed in Great Britain by
William Collins Sons & Co. Ltd, Glasgow

For Nick and Sue
A wedding gift

ACKNOWLEDGMENTS

Thank you very much, Marjorie Battcock, Tom Burns, Chris Ellis, Felicity Firth, Hal Haines, Tony Haines, Brian Higgins, Marjorie Sugden and Tiny Winters, for giving so generously of your time, your knowledge and your memories.

PROLOGUE

THE LUSITANIA
May 1915

A green cliff of water, towering. It rose. Higher, higher. Her hands were pressed into her bulky life-jacket. *Mamma, help me!* Seconds only and it came towards them, rearing, bringing with it bodies, debris, broken lifeboats. Nearer and nearer, higher than ever, crashing down on to the deck. Smashing into them, frothing and bubbling as it swept up her eleven-year-old body.

Her buttoned shoes were torn from her feet. Down now, down, down into the blackness. The weight of the world, of the whole ship, on her head.

Then, as suddenly, she was pushed up and up. She was fighting again. Thrashing. Up into the sea. Above the sea.

At first it was darkness. *Sacru miu Gesù – Mamma, help me!* Trying to call out. No sound. Her mouth full of water. Bodies thrashing around her. Drifting wood, chaos, moaning, weeping. Such a weeping and wailing. A man beside her, floating dead. She was with others yet utterly alone. Sunlight, high above them in the afternoon sky.

Then she heard the voice:

'Maria, *hold on, Maria.*'

And saw, coming as if from nowhere – his face. A face she knew and trusted. The face of certain rescue.

Five days ago in New York, standing amongst the crowd at Pier 54 and waiting to go on board, she had been happy. The *Lusitania*. Why, it's as tall as a hotel, she had thought. A floating hotel, six storeys high, rising out of the water.

The bustle, the clamour, people waiting to wave goodbye, hawkers selling miniature Stars and Stripes and Union Jacks – photographers, ciné-camera crews. All that noise and excitement, and I'm part of it, she'd thought proudly. The loading on: luggage and more luggage wheeled up the gangway, the scores of hat-boxes and cabin trunks piled dizzily on the trolleys. *And some of it is ours,* mine and Mamma's.

Five years ago, arriving in the States from Sicily, their possessions had come wrapped in cloth and sacking and tied with string. Now for this journey she had all these dresses and skirts and shoes, thanks to Mr and Mrs Ricciardi. Everything was thanks to the Ricciardis. 'Thank you, thank you,' she had said and so had Mamma.

But Mrs Ricciardi told them it was nothing, nothing at all. It was just so that Maria might feel at home with the other children. For they were to travel first class, as did the Ricciardis and their four children and nurse, Gina. Mamma must be near at hand always to look after the baby, Ettore. Mamma did anything Mrs Ricciardi asked. All she wanted was to please her. Maria felt the same.

Happiness was America now. It was New York and living with the Ricciardis instead of in a tenement. It was the change in their lives from when Mamma had been a kitchen helper and then done washing and sewing for Mrs Ricciardi. And from before that when Papa had been sick from a bone disease, and dying. Days of being so poor they wondered whether tomorrow would happen or who was to take care of Sicilian immigrants who fell on hard times.

The change had come about because only Mamma could stop little Ettore crying. The youngest Ricciardi child who'd cried day and night almost from birth, who refused food and grew peaky, who it seemed might die. Then one day in the nursery, Mamma had held him – and at once he had stopped. The next time, the same. For her, he smiled. For her, he gurgled. He ate, he laughed.

And it was because of that, Maria stood today with Mr Ricciardi on the promenade deck of the *Lusitania*, in her new white boots and her cream light silk coat, her dark curling hair tied up in a blue satin bow. She didn't look (Mamma said so) like a poor immigrant, but a rich little Sicilian-American girl. The Ricciardis were to spend one year in England. He was to set up a new office for his bank, Sacco's, in London, and Maria and her mother, as part of the family, were coming too.

Just then, a man holding a copy of the *New York Tribune* touched Mr Ricciardi on the arm. One page of the newspaper was folded back. Pushing it under Mr Ricciardi's nose, he pointed to a paragraph bordered in black.

NOTICE! Travellers intending to embark on the Atlantic voyage are reminded that a state of war exists between

Germany and her allies and Great Britain and her allies; that the zone of war includes the waters adjacent to the British Isles; that, in accordance with formal notice given by the Imperial German Government, vessels flying the flag of Great Britain, or of any of her allies, are liable to destruction in those waters and that travellers sailing in the war zone on ships of Great Britain or her allies do so at their own risk. IMPERIAL GERMAN EMBASSY.

'Had you read this?'
'I had,' Mr Ricciardi said curtly.
'And you're not worried?'
'I am not, sir.'
The man moved away. And then at last the all ashore gongs went. They were more than two hours late leaving. Three blasts of the horn, so loud she had to clap her hands to her ears. The crowd on the pier cheered as they moved. Confetti was thrown. Alphabet flags streamed from the masts. As the boat slipped past the Statue of Liberty and out through the Narrows, the sun broke through, glinting on the scummy water. Seagulls hovered round the hot black smoke from the funnels. The drizzle and stickiness earlier had made Maria's blue satin bow limp. As she stood at the rail, it flopped forward heavily, working loose.

Excitement and exploration took care of the rest of that day. She began by sliding along the greeny-grey linoleum of B deck corridor. She was able to get a good run until she collided with a steward. She was wearing her second best boots: they were more worn and slid better. When she thought she might lose her balance she clung to the round mahogany railing. Another delight was the elevator that went up and down between decks, from the Grand Entrance to the dining saloon. When she saw it almost full, she would rush along and squeeze in. Sometimes she stared at the people but when one woman said 'You're a rude little girl,' she was surprised. She had only been curious.

Mr and Mrs Ricciardi had a suite on B deck: day room, bedroom and bathroom. Gina, the nurse, slept nearby with Serafino and Gabriela and Franco. Maria and Mamma's room had a large brass bedstead and a small cot for Ettore. All the furniture was bolted to the floor.

When Ettore cried the first night, Mamma was able to stop him. Maria remembered overhearing Mrs Ricciardi in New York telling her friends, 'She's just wonderful, this woman. Speaks only a few words that aren't Sicilian – but children, well, she's only to *look* at Ettore and he's quiet.' Then later: 'Yes, we're taking her along. I don't fancy a year of hired nurses.' The wonderful thing was the way the Ricciardis had made Maria feel wanted too. Sending her to a good school (that had been hard, real hard at first), treating her almost like one of theirs. For over six months now the Ricciardi chauffeur had collected her when school came out.

The *Lusitania* sailed on Saturday. By the Sunday evening several of the children in first class were seasick – one of them actually vomiting in the dining-room and having to be removed in a flurry of warm water and damp cloths. As she lay with Mamma in the big bed, Maria felt the slight pull and heave of the boat. There was a smell too of paint mixed with seawater – it should have made her feel bad with its memories of that other terrible sea voyage. More than six weeks crammed into the bottom part of a cargo ship, Palermo–Genoa, Genoa–New York, tossed about, awash with vomit. Hunger, sickness – nearly everyone had seemed to be ill. If there was a doctor she never saw him. Six years old, she had thought the journey would never end. It became her life. She was frightened she would never know another. And then when they had at last arrived – she didn't want to remember now, what that arrival had been like.

Most of the time on the *Lusitania* she was free to do what she wanted except that she must spend two hours a day on her studies, including lessons in correct Italian (the Ricciardis' idea – although they were not being too strict about it on a sea voyage). But when she went along in her blue dress with the red bands, thinking she might play with the other children, they'd already made a circle that didn't include her. It was no better when she wandered down to second class although there were many more children. She talked to a Canadian boy whose lumber-jack father was coming over to join in the War. But the next time she saw him, he was with a group and didn't seem to know her.

Gina, the nurse, who had never been on the sea except for a trip round the bay, became very sick which meant a lot of extra work for Mamma. There she was, in the children's dining saloon, holding her own with some very superior nurses. Pushing Serafino and Franco around and seeing they ate up, answering any criticisms with: 'What you look at? You know Signor Ricciardi in

New York, very fine family? You don't? Then why you no shut your mouth?' Maria was proud of her – how not? She loved to see Mamma fighting back (where would they have been without?) but at the same time couldn't help feeling a little ashamed of this stout woman in black, without a proper nurse's uniform.

She hated her shame. To please Mamma, she tried again to play up on the boat deck. There was one girl, frizzy hair tied with a pink and white striped ribbon, nose tilted up like a pug dog's. She was accompanied always by her younger brother. 'Tell me, hokey pokey,' he said to Maria, 'what *is* that language you speak with your Mamma?'

Perhaps the Ricciardis had some idea she wasn't getting on with the other children, because next morning they invited her into the Palm Lounge where they bought her a strawberry ice cream. At a nearby table a man was explaining in a loud voice how he walked round the deck each day to keep fit. 'Six times equals four miles,' he told his companions. Mr Ricciardi asked her, 'Is that ice going to spoil your dinner?' but Mrs Ricciardi interrupted, 'Nothing spoils Maria's dinner.' It was just then, as she was scooping up the last melted bits at the bottom of the silver cup, that a man stopped by their table. Dressed in a light check suit, he had receding sandy hair which grew thick at the sides. His expression was serious, but his face looked as if it preferred laughing.

'Eric Grainger . . . I've spoken to a number of persons over the last two days – and I wonder if you're as concerned as I am that there's been nothing you could call lifeboat drill since we came on board?'

'Right,' answered Mr Ricciardi. 'But I don't think –'

'I do,' Mr Grainger said, 'and what my thinking tells me is that we're in a very dangerous position. You'll have noticed they don't black out the portholes properly? We're at war with Germany even if you Yankees aren't, and these waters are the war zone. U-boats – there've been rumours, you know. And some have received rather odd warning telegrams.'

'That's correct, sir,' Mr Ricciardi said. 'I had one myself.'

'And it didn't frighten you?'

'It did not – there's always someone wanting to scare the hell out of you. There was a warning in the newspapers too, but the Captain's British, he's experienced, and he's been instructed, I guess. If he hasn't fussed us with lifeboat drill then I reckon we don't need lifeboat drill.'

Mr Grainger didn't seem put out. He just lifted his hand in farewell, then moved on to the next table. Mrs Ricciardi said: 'Don't you listen, Maria. Don't you let them scare you.'

They stood up to go. Mr Ricciardi said, 'Somebody ought to put a stop to that guy. Going around scaring the wits.'

In the evening it was lovely and sunny and she tried to play medicine ball with the usual group, but the boy just called her 'hokey-pokey' again. She thought: I'm not going to cry.

'I don't want to play stupid games anyway,' she said, leaving them. 'I've got friends that are grown up.'

It was as if, because she'd said it, she had to make it come true. The next day was sunny. She didn't stay up on deck, but wandered about. She went into the lounge on D deck which she liked best, with its damask sofas and marble fireplaces and lovely domed ceiling. She saw the man from yesterday, Mr Grainger, on one of the sofas, and opposite him a young dark-haired man, sitting on the edge of his chair. She sat down on a smaller chair near them. The young man didn't look up but Mr Grainger glanced over, eyebrows raised in half recognition.

'I came through Canada quickly,' the young man was saying. 'I'm raring to have a go at the Hun. You can tell me, perhaps – England, how is she? Down at all? I mean, it hasn't gone like it should. All over by Christmas –'

'I don't like the way they're dug in,' Mr Grainger said. 'It's too static, is the trench system. Give me an open battlefield every time. Cavalry charges, even bows and arrows.'

'Do you know the States at all, sir?'

'My first visit. I've been to the nickelodeon. A few New York sights, but otherwise strictly business.'

'And what is that, sir?'

'A foundry in Middlesbrough, Yorkshire. Lately we've been interested in, and interesting to, the aircraft industry. I'm not giving away secrets when I say we've a casting process could help them a lot. Packard . . . I've been seeing them with a proposition which excites them a good deal. Let's say, the visit's been worth my while.' He glanced at his watch. 'I'll have to be off . . . I've liked talking to you. I've one son at the front already. I know how you feel.'

He stood up to go. As he was about to pass Maria, something came over her. She thought afterwards, I don't know why I did it. Out shot one of her legs so that he half-tripped, reached for

14

the small table, fell against it, and righted himself. He turned to her.

'Gee,' she said. 'Gee, I'm sorry, mister.'

'So you should be, little lass. So you should.' And patting her on the head, he walked away.

Just before lunch she overheard the man they called Staff Captain Anderson asking passengers if they'd care to contribute to the ship's concert on Thursday. 'Where are all our Clara Butts and Carusos?' But no one could be persuaded. 'It's the same in Second,' he said. 'I shall have to try steerage. A colourful lot there.'

She ran after him, 'Mister, I'll sing. I don't need a piano, I'd really like to do that, mister.' The officer seemed pleased. He wrote down her name and the number of her cabin. She told the Ricciardis and Mamma that she was going to sing in the concert. 'This ship's officer asked me to.'

Afternoon now, and she still had all this energy. Gina was as seasick as ever and very weak. The ship's doctor was to look at her. Mamma, very busy still, made Maria promise she wouldn't get into any mischief.

When she'd watched the waves a little and then ridden three times in the elevator between the first class lounge and the dining saloon, she went back to her old game of sliding along the linoleum, on C deck this time. Hand out, ready to grasp the shiny mahogany rail, a small run, a little push and, *I'm flying!*

A door opened just as she came to a halt, grasping the rail. A voice behind her said:

'It's our little tripper, isn't it? You all but had me over again.' She looked down at her boots. He went on: 'Don't you have anything to do but try and kill off elderly passengers?'

'Mister, I'm sorry. I sure am sorry.'

'What do you reckon we should do about it?' He took her arm. 'Come into my parlour, as the spider said to the fly. No, don't look puzzled – it's a rhyme, that's all. I'm inviting you to come and see my sitting-room. I'm lonely today. I miss my children.' When she hesitated: 'I shan't eat you. At least, not till dinner-time.'

'No, thanks, mister. I guess I won't.'

'Do I look like a spider?' He said coaxingly, 'Come on, there's a kind little lass. I've a phonograph. And some brand-new ragtime records.'

She felt silly that she'd held out because really she wanted to see inside everyone's cabin. He rang for a steward: 'I'm going to get you a lemonade.' Then as she sank into a big chair, 'Now tell me who you are so we can be properly introduced. My name's Grainger.'

'Sure, and you've a foundry and you've been in the States about a piece of metal and you've a son in the War –'

He smiled. 'Eavesdropping *and* tripping. What a cheeky one . . . But I can't say "lass" all the time. What do they call you?'

'Maria Verzotto, mister.'

'Not a little Yankee then, but an Italian?'

'No, I'm not, I'm Sicilian.'

'Italy, Sicily . . . The same, aren't they?'

'They are *not*, mister.'

'Right,' he said, 'I understand . . . But you live in the States?'

'Since I was six years. I'm eleven now. I didn't have one word of English when I came off the boat. But I learned real fast, didn't I? What Mamma and I talk, that's Sicilian . . . I'm going to sing in Sicilian tomorrow night, at the concert.'

'Are you now?'

'I'll sing a lullaby that Mamma sings to Ettore. That's the Ricciardis' baby.' She was finding it easy now to talk. The lemonade arrived. She sipped it and looked about her. His room was like hers and Mamma's except for a red bedspread and carpet instead of gold.

'You like first class, mister?'

'Second was heavily booked – and overcrowded into the bargain by some hundred and forty.' He sat back, hands in his pockets. 'I like my creature comforts, you see.'

There was a large box of candies on a table nearby. He untied the ribbon. 'Tuck in. They're meant for my family, but I've plenty more.'

She was greedy and ate several. Her mouth full of pistachio fondant, she craned her neck to look at his books: Rafael Sabatini, *The Sea Hawk*, Nat Gould, *Wizard of the Turf*.

'You like reading?' he asked. Scooping up a paper with one hand: 'It says here in the *Cunard Daily Bulletin* there's a strong possibility of Italy coming into the war as our ally. You've family over there still?'

'Yes, sir. My brother Mastro and Rosalia, that's my sister, they're married. They're in Monteleone where we lived. And I got two brothers, Rocco and Gaetano, they're in Detroit. They

16

came with us. Papa died. He got sick, something with his bones. We'd a bad time, mister – till the Ricciardis . . .'

She chattered on. He seemed really interested. When she'd done: 'My word,' he said, 'that's a lot to fit into eleven years . . . And now you're off to England?'

'I am, mister. Is where you live the middle of England?'

He smiled. 'No. *Middlesbrough*. That's in the north, by the sea. We've another house near the moors, where my family, our four children, spend much of the summer . . . Shall I show you my family?'

From the desk he took out several framed photographs.

'Here's James, our eldest – taken before he enlisted. He's in France now.' A blond moustachioed young man stared confidently at the camera: 'He's a fine-looking lad, is James. I rather depend on him . . . Then Ida.' Rimless spectacles, a large friendly face, smiling broadly. 'And Dick next.' A dark-haired intense boy, his mouth in a half smile. 'He's been very poorly, has Dick. Pneumonia. He's convalescing at Moorgarth, our house I told you of, at the moment.' Beside him was another boy, younger, dark, his features a heavier version of his brother's. He looked pleased with himself. 'And Peter. He's fourteen. And at school of course . . .'

Also in the picture with the two boys was a woman wearing pince-nez and her hair scraped back severely from a heavy-jowled face. She looked bad-tempered.

'And that's the boys' mother, Mrs Grainger . . . Now, here, we've a group. Dick, Ida, James – and our great family friend, Eleanor Dennison.' A tall woman, rather plain, smiled at the camera.

He took up the last picture. 'And this little one here,' pointing to a girl of about Maria's age with slant eyes and a pretty mouth, 'Jenny's eleven, like you –'

'But that makes five,' Maria said. 'You told me four.'

He said hastily, 'It's five. *Five*. Three boys and the two girls.' He took the pictures from her. 'And now, you wanted to hear the phonograph . . .'

It appeared that Dick loved ragtime. As well as some pianola rolls ('Clarence M. Johnson, that sort of thing,') his father had bought him a number of records. 'Irving Berlin – it may not be what he wants but I'm enjoying them.' He rang for some tea and they drank it together while the phonograph played, *I want to be back in Dixie*, and *He's a ragpicker*. Maria sang along.

'That's a bonny little voice,' he said. 'I shall have to listen out for you tomorrow.'

'I've got to go now,' she said suddenly. 'But I could come back, I guess. If you ask me –'

'I shall,' he said solemnly, as he saw her to the door.

She dreamed heavily. Maybe she'd eaten too many candies. She was shut in the wardrobe in Mr Grainger's cabin. Oddly, it wasn't upright, but flat on the floor. She didn't try to get out. She was safe in there. Safe from the Lion. She heard Mr Grainger's voice. Then doors opening and shutting. A creaking and a roaring. Mr Grainger said, 'You've no witnesses. You can't do this. My family . . .' The wardrobe swayed. Swayed with the waves on the sea. But it's bolted to the floor, she told herself. *It's bolted.*

'The Lion has a heart of stone,' one of the voices said.

'Have pity on me,' Mr Grainger said, 'I only did it for my family, for my five children.'

All at once she realized where she was. It was a linen chest, not a wardrobe. She wasn't safe at all. She must get out. She must escape, and save her cousin. She banged, desperate, afraid, on the lid of the chest. As it swayed with the sea, she thought: we shall all drown. *Agniulu Dei chie doje spiccata munti.* Mamma, help me, help me . . .

She woke suddenly. Mamma was shaking her. 'A bad dream, eh?' Ettore set up a thin wail, pulling at the sides of the cot. 'Now you've woken that bad boy . . .'

'I was dreaming of old times,' Maria said. 'It was a nightmare of old times.'

Her mouth buzzed. She could hear the flies, as she could feel them crawl about her mouth. Prickly pears, sweet painful taste. She had been eating a prickly pear. Pain and pleasure. In the heat the flies came to her sore, sweet, bloodstained mouth, lips torn by prickles. She tried to fight, to push at the humming mass. Someone took her hands away. She cried. This was her first memory.

Voices said, 'Hit her, she was told not . . . Hit her, she'll learn . . . Poor little one, wash her, throw water . . . Who has water to spare these days? She's with her sister. Let her sister take her back . . .'

Only one sister, Rosalia. Ten years older, and angry. Her dark heavy hair shaking with exasperation as she dragged or pushed

Maria about. Maria, always straying that little too far from home – in the village of Monteleone, up in the mountains. Vines and olive trees, sheep, shepherds, a main street that climbed, cobbled, with alleys twisting and turning off it. A little square with fountains where they went for water, of which there was never enough. A few years more and it would be Maria to fetch it, to stagger under the weight of the earthenware pitcher, her brother Arasimu groaning the other side.

Their house had two rooms, and a hole behind a door for a lavatory. She played on the floor which was made of mud. Indoors or outdoors – kneeling on the ground, absorbed, she didn't know which was which. The walls of the room were painted blue, like the sky. Some hens lived with the family. There was a copper stove for when it was cold, and an alcove with a decorated curtain, fringed with silk: she liked to twist and twist its tassels, then let them spin. Someone smacked her for that. Above the alcove was a loft, with wood for the stove, and grain.

On the walls were pictures of Sant'Antonio, Santa Rosalia, the Virgin Mary. Rosalia, Maria – how to tell the saints from the sinners, the living from the dead? Grandfather, two uncles she'd never seen, their photographs grouped together, flyblown, faded, moustachioed: the dead. The living were Mamma, and Papa who was thin and a little bent, but strong. Her eldest brother, Mastro, was thin too and his moustache grew low towards his chin in the same way. After Rosalia came Rocco and Gaetano, two brothers so close together they might have been twins – and so much older than Maria that they had always seemed large, vigorous. No photographs to remember the next two brothers – each had died after a few days. Then came Arasimu, two years older than Maria.

Arasimu. They fought like kittens, like puppies, in play, in anger. At night he shared the bed with her and Mamma and Papa. Then suddenly he was not there. Sounds of weeping and wailing. They wailed and then were silent, mourning Arasimu who had died of brain fever. She could remember nothing of his illness. They had sent her to her aunt's, to Za Rosetta's, five minutes away at the far end of the village. Her aunt's home was only one room, and the hole. Her husband, Zu Orazio, Papa's brother, was ill. Had always been ill. They lived on others' kindness and what Minicu, their son, got from work. Zu Orazio often sat outside the house with the women, his thin hands shelling beans. Za Rosetta had more time for her than her own mother. So did Minicu. Minicu was mischievous and curious. Wiry, small, like all that family. He was a tease and never minded his own business.

Za Rosetta told her stories and sang to her, Maria squatting beside her, as she made sweets which Minicu took up to people who were better off and would buy them. The doctor, for instance, or Don Cataldo, who lived in a large house not far from the church with only his housekeeper, and whom people called The Lion. ('Why?' she asked, for she was always asking questions. But either no one heard or they weren't telling, because they only answered, 'Why *not*?')

Once Mamma had taken her to see Don Cataldo. The room had a lot of furniture and was dark and frightening, as was Don Cataldo, although his manner was kindly. He had a great mane of white hair and a furrowed face. He stroked Maria's head. Mamma told her to kneel down. 'Down, down, Maria.' Then Don Cataldo asked some questions and gave her a blessing.

It must have been about then that Don Cataldo became confused in her mind with the Golden Lion of Za Rosetta's story. Maria's favourite.

A very rich man with lots to eat had three sons. The eldest asked to see the world so the father built him a ship and he sailed away till he reached land and saw a notice: 'Find the King's daughter in eight days and you can marry her. If you don't, your head will be chopped off.' He looked all over the palace and in every linen chest, but he couldn't find her so they cut off his head. At home the second son asked for a ship to look for his brother. The wind blew him into the same harbour. '*I'll* try and find the Princess,' but though he looked all over the palace and in every linen chest, he had his head cut off too. Then the youngest son set sail and a high wind blew him into the same place. On his way to find the Princess, he met an old beggar-woman and gave her some money. 'Can I help you, kind boy?' He told her about his brothers. She said, 'Go to a goldsmith, ask him to make a lion of gold with crystals for eyes and a music box inside.' Then she put the boy inside the golden lion and had it taken to the King, who wanted to buy it. But she refused, so he persuaded her to leave it for one night for his daughter to play with.

When she had gone the King lifted up some wooden floorboards. Underneath was a secret staircase. He took the Lion down, along a passage and through one door, then another . . .

The boy, who could see through the crystal eyes, counted seven. Then in a beautiful hall, he saw twelve girls all dressed the same. 'However shall I tell which is the Princess?' he thought sadly. When the King left, they all stroked the Lion and rode on his back till they got tired. The girl they called the Princess said she wanted the Lion to sleep with her. In bed, she said: 'Golden Lion, I love you. You are the most beautiful thing I have ever seen.' Then she stroked and kissed him. Suddenly the boy spoke from inside the Lion: 'How much I have suffered to find you!'

The Princess, frightened, began to scream, but her friends thought she was dreaming so they did not come. The boy spoke again: 'My two brothers died looking for you. I want to make you my wife – so I am hiding inside the Golden Lion.' When she understood this she was frightened again because she knew he would be killed too. How was he to know her from the others? 'You must give me a sign,' he said. So she promised to put a blue belt round her waist.

The next morning when he had been let out, the boy went to the King. 'I want to find the Princess.' The King was sad because he knew he would lose his head like the others. The boy lived seven days in the palace, eating fine food and drinking wine. He pretended to look everywhere and in every linen chest. On the last day he went into the King's room and asked to lift up some floorboards. The King was surprised but said nothing. The boy went down the stairs and along the passage and through a door . . . till he had been through seven doors. Then he was in a hall with twelve girls, all dressed the same. Just then one girl took from her pocket a blue belt – just like the Virgin wears with her white dress in the statues – and put it round her waist. '*She* is the Princess!' the boy cried, 'and she shall be my wife.'

After the wedding feast, the boy sailed home with his princess, a shipload of treasures and the Golden Lion. To the old woman he gave money so that she would never be hungry again. And they all lived happily ever after . . .

Like the old beggarwoman, Maria knew what it was to be hungry. It was the little animal inside which chewed at your stomach, ran around biting it after carelessly you'd let drop some crusts – lost them and cried for more. Many days in the winter there were none. Better in the summer, stealing the beans which Mamma sat shelling. Raw, hard. Another sort of pain. Bad days and good days – God sent them both but the Virgin took the bad ones away. Sometimes, if the talk was to be believed, it was the

Lion's fault. She was confused. 'Not the Golden Lion. He helps people,' she said. '*What* Golden Lion?' they asked, only half listening . . . 'Oh, some story of Rosetta's,' they said.

Or Minicu's. He told stories too, ones Maria could never remember, or didn't want to, full as they were of two-headed monsters, bears, hungry wolves on the mountain eating people. ('And all the village went up to look for little 'Ntonia and to hunt the wolf, but they found only *bones* . . .') She had bad dreams, and worried when Minicu went up into the mountains looking for herbs. 'Aren't you afraid?' But he only laughed at her.

Sometimes there was bread in the mornings, dry bread. Oh, it tasted good – with fresh water if they'd been to the fountain. Herbs perhaps. Stolen scraps, uncooked pasta fallen to the ground. At night a plate of pasta, the sauce so hot it made her eyes run. All eating together from two great dishes. Rocco with his big appetite, always the hungriest just as he was the largest and strongest. The dark hairs grew on his forearms and on his chest, a thick mat – curly like his head. He could frighten her. Not like Minicu but in a different way. When she knew he was angry, she was afraid. It was as if he turned into stone.

It was the summer before they left for 'Merica that Minicu disappeared. All Maria's family were going except Mastro and Rosalia: she was to marry a boy from Monteleone, Mastro a girl from the next village with a good dowry. Minicu could not go because of his parents.

She knew 'Merica was further than Palermo. But Palermo, for all she knew of it, could have been a village just beyond Monteleone. To go to 'Merica, they must sail on the sea. No one cried when people took the cart to Palermo, but Za Rosetta, whenever she spoke of their going to 'Merica, wiped tears from her eyes with her black headscarf, bit her moustachioed lip.

'Merica. Enough to eat. And money to send home. The Licari brothers were spoken of. Fifteen years ago they had come back on a visit with gold in their pockets and fine wool trousers and silk shirts and jewellery.

For some months now, she had been running errands for the trattoria at the foot of the village, taking the little money she earned straight home. One evening, she heard that Minicu was missing. He hadn't come down from the mountain. Za Rosetta sent Rocco and Gaetano searching. She and Mamma and other women from the village sat outside the next evening, waiting for news. Mamma was dandling the new baby from next door.

Mamma loved babies. Maria was meant to be sewing but, worried about Minicu, could not sit still. She was making a stocking and her needle was rusty. She rubbed it in her hair as she'd seen the others do. Talk went on round her. Wailing. Za Rosetta sat with them and was comforted. There wasn't a man in sight. 'I should have gone to church,' Za Rosetta said, 'O Lamb of God, find me my son, find me my Minicu.'

A kitten rubbed its head against Maria's legs, then flinched as she raised her hand to caress it. She was silly about animals, worrying even about the hens and turkeys. A scrap of material dangling in the air floated to the kitten who caught it and tossed it. His bones showed through his scraggy parted fur. 'Give that me,' she called. But he slunk off. From boredom, from distress – she ran after him. He darted up an alley, down another. Barefoot, panting, she followed.

The houses came to an end: round the open door of the last one the kitten disappeared. She followed. Inside, a room like any other, but no alcove and curtain. A hunk of dry bread stood on the table. There was no sign of the cat. Of anyone. A hen scrabbled in the corner. She was hungry and thought of biting at the bread. But if someone should come? If someone was pissing in the closet? And she was curious. Had always been curious. 'Little cat, where are you?' she whispered. *I won't think about Minicu.* She decided to peep in the linen chest, lifting the lid carefully: it was half full of coarse sheets.

Then she heard voices. *Sacru miu Gesù,* if I'm seen. She hurtled into the chest, lying quiet, crouched. Scarcely daring to breathe as they came into the room.

'Bolt the door. Quick. Look around. The watercloset, anyone over the hole?'

'No one – she's at church praying for Granddad's soul.'

'Keep your voice down. Quick – they're asking about Minicu . . . What happened?'

'What do you think?'

'Just tell me. You were there. They told you to dispatch Gaspare, didn't they? I'd have been there if I hadn't been sick . . . The Lion's orders, were they?'

'If you say so.'

'Getting rid of Gaspare – it wasn't difficult?'

'Alone with his sheep. He'd barely turned his head before we –'

'All right – he had it coming to him. Pass that carafe, I've a

23

dusty thirst . . . Just tell me where Minicu comes into it.'

'The shot – he couldn't not have heard.' The voice had a tremble, an edge. 'And he saw us, two of us with guns. I hid my face, but Pietro, he knows Pietro. We couldn't . . . We'd no choice.'

'The body?'

'Ask the vultures –'

'Who ordered it, then, dispatching Gaspare?'

'The Lion, who else?'

From somewhere, the kitten mewed.

'We only did what we . . . A man must obey. And who can one trust? Were we to trust Minicu? My life would go if I –'

'The Lion . . . The Lion has a heart of stone . . .'

The voices stopped. The door was unbolted. Steps fading away. Silence.

She lifted the chest lid, trembling – her legs so weak she could at first hardly walk. At the end of the alley she began to run. And run.

Back with her family she was silent and sad. They were all sad. She told no one what she had heard. Not even Rocco. Least of all Rocco.

In the brass bed of her *Lusitania* cabin, she was woken by a creaking sound. Bump, bump. Wood against metal. She had been sleeping again after the nightmare. Ettore, being dressed by Mamma, tried to get on to the bed to tug at Maria's hair. But she was impatient, wanting to be up and out. On the promenade deck, on the starboard side, several lifeboats, uncovered, were hanging out on the side, their keels above the railings. It was the creaking of the unused davits that had woken her. Some smaller wooden boats with collapsible sides were fastened beneath.

Standing nearby was her new friend, Mr Grainger. 'Good. The equipment's good. It's the drill that isn't. Boats – they tell me there's a margin of six hundred places over what's needed – we'd not be another *Titanic*.'

'What's that?' Maria asked.

The sun had come out and was sending shadows of the heavy lifeboats across the deck. 'Tomorrow we'll see land. Not England – Ireland.' He chucked her under the chin: 'Not Italy – Sicily, eh?'

'Can I come and hear your phonograph?'

'Of course, Miss Verzotto. Come after breakfast.'

She sipped ice-cream soda, ate more candies, and sang along with the records. *'The world goes round to the sound of that International Rag . . .'*

'I like to hear about your family,' she told him. She thought suddenly and longingly of her own. Papa, Mastro, Rosalia, Rocco, Gaetano – dead Arasimu, dead Minicu. It wasn't the same with the Ricciardis, however kind they might be. Nor had they said what was to become of her and Mamma once Ettore was a big boy. After the visit to England . . .

'I miss them,' Mr Grainger said. She wondered if he worried a lot about James, fighting in the War.

That evening because of the concert she wore her best frock for dinner: white silk with a bright red sash and lace panels. Mrs Ricciardi looked beautiful and fashionable in violet chiffon and satin. The concert in aid of the Seamen's Homes was in the boat deck lounge. She and Mrs Ricciardi went up in the elevator while Mr Ricciardi climbed the grand staircase. Maria's feet, in glacé kid slippers, sank into the deep pile of the lounge carpet. She saw Mr Grainger a little way away, almost hidden by one of the palm trees. When Mr Ricciardi was discreetly pointing out Alfred Vanderbilt, she told him, 'Over there – that's my new friend over there.' Mr Ricciardi said only, 'Oh, *that* guy.'

The concert was part interesting, part boring. When someone played *I love a piano*, she wanted to join in: *'I know a fine way to treat a Steinway . . .'* For her own song, she waited only to be asked. Waited and waited. She became so mad at not being on the programme that she didn't join in the chorus of *For he's a jolly good fellow* which the other passengers sang for Staff Captain Anderson.

Her last whole day, she was woken by the sound of the foghorn. Tomorrow morning they would dock at Liverpool. On her way to breakfast she stood at the rails, looking out for land. She saw only mist. Mr Grainger, beside her again, told her how sorry he was not to have heard her sing. 'If you'd like, come and help me pack later this morning.'

She didn't know what made her so hungry. She worked through stewed fruit and porridge, brown hash and eggs, cold ham and lots of fresh rolls and three cups of cocoa. Mr Ricciardi, who had come down at the same time, complimented her on the roses in her cheeks.

The fog cleared and the sun came out. The sea was calm. Gulls, calling, followed the ship. Mr Grainger was sitting reading

The Sea Hawk on the promenade deck when she went to fetch him. Back in his stateroom, she stacked up the piano rolls. She looked at the photographs again. There was one she hadn't seen before. A pretty young woman wearing a frothy blouse, with curly hair and a laughing face. 'And who's this?' she asked.

Taking the picture, he placed it with the others. He seemed a little cross. 'That's Mrs Grainger's sister. Miss Rowland. The children's Aunt Dulcie.'

Maria said, 'She's really cute-looking, is she nice?' He didn't answer her. Later, when she'd asked yet another question about Dick and Ida and Peter and Jenny, he turned to her:

'Well, Miss Verzotto – what do you say while you're in England to spending a few weeks with us? Staying in the North Riding at Thackton-le-Moors?'

'Yes, sir. Yes, *please*.'

'That's settled then. We'll exchange addresses tonight.'

Back on deck, he showed her land through his binoculars. She could make out some church steeples and rooftops in the villages. The calm sea glistened bluey-green in the sunlight.

She could hardly wait for lunch-time to tell the Ricciardis about her invitation. But they had the second sitting and she must amuse herself till then. She wasn't sure what Mamma would think – she was nervous enough of England as it was.

'I don't see why not,' Mr Ricciardi said. 'I'll have my company investigate him . . .'

She was so excited, what with that, and the landing tomorrow, that she took a long time to finish her meal. Mamma, who'd eaten with Gina and the children, would be putting Ettore to bed for the afternoon. Maybe she'd go later and tell her about Yorkshire.

The orchestra in the balcony was playing, *The Blue Danube*. She hated that kind of music. Plonk-plonk, it went. Plonk-plonk. Neither of the Ricciardis wanted any pudding or dessert. Mrs Ricciardi had a headache and thought she would lie down. Mr Ricciardi said to Maria, 'Your ice-cream'll be along soon – you'll be OK?' She said Yes. She'd asked for pistachio. When it came, there was no spoon with it. There wasn't a wafer either. She was about to call out, 'Hey, mister!' when something happened.

A violent shock. A loud booming. Her dish, her glass, the vase, knives, forks, pepper, salt – all seemed to jump. A rumbling noise beneath her. It's an earthquake, she thought. She remembered stories of Messina. The tidal wave and ships broken up.

She gazed terrified at the cherubs on the domed ceiling. All around people were trying to right themselves, their effects, their tables. The orchestra played still. Plonk-plonk. An army officer sitting with two women at the next table, exclaimed in a loud voice, 'That's it, they've got us – *they've got us!*'

Splintered glass from a porthole fell on to the floor beside her. Everyone getting up to go now. She was suddenly unable to move for fear. And still *The Blue Danube*, plonk-plonk, plonk-plonk. She asked the army officer, 'Is it an earthquake?'

He was shepherding the two women out. 'Good God, child. Where are your parents?'

But she didn't wait. She ran out. She could still hear the band. Sounds of splintering glass. Outside, people were coming from every direction. Should she run to the Ricciardis? No, better go to Mamma and Ettore. Gina and the children, were they in the nursery?

Suddenly she wanted Mr Grainger. He would know what had really happened. He would know *what to do*.

The elevator opened. 'Hurry,' someone said. She was right by the door. An elderly man took her arm: 'You coming up, little girl?' She shook her head and moved away. Two people pressed past her. The grille shut.

She moved towards the staircase. She realized now that the deck, the whole boat, was sloping. Nothing was safe any more. Nothing. In her panic she couldn't remember which was Mr Grainger's cabin. Better perhaps to go to the promenade deck where he'd said he'd be reading? But why should he be there? How silly. He has gone to safety, she thought. She could see no one she knew. It seemed everyone was looking for their children. A waiter from the dining-room stood near her. He called out, waving his white-coated arms:

'Take your time, she's not going down. The *Lusy* is *not* going down! *Calm*, please.'

There was a message over the ship's loudspeaker. She could not hear it. She could not understand it. She climbed the swaying, tilted staircase, hurrying now towards B Deck, to their cabins.

It was just before she reached them that the lights went. A stewardess carrying two children came round the corner of the corridor. 'Follow me,' she said to Maria. 'The power's gone . . .' Her words tailed away as Maria hurried in the opposite direction. I want Mamma, she thought, I must find Mamma and the Ricciardis.

In the half-light she found the cabin. The door was open. Inside all was disorder: drawers fallen out, shoes and boots scattered. The lifebelts were on top of the wardrobe. She climbed up. But there was nothing there. She stumbled and ran out, calling for Mamma, calling for the Ricciardis.

Now she was truly frightened. To go up or go down? To go where? Someone would give her a belt surely? A plump young man holding two jackets put one on her. She could hardly keep still as he fastened it. 'This way to the boats,' he said as she began to run away. There was another message over the speaker. All would be well, it seemed to say. The *Lusy* was righting herself.

There were no lights anywhere. Down again by the dining saloon, she tried to climb the staircase to the Grand Entrance. But the ship's list was so strong now that almost at once she stumbled and slipped, and fell down again.

She heard the screams first, piercing above the other confused sounds. She saw, half way up, the elevator cage. That same elevator she'd almost gone in only minutes ago. Trapped, frantic with terror, the occupants beat their fists against the metal grille.

When she at last reached the starboard deck, the list was so great that part of it was almost under water. She was shivering, shaking. Calling: 'Mamma, Mamma, Mr Ricciardi, Serafino . . .' A lifeboat filling up, people scrambling, pushing. A man standing near said, 'Make way for this child, let her on, there's a child to go in here.'

The boat was almost full but people were still pushing. She had just been lifted in when suddenly, standing near the boat, was Mr Grainger. At last, Mr Grainger.

'Out,' he told her, 'at once. It's not safe.' Someone protested for her: 'Is he after the place himself, then?'

'Get out,' he said, lifting her up and back on to the deck. 'Daft lass. I came straight to the dining-room to look for you. Stand still. Your jacket's wrongly fastened. You'd not have a chance . . .'

As he twisted and pulled, altering the fastenings, she saw that the boat was being launched.

Not launched. Spilled. Mr Grainger put a hand over her eyes. 'Don't look. You're safe for now. Wait here – a few moments. *Don't move.* I've two kiddies to help and I'll be back.'

. . . At first it was darkness. *Sacru miu Gesù – Mamma, help me!* Trying to call out. No sound. Her mouth full of water. Bodies thrashing around her. Drifting wood, chaos, moaning, weeping. Such a weeping and wailing. A man beside her, floating dead. She was with others yet utterly alone. Sunlight, high above them in the afternoon sky.

Then she heard the voice:

'Maria, *hold on, Maria.*'

And saw, coming as if from nowhere – his face. A face she knew and trusted. The face of certain rescue.

PART ONE

1916 – 1935

I

'. . . *When I tell them, and I'm certainly going to tell them –*
they'll never believe me . . .'

She'd tied a large blue bow round the puppy's neck. She held
him in her arms now as she pedalled the pianola, rubbing her
face into the silky coat. Dear spaniel Trimmer. Outside the snow
fell but inside the fire burned brightly, in the stuffy upholstered
morning-room of the Graingers' house in Linthorpe Road. ('How
do you like the cold North?' people asked her this January of
her first winter. They'd asked the same when she'd arrived in
Middlesbrough last May, after the *Lusy*.) She played the same
roll over and over. Even after nine months she hadn't tired of
the novelty. When she went to Thackton-le-Moors, it was the
one feature she missed. The Ricciardis had not had a player
piano.

'. . . *that from this great big world you've chosen me . . .'*

The door opened a crack, then closed again. Trimmer jumped
from her lap. It opened fully and the Grainger son, Peter, came
heavily in.

'*That* again. Don't you ever?'

'If you don't like it –'

'Never said I didn't, did I? It's just you're always sat there . . .
Blast that puppy's teeth . . . Shouldn't you be helping somebody?
Mother, Aunt Dulcie?'

She went on pedalling. 'Mind if I sit down?' he asked.

'It's your house –'

'Yours too. Your *home* now – I suppose.'

She watched the piano roll go backwards. 'You don't like me
too much, do you?'

'I don't like anyone *too much*.' He snatched up Trimmer.
'Dick's a menace, getting you this animal . . . Anyway, it's Jenny
who doesn't like you. I like you a lot. It's just –' he shrugged his
shoulders '– you behave as if I'm not there.'

'Well, you're not a lot of the time.'

'School, I have to go to school. And it just so happens I have

33

to go *away* to it.' His voice was sulky. It swooped too, from high to deep suddenly. She said:

'At your age, at fourteen, my brothers were working. *And* they were grown up.'

'If I could be grown up, I would.' He let Trimmer drop. 'You make me sick –'

'Sick ill, or sick vomit?'

'Oh *God*,' he said, putting his hand to his mouth.

He went noisily out of the room. She felt as if she'd been slapped. The joy had gone out of the day. Trimmer had curled into the fireside chair. She left the pianola and went over to him. She felt the tears coming, like a choking. She plunged her head into Trimmer's coat. 'Mamma. Mamma.'

When had she last cried for her mother? Christmas, perhaps. She didn't cry much because she thought it wrong, except that she had lost so much.

Best not to think how much she had lost. Those days in Queenstown after the rescue, lying tucked up in the overcrowded Queen's Hotel, shivering, exhausted. Uncle Eric sitting on the end of the bed: 'For now I'm taking you home with me, then we'll see . . . The States maybe – or even go back to Sicily?'

They hadn't spoken of it again till they were on the train from Liverpool to Middlesbrough. He explained that they wouldn't be going yet to the house in Thackton-le-Moors but that he would take her as soon as possible. Still stunned, frightened, she clung to his hand as they walked the long platform at Middlesbrough. Strange people. Strange town. The whole family almost, walking out of the framed photographs in Uncle Eric's cabin. Aunt Maimie, Aunt Dulcie, Dick, Ida, Jenny. They overwhelmed her. Only Peter away at school and James at the Front, absent.

No one spoke to her then of dead Mamma or the Ricciardis – who had loved her and been kind: Gina the nurse, Serafina, Gabriela, Franco, baby Ettore. At night their bloated, drowned faces passed before her while she shook with terror and sorrow. *Sacru miu Gesù.*

She wouldn't have wanted to go back to Sicily. But the remaining Ricciardi relatives could not be expected to take her on. Her brothers Rocco and Gaetano, perhaps they could do something? They were in Detroit – but where? Detroit wasn't a village. If Mamma had had (and surely she had) a scrap of paper, an address, it had gone.

In Monteleone they would know. As soon as he'd rested a little, recovered from the worst of their ordeal, Uncle Eric had begun the inquiries necessary. But the distances and difficulties were great. Weeks, then months, passed as they waited for answers. Letters went to various authorities in Detroit in an attempt to trace Rocco and Gaetano Verzotto, the one thought to be waggon-driving, the other a bricklayer. The priest in Monteleone was written to. It wasn't till the autumn they learned that both Rocco and Gaetano were in Italy, training in a mountain regiment. Italy had joined the allies in that summer of 1915, and they had come back to fight.

No question then of living with her brothers. For a while after that news, the future hung, unmentioned. Then in the late autumn when she was already settled in at school and had grown to feel that the Graingers' was indeed her own home – Thackton even more than Middlesbrough – Uncle Eric had said one Saturday at Moorgarth, sitting before a log fire, toasting muffins, 'What would you say to being adopted properly, Maria? All the legal knots and bows properly tied?'

At that very moment she could not think of anything she wanted more. To live for ever after, with Uncle Eric and his family.

And so it was. Yet in this game of Happy Families, it wasn't possible to like or get on with all of them. When the photographs came to life it had been Uncle Eric's wife (Aunt Maimie as she was to call her) that she had felt the least happy with. In the picture she'd seemed formidable. In real life she was that, but also florid, stout, and discontented. She didn't care for being at Thackton, yet everything was wrong at the Middlesbrough house too. Uncle Eric paid little attention to her grumbling. He was good-tempered with her, only occasionally losing patience, telling her not to be a fool. Then she would bridle and Aunt Dulcie, making the peace, would reach out and touch Uncle Eric. 'That's right, take sides,' Aunt Maimie would say crossly. Then pretty Aunt Dulcie would react uneasily, biting her lip. Maria wondered what it must be like to be Aunt Dulcie. (She didn't wonder what it was like to be Aunt Maimie. It must be hateful.)

Aunt Maimie, when she found Maria alone, often remarked on her 'physical development'. 'Your chest, dear, your *breasts*, there've been big changes since you first arrived. You're sure you know, dear, what being a woman means?' Once she leaned very close, her sour breath against Maria's cheek, 'Little girls

35

from hot countries.' She patted Maria's hand. 'I think you can expect something soon. Promise to tell me, dear.' Maria had thought she would die of shame rather than do that. And when just before Christmas it did happen, it wasn't to her she spoke or even Ida, but to Aunt Dulcie.

Aunt Dulcie, so pretty, so soft, so warm and caring. She was twelve years younger than her sister Maimie, and had come at the age of eighteen to live with the Graingers after the death of her mother. She had been there ever since. Maria was surprised she had never married. 'Why aren't you?' she had asked the second week there. But Aunt Dulcie had shrugged her pretty, fashionable shoulders and returned to her sewing.

She and Aunt Maimie worked hard for the Cause. War work at the Babies' Centre in Middlesbrough; childcare, sewing, knitting. In the evenings Uncle Eric was often busy on committees: Belgian Relief or the North Riding Distress Fund. Ida organized sewing parties with shirts and pyjamas already cut out.

James, Ida, Dick, Peter, Jenny. Perhaps the easiest was Ida (robustly helpful, explaining in her brisk, jolly way, 'This is how we do things here. You'll soon get used to it . . .') The kindest was Dick. Dick would be joining the RFC, the Royal Flying Corps, as soon as he became eighteen, then the family would have him to worry about too. As she had Rocco and Gaetano. Dear Dick – who exasperated Uncle Eric. Too dreamy, too intense. He was clever with his hands and understood the technicalities of work at the foundry – but he could not charm like James.

Although she had seen James only once, she felt she knew him almost as well as she did the others. She shared in his letters from France: James, the Graingers' pride and joy, who had come on leave in November and been seen to be even more fine-looking than in the photographs. Although such a short time at home, he'd been happy to talk with his father about the Foundry and its problems. He couldn't wait for the guns to stop, he said, so that he could be part of it again.

And then there was Jenny, difficult Jenny, appealing always to Aunt Dulcie when she was in trouble ('I wish Aunt *Dulcie* was my mother,' was her constant cry). Jenny had her father's eyebrows, bushy and growing close together, above green eyes. She had too the clean-cut family cheekbones, so marked in Aunt Dulcie.

Jenny disliked Maria. Jenny, watching her at meals, wearing

her little secret smile as if she knew something Maria didn't. (She did of course. She knew that she belonged here.) Jenny, hiding her school exercise book: 'You were trying to look, weren't you? You can't pinch my school work, you have to do it by yourself.'

'I don't want your stupid work,' Maria had cried (was it to be the *Lusy* all over again?) Jenny peering over her shoulder: 'If that's meant to be a map of Italy, you've got it wrong. Sicily's only little. Look, you've made it as big as Spain –'

'It *is* as big as Spain!' Tears of rage and frustration welled up, while Jenny smiled the smile that turned up the corners of her mouth, narrowing her eyes to dangerous slits. Too late Maria thought of a reply:

'It's art, Jenny. You may be crazy enough to think it's geography, but it's art. I can do it just any way I like.'

It had been in September she began at the Grammar School in Albert Road. The boys and girls were in different wings. She had been strange and lost, with only a mocking Jenny for support. The other girls had been told about her history. They were surprisingly kind. Because she was a Catholic child, Uncle Eric had to get a dispensation from the Bishop for her to attend a Protestant school. Every Sunday when the Graingers attended St Hilda's, she was taken to Mass by an Irish family, the Mulligans. When they were in Thackton, Aunt Dulcie's friend, Miss Dennison, took her by motor to the church in Egton – a village which, Miss Dennison explained, had stayed Catholic since Penal times.

The Dennisons' house, Park Villa, was on the road leading into Thackton-le-Moors from Moorgarth where the Graingers lived. Eleanor Dennison, tall, perhaps a little severe, had smooth brown hair up in a bun, and strong features in a long face. She was kind, inviting Maria to breakfast after Mass. Her mother, who went with them, frightened Maria. Her voice although quiet, was like someone spitting needles.

Miss Dennison kept two beehives at Park Villa and last July she'd allowed Maria to help her with taking off the first frames of honey. In August they had gone together to take the bees out on to moorland, to gather heather honey. Miss Dennison talked to her of Italy and Italian art, about which Maria knew nothing.

Thackton. How she loved it. The first time arriving at the small station in darkness. The porter with the lantern calling, 'Thackton-le-Moors, Thackton-le-Moors.' The gig up to Moorgarth. Elsie Thackeray, the housekeeper, waiting to meet them.

The tureen of bacon and pea soup, the freshly baked bread. The feeling of home. Much more than Middlesbrough, Thackton was to be her home.

Thackton-le-Moors was in Eskdale, named after the river Esk. The dales or valleys of Yorkshire ran from north to south like the fingers of a hand, between the high moorland ridges. You could tell which way you were going, Dick said, by the rain or wind on your cheek. There was plenty of rain and wind.

Last summer she'd been with Ida and Miss Dennison, gathering sphagnum moss on the moors. It was used for dressing wounds in hospital where it could help avoid the dreaded gas gangrene. In the late summer they'd picked bilberries – envying the man who used a bilberry-gatherer like a giant comb, raking up an hour's work in one swoop.

Moorgarth. The stone farmhouse which stood on the road leading out of Thackton towards the coast had once been a silk mill. But a wall and gateway outside, and the old fireplace built into the foundations of the farmhouse were all that remained of it now. The farmhouse door was reached by walking round into the courtyard which, with its worn flags, was built in the shape of an L. The bedroom she shared with Ida, Jenny and Aunt Dulcie, looked out on to partly cultivated land – a regular pattern, crisscrossed with fields, green or gold. Farmsteads were dotted about. Clumps of trees followed the river Esk as it meandered. And the train from Middlesbrough to Whitby could be watched, puffing white in the sunlight but at night a toy train, just visible by its dimly lit wartime carriages (a section of line had been taken up to contribute metal to the war effort). Behind all that, high up, was moorland and the long flat-topped ridge known as Thackton Rigg, with its dark patches of dead burned heather, its path winding over, out of sight. Last summer she had watched the colours changing, from green to amethyst, to purple, to russet.

The stables and cattle sheds were filled with bicycles and games except for the one in which Dick kept his cream mare, Eulalia. (He wanted her to ride but she was frightened.) Moorgarth wasn't farmed but the Graingers had the ancient right to graze eight sheep on the land attached. Although there were none there, there were plenty in the village itself. Strolling up the main street, black-faced and solid. So heavy and humorous beside the lean biblical sheep of her childhood.

The sheep of Monteleone, the mountains of Sicily. And Minicu. She did not often think of Minicu these days. She kept him buried with lots of other frightening memories. It was enough to mourn Mamma and the Ricciardis.

But some of it was unwittingly dug up through Dick's kindness. He had brought her a pile of books from his childhood. She hadn't bothered much with the pirates and Indian mutineers (just as she hadn't with Ida's schoolgirl heroines who never cheated, while taking the blame for those who did) but had fallen eagerly upon the volumes of fairy tales. It was in one of these she'd come upon *The Golden Lion*. Although some details were different, it was Za Rosetta's story all right. Translated now from the German, it had come a long way. When with delight she pointed it out to Dick, he said, his eyes lighting up:

'Oh, but that was quite one of my favourites – I used to pretend *I* was the youngest son hiding inside the Lion . . . Once I even had a nightmare about it and wouldn't be in a room with a closed door. I was a great nuisance as a child.'

'It isn't frightening,' she said, 'but it could be. I used to mix up the Golden Lion with a real person who –' She broke off.

The Lion. We don't think of him. And we never speak of him. Kindly man with large hands, friendly pouches beneath his eyes, a head of hair like a lion's mane. Mamma: 'On your knees for his blessing. Down, Maria, down . . .' ('The Lion has a heart of stone. Where is Minicu? *Ask the vultures* . . .')

Dick's kindness, thoughtfulness. Trimmer had been his idea, a present for her first Christmas. The family bulldogs, Pepper and Salt, were friendly but belonged to everyone. Dick had suggested a spaniel puppy, golden, from a litter which Tom Reeves had just bred (Tom was the Dennisons' gardener and the youngest of five boys. Three of his brothers had been killed already.) It was Uncle Eric who had christened the puppy. 'Why Trimmer?' she'd asked.

'He who runs with the hare and hunts with the hounds,' Uncle Eric told her. 'A trimmer. But don't bother your dear little head with that.'

How she loved Trimmer. Here at Linthorpe Road where she had a room of her own, no one knew that he slept tucked up in her bed (at Moorgarth where she shared a bed with Ida, he would howl at intervals all through the night). She buried her face now in his coat, dried her tears with the blue bow, and kicked the pianola stool, hard.

That's for Peter, she thought.

The door opened, quietly. It wasn't Peter back. It was Aunt Dulcie. Tears ran down her face. She held a paper in her hand.

'I was looking for – Maria dear, where is everybody? I – you see, perhaps I shouldn't have opened this. But I guessed. I met the telegraph boy as I came up the drive.'

Maria stood very still, Trimmer in her arms. Aunt Dulcie said, mouth trembling, tears falling:

'I shall have to tell his mother. And Eric, Mr Grainger . . . It must be I who tell him. You see, Maria dear, James has been killed.'

2

At first Dick thought it was the wind in the 'plane's rigging. Then he heard the crackle of flames, the whipping, the roar. Petrol. Smoke, heat: orange heat. This is the Orange Death, we call it the Orange Death. A figure, a man, stands up in the 'plane, flailing the air. The rush of air fans the flames, but he stands up and beats them. And all the while the plane is going down. Down, down. A spiral. A roaring furnace. The flames roared in his ears. Fire sizzled flesh. Mouth twisted, wordlessly. Seconds that are minutes that are hours. Oh God, *let me die*.

'You were screaming in your sleep again,' Rattler told him.

'I'd a nightmare. The usual.'

'If you're like this now, how'll you be in France? Littlewood's brother's been out three months. He says –'

'Cut it, Rattler –'

'Bloody lucky, those training Avros yesterday, they didn't catch fire – clashing in mid-air like that. What a sodding way to go.'

'*Clear out*, would you?'

He was sorry a moment later. But neither Rattler nor any of the others would expect an apology. They were a good-humoured lot – as was Dick most of the time. Lieutenant Richard Grainger RFC. There was a great deal to enjoy in flying. And it was smart and exciting to be a 'birdman', about, this summer of 1917, to be posted to France. Yet, these fears. Shot down in flames. Perhaps, as he suspected, everyone else had them secretly? When the nightmares returned again and again, he would ask himself: How did I come to be here? Why?

The *Lusitania*. He had been sixteen when she was torpedoed. The Christmas before, 1914, he had left school to work in the foundry. In the spring of 1915 he became very ill: double pneumonia. Dad sent him to Thackton, with just Ida and the house-keeper Elsie for company, to convalesce. Riding, eating, walking, resting. One day in early May he'd been on his way back to

Moorgarth when a despatch rider, goggled, helmeted, stepped off his Douglas cycle in the village:

'Had you heard, the Germans have sunk the *Lusitania*? The bastards.'

Hurrying back to Ida, then running down with her to rouse Mrs Clarkson at the post office. Putting a call through to Middlesbrough and hearing there was no news yet of survivors. Then going back, not to Moorgarth, but to the Dennisons where there was a telephone (and a plainly shocked Eleanor, caring, it seemed, as much as if it were her own father). The call came at eight the next morning. Aunt Dulcie's voice: Dad was safe. Yes, it was certain – the telegram had come directly from him. She was making the call because Mother was too upset. Mother had had a fainting fit on hearing the news.

The day before going back to Middlesbrough to welcome Father home, he went for a last ride. He could see from his window his cream mare, Eulalia, grazing. As he crossed the yard, her nose, eager and questing, came over the wall. She arched her head in anticipation as he produced from his pocket a wizened apple. She ate it, yellow teeth bared. Her cream-coloured coat was caked with mud where she had rolled in it: pale curly mane matted, folded back on itself.

Caressing her, 'My Eulalia,' vowing yet again 'You shan't be cannon fodder,' he felt himself unsettled, like the weather. Part of the general anger. Yesterday old Mr Outhwaite in the chandler's had said, 'There's not a German in England'll sleep safe in his bed tonight.' Riots in Liverpool and Hull. More Germans interned, rushed to the Isle of Man. 'A fine grown lad,' the words hung in the air. 'A fine grown lad like you, you'll be wanting to go.'

He didn't. Although had he wished, he could have passed for seventeen, even eighteen. Nor was he really indispensable in the firm yet. He knew quite a lot technically and would soon know a lot more, but when the time came the firm would manage well enough, would help the war effort, without him. He thought of Dad's journey to the States (how successful, they would be hearing from him); the acid-resisting bearings, Dad's own invention, which had so interested Packard. Whatever the outcome (and surely it would mean increased production?) they could manage without him. James was the greater loss. James, while not eager to fight, had been full of a sense of duty.

Running his fingers through Eulalia's knotted mane, Dick

thought: I could not bear to be a soldier. An officer, leading his men out of the trench, first and fearless.

The mood followed him throughout the ride. As he came up on to Thackton Rigg, he stopped for a while. Listening. Down in the valley a dog barked. Then he heard a skylark sing, saw the bird begin its ascent. He leaned forward a little in the saddle: the lark was singing still, spiralling now, higher, higher, until, although he strained, he could see it no longer.

Air, sky, the natural habitat of birds. What must it be like alone up there? But of course, he thought suddenly, I don't need to be a soldier, don't need to live underground. Life of a mole, sniped at, gored by bayonets, buried at any moment by an explosion. *I shall fly*, he thought. When the time comes, I shall fly. Up, up, into the sun. Wings opening into the sun. A skylark.

The next evening (could it be only a day since he'd watched the lark ascending?) he stood with Ida and Aunt Dulcie beneath the glazed arched roof of Middlesbrough station, watching anxiously for the familiar figure, bushy eyebrows, assured stride, walking the length of the platform. And then . . . But what was this? He had expected Dad to be differently, perhaps oddly dressed – after all he had lost everything. But that Dad wouldn't be alone . . . Yet here he was, unlikely check coat and, holding tight his hand, a small, plump, dark girl, in a plaid coat-dress and with a scarlet bow in her hair.

Maria. Maria Verzotto. About to alter all their lives. Her voice: strange, partly American, partly something else. Her quaint way of speech, her boldness, followed by attacks of painful shyness when she would attempt to hide in Dad's coat. She was to call Dad 'Uncle Eric', but often she forgot and would say just, 'Mister. Hey, mister . . .'

She had lost not only, tragically, her mother, but also the rich Americans who had semi-adopted her. She was to stay in Middlesbrough with them until her future could be decided. Aunt Dulcie took her to Wilson's the draper's to kit her out. At Thackton two weeks later, Eleanor Dennison's help was asked. Like her, Maria was a Roman Catholic.

Maria. Better not to remember how some of them hadn't liked her. Jenny's jealousy. Peter's sulks. Mother was difficult too. 'I trust I'm not expected to put myself out for – that,' she had said forbiddingly, within earshot of Maria. 'Let Dulcie bother.'

Dick had liked her at once. It was he who'd shown her the player-piano (the ragtime rolls, the gramophone records so lovingly bought by Dad in New York, at the bottom of the sea now). Those first few weeks, still lost and bewildered, she'd seemed her most contented when she sat pedalling, occasionally singing along.

Gradually after her arrival life had returned to normal, wartime normal. He had gone back to work at the foundry. No one spoke of his enlisting. Rightly they worried instead about James who, further cause of family pride, was awarded the MC after the battle of Loos in September. In the autumn he came home on a fortnight's leave. Handsome, confident, and tired. Tiredness gave him a distinguished air, as did the no longer new Sam Browne and the soft cap, battered now, worn carelessly at an angle. Frequent fast, nervous cigarette-smoking. He refused a cigar from Dad the first evening although he accepted a brandy and three whiskies. At the foundry he walked round the floor with Dad, Dick in tow, and asked the right questions.

Where do I fit in? Dick had thought then. In the middle – Mother's least favourite son. Dad's – what? Not a favourite there. It was James the firstborn, the natural inheritor, who effortlessly did everything right. *'My son, James.'* Who could forget Dad's face when he presented James to anyone? And then, five months after that last leave, he had been killed. Within hours, Dick had seen his mantle falling, slipping easily on to Peter's shoulders. A distressed Peter who declared, uneasily emotional, voice breaking, 'If it wasn't for school, I'd step in tomorrow . . . I'll make the works what *he* would have done – you wait and see.' And then, fiery red, he had burst out sobbing and left the room.

Dick, struggling with emotions that wouldn't go into words, had felt his face stiffen, his lips swollen and dry. (James, running out from the trench, shot like a fox who leaves his lair? or buried underground in a shower of dust and metal?) All he could do was blurt out:

'Did they – will they tell us how he died?'

Silence.

'Dick,' Aunt Dulcie said reprovingly. 'Dick. In front of your mother . . .'

He applied to join the Royal Flying Corps just before his eighteenth birthday. The interview went well and he expected to go within a week or two so that he could begin his new life before courage cooled. But he heard nothing till the early cold days of October, when he was sent for to go south to Stamford, in Lincolnshire. At first it hadn't been too bad. Excitement and comradeship. That perhaps was what he'd been missing since leaving school. Walking with, or without, father on the foundry floor, had been no substitute for shared experiences. Now it was new, quickly-made friends. Judson, Littlewood, Rattler, Price-Davies, Snelgrove, Osborne. Same problems, excitements, joys and sorrows. *Same fears*.

He trained on a Maurice Farman and then an Avro, after a while in ground school. His friend was Rattler, with whom he was billeted in a room above a gunsmith's. He had two hours of dual instruction. His instructor was only twenty and looked younger than he did: yellow down where a moustache was intended. Dick learned with hushed fear that only the month before, two instructors had been killed by their pupils. It wasn't necessary to fly over the German lines to meet death.

Machine-gun class he found too easy and consequently dull. 'The return of the fusee.' 'The tripping of the lock.' Rattler whispered loudly: 'What about the tripping of the light fantastic? Tonight's the Bunny Hug *if* they let us out in time.' He had his eye on some very attractive nurses stationed nearby.

A chap named Wheatley went up to loop without permission, and crashed. His wings fell off. 'I'm not interested in stunts,' Dick told Rattler. But it was all Rattler wanted to do. He dreamed of swooping like a bat, beneath a bridge, closer, closer to the ground. People beneath him scattering in terror. Skimming the tree-tops, circling church spires, dicing with danger.

It wasn't what Dick wanted. Surprisingly in all those days of training, he had never lost that first vision of a lark soaring. The day he took his altitude test, more than nine thousand feet up, he saw in the distance what he thought was a bird. It was another plane. After a while it began to spin. Spinning, spinning, and disappearing beneath the clouds. He went up and up, his wings ice-covered from the clouds, dense white, that he'd passed through. And then above, a sky of such blue. That very blue into which the lark had soared. Underneath him the white clouds were snow-covered mountains. How far could he see? If not to heaven then at least to France and beyond: Germany, Hungary, Russia. Happy, so happy in his loneliness. As alone, solitary, as that lark had been.

*

Autumn of 1917 and they were in France. Added now to the other smells of flying, the castor oil, the varnish, the petrol, was the smell of fear. The Germans had parachutes. The British had not. Better a machine-gun blow you to smithereens, even to drown in mud, than to fall from the skies – a ball of fire trapped in a machine. Price-Davies told him:

'If you're going to be ushed out in a blaze of glory, then for God's sake, carry a revolver.'

There were good times. His friends saw to that. Littlewood, who'd achieved a bullet wound in one ear, wondered if he should wear a ring in it? 'Bound to impress the ladies.' Not that Dick was very much gone on girls. At home there had been no one – unless it had been Nancy Carstairs in the days of dancing class. Nancy Carstairs from the richest family in Middlesbrough. At parties she had chosen him always, and just after his seventh birthday he had asked her to marry him. Since then, it was rumoured that she was sweet on him. At training school in Lincolnshire there had been the nurses. Forbidden meetings, jaunts. Eve, the vicar's daughter from Wiltshire, who had flirted, held his hand, laughed at and excited him. She had had only two topics: teasing him and admiring herself. He'd liked both. But for all the evenings he'd spent with her, alone together only when walking the short distance home, there seemed nothing now.

They didn't speak much of their fears. Better not. In the evenings in the mess, sounds not of a lark singing, but of a bunch of boys. Dick at the piano, stomach in knots, head throbbing.

'Rag it, tickle the old ivories, Grainger.' Often, too often, there was a death to celebrate. They sang:

'. . . *The young aviator lay dying, and as 'neath the wreckage he lay, To the Ack Emmas around him assembled, these last parting words did he say.'*

Littlewood, Judson and Price-Davies were all dead by early September. The next week Dick received a 'lucky' light shoulder wound. Soon after he left the hospital, he learned that his squadron was to go on to Home Defence.

Rattler was not pleased. 'Gothas and Zeppelins – not the same at all. I'd much rather get the Hunfamous Hunarinos in a straight fight . . .'

'. . . *Take the cylinder out of my kidney, the connecting rod out of my brain, From the small of my back take the crankshaft, and assemble the engine again . . .'*

3

A sharp cold morning in January 1918. Mrs Dennison's voice, at nearly seventy as firm and clear as a young girl's, came from upstairs: 'Eleanor, what are you doing, are you down there, Eleanor?'

Eleanor, tempted not to answer at all, had learned over the years that it didn't help. 'I'm writing to Basil,' she called up firmly, 'and am trying to concentrate.'

That should have silenced her mother, but instead, mention of her beloved priest-son brought her, slowly and heavily because of her increasing lameness, down the stairs.

'Wait, please, Eleanor, I have a message. The memorial cards for Mrs Struther –' She was approaching the desk, small plump hands clasping her cane. Below the net which tidied her wispy front hair (and tonight would leave a red mark) little gold-rimmed spectacles. Behind them, cold pale blue eyes.

'Did you hear me, Eleanor?'

'I must finish what I'm writing first –'

'I don't care for your tone. Basil is more likely to wish for a message from me than anything you might have to say, my dear.'

Eleanor's lips tightened to keep back the angry words – full lips that became suddenly thin.

'Tut! I've come downstairs without my knitting. Run up, would you, Eleanor?'

Despising herself, Eleanor went. Heavy, angry, so that it seemed to take her as long as it would have done Mother. She wanted to drag the khaki sock from its three needles, to pull and pull the thread: her fingers ached with renounced mischief.

'At last. I wondered if perhaps you had decided to stay upstairs contemplating a work of art?'

Back at her letter, Eleanor thought suddenly, painfully, of Eric Grainger, and of how she loved him. 'It seems to me,' her mother was saying, thrusting in the needle, smoothing the khaki stocking stitch, 'unnecessary to have told Basil of my small upset with the coalman –'

'Kindly *do not* read my letters!'

'Temper, my dear, temper.'

Agitated, Eleanor addressed the envelope. 'The Reverend Basil Dennison, SJ' Her hand shook. A duty letter, its contents dull and uninspired, and even then Mother had found matter for discontent. It's as if she knew, Eleanor thought, that I don't care much for Basil, just as I don't care for my sister, Margaret. God must know, have always known, which of the family I loved best. Or why else would He have taken them away?

Six of them: the children of Lieutenant-General Roland Dennison and Dorothy Cicely Lockwood-Turner, married in Egypt in 1873. Guy first: Eleanor marvelled later that he should have been at once so perfect and so nice. Remembering a lawn in sunshine and a godlike being with curly hair, taller even than Papa, who'd swung her round and round ('Stop, stop, *do it again!*') For three happy years she had been able to follow him about. Worshipping. But even in those days, it had not been right with Mother. That voice, haunting her earliest memories, cutting, accusing. Father was often fierce but, heard from behind the nursery door, not truly frightening. It was the reassuring boom of a foghorn (seaside holidays at Cromer), the excitement of a thunderstorm.

After Guy, another son, Arthur, who had lived only ten months. Then Margaret and after they were back in England, Basil. And Barbara. *Babs. My sister.* When anyone said, 'sister', Eleanor thought always of Babs (why never of Margaret with her Guards colonel husband and her four lively children, the eldest already asking how soon could he 'have a go at the Hun'?) Babs, eighteen months older than Eleanor and, after Basil went away to school, her chief companion, friend and protector.

She and Babs were to be educated at the convent Mother had attended in the eighteen-sixties. Margaret had left the year before and their questions bored her, while they regretted all the times she'd talked of school and, uninterested, they hadn't listened. She was going out to India that autumn to act as hostess for Guy whose regiment was stationed in Naipur. Her mind was on that, and on the wardrobe she would take.

September 1895 saw them at the Convent of the Resurrection with its views of the Sussex Downs from the high dark windows. The nuns were called by their surnames prefixed by Mother. Some were quite young, but all seemed to Eleanor to hint disapproval in a way that reminded her of Mother. Indeed when she answered them: 'Yes, Mother, No, Mother,' there seemed little difference.

Altogether she wasn't too happy in this dour stone building with its long corridors, strict rules, cold mornings and lumpy porridge. But it was all right because of Babs. The nuns spoke of her as *'dear* little Barbara'. That never happened to Eleanor who was not little – indeed she'd grown so fast that, standing straight, her head cleared Babs by a full two inches.

Babs was naughty ('Let's commit a teeny half-size sin, the sort Our Lord'll hardly notice and Mother Etherington not at all . . .') but never brought any wrath down on herself. Her face wore the right expression. Eleanor's did not. 'Bold,' the nuns said, 'I don't like your *bold* manner, Eleanor. Why can't you be more like Barbara?' Praise and comparison that could have made her dislike Babs. Only Babs didn't want to be good – though she rather fancied, she said, a broad blue Child of Mary ribbon. She puffed out her small ripening bosom in anticipation.

In the summer of 1896, Babs, thirteen now, became ill. The illness began with a nagging pain which Mother Kenward, the Infirmarian, thought was constipation. Babs said: 'She asked me if I'd been, you know, on the throne. "Have you done your duty, dear?" and then gave me fizzy Eno's.' But after two mornings of fruit salts Babs had still not been able to do her duty. Castor oil followed. Pain then, violent ineffectual griping, cramping. Babs was in the infirmary. The school doctor was sent for.

'I want to see her,' Eleanor said, lips trembling. When Mother Hilderson told her, 'Later, after lessons,' she repeated, 'I want to see her *now.*' The nun, irritably tapping her hand: ('Is that the way to speak to a Mother?') told her: 'Very well. But five minutes only.'

The doctor had just left when she arrived panting at the infirmary door. She rushed over to the iron bed: 'Babs, they won't tell me what's wrong, are you going to die?'

'Silly, rumpty foo,' Babs said in a brave voice. Eleanor sat on the end of the bed while Mother Infirmarian hovered. 'The doctor asked where Daddy was and I said in Egypt. I terribly wanted you to come and see me.' She clung to Eleanor's outstretched hand. 'I'm frightened,' she said, 'the pain . . .'

Eleanor laid her head on the high pillow beside her sister. 'Babs . . .'

Mother Infirmarian pulled her away. 'What a lot of fuss. Back at once to your classroom.'

Babs had a fever next time she was allowed in. Word went round that Barbara Dennison was very sick. Eleanor overheard the head girl talking: 'They say it's a bowel obstruction.' It was to be years before she knew the truth. The ineffectual, irritating laxative followed by the heavy purge. The ruptured appendix. Peritonitis setting in. Fever, more pain. Their father, cabled. Mother, ill in bed – too ill to travel, she said.

Babs's face was heavily flushed, her legs drawn up under the blue cotton blanket. She breathed raspingly, and when she spoke her voice was so faint, Eleanor had to bend right over the bed. Another time, Babs was asleep when she came in. Eleanor wanted to sit by the bed and hold her hand, but Mother Infirmarian shooed her away. 'She's always worse after you've excited her.'

But as Babs grew more and more ill, Eleanor didn't want to leave her. She wanted to sleep in the infirmary with her. Mother Kenward discouraged this, sending her back whenever she made further, frequent visits without permission.

One evening, escaping from her dormitory before Lights Out, it seemed to her that Babs was much worse. She lay mouth open, face flushed, breathing heavily. Eleanor said:

'She shouldn't be like that. I want to talk to her. Babs, talk to me!'

The nun took hold of her arm. 'Don't disturb your sister. You are a thoughtless child.'

She pleaded: 'The infirmary – it's nearly empty. *I want to be with her.*'

'The infirmary is for sick people . . . Don't be difficult, child.' Her voice although exasperated was kindly.

Eleanor began to whimper. That was a mistake. They would never allow her to stay now. She knew even as she wept.

'You'll wake her, if you go on. She needs the sleep.'

'She isn't asleep,' she cried, almost screaming in her panic, 'she isn't asleep, she's *dead*.'

Mother Etherington from the dormitory had come in. They reasoned with her. 'Look, child, you can see her breathing.'

They were kind still. Reasonable. They promised her if there was any cause for worry, they would send for her. 'You promise?' she begged tearfully, looking over to where Babs lay, tucked tight in the high iron bed. Back in the dormitory, she could not sleep. She lay, chilled, behind the curtains of her bed. Praying.

Oh, how she prayed. Six decades of the rosary. The *Memorare*, over and over. *'O Blessed Virgin Mary, never was it known that anyone who had recourse to thee . . .'*

She must have slept a little because when the heavy bell sounded it was as if through a fog, the words insistent, *'Vigilate et orate, vigilate et orate,'* as the prefect went down the beds. She splashed water, dressed hurriedly, forgetting the sash for her cotton frock. Then as the others looked on, without speaking she rushed from the dormitory.

Mother Kenward came to the door. She put a finger to her lips. 'Hush.'

'Where is she? I want –'

The nun took her by the hand. 'Quietly, my child. I have to tell you –'

'She's dead, isn't she? She's *dead*?'

'Our Lord has taken her. You see –'

'You promised,' she cried, 'you *promised*!' She rained blows on the nun's habit. She shouted, 'Was she alone when she went to Jesus – when she *died*?' That terrible dark word with its long corridors, leading where? (Not to hell – however naughty Babs had been, they had not been grave sins.)

The nuns made excuses. Eleanor had been tired, of what good to wake her, to frighten her? And Babs had slipped away. She had never woken. It had all been too late to do anything.

She went numb after that. She was numb for a long time. She felt terror whenever she thought feeling might come back. Mother was angry with her for not wanting to talk about Babs. 'I myself suffered deeply, confined to bed, unable to visit her. The nuns tell me you were very difficult and hysterical. That cannot have helped.'

Hard times. Times of heavy winter-cold sorrow: reproached by the nuns for not honouring Babs's memory, reproached by Mother, watching her body grow taller and heavier, carrying before her unwanted embarrassing breasts. Looking in the glass and seeing that she would never be beautiful. She cried only when she was alone or when she dreamed, as she did sometimes, that Babs was still alive. So that it was somehow not so much of a shock, she was in a way prepared, when three years later, in the Boer War, her beloved Guy died. His regiment had been sent from India to South Africa at the beginning of the fighting. He was dead within a month of enteric fever. Margaret, about to be married to one of his brother officers, sailed for England.

Her fiancé survived, came home (and now in 1918 was still fortunate, having a staff post with Field Marshal Haig).

At seventeen she left the convent. She did not have much social life. She enjoyed good clothes, but not the frills that Mother insisted on. She remembered a dreadful yellow-spotted chiffon ball dress with ruffles. Mother told her: 'You quite spoiled it, Eleanor – a solemn face weighs a frock down so.' Once someone described her as: 'A handsome girl. Rather splendid-looking, really.' Mother, hearing, snorted gently.

In 1905 when she was twenty, Father, who'd been retired some time, decided they should live in Yorkshire. He bought Park Villa in Thackton-le-Moors, an 1877 house of red brick, gabled and with a generous garden and small orchard behind. It stood on the road leading out of the village. Two rooms were set aside for Eleanor. It was taken for granted she would be staying as mother's companion. No one so much as mentioned 'When you get married'. Father, who seemed never to notice that she and Mother did not get on (Mother was always so charming to him, so full of flattery and solicitude), told Eleanor, 'It's good for your mother to have you there. When I go . . .'

By this time Margaret was busy with three children, and following her army husband around. Basil had been already some years with the Jesuits. He told Eleanor that it was Guy's death which had shown him his vocation: 'Even though I knew, as son and heir, it might be my duty to have a family. There was quite a conflict.' All this, in his dry voice with its almost querulous tone. She had wished she could like, even love him a little. But they had never been easy together. In his twenties he had already begun to seem elderly, with his fine thinning hair and his narrow-bridged nose which looked always a little disdainful.

He was critical of Eleanor, suggesting that she didn't take enough care of Mother. 'You are not a very spiritual person, Eleanor,' he said on the eve of his ordination. 'I speak of course as a brother, not as a priest.'

'A priest *to be*,' she corrected him.

'What's in a day?'

'Everything. If you believe that God is about to change you, make an indelible mark on your soul –'

He interrupted: 'You've skilfully changed the subject. As so often, I suspect, in your life, turning it to your seeming advantage.'

She gave up, did not think the battle worth fighting. So many people now she must guard herself against, so few to whom she could open her heart. Perhaps that was why, around that time, she fell in love with art. Her emotional life became completely bound up in it. She had no talent of her own – any attempts she made were heartbreakingly bad. She cursed her inability to capture in watercolour the gentle yet sometimes violent colours of the Yorkshire landscape: subtle greens shading into brown, yellows both muddy and brilliant, the slash of purple in late summer. She hated her stiff dilettante efforts.

Gradually as she came to know more about technique, she was able instead to marvel at what others had achieved. And most especially in fourteenth- and fifteenth-century Florence. All her gift money went on albums, reproductions, histories. Giotto, Cimabue, de Fabriano, Fra Angelico, Uccello, Botticelli, Filipo Lippi, da Vinci, Raphael. Madonnas and Venuses jostled for space on the walls of her bedroom. She feasted on them, tried to enter them. Heard them as if they were music. It seemed to her that they had life and breathed. Or rather, that she only breathed when she looked at them. She would feel afterwards as if she had gulped fresh air.

Ah, those colours, the brightness falling into her drab life. How she longed to visit Italy and most especially Florence. Perhaps if she had asked Father directly, he would have said Yes? But the project, the desire, had been so secret she hadn't been able to voice it. (To have had Mother mock her . . .)

Within a year of the move Father died very suddenly, of a heart attack. In his Will, he left her Park Villa – and Mother. Park Villa was to be Mother's home for the rest of her life, Eleanor never thought of the house as other than a gift on paper. While Mother lived she was, if anything, worse off. She had little or no money of her own: a handful of stocks and shares about which she knew nothing and which she would not have dared to sell. For everyday pocket money she had still to ask Mother. If she were to marry, her husband would have to live at Park Villa.

But she did not expect to marry. She felt certain of this. It was not enough to be 'handsome'.

Once, before the move to Yorkshire when they were living temporarily in London, Basil had brought home a fellow student. A slight, intense boy with a shadowed face – not unlike Dick Grainger. She had felt his eyes on her all during the evening. It was a strange sensation; it had not happened to her before. He was to be a priest, so, she thought, it could not be that he was interested in her. Too shy to look at him, she felt nevertheless a great need to mother him, to tell him that it, that everything, was *all right*. When he left she felt a sudden desperation that he should be going and she might never see him again. Often it was on the tip of her tongue to ask Basil about him. When she at last did, she learned that he had gone to a mission in China. For years she felt irrational guilt about this wicked love, desire, if that was what it had been. A priest. A priest to be. How wicked.

'Anything more to go in Basil's envelope?' Eleanor asked. Smell of hot wax. She stamped on the Dennison seal.

'How careless you are with the wax . . . The Grainger boy is on leave – you knew that, I suppose? They say he's very nervous. About what, I can't imagine.'

'He's at the controls of a plane,' Eleanor said sharply. 'That should be enough. Home Defence.'

'Fooey, Eleanor. Flying in *England* – it's hardly the trenches, you know.' And when Eleanor didn't answer: 'Always the best that go – James was a splendid boy. No wonder Maimie Grainger is so shattered still. I told her, "I know what you're suffering – I lost my firstborn, a firstborn is special." '

I know, I know, Eleanor thought. Those who come after are also-rans. She waited. But instead, another predictable:

'A priest now – a priest is rather special. And then a daughter who marries –' She lifted the sock: 'Time to turn the heel already . . . Grandchildren, a gift. Margaret has more than made up for you –'

Eleanor stood up. 'I'll walk to the post –'

'Don't interrupt me, just because I suggest you are less than perfect.'

'I'm very *im*perfect, I know. It's not for want of your telling me.'

'That tone again – I don't know what's wrong with you, unless it's constipation. I suspect jealousy.'

'Jealousy?' She stopped by the door. 'Jealousy? Of whom?'

'Basil, of course. For being a priest. God's anointed.'

As she changed into her outdoor shoes, she smelled lunch cooking. Savoury oatmeal pie. Because of the wartime food shortage, today was a meatless day. A wave of disconsolate hunger swept over her, merging with her anger at Mother.

At the post office, Mrs Clarkson, the postmistress, told her: 'There's a telegram come for Reeves.'

Eleanor hesitated. 'It's Tom gone, isn't it?' When Mrs Clarkson nodded, she said, 'I'd hoped . . . Mr Grainger tried to do something, you know. To get him transferred.'

'I ken. But there it is. Four gone in three year. And now Tom. I'd thought Vicar'd mebbe break it them, but he's ill abed – And this telegraph business, I don't reckon nowt to it. Lad'd never get a bike over t'moors.'

'Someone should walk over there. I could.'

'It's a way, Miss Dennison. Alone?'

'No,' she said, suddenly thinking of it, 'no, I shall ask one of the Graingers.'

Dick only was at Moorgarth. He agreed at once. 'I'm only idling,' he said, 'and already tired with it.' They decided to set out as soon as possible. 'Two hours to cross the moor,' he said. 'An hour there and two to return – We should be back before the light goes.'

'Daylight saving, tampering with the clock and upsetting people, will be some help,' Eleanor said. Home again, she ignored her mother's protests, saying: 'It's the least I can do. Tom was our gardener.'

They set out at a steady pace. If he kept back for her, she didn't sense it. The going was hard: as they left the fields behind and began climbing the moor to the west of the dale, they made their way through boggy patches and sedge grass. Damp, beaten-down bracken fronds clung to their boots. The sky was the grey of winter, shading from pale to metallic. But the moor still hinted at autumn with its strong russet tones.

She said, 'I think we do right to go in person. A woman should be there – and you, Dick, you're a familiar face.'

'The Reeves lads,' he said, 'when I was in short trousers, they were like gods to me. They could order people about. Tom had the most authority of all. I envied him.'

'But now –'

He interrupted, his voice sharply bitter, 'Oh, but some might. For him it's all over and done with. They can't shoot him down in flames, can they?'

They sat half an hour at the farmhouse. Eleanor had suggested the kitchen, but almost at once after hearing the news Mrs Reeves had sent her grieving daughter Ada to lift the blinds in the parlour, and set a match to the fire. Stiff with cold and sorrow, she sat with her guests. 'I can't rightly believe it,' she said over and over.

Ada brought in a tray of tea and hastily made griddle scones. 'You'll take a bite, a sup?' Mrs Reeves asked anxiously, as if to clutch at Eleanor. They could not have left without seeming heartless. But when they stood up to go she saw that it was already quite late, and the light beginning to go.

A bumpy grass track led away from the farmhouse. The air in the darkening sky seemed heavy, pressing down on her. Walking beside Dick, she felt an immense tiredness: the weight of sharing for a little while someone else's sorrow. She wanted to say something of this to him, but could not find the words. She said instead, 'I shouldn't care for this walk back if there were snow.'

Dick said, 'We've often walked in snow, you and I. Long family hikes – except there doesn't seem to be family now. We all go, we have to, our separate ways . . . Will the world ever be the same again?'

'How can it be?' She sensed the anxiety in his voice, but didn't know how to allay it. She asked him the time and he took out his watch, but the light was so far gone that he had to strike a lucifer.

'Later than we thought,' he said. 'We must hurry. I don't like . . .' he sniffed the air: 'a smell like fog.'

They were trudging the rough grassy road still that linked the Reeves's and other scattered farmhouses, at the point where the enclosed land ended. In the distance, scarcely visible now against the darkening skyline, was Thackton Rigg. Along the top of it a road ran directly to the village. He said:

'Once up there, even if there's fog or mist we'll at least be able to find our way.' They left the track and began to make their way slowly uphill, walking at an angle through sodden heather, Eleanor stumbling occasionally, Dick asking, 'All right? Take my arm.'

And then the mist fell. As suddenly and as totally as a blanket of snow. One moment the Rigg could just be made out. The next, in front of them was only a cold swirling. Eleanor put a hand on Dick's coat. She said as calmly as she could, 'I can see you – just.'

His voice pierced the gloom. 'We can't go down again, you know. I wouldn't trust us to find the rough road. And if we're not on it we'll never find the farmhouses. Any of them.'

Eleanor said, 'Logically we just have to keep walking slightly upwards. Then we *must* reach the ridge top.'

But it wasn't like that. From the first moment of cold white threads, muffling them, she had known they would become lost. She was filled with terror even before it happened. She had never realized how much she relied not just on the ground beneath her feet, but on the sight of expected things. Landmarks. North, south, east, west. Here now, was that terrifying game of childhood. Blindman's buff (twirled once by Basil so ferociously that when he'd stopped, she had keeled over).

'Something's wrong,' Dick said. 'We should have surely hit the road by now.'

The fog was if anything denser. Soon the light would go completely. She was afraid she would lose him. 'Don't move far away,' she said, her capable manner deserting her: no longer thirty-two-year-old Miss Dennison, but a frightened girl.

They continued, still seeming to climb. Occasionally the ground would dip, puzzling, frightening her. Moorland she thought she knew well became now as foreign, as treacherous, as something in a fairy tale. When Dick said, 'Eleanor – we're lost,' he voiced what she already knew.

They linked arms. 'We are,' she said. 'What shall we do?'

Dick made a plan, cheered her, soothed her. She heard in his tones for the first time echoes of Eric. She had never thought him like his father. Only in James had she seen, though physically different, some of the easy charm that Eric must have had as a young man. He said, 'I wish I knew where we'd gone wrong. I was leading, after all, it's me who's landed us in this mess. Our families will be terribly worried. Your mother –'

Oh, let her, Eleanor thought angrily, still irritated with her from the morning. She said, 'It will do her good to worry about me. I am with her too much, you see. Margaret makes a virtue of scarcity. And then she has given her grandchildren, which I have not. I am nothing –'

'You're not nothing to us. To the Grainger family,' Dick said hotly. She could feel the warmth of his defence of her. He said sadly, 'If I'd Eulalia here, she'd know the way home. She always did. I'd never to guide her back.'

'How do they know? Smell?'

'Smell. Instinct. Something we haven't got or have lost. Look at homing pigeons. Carrier pigeons.' But talk of carrier pigeons brought thoughts of War and the Front, messages winging to and fro. All that world that had been too much with them that afternoon.

Dick's plan was to search out a sheep hollow, preferably one with tallish heather around it. (Could it not have been sheep hollows deceiving them just now, so that they'd mistaken rising ground for falling?) Sheltering in one of these, they would make out as best they could until daylight.

The griddle scones and the tea seemed long ago. But she wasn't hungry. Only cold. Her coat was heavy and damp, her feet swollen as if iced in her boots. Her fingers, stiff inside her leather gloves, wouldn't bend.

The silence seemed part of the mist, as if any sound near them must be muffled by it. Once they heard sheep but so distant it might have been in another country. In the hollow where they huddled together, half-lying, half-sitting, Dick was so close she could feel his warm breath against her frozen face. He had offered her his scarf, wrapping it round so that just a space was left for breathing and talking.

Dick, dear, dear Dick. In the stillness and the silence, the gaps, easy, between conversation during this long, long night, she thought: If I could only tell him. The fancy took her, the longing, compulsion almost, to say to him, 'Dick, I love your father. I love him more than anybody or anything in this world or the next. He is God the Father, the Son and the Holy Ghost. My love for him is every wicked blasphemy you can think of and it can only bring down on me retribution, but I am quite powerless. Every time I go to Confession – you've heard of Catholic Confession, Dick? – every time I go I know what I should say, because it is wicked and not at all permitted. *But I cannot help it.*'

It was the summer of 1908 she first became friends with the Graingers. They had bought Moorgarth the previous winter. (She learned later that the deeds for the purchase had been a Christmas present to Maimie, parcelled up under the candle-lit tree in Linthorpe Road. At the time the story had seemed to her romantic; later, merely ironic.)

The Graingers walked in all weathers. She discovered this one blustery July day, cold enough for March, when she met them up on Thackton Rigg. She was fleeing Mother, needing that day an escape that was more than just running to her room and immersing herself in Giotto.

How had Mother upset her? Through Babs, of course. Yet again, the reproach: '. . . that you should have gone to your bed and *slept*, when you knew she was dying. I had my illness, of course . . . But for *you*, it was possible. Coward.'

White with anger and pain, Eleanor had left the room, slamming the door first, then striding out not too well shod, and regretting it. The weather growing worse and worse.

Four walkers came into view. The Grainger family: father and three older children: James, Ida, Dick. She had met them once only under rather stiff social conditions. She could not recall much of the occasion. James, knickerbockered and tall, must be about fourteen, and Ida twelve. Dick, limping behind, could not have been more than nine.

'It's Miss Dennison, isn't it?' James said. He was in the lead. Their father and Ida joined him a moment later. Eric laughed, took off his hat. Ida, turning, called back to Dick: 'All right, slowcoach?'

James said to Eleanor, 'Poor sort of summer weather we're having –'

Eric interrupted: 'I can see Miss Dennison is used to it, and doesn't need the heavy protection we do.' Then as Dick arrived beside him: 'Well, son, here is one of our neighbours.'

'He can usually keep up,' Ida said. 'It's a heel rubbed or something.'

Eleanor said, 'I'm not going any further. Not in this footwear – I mistook the weather. Why don't I stay with Dick a while? Walk him down at his and my pace?'

'That's very civil of you,' Eric said, 'if we don't put you to trouble.' He turned to Dick.

'Yes, please,' Dick said, 'If she – if Miss Denson –'

'*Dennison*, Dick. Say it correctly, lad.'

Dick and she set out well after the others. He had found a sheep skeleton he wanted to show her. They gazed a while at a mackerel sky growing slowly clearer, revealing the pattern beneath them of fields crisscrossing the hillside, the road below, and beyond that the dark form of the woods following the river as it twisted out of sight. She walked slowly to accommodate herself to his pace. The others could not be seen now. Dick took his boots off. 'Otherwise I'll wear a hole in my stockings. But I'll have to go even more slowly now, because of the stones and turning an ankle.'

They came to where the bracken, green now and toughfronded, brushed against their legs, calf high. They had to force their own path. Dick seemed not at all shy of her.

'Did I tell you about my pony?' he asked, pushing the bracken apart with his hands. She thought she had seen a black pony, grazing in the field behind Moorgarth. It was an early birthday present, he said. The others weren't interested in Hero: 'He's all mine, he needs me to feed him. Tom or Ernest Reeves, they look after him when I'm in Middlesbrough.' One day, he told her, he was going to have a cream mare. He would break her in himself.

By the time they arrived at Moorgarth, the others had been back nearly half an hour. Easily, gladly, she accepted their invitation to tea. She sat in the warm oak-beamed room before a roaring fire. Behind the floral chintz sofa and armchairs was a white-clothed table laden with food, where Peter and Jenny sat with a nursemaid. They were joined by Dick, who'd had his heel dressed. It was more like a winter afternoon tea.

She ate prodigiously – she who so often watched listlessly Mother chewing with precision her two muffins, her slice of seed cake. She ate scones thick with butter and newly made strawberry jam, victoria sponge, eccles cakes, potted meat sandwiches, ginger parkin. She was almost ashamed – and at the same time happy.

Maimie Grainger was missing ('Ma is resting,' James had said), but Dulcie was there. Eleanor was half way through her second scone when this small, breathless, elegant figure came hurrying in: kissing Jenny, patting Peter's head, exclaiming at Dick's bad luck. Coming to sit on the sofa near Eleanor's chair, and beside Eric who, legs stretched out, was reading the *Whitby Gazette*.

'I've been meaning to call,' she told Eleanor. 'We met at the Crowthers', so briefly though, and I spoke only to your mother, I think?' Then began a conversation which seemed hardly to have stopped since. Dulcie, who had become her dearest friend. They talked about moorland scenery and watercolours and Dulcie's terrible sketches. Eric looked up to say with a smile that, yes, they were rather dreadful. Eleanor comforted, said delightedly they could not possibly be as terrible as hers.

Soon they were speaking of real painters.

'You haven't been to Italy? Oh, but you *must*,' Dulcie cried. 'I went first about your age, and although the art was of course quite wonderful – the fashions also. I am quite mad, don't look at me, I am quite mad and frivolous about clothes, and shoes and hats. Maimie, my sister, has no patience with me at all.'

Suddenly in the room, caught in the air, a scent only, of danger. (Was it to do with Dulcie, and the excitement she brought in with her? Did it come perhaps from Eric?) Dick spoke from the tea-table:

'Dad, next time we go walking, can Miss Denson please come with us?'

Eric, looking up, smiled. 'Of course. Any time. Whenever she wants to join us.' For a few seconds she felt flattered, needed. And then in her moment of happiness, she remembered. Mother, left in unexplained anger.

'I have to go, I really must, at once.' She stood up awkwardly, the words tumbling out. A schoolgirl again. Everything suddenly spoilt.

Later, she was able to relive and treasure the afternoon. Holding it safe even when Dulcie came to call the next day, ignoring Mother's criticisms ('a frivolous little thing'). Dulcie, who wanted to be her friend. Meanwhile, Eric was as good as his word: she was invited to walk with them for the remainder of their summer visit, and then again during autumn week-ends.

But loving Eric – what of that? Why, when it happened, did it surprise her so totally? Of course, she was to think later, I should have been loving *someone*. Her heart: the trouble had been with her heart. Somehow in the years since Babs's death, and Guy's, her heart had shrivelled. A heart, smaller than it should have been. Unoccupied too. Perhaps that was why, she thought later, she had been so eager, so quick to give Eric not just a place in it, but the whole of it.

Although it happened suddenly, she could look back and see that it had been coming. They had all been out walking. It was late autumn. She was behind yet again with Dick who wanted to gaze down into the quarry. Ida and James were far ahead. She saw Eric stop for something. As she and Dick came up, he was crouched down. Standing behind him, she saw the width of his heavy jacket, the collar half up, half down. Without thinking, she reached out to arrange it – then drew her hand back as if burnt. In her confusion, she said hastily,

'Here we are! Not so far behind –'

'I found this, Eleanor dear.' He was rising to his feet. She saw cupped in his hand a sprig of bell heather, still with its deep purple. He looked directly at her. 'Take it.'

She knew then suddenly that she *was* dear to him. Part of the family, another daughter perhaps – but dear. Something happened in her heart as he spoke. She took the heather, stammering her thanks. She had to look away. She blushed like a fourteen-year-old girl.

For the rest of the outing she was torn between wanting to be with him, and wanting to be alone so that she could think of this momentous thing that had happened to her. *I love Eric Grainger*. She passed a night and then a day of such beauty. Instead of walking, she floated – no longer the awkward Eleanor. The wonder was that Mother didn't notice. Every minute she could feel her heart growing, swelling, with love.

Except . . . what could Eric *want* with her heart? He hadn't looked, never would look at her, as a woman to be loved (as she, for ever and ever, would love him?) And nor was there any way that she could ever tell him her secret.

Opposite Mother at the dining-table that next evening, curtains drawn against a sleet-filled sky, she saw that it was all quite quite hopeless. A pastel of Guy, aged eleven, faced her on the dining-room wall. She imagined she saw reflected in the glass, Eric's eyes, crinkled as they were when he smiled. Smell of cologne, cigar smoke. Eric held out his hand and touched hers. It was warm as he clasped her fingers in his palm. 'I found this, Eleanor dear –'

Sitting at the table, she gave an involuntary jump, as if burnt. Burnt. Of course she would burn. Loving Eric was a sin, a mortal sin. *Thou shalt not covet thy neighbour's wife*. It was so clear, the commandment: it meant – she had never realized it – nothing less than this painful longing. So why, oh why, had she not thought? How could she, a good Catholic girl, love, long for, desire (oh, beautiful wicked word), a *married* man?

The need now, this icy night, to declare her passion, was overpowering. She began to imagine that the whole fiasco, the taking of the wrong way, the being lost in a fog, was destined so that she could unburden herself, confide in this boy she had known from childhood. That what she could never say to Eric she could somehow tell his son. But what would he do with such a confidence? Would it not add horribly to all his other worries? Would she ever be able to speak to him again, alone? To look him in the face?

And yet . . . 'Dick, I –' she began. 'Your father –'

'What did he tell you about me?' His anxious boy's voice. 'That I'd never be like James? That I'm reckless with the motor?'

'No, no. Nothing like that.' I cannot say it, she thought. Must not. It is he who must talk. What had he said only this afternoon, about death in flames?

'You're frightened,' she said. 'Aren't you?'

'That we shan't survive the night? If we hadn't been able to find a hollow . . .'

'No, Dick dear. About – flying.'

The damp fog was a heavy grey blanket, pressing them down into the wet heather. Teeth chattering, he told her of his nightmares. 'I don't often talk like this.'

'But you ought. You must have someone to whom you can say it. You cannot expect to be brave and heroic all the time.' She thought of Dulcie. 'Your aunt, have you spoken to her?'

He said simply, 'I couldn't bear she shouldn't think well of me. When anyone criticizes me at home, she says, "Dick is all right." My mother, I couldn't speak to. And Ida thinks all men are brave – she'd show breezy common sense if they weren't.'

They lay huddled together in the ling bed. She thought: *I am sleeping the night with Eric's son.*

She talked of her love for art. 'If only I could paint or draw . . . I plan to go to Italy,' she told him. She did not mention money. How could she afford a trip when she was dependent on Mother even for a packet of pins? 'It's a long-cherished dream to go to Florence. To see the Fra Angelico, the true colours –'

The slow coming of daylight found them unbelievably stiff and cold. But they could see, even if not very far. And after a little, they heard below them the sound of a horse and cart. The carter giving commands. The rattle of harness.

They made their way down painfully, following the sound, Dick calling: 'Holloa, whoa, holloa.' The moorland was rimed with frost. He went ahead of Eleanor. He called back then that they had been noticed.

The carter helped them up. They sat exhausted, aching, humped against the sides of the cart. He offered to turn at once for Thackton. They went to Moorgarth first, at Eleanor's insistence.

There was a lamp on downstairs. A distraught Dulcie: 'Eric set out at first light. He has some searchers. You can't imagine what we've been thinking. The very worst . . . Eleanor, you must go at once to your mother, dearest . . .'

'How could you have upset me like that, Eleanor! Rushing off after luncheon with scarcely an explanation. And then to have caused such worry. It shows a person totally devoted to self.'

'Really I need to go to bed – or if the water can be heated, a bath . . .'

'Is that all you have to say? After my night of suffering?'

'I'm tired. And very, very cold. We might have died, you know –'

'Are you telling *me* what the worries should be? Eleanor, I despair. I cry to Our Lady in Heaven. Eleanor, what are you for? What is your purpose?'

'I don't know. Or care. And am going straight upstairs –'

'Don't care. Yes, that is it. I must care for *you* since you are not married. Better you should be a nun. If they would have you. Though I doubt they would take anyone of so little help to them. But you are afraid to ask, are you not, in case they refuse you?'

'Mother, I don't want to be a nun. I just want a bath.'

'There you go again. Creature comforts before anything else. A fine nun *you* would make, Eleanor.'

4

When Aunt Maimie came into the room, Maria did not show her the letter, although it was usually difficult to keep anything from her. Aunt Maimie sat down heavily, then plumped the cushion behind her. 'Perhaps you'd ring for Elsie, dear. She could bring me a nice cup of tea.'

The letter was from Rocco. Between the ill-written pencilled lines, already faint, she saw his face. Heard his voice. He and Gaetano were fighting. Uncle Eric had shown her on a war map the exact line of the Italian front. Rocco wrote that the life was hard and that he envied Gaetano who stayed doing everyday tasks and chores at base. He grumbled, 'I didn't know about fighting, this sort, when I made my decision . . .'

'And what has the postman brought little Maria?'

I don't have to tell her anything, Maria thought. But already it was a summer afternoon spoiled.

Summer of 1918. In March and April there had been terrible reverses in France. Towns and villages evacuated, the line going back. But now the Americans had landed and begun fighting. She had seen them in an illustrated paper in their high, broad-brimmed hats, looking so smart, so confident, so *new* to it all, and had had a sudden fit of longing for America.

Except that she was quite happy to be at Thackton. It was Thackton all the time now, which would have been lovely except that Aunt Maimie was there too – behaving as if she feared at this late date a German invasion (Aunt Dulcie, laughing but exasperated, said, 'It's not Germans worrying her, it's germs.') The germs that scared her were Spanish 'flu, already an epidemic among the Fleet in northern ports. It was a swift killer: healthy men, dead with pneumonia in a couple of days. 'Middlesbrough is a port, of course,' Aunt Maimie had said. 'The germs will travel by trawler.' It had been all Uncle Eric could do to stop her removing Peter, Maria and Jenny from school.

But even Aunt Maimie, walking restlessly round the house, irritating dear Aunt Dulcie, even she couldn't spoil the beauty of these summer months. This afternoon Miss Dennison would be taking her bees up to the heather. Two hives. They were to go with Thompson the carter. After Mass on Sunday, Miss Dennison had invited Maria to come too. The bees would be left to make honey on a stretch of moorland near Goathland.

Maria went out often, and usually alone. She just walked. This aimless wandering soothed her. High up on Thackton Rigg, she could worry in peace about Rocco and Gaetano. Dick too. Seeing swallows, flying high because of the hot weather, wheeling and screaming in the summer evening, she would think of him in the air. She picked harebells, taking them home to press. She put some in the exercise book where she'd copied her version of *The Golden Lion*. Pale in the strong sun and the wind, they took on a deeper blue as they dried.

She wandered too by the river Esk, sometimes taking along her crochet. At the water's edge, she watched cows on the opposite bank. Midges rose in a cloud about her straw hat. She was bitten by horseflies. 'Clegs,' Elsie called them. 'Nasty dratted things . . . Clegs,' she said over and over, making them sound like Germans who bayoneted babies and crucified Canadians after they'd cut nuns' breasts off, as they did in Aunt Maimie's stories.

Sometimes she sat on the moors, pretending she was a shepherd. The blackfaced sheep, thick shaggy fleeces overhanging their spindly mottled legs, ambled past or stared without curiosity. They didn't seem to know or care that she was perhaps only here on a visit. (Or so it seemed to her sometimes. For tomorrow it might all go. Tomorrow Uncle Eric might lose patience, find displeasure in her, wish he'd never adopted her.)

Rocco's letter: some of the pencil was quite lost, two lines censored. He thought of the family a lot, he said, especially Mamma. What sad, bad times there had been – so much sickness and death. 'If I live, *if*, I don't know whether to take a chance in our home again or go to 'Merica –'

'Maria.' Aunt Maimie's voice: 'Maria, I'm speaking to you.'

'I rang for the tea, Aunt –'

'The *Unseen Hand*, Maria, dear. Our secret enemies. Pro-Germans. You remember my telling you? And now there's worse – a conspiracy to spread *vice* here, Maria.' She paused, breathing heavily, 'You know what vice is, dear?'

'Sure.' Then proud of her way with words, 'It's being vicious –'

'I don't like "sure", Maria. It sounds a bit Irish even if you picked it up in the States.' She folded her hands on her lap. 'They plan to make our boys at the Front no good through *venereal* disease. And then to spread terrible vices all over England . . .'

'Yes. OK.'

'*OK!* What language . . . You know what venereal disease is, dear?'

Maria moved uncomfortably. The room was unpleasantly hot. Outside in the courtyard Trimmer gave several sharp barks.

'Revolting, dirty illnesses which women catch from men, and men from women who . . . You see, the poisons enter through certain parts . . .' Her face was flushed, excited. 'There is the Black Book – put together by *them*. Nearly fifty thousand names, all British subjects who could be blackmailed through their weakness – mostly the vice that the Bible speaks of in Sodom. You know about that, dear?'

'I might.' She caught the faded, sweetish yet stale smell that always hung about Aunt Maimie, lingering even in her hats. She felt faintly sick.

'Roman Catholics don't read the Bible, I know, but in Sodom –' her voice was husky with pleasure '– the men committed their disgusting act *with other men*. Putting their – member in a certain place. Like animals, Maria. Beasts –'

'Where is this book?'

'In Germany, of course. But a lady was shown it by two British officers in a hotel here in Yorkshire, while they were having afternoon tea . . .'

Aunt Maimie's voice droned on. She tried to snatch a glance at her letter. She thought of Rocco and America, and of how it had been.

'I want you to come to me if there's ever anything you need to know. After all, you are almost fifteen . . . How much do you know, dear, of what men do with women?'

When had she not known? Child in Monteleone. Sounds in the night, all sleeping in one room, how many to a bed? Animals were the same and what matter? She had always known. Only in America had it been perhaps different.

'Merica. That was to have been Paradise.

Dreadful voyage, dreadful landing. Sick, weak, confused, herded into the lighter. 'There's Ellis Island.' Red buildings. Oh, so weary, climbing the long flight of slate stairs up to the Great

Hall, its sheer size terrifying her. At the top of the stairs stood the white-coated doctors. Waiting. Watching out for the deformed, the lame, the breathless. 'Hold your head up,' Mamma said. They had to walk in circles. Fingers pulled at her eyes, poked her chest. Tongue out, tongue in. Undress, dress again.

The Verzotto family were all right. The son of the woman who on the boat had had the bunk above, his coat lapel marked with coloured chalk, was put aside in a cage with others. He was not all right.

Questions, questions. She had not understood half of them. The interpreter asked, was Papa an anarchist? Herded from one part of the building to another, they passed through in their thousands. As many as ten in a day. The sheep on the mountainside back at home had more dignity.

New York which they'd glimpsed across the bay. New York was 'Merica. 340 East 108th Street. She scarcely knew her numbers but she had that pat. If nothing else it was, after its fashion, home. They shared with the Cusimano family from the boat. Sicilian but not from Monteleone. Eleven children in all. Herded together now just as they'd been on the boat. Neapolitan families mixed in nearby tenements. Natural enemies. Rocco coldly swearing death to them all. Gaetano following him blindly.

They were cold all their first winter. There were three rooms among them and a real lavatory in the hall. And water, that was the wonder, water always. Their only heat was the stove in the kitchen. Rocco and Gaetano and the Cusimano boys got used coal from the dumps. Any firewood they had was stored in the bedrooms piled high to the ceiling.

The two families were united against Neapolitans but nothing else. Mamma and Mrs Cusimano had a feud. Mamma had brought some bed linen with her from Sicily. Worn, mended, but still bed linen. Mrs Cusimano had none. Her family slept with sewn-up cement bags for bedding. Out of jealousy, Mrs Cusimano cut up one of the Verzotto sheets.

Her memories now were of noise. Noise. And fear. The teeming streets, the cluttered iron fire-escapes, cluttered and clattering – the shouting, clanking, banging. The language was familiar, the smells; washing, brightly coloured, was strung from window to window just as at home. But it wasn't Monteleone. It was the big city. Thudding, jangling, whining, blare of motor horns, rumble of overhead railway.

At night there were bedbugs. They came off the wall. She was bitten badly. To escape, Rocco, Gaetano and the older Cusimano boys all slept down in the stables among the wagons. Better the flies off horse dung than bedbugs.

The iciness of the first winter, followed by the stifling heat of summer. No longer the relentless Sicilian sun but an airless, noisy, always noisy, heat. Papa, calling out his wares, pushed a cart loaded with cabbages, tomatoes, onions, squash. So, it seemed, did everyone else. In the fall Rocco and Gaetano left for Detroit with the three eldest Cusimano boys. Soon after Papa fell sick. He looked so small suddenly, seeming to shrink as they watched. There were medicines they couldn't afford and which did no good. Mrs Cusimano boiled up herbs for him.

Lean times, bad times. When Papa got very bad he was taken to St John's Floating Hospital. She did not see him again before he died. Pott's Disease was the name of his illness. She had bad dreams for a long time afterwards.

Often she didn't know what was what. Wondered what was happening. She was hungry still. Not as hungry as sometimes in Monteleone, but hungry.

Days and nights, weeks and months merged. Mamma had a letter from Detroit and some money. Mamma was always hungry, always worried. Another family joined them and there was as little room as ever. Mrs Amato had four children and a baby. Her husband was in prison. She and Mrs Cusimano screamed at each other. Mamma tried to keep the peace.

Then the two younger Cusimano boys got into trouble and were put in the Catholic Protectory. Soon after the eldest was sent to Elmira Reformatory. Maria didn't miss any of them. Their mother wailed and shouted. Mamma waited to hear more from Rocco and Gaetano but, apart from the money they'd sent for Papa, they never wrote.

Meantime she knew everything. As at home she'd known about animals, she knew everything, and knew it was nothing. She saw Gaspare Cusimano and the older Amato girl in the lavatory – the catch on the door not properly fastened. Gaspare waved his fist at her and laughed.

Lean time, bad times. She and Mamma huddled together in a makeshift bed. Cold and hungry. Hot and hungry.

One day a softly-spoken lady dressed in white came round the tenements. She brought them a coloured picture of Italy. A bridge over still water. 'That's Venice,' she told them. She said the picture was theirs to keep. She read out the wording underneath: 'A cough may lead to consumption.' There was an address to go to for advice. Mamma fastened the picture on the wall, covering over the crushed bedbugs.

It must have been the spring of 1913 when another lady called. She was very elegant, much smarter than the lady in white. She was what they called a 'do-gooder' and she had with her a list of posts in the homes of well-off Italian families. There was a live-in kitchen help in Brooklyn Heights. Mamma said she couldn't go because of Maria but the lady thought this might be all right. Mrs Cusimano, raising her fist in the air, said that she'd leave all *her* family willingly, *and* all those dirty Amato brats – to say nothing of Mrs Amato.

She and Mamma had gone to the Ricciardi's house. She had loved their home from the start, though its grandeur had frightened her. She remembered Don Cataldo's house in Monteleone. It also had frightened her. (Don Cataldo, the Lion she had once thought Golden. Forget now about Minicu. Never, never speak to anyone of what I heard.) There were luscious thick carpets, heavy velvet curtains, paintings, ornate furniture. She loved the scent in the house of wax polish, lemon oil, the exciting smells of meat cooking in rich sauces. There was always enough to eat in the kitchen. She began to forget the pains of hunger. The worry of hunger.

She was to keep out of the way, which had not seemed too difficult. She met Mr and Mrs Ricciardi, who were very nice to her and said they wanted to give as many chances as possible to immigrant families in distress. She was washed and scrubbed and deloused and given clothes and sent to school.

Then, a year later, came the day when Mamma saved Ettore's life. Ettore, the new Ricciardi baby, who had cried, it seemed, almost every minute from birth. Who ailed and scarcely ate. Who might not live. Maria and Mamma, dressed in their best, coming back from Sunday Mass with the baby's nurse. Nurse Maranzano, tearful from lack of sleep and apprehension: 'And now Mrs Ricciardi cries too, all day and half the night.'

Mamma asked to see Ettore. She and Maria would visit the nursery and say an Ave Maria. Skinny, wailing child. Mamma putting her shawl aside. 'OK, I pick him up?'

It was the Virgin Mary or the Lamb of God made the miracle, but miracle it was. Ettore hushed. And then half an hour later, still in Mamma's arms, taking a bottle. Sucking greedily, contentedly.

From that day on, no one else would do. For Ettore had not changed. The miracle would work only with Mamma.

Mrs Ricciardi, with tears in her eyes, clasped Mamma's hands, clasped Mamma to her.

And from then on, everything was different. Their whole life. Mamma was to have main charge of Ettore. Mrs Ricciardi's gratitude, spilling over, became love for Maria too. Nothing was too good, too expensive, for Mamma, and her daughter. But Mamma wanted nothing much really, so it had been Maria of whom they (for it was Mr Ricciardi too now) had made a fuss.

Her clothes became expensive, her school changed. She was their pet. Their eldest child almost. She loved to be with them, to go on outings, picnics. Where once she'd dragged her feet, she skipped. Grew pleased with herself. Cheeky.

Then had come the news of a year in England. *A year in England.* She didn't bother about the future, what she and Mamma would do when Ettore grew old enough not to need Mamma. Wearing her new white boots and her cream light silk coat, she had stood, with Mr Ricciardi, on the promenade deck of the *Lusitania* . . .

Restless now, she was about to make for the door.

'Don't go, dear,' Aunt Maimie said, 'I was so enjoying our little talk.'

But just then the tea came in. And with it, Jenny.

'There's a cup for me on the tray.' She ignored her mother. Maria wondered if perhaps she'd been hovering outside. Elsie poured out and after they'd all drunk a cup, Aunt Maimie announced she was going up to rest.

Alone with Maria, Jenny dipped her fingers into the bowl of rose petals. She let them fall in a shower.

'Ma doesn't like you, you know.' (But this was old stuff.) 'And *I* don't like you, either.'

'What do I care?' Maria cried, reaching for Rocco's letter, hiding it.

'You'll care if you can't live with us any more. I've heard Ma say you're a *cuckoo in the nest.* But Aunt Dulcie sticks up for you, I wish she wouldn't, it makes you *stuck up* . . . That's a joke.'

Maria didn't answer. Silence was her best weapon. She remembered one day two years ago now when they had fought. Maria hurling her stronger, heavier body against Jenny's; Jenny who had insulted her family, her country. The two of them, beating each other about the head. Separated finally by a shocked Ida. 'If Dad heard about this.'

There were tears in Jenny's eyes now. Her voice harsh:

'I want Aunt Dulcie to love me the *best*. She did before you came. She paid me the most attention of all. I was her special dear favourite.'

How I hate all this, Maria thought. Jenny was still talking: 'I've wanted to say this for ages and ages, and now I shall. I wish Aunt Dulcie was my mother. Then she'd have to go on loving me the best.'

'I'm going upstairs,' Maria said. 'Talk to yourself –'

'You're going to the bees later, aren't you, why should you take Miss Dennison's bees, why *should* you?'

'No, I'm not. I shan't go.'

'There!' she cried triumphantly. 'I've made you not go.'

'No. I made myself not go. I changed my mind –'

Jenny burst into tears. 'I wanted to like you,' she cried, running from the room. 'I *wanted* to like you!'

Dear Eleanor [Dick wrote from France],

I've been most awfully slow about answering your last letter. Although I rag the piano in the evenings in the mess, life is really just eat, drink, sleep (sometimes) and fly. The only reason I've a chance to catch up with mail is this atrocious weather which has grounded us.

My friend Snelgrove has got the DSO. He seems to bear a charmed life. And his nerve is still pretty good – but can he go on? Rattler is still around but we lost Evans and Barker and Spence this last month. Part of me doesn't *want* to make friends now.

You see, dear Eleanor, I'm not afraid to die, just of *dying*. And that sort of thing day after day, it eats right into you. You know some of my fears, don't you? I keep thinking not just of the flames but if, say, when I was diving, a wing pulled off – or my motor cut out when we were trench strafing. I tell you about these fears because of our talk together that night last winter. (If we had died then! Except, they say it's a very peaceful way to go.)

This isn't really a very cheerful letter. I can only say I'm sorry. I don't think somehow, from what I know of you, that you'd want me *not* to write it. Or not to send it you.

Rattler is just back from leave, and had a ripping time. There's certainly no hardship with food in London for people who have money. He ate at Romano's on a meatless day and had – guess? Hors d'œuvre, and shrimp soup, and an omelette and then noodles and grilled salmon and vegetables *and* bread and butter pudding. He didn't mind the shortage of rolls with the meal!

Is that more cheerful? Now I must end. I can't believe it is already more than six months since you and I were Lost on the Moors. I only wish I were there now, or could believe I ever shall be again.

Your loving friend,
Dick Grainger

A month later, in the middle of August, his squadron moved to an aerodrome at Bertangles near Amiens. One early morning, a few bombs strung under his fuselage, he, Osborne, and newcomers Hammond and Marryat, flew about four miles across the lines, going after German transport. Machine-guns sprayed them from the ground with tracer, a few field guns took a crack at them, but they were back safely for bacon and eggs.

Later that same day all four of them went on a high patrol. Within easy reach of their own lines, Osborne chased after a two-seater 'plane. And then at fifteen thousand feet Dick spotted below them a group of Fokkers: the dread, Mercedes-engined DVIIs, so able at high altitudes.

For the moment cloud hid the four of them. To escape, he and then the other three climbed. Up, up, to twenty thousand feet. But the Fokkers – as many as five – climbed higher. And higher. At altitude the thin air was exhausting. I can't breathe, Dick thought. He swallowed desperately, to clear his ears. The Fokkers were right above now. Then he saw Marryat go down, Turning, Dick lost height. His engine spluttered. He turned again. Down now to twelve thousand feet. In the rear, Hammond was picked off.

And it was then it happened. A searing pain in his right shoulder. Seconds later, a blow to his jaw. His whole head, hammered. Blood spurted, soaking his jacket. Pain. Confusion. His right arm would do nothing. Faint, dizzy, he fought the blackness as the world spun – as his 'plane spun. Blackness rushing at him from all sides. Again the world spun. His plane spun. Falling, falling now.

A rush of cold air, and pressure, as suddenly he was conscious again. Beneath him was the ground. Near. Too near. Somehow – afterwards he could remember little of it – he pulled his 'plane out of its spin. He hit the ground at nearly a hundred miles an hour, just the right side of the British line. Bouncing and sliding, his Camel, its undercarriage torn away, flung its fabric for yards around. Then it turned over. It did not catch fire.

Osborne, Hammond and Marryat were all killed.

He was in his room at Thackton, hidden inside the Golden Lion. He could not see through the crystal eyes. He heard banging of loose floorboards as they were lifted. Now he was being carried down. A door opened. A passageway. Another door, another passage. Where am I? Inside the Golden Lion, of course.

He thought: The story has a happy ending. *But the pain, what about the pain?* The pain was only that it was dark and he was inside the lion, and afraid. The lion who was made of gold. He ought to be able to see through the crystal eyes – only it was dark, so dark. Cramped inside the lion, he felt only pain, advancing, retreating. Pain.

The hall – this was the 'lovely hall' of the story, but he *couldn't see it.* Here somewhere were the Princess and her eleven friends. He could hear music. Laughter. Voices of women. A face appeared before him and then was gone. He struggled to get out of the dream. The face came again. He fought his way into the light.

'Hello,' he said, 'hello, are you the Princess?'

'No, love. I'm Nurse Ackroyd. We're looking after you. You're very poorly.' A hand touched his forehead. He knew it was the Princess's hand, just as he had known it was her voice.

Now he was awake properly. He saw his legs before him but couldn't recognize them. White objects. One of them hung from the ceiling. His head aching, stabbing: too stiff to move. Face raging with pain. No hands. Where were his hands? Then a voice, from far away. His own?

'I always thought it was going to be fire,' he said. There was a different face now. Not the Princess. She said absent-mindedly, adjusting his hoist, 'What's that? What fire?'

'*Orange Death*,' he said.

'There, there,' she said soothingly. He could see she was young and pretty with fair curly hair beneath her cap.

They told him later what had happened to him. He was in No.

4 General at Amiens. He had been unconscious for four days. He had a flesh wound in the cheek, quite clean, a severe wound in the upper shoulder, a scalp wound, and two very badly fractured legs. He was told also about the rest of the patrol.

After that he seemed to go in and out of consciousness. Light and dark – sometimes it was dark and yet there were daylight noises. The sound of a gramophone, loud, raucous. *'Where does Daddy go when he goes out?'* Men's voices joining in, *'It must be nice where Daddy goes . . .'* Sometimes an unbearable brightness. Once he heard some poor chap shouting, then his own name in a sharp tone: 'Lieutenant Grainger, can you hear me? You're disturbing your brother officers.'

The days passed. Letters came from home. A hamper from Selfridge's. He was put down for a bottle of Guinness a day. He heard that some friends had been to see him but because he was unconscious at the time, they had had to go away. He felt ashamed of the times he hadn't visited comrades, when he had superstitiously kept away. ('They're all right. A Blighty one. Soon be going home.')

'When am I going home?' he asked.

'What a question!' It was a nanny's voice, like a nursemaid that he remembered, a girl called Maddie with rippling wavy hair and a voice that was always like a reprimand even when she praised. 'What a question! And you with two legs like that –' She was the pretty fair one, Nurse Lewis. She and Nurse Maxwell, a stocky, efficient redhead, were the ones he saw the most of.

'Where's Nurse Ackroyd?' he asked, suddenly remembering.

'Nurse Ackroyd's on leave. Gone to be married.'

Days passing. Dressings, pain, sleeping draughts – and more pain. The hospital was his life. And the routine, there was something almost like hope about the routine. He could be certain that at eleven every morning, Sister would pass and say, 'Did you get your Guinness today?' Or sometimes: 'You look a little plumper. But isn't that lying in bed being fed potatoes, and milk and butter? Like a pig,' she would say, laughing. Yes, like a pig. Except that he wasn't being fattened for slaughter any more. All that was over.

Over, and then what? His legs. What about his legs? He didn't like to ask. They had told him nothing more. The surgeon spoke to Sister in vague terms: '. . . don't like the look of . . . think perhaps we ought . . . the hoist.'

Nurse Ackroyd came back. She appeared one unexpectedly

chilly morning: dark cardigan with red piping, thick waving hair showing beneath her cap. It was *her* face all right. She had the voice of the Princess too. Low, quiet, firm. She wasn't pretty, though. Large features, too high a colour. She was older than the other nurses.

'Well,' she said, 'you've improved! I'd never have recognized you.'

'I'd know you,' he said boldly. 'Anywhere.'

'It's my nose,' she said, 'I've this large conk. My husband –' she repeated proudly '– my husband says, sailors at sea would be happy to catch sight of it.'

Nurse Maxwell brought him his medicine. She told Nurse Ackroyd, 'Our birdman's been asking after you, Gwen. Twice.'

'Well I never. And I thought you didn't even know I was there. It's odd the things people remember.'

He realized then she had a Yorkshire accent. Later he asked her: 'Is it true you went on leave to get married?'

Her eyes lit up. 'They told you, did they? Really, they're . . . I'm so happy,' she said. And indeed she looked it. He could see it in the glow of her skin. 'I'm really Nurse Latimer now but they call me Ackroyd here still. That way folk don't get confused.'

Standing by the bed, keeping an eye open for Sister, she talked about her husband. 'Cyril – Captain Latimer – he's back in Belgium but he's due for a staff job any moment. Before we wed, he'd been out thirteen months without leave. They kept cancelling, you see . . . But in the end we'd ten days together. It was grand –'

'Where did you go?'

'Tenby, in Wales. Cyril has cousins there. It was quite wild. We went over to Caldey where the monks are and got caught in a storm. The war seemed a million miles away. I'm so happy,' she said again. 'We're both so happy.'

'You look it,' was all he could say. He could smell it: the scent of happiness, overcoming the bitter astringent disinfectant, and the sickly sweet gas gangrene (not his, thank God, but the poor devil on his right).

He lost count of time. How many weeks had he been here? He heard from home that Aunt Dulcie had made attempts to come out to him. (Dear Aunt Dulcie.) About his health, no one told him very much. He supposed he was making progress. Some nerve, peroneal they called it, had been crushed in his leg and there was question of its long-term effects.

A slight lull in the action gave the nurses more time to talk. Nurse Maxwell confided in him her plan to go to Girton, Cambridge, after the War. Nurse Ackroyd showed him photographs of her honeymoon. Her husband was a large moustachioed man, smiling in every picture, pipe-smoking in some. She said, 'Cyril's really clever . . . Anything to do with motors. He's very inventive. After the war there's bound to be openings.' She had lost both her brothers on the first day of the Somme. 'They were in the Bradford Pals. Joined the same day. Mother took it very hard.'

He smoked a lot, read John Buchan and Baroness Orczy, and made friends with his neighbours. 'When can I go home?' he asked almost daily.

There was a sing-song and entertainment in the ward. An elderly Englishman, an elocutionist who'd lived in Amiens for twenty years, recited a dreadful monologue about a puppy that carried messages through the trenches. Many of the patients were too ill to give him the bird. Dick was too polite. Later, walking the ward, he stopped by Dick's bed. Seeing the notice at the foot: 'Ah, Icarus is amongst us!' he declaimed.

Next morning the surgeon on his round told Dick he would be going home in two or three days. It was then he said: 'I have to tell you that, consequent on your injuries, your walking will almost certainly be hampered. That is, you may, though not necessarily, need a stick. One leg will be shorter than the other . . .'

'For ever?'

'Ah, permanently, of course. You have been a very fortunate young man. To have survived at all and with comparatively so little damage.'

Permanently. For ever. A cripple, he thought, I am a cripple.

He cried when Nurse Ackroyd was dressing his shoulder. She told him, 'They don't know it all. And using a cane, or a walking stick – I shouldn't wonder if you won't look even more distinguished.'

Her compliment warmed him, even though he guessed she spoke like that to all of them. He said now, impulsively, 'You know, when I first saw you – when I was just coming round – I thought you were a princess.'

'Well I never,' she said, throwing back her head and laughing. 'You've a good line in compliments, have you birdmen.' She rumpled his now unbandaged hair. 'Princess, indeed.'

5

Christmas of 1919, the second since the Armistice but the first
since the Peace. The war was truly over and everyone seemed
keen to celebrate. But apart from a family outing to see Mary
Pickford in *Daddy Long Legs*, the Graingers had not had many
parties, so Maria felt quite excited about the fancy dress dance
to be given by the Carstairs family (all ages over twelve invited,
although older persons need not dress up).

She was to go as Lady Teazle. Ida explained that she was a
character from an eighteenth-century comedy. The outfit could
easily be hired. When it arrived – pale blue tiered crinoline,
white wig, beauty spot – Maria said: 'It might as well be Marie
Antoinette, why don't I go as Marie Antoinette?'

Dick left just after Christmas to stay with an RFC friend in
Devon. A pity to miss the party, everyone said, since the Carstairs
girl, Nancy, was known to be very taken with him and frequently
asked him up to tea.

Jenny was Spring, in a grey and silver-green outfit with a
three-pointed cap. Her slant eyes made her look like an elf. She
pirouetted in front of the glass, gloating over Maria. She said
childishly, 'You won't be able to move in your outfit.'

Ida was Britannia. With sceptre and helmet she appeared even
larger. She had been training for teaching all this year and
planned to go to London for more training in January. Jenny,
restless, would have liked to join her. She talked incessantly of
going to live there as soon as possible. But Uncle Eric wanted
her to stay at school. This winter she had sat her Matriculation,
there was talk of her doing her Higher Certificate. 'Two more
years,' she said with disgust.

Maria had also sat her Matriculation, and left school. Her
future wasn't sorted yet but it didn't matter. Lately she had felt
a general tranquillity. Like her adopted country, she was at
peace. She had at last settled in.

Now there was no fighting, she didn't have to worry about
Rocco and Gaetano. But since the last letter which said they

were out of the army and home again in Monteleone, she'd heard nothing. She wondered if they would go back to the States, where they would surely be welcome since they had fought on the right side? Perhaps they had already left – although Rocco's letter had hinted at vague ideas for making money in Monteleone. He'd complained too about older men in the village who had done well while he and his friends had been fighting. The Old Brigade, he called them. Profiteers.

Her own future? Uncle Eric never actually said anything. Aunt Maimie (oh, that dreadful Black Book) muttered occasionally, 'We shall have to do something for you.' Aunt Dulcie said, 'You'll soon be meeting – young men.' Ida was the most direct: 'You're so grown-up looking and bonny. It'd not surprise me if you were married soonest of us all.'

Marry? But whom, when, where – and would it be all right? If she were to end up like Aunt Maimie, or as bad, Aunt Dulcie or Miss Dennison, who hadn't married at all. If she'd stayed in Monteleone, mightn't she perhaps be married already?

But she lived here now, in Yorkshire, in Middlesbrough and Thackton. This family, and most especially Uncle Eric, was her family now. Rocco and the others were faint voices. She heard them clearly only when Rocco wrote.

How did she get on with the Graingers these days? She could manage Jenny better now she was more used to the jealousy. Jenny felt superior because she was certain that, after leaving school, she'd be allowed to go to London and to work in an office. She flung her ambitions at her father who said good-humouredly, 'We shall see what we shall see.' Jenny answered cheekily, 'When shall we see it?' and then: 'I want to live in a little flat. I shall, with Aunt Dulcie. Aunt Dulcie would love London, wouldn't you, Aunt Dulcie? We could live in Chelsea or Mayfair or somewhere. We'd be so happy together. Wouldn't we, *wouldn't we*, Aunt Dulcie?'

Peter was another matter. She preferred it when he was away at school, at Rossall. Next autumn he would go to Durham University. He had grown up as handsome as promised: thick black hair, brooding poetic face – beside him, dear Dick seemed peaky, anxious. But in looks he was set to rival even the memory of James. But he didn't see it like that, complaining, 'All Dad thinks of is James. None of us are any good. Not Dick, not me. It was all on James . . .'

In November Uncle Eric and Dick had been up to London for

the Motor Show, the first since the war. Uncle Eric bought a new motor, a twenty-five horse-power Crossley Touring Car. Peter was jealous. If it hadn't been for school, he would have been the one to go. 'Dad knows Dick prefers horses to horse-power.'

A poetic face and mouth, except that what came out was scarcely poetry. She wished she could like him. All last summer he'd been unkind to her. He hated her to play the pianola:

'I hate to see your legs go up and down, up and down. They're disgusting.'

'Don't look, then.'

'Shan't.' Another time he said: 'A fellow at school asked me if you smelled, he said he'd been in Italy and they all smelled.'

'*You* smell,' she answered coldly, but her mood as she went out, slamming the door, was heated. In her mind she kicked him, tugging his thick hair, pulling it out in handfuls. Later that same day as she was going up the stairs, she felt a hand on her stocking. When she tried to move she couldn't. Peter was half-kneeling on the tread behind. Suddenly he had hold of her legs tightly. If she hadn't leaned forward, struggling, trying to kick out, he would have had her over and into his arms.

'What are you *doing*? What a silly joke –'

'It's not a joke. It's ever so serious. Sorry for what I said about your legs. They're ripping – I like 'em.'

'*Let go* –' She kicked out. He lost his balance, then just in time recovered it. He was so angry his sulks were almost tears: 'Blasted little . . . legs like bits of macaroni, uncooked macaroni . . .' He pushed on past her and up into his bedroom.

Uncle Eric was away for the party. Aunt Maimie didn't wish to attend. Aunt Dulcie would go with them but not in fancy dress. She wore a jade-green and gold brocade frock and looked very elegant.

The Carstairs had also lost their eldest son, at Arras in 1917. Molly who'd married in 1915 was a war widow living at home again. Pip, about to go up to Oxford in 1914, had fought through the war and was now at University. Nancy, the daughter said to be sweet on Dick, was twenty. The youngest son, Thomas, was twelve. Sybil at fifteen was the nearest to Maria's age: Maria liked what she had seen of Sybil.

Lady Teazle. Marie Antoinette. Without doubt it altered her: olive skin against the white wig, the realistic beauty spot, tight-fitting waist of the tiered dress – so unlike the everyday Maria.

Ida as Britannia, holding her awkward sceptre, looked like – Ida. Jenny, pixie-like, jumped up and down. They were on the upstairs landing, waiting for Aunt Dulcie who was to accompany them. Peter, who hadn't wanted to go and now had a heavy cold as an excuse, came out of his room in a dressing-gown, handkerchief held to his nose. 'Don't make a din coming back, waking me up,' he said.

On the way Jenny was restless, complaining that her Spring costume was uncomfortable. Aunt Dulcie told her she was a lucky girl: 'Your father could easily have put his foot down. Grown-up dancing at fourteen . . .' Jenny, crestfallen, grew quiet, as she did always when Aunt Dulcie scolded her.

The Carstairs house: large; imposing, the lamps outside showing up the white of the Palladian columns. Inside the party had begun. 'I knew we'd be late,' Jenny said, 'it was fussing over Maria's stays. She's too fat anyway.' Maria didn't bother to answer. Mr Carstairs was not to be seen. Mrs Carstairs, a large, solid, round-faced woman in puce and black lace, clasped Aunt Dulcie's hand. She congratulated the girls on their outfits, her eyes wandering over the hall. A party of what looked like zoo animals were just entering. Through an open door a small band could be heard, playing a toe-tapping tune. Mrs Carstairs told Aunt Dulcie: 'The young keep asking for negro music.'

Sybil, leaning over the rails of the landing, wrapped in a blue dressing-gown, her thick dark hair in a pigtail, called out in a croaky voice, 'Hallo, everyone!' Mrs Carstairs explained that Sybil had a nasty sore throat.

There was a minstrels' gallery in the room where the dancing was. Some of the older people were sitting up there. Aunt Dulcie joined them. Maria 'lost' both Ida and Jenny as soon as possible. She wandered about, bumping her hooped skirt into people. A glass of hot punch was pressed into her hand. A voice said:

'Who are you – if one's allowed to ask?'

'Maria Verzotto.'

'Never heard of her, I *am* ignorant. Historical?'

She said stupidly, 'Marie Antoinette, I mean. Tonight I'm Marie Antoinette –'

'Of course. I should have guessed. You look pretty like her – Well, *pretty*, anyway . . . But before I ask you to dance – who am I?'

Wig not unlike hers, tailed coat, ruffles of lace . . . She couldn't guess. Then she saw beneath the lightly floured face, the Carstairs son. Pip.

'Waltz with me,' he said, taking her hand. He towered above her. 'And have a guess as we spin round.' The band played *Destiny*, as if there'd never been a war.

'Actually,' he said, 'I'm the Scarlet Pimpernel. My task could well be to rescue you. Would you like that?'

Ida waltzed by in the arms of Mr Carstairs.

'I'm not very good at the foppish bit,' Pip said. 'I'm not sure I'd convince.'

He talked. How he talked. Maria didn't need to say a word. He told her: 'It's really been a year for fancy dress. Oxford's been full of them. I had the idea for this one early last term –'

'You're studying there?'

'For my sins, yes. No, thank God rather – just to have survived is pretty marvellous. Now part of me only wants to enjoy myself. To learn of course, but to have a *good time*.'

'When the fun's over, what'll you do?'

'Oh, the family business. Naturally. I'm heir to it.' He broke off. 'The Graingers lost their eldest too, didn't they? Frightful, that.' He repeated it several times, nervously: 'Frightful.'

Maria said, to change the subject: 'A waltz is wrong, isn't it, for us? We ought to be doing a minuet.'

'Even a waltz is too staid for me. The real me under this wig . . . I'm trying to encourage the shimmy shake this evening, but the Mater's not being very helpful.' As *Destiny* ended, he asked, 'Do you have the next dances booked?'

Not yet, she told him. He immediately booked two more for later, 'I'd really like to go on dancing with you now but *noblesse oblige*. Host and all that. I'm going to introduce Mr Lowe to you. He always likes the same girls that I do.'

Mr Lowe was Friar Tuck, and jolly with it. His own hair was balding naturally in the form of a tonsure. Maria envied him: her head beneath the wig felt hot and scratchy. He told her he had been in for an Army heavyweight. 'The war, that ghastly show – should have been fought in the boxing ring.' His face shone with enthusiasm. 'The Carpentier fight last month. Now that *was* something – over in seventy-five seconds. Unbelievable. Carpentier, so quick on his feet, taking the offensive, getting Beckett's face with a left-hander, then a few body blows while they're in a clinch – and finish him off with a right hook to the jaw. *Wonderful*.'

Back with Pip again. 'I'll tell you a secret,' he said, 'except perhaps you know. Dick – it's a pity he's not here tonight. My sister Nancy . . .'

He pointed out a small wan figure dressed as a Quaker girl, sitting up in the gallery. 'I must get Bertie Lowe to dance with her.'

The evening whirled by. She could only call herself a success. In the next half-hour her card was completely filled up. She noticed that Ida sat out a lot, sometimes with Nancy Carstairs. Jenny seemed to be eating and drinking most of the time together with two boys dressed as the Princes in the Tower.

At one o'clock they were collected with the motor even though the invitation said, 'Carriages two a.m.' On the way home, Aunt Dulcie said, foolishly perhaps, 'Marie Antoinette was quite the Belle of the Ball.' An overtired, overfed Jenny said angrily, '*I* wanted to be Good Queen Bess only you wouldn't let me – I just got *Spring*.'

'Hush, hush, dear,' Ida said.

Maria crept along the corridor to her room. She was still undressing, pulling at the tight laces, wishing she hadn't refused Ida's offer of help, when she heard the creak of floorboards outside. A knock at the door. She thought: I hope Jenny hasn't come to be nasty.

'If it's Ida, come in –'

But it was Peter, handkerchief in hand. He looked angry. He said, 'I thought you were never coming back. And the din you all made. After I'd asked you, too.'

She had pulled a wool wrap from the door hook to cover herself. 'Did we wake you? I'm sorry. And when you're ill.' She said it politely, without looking at him.

Silence. She went on, 'Is that what you came to say? Because if . . .' She folded down the corner of the sheets.

Then as she turned round, 'No,' he said, 'I came to show you this.' His dressing-gown was open. The handkerchief was wrapped round – yes, it was . . . She saw it pointing upwards, circled at the base by the white cotton.

'Look at it. Go on, look at it.'

'Peter – I don't – *Get out of here* –'

'Go on, look under the hanky.' With his free hand he grasped hers and placed it over the handkerchief, trapping it.

'Something's wrong. You're sick. You shouldn't be doing that, you shouldn't be in here at all.'

'Rubbish,' he said, holding her hand tighter. His voice was hoarse but very deep, as it had been for a long time now. 'Daft rubbish – you know all about it, don't you? You know what you want. *I* know what you want –'

'I don't,' she said angrily. '*Let go!*'

He had placed his foot on hers. 'This hanky's wet. You know why it's wet, don't you?'

'Let me go. My foot hurts –'

'Foot hurts, foot hurts. There's more than your foot'll hurt if you don't behave –'

'What have I done wrong?' she said, breaking away. Hurrying towards the bed, as if it represented safety.

But how could it? She should have made for the door. He was talking at her again now, stopping once to cough heavily. 'Don't think you can just –' he began.

She made for the door. But he was quicker. Darting from side to side to block her.

'Don't tease,' he said, 'don't dare tease me –'

'*You're* teasing,' she said, pushing her face at him, 'Let me out of *my own* room. Or get out. I don't like what you're doing. I don't like you.'

Fateful words.

'Don't like me, eh? But you're going to want me. Any girl who sees this – what I showed you – she'd want it –'

'Let me out! Or *get out* –'

He lunged forward, wrapping her in his arms, so tight she could hardly breathe. He said, 'I'm a big boy, I'm grown up – more grown up than Dick. I look older, I *am* older, really. Maria, M, M, M, Maria, you know when I'm rude it's because I want you. I'm always watching – waiting for my chance. Then I'm rude and horrid. I know I'm rude and horrid. I don't mean to be. I only want – you. Now. I thought I'd never get through the evening. I did it twice before midnight. Just thinking, and waiting.'

His voice was urgent in her ear. She couldn't move. She was trapped in the linen chest. Outside the Golden Lion prowled, seeking whom he might devour. Trapped. Trapped. And deathly afraid. The waters rose on the deck of the *Lusitania*. She would never escape.

He pulled open her wrap. He had hold of her still, her arm pinned down. He tore at her underslip, crumpling the cotton, wrenching aside the knickers. 'Let go, let go, let me in, I know what to do, let me do it –'

As he forced himself into her, she dug her fingers into the bedcover. Tearing at it. On and on the pain. His face, evening stubble, pressed now into her collar-bone.

The waters rose on the deck of the *Lusitania. Sacru miu Gesù. Help me, help me . . .*

Then she was suddenly someone else. The animal who submitted. Patient, pained, mounted animal. A few more moments and he lay heavily, flaccid, across her body. Her ribs, crushed as she tried to breathe. He pulled himself up on his elbows, then fully upright, standing by the bed. His dark face shone with sweat. He said: 'Well, that's it. I hope you enjoyed it.' When she didn't answer:

'Girls like you, peasants, because *that's what you are*, they like that sort of thing. You kept showing me your legs going upstairs, I don't know how I'm supposed to not give you what you want.'

He was fastening his dressing-gown cord: 'You don't tell anyone, *anybody*, do you hear? I'll deny it anyway if there's any trouble, which there won't be. I know what I'm doing. Clissold at school, his dad used to live in Paris, he told me . . .'

At the door, he said, 'You don't think I'm going to pay you, do you, you don't expect to be paid?'

She could remember little of the rest of that night. Only that, curled in a ball, sore, frightened, in pain, she had sobbed for Mamma and the Virgin Mary and Za Rosetta.

Her eyes were swollen in the morning. She splashed them with cold water. She saw blood on the bedcover and tried to sponge it off. Between her legs felt raw now with an ache like toothache. She didn't want to touch, even to wash herself.

Aunt Dulcie and Aunt Maimie were breakfasting downstairs. No one else was up. Aunt Maimie expressed concern at her fatigue: 'You're sure you drank no strong cider, dear?'

'She was dancing with Pip Carstairs,' Aunt Dulcie said. 'Quite a gay blade at Oxford, I hear. They lead a fast life, some of these returned servicemen. He couldn't believe you were only just sixteen, Maria dearest. He thought you at least eighteen.'

She avoided Peter that day. But he treated her as if nothing had happened, although she caught him once glancing at her warily. Later he said to her, 'Remember what you promised.' She told him, 'I don't have to keep that sort of promise.' But she knew she would tell no one.

He said, 'If there's any fuss or complaints – I'll say you started it. That you threw yourself at me. They'll believe me. Everyone knows a man can't say No.'

His threats frightened her. And, might he not do it again? Although she would not, could not, tell anyone – how she longed to! She counted the days until he returned to school. Dreading the nights. Why can't I ask for a key to my door? And yet she could not.

She felt she had sinned. Going to Mass three days later with the Mulligans, she stayed away from Communion. She knew she was unclean even though she had washed herself several times over. Yet if she went to Confession, what would she say? She wanted with a terrible longing to be in Thackton. With Dick and Aunt Dulcie. There, and only there, could she begin to heal.

It was a snowy day when at last Peter left for school. Sitting in the new Crossley, wrapped in a rug, being driven to the station. Everyone came down to say goodbye. He was kissed by them all. She felt as she smelled his skin a fierce wave of terror. And of hate.

6

From where Eleanor sat by the window, she could see Ruddock the gardener going to and fro with the wheelbarrow, his back hunched, his legs bandy. Almost spring now, hope of summer to come, and perhaps warm afternoons sitting at the wooden table in the far garden. Tea and sandwiches, and pretending for a while that nothing had changed (Babs had not died, Guy was not buried in South Africa, there had never been a Great War). Summer and perhaps Eric on his way from the station to Moorgarth, looking in on them, charming Mother, making them both laugh.

And making my heart grow heavy, she thought. But wasn't the heartache worth it just for those precious moments? Moments that Mother knew nothing about (if I may not love purely, she thought, at least I can love secretly). But meantime the best afternoon of the week was today, when Mother was driven to Lady Grimshaw's to help with the disabled, and she knew that for at least three hours she would not hear those modulated but acid tones. 'Eleanor, *what are you doing down there?*'

What am I doing? I am sitting, my hand stroking the soft wool of my green dress, now on the shoulder, now on the knee. For a second I shut my eyes. If only I dared be so wicked as to imagine that Eric's hands stroked mine, stroked *me*. Knee, shoulder. More and more. And more. Wicked. I know with my reason that it's sinful even to *think* about thinking about it. But oh God, oh God, we cannot choose whom we love . . .

The bell rang and she jumped. Dulcie was shown in, calling unexpectedly. Eleanor hadn't even known she was in Thackton. Her first thought on seeing her was that her hair had lost its springiness. Limp, unlikely. (Impossible, though, for her not to look well dressed: an outfit in brown duvetyn trimmed with nutria, far too smart for the country, the skirt just a little shorter than anyone else's.) And such an agitated Dulcie. A few sentences of small talk, Eleanor ringing for tea, and then:

'Eleanor dearest, has Maria spoken to you at all? You see, dearest, something terrible has happened –'

'I know nothing.' Thoughts, pictures, raced through her mind. Disease, Sicily, some ghost from Maria's past.

'I thought – because she was here a few weeks ago, and because you take her to church and . . . that perhaps she'd confided in you?'

A few seconds' silence, then: 'May I know?' Eleanor asked.

'You must,' Dulcie said. 'You must. I can't bear . . . this wretched knowledge. Forgive me that I'm so *agitated* –'

Eleanor listened, appalled. She didn't want at first to believe it. Distaste, horror, disgust, pity, above all pity, warred within her. Also, and this must be pushed down at once, a fearful sick excitement. Eric, she thought: What will he do, how will he take it?

'Eric is distraught. He's been over to Rossall already to speak to Peter. It appears she led him on . . . He was almost – seduced. I don't know what we are to think. A girl who was loved, adopted – and then. But it takes two, does it not?'

'Maria, though . . . What does she –?'

'She won't speak of it at all. She spoke only enough to tell me. She has become hard and silent and knowing. And yet one is sad, and sorry for her –'

Her own foolish questions. 'But is it certain?'

'Certain,' Dulcie said sadly. 'Maria isn't a hysterical child, or given to unnecessary dramatics. She's – seen nothing for three months now . . . I'm taking her to Dr Cartwright on Thursday but he'll only confirm –'

Eleanor said, 'Practicalities. We must think about them at once.' Her heart in spite of all, had gone out to Maria. (Sixteen. Myself at sixteen. Would I have known even what was happening to me?)

Dulcie said, 'I've tried to tell myself she's Italian, has developed earlier, that perhaps in some way it's all different, not so serious, so terrible. But . . . Oh, *what is to be done*?' she cried, drinking her tea in small anxious sips. Then, more calmly she said, 'They must not marry. That is the one certain thing out of all this. No one is to make them marry.'

'But do you fear that? Who's suggested it? *She* hasn't, surely?'

'It *is* a solution of sorts, dearest, and some would advocate it . . . But an eighteen-year-old boy and a sixteen-year-old girl. Impossible.'

'Not impossible. Just inadvisable. And wrong. It would be so wrong.'

'Eleanor dearest, in the last twenty-four hours I must have thought of everything. And come up with nothing.' Her voice trembled. 'I wanted, you see, for Maria's sake to be someone who would take over – to remove the worst of the worry from her. *"Leave it to me,"* I said with authority. You know me, I can be very just so – when I wish.' She broke off a piece of seed cake but forgot to put it in her mouth. 'No, they mustn't marry. But equally she cannot rid herself of the child. She must be protected, supported, in case she should even *think* . . .'

'It mustn't even be mentioned,' Eleanor said.

'If she'd been a servant, she could have been married off. Someone local, farmer, shopkeeper. For a consideration, of course. Some of Maimie's money.'

'Maimie doesn't know?'

'Maimie *must* not know.' Dulcie had gone quite white. Her hand shook as she picked up the cup. 'As I said, dearest, that solution is only possible with the servant class. Maria is not that. She was our sacred trust and we've betrayed her. A girl should be safe in her own family. It's not as if –' She broke off. Going on, more calmly: 'It must be adopted, of course. There must be somewhere she can go. A Home. Somewhere where it would be all right and she could have it and come back to us . . . Only, no – she could not come back . . . You see, oh, Eleanor dearest, I'd wanted *so*, by the time Eric arrives, to have some thoughts together.'

Her mouth was working. Suddenly she burst out: 'You know, it's upset me even more than it should because –'

'Because what, darling Dulcie?'

'Because it's my story, *our* story, again. Oh, it isn't, of course, of course it isn't our story. It's Maria's. Ours was quite different. We loved each other –'

'Dulcie, you don't make sense. *Tell me.*'

Tears beaded in her eyes: 'I know I don't – make sense. And it didn't. At the time it didn't. Victims. We were all victims. So long ago now. Fifteen, sixteen years . . .'

The carriage clock struck the half-hour. Mother, Eleanor thought – willing her to stay away. She said: 'Fifteen years ago. You and I hadn't even met.'

'If you'd known me then, if we'd known each other, dearest, I would have confided in you. But then, ah then, I had nobody. There was some dreadful reason why – each person – couldn't be the one confided in. Then later when I'd got to know you and we'd become friends, it wasn't – there never seemed a time for such a dreadful secret. And what would you have thought of me? I couldn't have borne you to have thought badly of me.'

'But you can tell me now. *Please*, Dulcie dear.'

'Jenny. It's Jenny. She is – mine. Jenny's my child.'

(Oh Mother, do not come home now.)

'Our child. Eric's and mine.'

She stopped and looked over at Eleanor. Her hands were joined, twisting on her lap. 'You see, Eleanor dearest, you *are* shocked. A Roman Catholic – what must you think! A married man. And then –'

Oh, but yes, Eleanor thought, yes, I am shocked. Shocked. As one who receives a blow. She said, 'You don't need to tell me if you don't wish.'

'No, I want to, truly. I've wanted to tell you –' She laughed drily: 'You know, the other day I could almost have told *Maria*. And would have, if I'd felt it would have helped. But you can see now why, when I heard her tale, I thought: Oh dear God, is it to begin all over again?'

'Jenny knows none of this?'

Dulcie shook her head. 'And must not . . . Remember, "Oh, I wish Aunt Dulcie was my mother, why isn't Aunt Dulcie . . .?" It used to wring my heart. It still does . . . It's all been so difficult – and yet I wanted to go on living with Maimie and Eric. I *chose* to. Eric had asked that it should be so . . . Everything to be as it had been.'

Everything? Eleanor asked herself.

'No, not everything, of course. We had been in love, had a love-affair, and then became – what? I often wonder. Never, of course, what we'd first been. Sometimes a glimpse of that light-heartedness when I was Maimie's little sister come to live with them, to be a help and support . . . It seemed such a good idea then, you see. There were difficulties, of course – Maimie spoke of Eric with impatience, I could only see his charm. She said, "He only wanted my money. To start the business, to start the foundry." His father – he was much influenced by his father, Eleanor. And anyway, it had happened. It was done.'

Eleanor's heart thumped still, her mouth was dry.

'And then he and I, thrown together by her illness. Threatened consumption (she who's so stout now). I sometimes played hostess when she was indisposed. But it wasn't like this tale of Maria's. No. We *loved* and knew nothing could come of it. Your wife's sister – what does the Bible have to say? And the law too, the law of England. There was of course never meant to be an accident –'

Eleanor glanced anxiously at the clock. Mother: putting on her coat, scarf, gloves.

'And then and then – running to Eric, for I had to run to him – telling him what I feared. My sick terror, Eleanor. At first I'd wanted to keep it to myself – just as Maria told me *she* did. To disappear, telling no one. But where, and how? Yet when I told Eric, when we began to share the horror, the realization of what we'd done, it seemed, you know, that sharing made it not better but somehow worse.'

(Oh, let it rain, let it *snow*. Let Mother be delayed.)

'And then he told Maimie . . . He told her there and then. That same day. Once over the first shock, you see, he behaved with great decisiveness. And Maimie said, quite calmly, "I guessed something of this. What you deserve, the two of you, has happened to you." Not a word of real reproach. I wish she had. She merely looked superior, as if we'd been naughty children. "What are we going to do about it?" she said. Eric told her, "Dulcie will keep the child, somehow." You see, I couldn't let my child be taken by strangers. He knew this – and yet what was I to do, Eleanor? An unmarried mother. It was not to be thought of . . . In Bohemian circles possibly. But not in our world. And then Maimie said, amazingly, "The little bastard had better be ours, then. Isn't that what you're trying to ask?" Eric said yes, but in that case it wouldn't be a bastard, would it? Cheeking her, you know, at a moment like that –

'It was given out, you see, that Maimie was to go to Switzerland because of her lungs. The dangers of childbearing after a consumption threat . . . By that time Dr Cartwright was in our confidence. And of course she could not go without me for company. What a story! And yet people believed. It had somehow plausibility . . . She left very soon, I followed three weeks later. Eric's sister Harriet came to be mother to the children. Maimie and I were several months in the Valais – a village above Montreux. The nearest thing to hell on earth. Cooped up together with a hate, on her part, untinged by any charity. I used to think: When all this is over I shall go away, ignore the child, allow Eric to rear it as his own. But . . . I had Jenny, and a month later we brought her home. Born prematurely, we said, but healthy. Beautiful, and Maimie's. I wanted her, you know.' Her voice

broke. 'I *could not have borne* to leave her. My intentions –
everything went by the board.'

The outer door banged. 'Mother,' Eleanor said.

'Is that the time?' Dulcie hesitated.

The door opened:

'Miss Rowland – Dulcie, my dear, how delightful to find you
entertaining my bored – I almost said *boring* – daughter . . . I've
had such a busy afternoon. Lady Grimshaw says she doesn't
know what she would do without me. Did you hear that, Eleanor?
I don't think Eleanor appreciates me, you know.'

She lived through the next few days, her mind in a ferment. Poor
Maria – Maria with her quiet beauty, looking so often like a
young Madonna (Raphael's Madonna of the Chair, second from
the left, half way down her bedroom wall), and now to be a
mother because those heavy-lidded eyes, that ripe body, had led
her, and Peter, astray. But lying in bed at night, she could think
only of Eric – and Dulcie. Such a shock and yet she seemed
always to have known. I knew without knowing, she thought,
remembering the scent of danger (had it not been danger?) she
had caught on that first visit to Moorgarth.

The day after Dulcie's visit she walked up to the house. But
Dulcie had left, gone back to Middlesbrough, Elsie said. The
family would all be coming down on Friday.

She saw from the window of her room the train arrive at the
station. *They are here.* It was all she could do not to stand at the
front gate waiting for them, for Eric, to pass. She felt heavy with
powerlessness. She could be kind, she could listen, sympathize,
but what could she *do*?

After the evening meal, her restlessness overwhelmed her. To
escape from Mother, she dressed for outside, saying she was
going to visit an ailing friend.

She walked along the road in the moonlight. Almost full moon
– lovers' moon. She took the turning before the Robin Hood
Inn, past the neglected cattle shed and down the grassy lane.
Damp glistened on the drystone wall, the only sounds her
footsteps, the sighing of the night breeze, rushing water in
the beck. The fence was broken, someone had repaired it
with a piece of iron bedstead: soon the water would make it
rusty.

She felt very calm suddenly. A cloud passed in front of the
moon. Beneath her feet now the crunch of dead bracken. Her

heart, which had been racing all evening, beat steadily. *I know what must be done.*

She stood still. It was as if someone spoke for her. Not God – but someone sent by Him? We are here on earth to help each other, she thought. Not just the 'to love and serve God in this world and to be happy with Him in the next' of the penny catechism. No, let us love one another as God loved.

Eric, hurt, confused by the news Dulcie has given him. But I, who am not allowed to love him – I can help. Thirty-eight – I don't expect now that I shall ever have a child, or a husband. But Eric's grandchild (why not?) can become *my child.* Oh dear God – To help Maria. And to help the baby, the helpless baby.

She turned towards home, resisting the temptation to go on into Moorgarth – to tell them *now* . . .

This was the Plan. Italy, with all her art treasures – why should she not visit Italy? Maria and I, we shall go together. Everyone will hear that she has gone to London to join Ida and to do, say, secretarial work. In Italy I shall find a convent for Maria. Yes, a convent. The nuns will be kind. (Forget Babs's death.) About this they *must* be kind. When she is settled, I shall come back. Then another visit when the baby is two or three months. I shall bring it back. Adopt it. Mother cannot stop me. I own the house, after all. The baby will be an Italian orphan that I have befriended (God knows, Maria looks Italian enough – and Peter is dark-haired . . .)

She stopped at Wilcock's field, leaning for a few moments over the gate. In the elms at the far end, the rooks were silent. Gone to rest. *It will be all right*, she told herself. Oh Eric, how I love you.

'Mother, I'm going to visit Italy. Tuscany. Pisa, Florence . . . to see for myself some of the paintings I've loved for so long –' Her voice surprised her with its defiant note.

'Did you hear, Mother? A trip to Italy. By myself. At the end of this month.'

'The very idea! So sudden . . . Who's to see to me, I should like to know? And you aren't accustomed to travel – have you ever travelled by yourself? Even with everything arranged by Cook's you will manage to lose yourself or your belongings. I remember that time at the convent . . .'

7

My future, Dick thought. It stretched before him, impossible to change. But, he thought, *at least I am alive.* (Dry, unemotional voice of the surgeon: 'You are of course very fortunate to have any use of your lower limbs . . .') He had only to glance around to see how much worse off others were. Apart from one leg shorter than the other, and a foot that dragged slightly, he was fit and healthy.

He supposed that one day he would forget the horror of those last moments . . . The strange thing was that part of him yearned still to be in the sky. Was it because he missed the companionship, friends of his own age, united in a common cause? He missed not only the dead (Rattler, survivor of the war, shot down over Petrozavodsk, fighting with the North Russian Expeditionary Force), but the living too. He had been to stay with Snelgrove just after Christmas. Snelgrove's father wanted him to work in a bank. 'A bank, Dicko, for God's sake . . . At least old Rattler was doing something useful, ridding the world of Bolshies . . . What about a flying circus, old chap? Joy rides at bazaars, fêtes, that sort of thing? Hell of an excitement for them and at least we get to fly. The Aircraft Disposal Board, they've some Avros on hand. God knows, we know what to do with those.'

Or what about a commercial air service. 'Handley Page converted double-engine bombers and supplied them to Imperial Airways for the London–Paris venture. It's not doing badly. Bit weather dependent, but definitely the thing of the future.' In March he'd come over to Thackton. His enthusiasm was contagious, and Dad became quite excited by the idea of a Vickers 'Vimy', a much smaller machine with two Rolls-Royce engines, very suitable for conversion. But it all came to nothing. Dad saying only, 'Enough talk of madcap ventures. A family firm needs *family.*'

And then came the business of Maria. Early in the year she'd seemed, if not physically sick, then sick in soul. She had walked about hunched, complaining of the cold. At Easter she'd stayed on at Middlesbrough, Aunt Dulcie with her. Peter, back from Rossall, was edgy and semi-defiant about something.

It had been Dad who told him the facts. It seemed to Dick the most appalling mess and wickedness: he didn't like his father's man to man approach, didn't like the plans they had made to solve the problem. Eleanor so noble, Eleanor taking on the child. He would like to have heard from her own lips of this plan to leave Maria in Italy while pretending she was in London, with Ida. (Oh, what a tangled web . . .)

Peter, tackled about it, had said only, 'Wouldn't you like to know, *brother*?' No one but Dad, he told Dick, had the right to ask him anything. Impossible to speak of it to Maria. He could only suffer for her. (What dream world had he been in while all this was going on? He who had never seen her as anyone but a sister. A beautiful sister.)

The week before Eleanor and Maria left for Italy, he was sent to Bradford for a few days. The work was to do with people – more human contact than casting. The programme left him quite a lot of free time. He took a tram out of the town and walked at his own pace. The weather was bracing, with April gusts that threatened to turn into showers.

By half past three on the last day he had finished his appointments. Stepping off the tram in the centre, he noticed the darkening sky. A chill wind, the sooty air smelling suddenly of a winter afternoon. He turned down a side street, crossed Westgate and into Barry Street. Already lamps were going on. He discovered a sudden need for a steaming pot of tea and buttered teacakes – now.

Down another street, round a corner, past some offices, a cutler's, a draper's, and then: a café. The Adelphi Tea Rooms. Half-nets hid the interior from view. Inside was quite small with dark oak furniture. It smelled of the tea he now longed for. A waitress, small and pale with a spotty face, hurried by, her tray piled high with teacakes and currant loaf. He sat at one of the round tables and tried to attract her attention. 'I'm that rushed,' she told him.

He studied the menu. York ham and salad, plaice and chips, potted shrimps . . . tea, cocoa, Horlicks. He looked up.

'Well, if it isn't!' exclaimed Nurse Ackroyd. 'Our birdman –'

She stood beside him, pencil and pad pulled up ready from her white apron. She was dressed in plain black with a frilled head band, the same as the young girl.

'You'd best give your order quick,' she said, smiling. 'There's a real rush on this afternoon. I don't know what's come over folk.'

'It's wonderful you remember me,' he said, feeling the blood rush to his face. 'All the chaps you must have nursed.'

'Get away, Lieutenant Grainger – I never forget a name . . . Give your order, there's a love. The girdle scones are homemade, I'd go for those. And the potted shrimps, they're from my cousins in Morecambe. They're good.'

'Yes, yes. All that. And a pot of tea. Strong, please. Only what in heaven's name are you doing here? You can't be just a waitress. I mean, not after . . .'

She touched his shoulder. 'Other folk are waiting.' (Memories of hospital. How many times had she not touched him, and sped away from his bedside?) She added: 'It's my place. I own it and run it. Anything wrong with that, now?'

She was gone before he could answer. He watched her take three other orders, then run to the telephone by the pay desk where an elderly woman sat.

At the table next to his were a mother, father, and small girl. The girl was in outdoor clothes: large blue hat and thick buttoned coat. The mother placed a white napkin under her chin. Dick watched fascinated as she crushed, in strong little hands, fingers of buttered toast. The butter ran down her hands and on to her coat cuffs. Her father slapped her, then, buttery from touching her, began licking his fingers. The mother said, 'You're disgusting.' The little girl let out a thin scream of frustration. 'I said not to bring her,' the father said, 'she's not like the others, she's not reasonable . . .'

His tea came. There was a tiered stand with an assortment of cakes, creamy and plain. Gwen said, 'The madeira cake's homemade.'

He said, 'When can I talk to you?'

'Well, I shouldn't think just now,' she said, disappearing almost at once.

As he sipped his tea, he decided what her story must be. Her husband had fallen on hard times – perhaps had had Spanish 'flu and not recovered properly? His earlier image of her: homemaker, sitting comfortably by the fire, one or even two children, gone up in the world a little . . . Anything but this.

His thirst was even greater than his appetite. He emptied the teapot and the hot-water jug, and asked for more. Then he ate his way through girdle scones, bread and butter, potted shrimps, both slices of madeira cake.

She came over when he hailed her. He hated doing that. 'Have you had enough, do you want your check?' But he told her, 'I'm not going. Not till we've talked. A surprise like that, an old friend, and you think I'd just come in and stuff myself and leave.'

'That'll be ninepence,' she said laughing, handing him the check. 'I'd like old friends to have it on the house, only . . . You can have another pot of tea, though.'

'I'm stopping here until we can talk,' he said. 'I can sit somewhere else if you need the table.'

'Listen, Lieutenant Dick, you'd never do what you were told on the ward, would you? Go away now and come back about half seven – We eat then before clearing up.'

He had a ticket for the Alhambra that night. He took it back for resale. At the hotel he put in a call to Middlesbrough and reported to Dad about the day's meetings.

The café door was just being locked as he came back. Gwen was standing there with the little waitress – he hoped she wouldn't be staying. But she said goodbye almost at once, hurrying out into the dark street. Inside the lights had been dimmed except for the corner by the kitchen. The elderly woman from the pay desk was sitting already at a table.

'We're just getting our tea,' Gwen said. 'Are you ready to eat again?'

There were plates of ham and salad and slices of already buttered bread. He was surprised by his sudden sharp hunger.

'I'll just get it,' she said, leaving him alone with the elderly woman. He asked her, 'Are you Nurse Ackroyd's mother?' feeling foolish as soon as he'd said it. Nurse, indeed . . .

'I am.' She said it with finality, closing her mouth firmly after speaking. She ate with a fine appetite, occasionally glancing over at the curd tart lying waiting at the end of the table. 'Where's our tea, then? Didn't Gracie mash it before she left?'

Gwen asked him what he was doing now, and why was he in Bradford? 'You never live here by any chance?'

I wish I did, he thought suddenly.

He knew the time would come when she would ask him about his limp. She said:

'That leg, the one that didn't quite, does it trouble you?'

'Sometimes.'

'When they sent you home, I thought maybe it'll not be quite right. You were lucky as anything – keeping it.'

'I know my luck. Don't think I don't.' He felt bitter once more for others. 'My friend,' he said, 'the one who came to see me – you won't remember – he was killed in Russia.'

'I'm sorry,' she said, not admitting if she remembered or not. Her mother tut-tutted.

'It's for you to answer questions now,' Dick told her. 'Why here, why a café? What happened? You were going to have a family . . . Your husband – What *happened*?'

She said, 'He got killed. That's what happened.' The slice of bread she'd just taken up remained in her hand. 'All those months in the trenches, safe. He was just unlucky, you see – he got that staff job – but then this castle, château place they were in, it got a direct hit. Cyril died at once.'

It was his turn to say, 'I'm sorry.'

'So you should be,' Mrs Ackroyd said. She spoke with a dull anger, though continuing to eat. She reached for the curd tart: 'My lass's life in ruins. Five weeks wed only. Then we'd trouble at home. She's not said, has she? We lost Father, lost Mr Ackroyd, Christmas 1918. He left nowt. A good man like that – nowt. Only owing. And our two lads, gone. It looked as if we'd maybe to be beholden. But then our Gwen had her idea –'

She told him how they'd bought the tea rooms, of how Gwen cooked and baked for it. In the summer Gwen had made ice-cream, the two sorts: it had been really popular. Another eighteen months and they'd be out of debt. 'A year ago Friday week, we opened. It's been hard. And'll be hard again, I don't doubt.'

Gwen said, 'Don't mind her. She grumbles. Always has.'

Gwen didn't grumble. She glowed. Not as he remembered her after the honeymoon – there were dark lines under her eyes now, something dark behind the eyes too – but with the glow of achievement.

'So you're the manageress, the owner?' he said. 'You don't dress like one.'

'It puts folk off. Too stiff. This way, they tell me their troubles.'

'I wonder you've the time. You'd none for me, today.'

'Hark at him!' And she began to reminisce about No. 4 General. Telling her mother stories of how the boys behaved. Reminding Dick of the elocutionist and his dreary monologue.

'You see, you remember us all,' he said triumphantly.

'Of course I do –'

It was time for him to go. He saw Mrs Ackroyd grow restless, pouring the dregs from the teapot but not refilling it. He didn't want to outstay his welcome. (And it had been a welcome, had it not?) He wanted to ask Gwen, 'When can I see you again?' But somehow he couldn't.

'You've done wonderfully,' he told her. 'It's a fine place.'

'When you're next in Bradford you'll know where to come for your tea, won't you?'

Walking back to his hotel, it was as if he trod air. The limp was there, but didn't matter. As he closed the door of his small bedroom, he stood a moment looking at the narrow white-covered bed. He wondered if she slept in one like that. Alone.

A princess, he thought. The Adelphi Tea Rooms, Bradford. Run by a princess.

8

'Are you sure you're warm enough, dear?' Eleanor asked. 'You're not worried – about going on the sea? Not frightened?'

It seemed to Maria that ever since they had left Eleanor had been fussing, showing concern, when all she wanted was to be left alone. This morning she'd been sick, waking up in the small London hotel, nauseated and frightened.

She wasn't afraid of Italy. Or was she? This strange northern Italy where she was to be left, in its own way a foreign country compared with Sicily. And she would be alone. All the faces that since 1915 had grown familiar would be absent.

The sea crossing. Sitting up on deck, thoughtfully wrapped in a rug by Eleanor, staring at the grey choppy waters of the Channel. A chill April day. Five years ago next month, death has chased her across the deck of the *Lusitania*. And Uncle Eric had rescued her.

He had not come to her rescue this time. No one had. She could not call it rescue, what they were doing to her now. And Uncle Eric: she'd scarcely been able to look at him, so certain had she been of his anger, his disappointment. Those terrible weeks when, Peter back at school, she'd thought she could bury the horror deep inside her. Forget, she'd told herself from one dread day to another, forget. But of course buried deep inside had been, not the awful memory, but a baby.

She knew too much, she seemed always to have known too much. Her body, now heavy, now light, but always different, spoke to her. Running errands for Aunt Maimie, helping Aunt Dulcie with her war wounded, she moved as if sleepwalking. It was a nightmare from which she couldn't, however hard she tried, wake. Then suddenly it was the third month and still nothing had happened. She knew she would have to speak.

Not to Aunt Maimie. Never Aunt Maimie. (The nausea she'd felt when, taking her hat from her, she had caught that unmistakable sour stale smell. Aunt Maimie and the Black Book . . .)

Watching Dick's kind face at the supper table, she'd thought: I wish I could tell *him*. He had looked at her and smiled and said that she was very quiet these days. 'Winter'll soon be over,' he said.

In the end it had been Aunt Dulcie she told. Finding her alone, sorting a pile of linen, she stammered it out, wanting to weep, but not able. 'Something awful's happened.' Saying it twice, then blurting out the truth: 'Expecting, you call it, don't you? I think I'm *expecting* . . .' The shock and horror on Aunt Dulcie's face – and all that before any questions about the father. 'Peter and mine, it'll be . . . Peter's the father.' And then, oh horror, Aunt Dulcie, her eyes filling with tears: 'Maria, how *could* you, darling?' Maria had known then that she had done wrong, that the shame she felt was real. She would have explained, but no words came. 'He did it to me,' was all she could think of, but even that she couldn't manage. By now Aunt Dulcie was really crying. She threw her arms round Maria. 'So young, both of you, it's . . .' Then: 'Leave it all to me,' she said, 'let *me* worry, Maria dearest . . .'

The next morning Maria began a heavy cold. Aunt Maimie fussed, as if Spanish 'flu lingered still, and told her she was to stay in bed. Aunt Dulcie came and sat on her bed, saying: 'Sleep and rest. We shall think of something.'

The third day she was downstairs early. Uncle Eric and Dick had already left. Aunt Dulcie said, holding her hand tight: 'Eric is staying home this afternoon. He wants to speak to you while Maimie's out at whist.'

His face wore an expression she had never seen before. He told her to sit on the leather sofa. He remained standing by the fireplace. Aunt Dulcie, in one of the armchairs, looked at her hands. He said, his voice almost breaking, 'Maria, Maria, what have you done?'

She was silent. He went on: 'The shock. It's been terrible. I can hardly bring myself . . . I was over at Rossall yesterday, where I spoke to Peter.'

She said, without looking up, her first moment of hope, 'You know, then?' It was as if the curtain parted and light flooded in, 'He's told you what happened?'

'To my everlasting regret, yes – I wish I hadn't to hear it. He said . . .'

She could not believe it. She hadn't been able, had not dared, to tell the real truth. But this – this travesty . . . That he should

101

suggest *she* had been the wicked one. She muttered in a voice small with desperation, 'Is that what he says?'

'It is.' He said gently, 'Have I to suspect my own son of fibbing? I'd to drag it from him. I wish it *weren't* so.'

Weights dragged her body, head, hands, down, down.

'He's to blame, is Peter. It takes two. He's heard from me about that. But to have *led him on* . . . You've disappointed us so terribly. A girl we took into our home and trusted.' She heard his voice through a black fog, could smell the blackness.

'We'll continue to love you, of course. Even if it weren't our duty, we'd do that. We'll continue to love you, but we can't forget . . . We'd expected a lot from you, Maria. But it seems – and I blame myself, that blood will out. Latin, Mediterranean, whatever . . .'

A stone, lying stuck in her throat. 'I didn't –'

'Didn't what?'

She was silent. No tears were possible. All of her rock hard. Her mouth tightened. She longed suddenly with a great intensity for Mamma. For her childhood. The past. Not safe perhaps, but shared.

She remembered little of the next few weeks. A visit to the doctor with Aunt Dulcie. Later in Thackton, again with Aunt Dulcie, a special visit to Miss Dennison who was to help them. She realized they had made their plans without consulting her. Sitting up in Miss Dennison's bedroom, she heard what was to become of her – and the child.

Miss Dennison was gentle with her. 'I shall never at any time reproach you. What's done is done. And for the girl, it is always worse.' She told her, 'You and I are going to be a long time together – I should like you to call me Eleanor.'

At Moorgarth, Elsie, who had been told only that Maria wasn't well, plied her with food. Maria was two weeks there, going over to Park Villa almost every day. Mrs Dennison asked her, 'What do you think, my dear, of my daughter's sudden urge to travel?' It was assumed she was teaching Eleanor Italian.

Letters, winging to and fro. In Middlesbrough it was given out that Maria would leave to do secretarial training in London. She would live with Ida.

Eleanor said: 'I've asked my brother, the one who is a Jesuit priest, to find us somewhere to stay. And he has given us an introduction to a friend, also a priest, who will choose a convent for you.' Perhaps she saw something in Maria's face because she went on hurriedly, 'I of course had to confide in him, dear. But as you'll know, a priest . . . Our secret will be absolutely safe.'

Florence was to be a sightseeing tour for Eleanor. After her departure, Maria would move to a convent and stay there until the birth. When the baby was about ten weeks, Eleanor would visit Florence again. The baby would be weaned and she would bring it home, ostensibly an Italian orphan – adopted on impulse. Basil's priest friend would help with the legal side. A few weeks later Maria would return – straight to London, and Ida.

The days before they were to set off, back in Middlesbrough now, alone in her room she wept into Trimmer's silky coat. He too she would be leaving for ever. Her love for him seemed to hold concentrated all her sorrow, and terror.

All the time she wondered who knew of her shame? Aunt Dulcie, Uncle Eric, Eleanor and Ida. Who else? Looking at Dick, she would wonder, does he? and not dare to ask. That he should think ill of her, it wasn't to be borne. Jenny, she was certain, sensed something but it was masked by her jealousy at Maria's going to London. 'It's all so sudden, and she hasn't even begged. Dad, Aunt Dulcie, why can't *I* go?'

But the worst of all, now in this waiting time, was having to live with Uncle Eric. Peter she did not have to worry about – he would not be home again until after they had left. Aunt Maimie seemed amazed only that it should all be happening so quickly. Ida, home for the weekend, told her, 'An opportunity suddenly came up.' To Maria, she was robust and consoling. She never referred to the child. She said only, 'We shall have some good times together.'

She tried never to be alone with Uncle Eric. With others there, he was pleasant enough, although even then she could sense his anger. Her last evening, taking her alone into the drawing-room, he explained that afterwards, she could never come to Thackton.

'It would make an impossible situation for Eleanor. You'll visit us at Middlesbrough. There'll always be a welcome.'

Would there? She could not believe it, just as she could not believe he was the same Uncle Eric she had tripped up on the *Lusy*, in whose stateroom she'd fooled around eating candy. His pet, and her dear friend.

She was sick again on the train as it travelled through clean bright Switzerland, washed by morning light and spring sunshine. The rich, creamy coffee they'd drunk at the frontier lay in the pit of her stomach, then rose in fatty globules. She went and stood in the corridor. Eleanor said, 'You look very white. Do you feel sick?'

Concern, endless concern. She wanted to cry out, 'I'm not sea sick, train sick, baby sick, *I am heart sick*.' How could she feel anything else, with this load of shame, which she alone had to carry? They had not asked her what she wanted. (And if they had – what would she have answered?)

The tinkling of sheep bells, a reminder of home, of Sicily, woke her early her first morning in Florence. She crossed the chill floor of her room in the pensione and threw open the shutters. A ramshackle two-wheeled cart piled high with glass jars was crossing the Ponte alle Grazie. The driver walked alongside cracking his whip at the unevenly matched pony and mule. There was a brass horn hung with bells at the front of their wooden saddles. It was this sound that had reminded her of home. Other carts followed. A whole procession. She remained a long time watching.

She and Eleanor had separate rooms at the Pensione Cafferkey. Although she was lonely she wouldn't like to have shared – she knew that at night she would weep. The pensione was run by two Irish maiden ladies. The elder Miss Cafferkey did all the talking. She blinked a lot as she spoke and had a hairline so low it gave the illusion of a bandeau. 'Pet,' she called Maria, telling Eleanor, 'Isn't she the dearest little thing?' The younger Miss Cafferkey was small and round and wore a surprised expression. The cooking at the pensione depressed Maria. It was not Italian at all. 'Good plain food,' Miss Cafferkey explained. 'Not to surprise the visitors' stomachs. None of your greasy oil and only the littlest raw salading.'

Maria wore a wedding-ring and was known as Mrs Gardner. Eleanor was a Miss Davis. Earlier she'd explained to Maria: 'My brother thinks it better we stay here under assumed names. Many English people come to Florence in the spring . . . I think, dear, we may need to give little fictitious accounts of your background.'

With some of her old spirit, Maria had said, 'Let's sort it out then, let's get our story *right*.' It seemed to her sometimes that Eleanor perhaps had not after all thought of quite everything. In slow anger, she thought: If I'd had to do it, I'd have done it better.

In the small garden of the pensione the anemones were almost over, but the magnolia was in bloom. Pots of hyacinths and freesias stood on the flagstones, tight-skinned grape hyacinth grew profusely. She and Eleanor hired bicycles for three days from a shop in the Piazza Beccaria. Eleanor, hatted and gloved, her high-necked blouses fastened always with a brooch, led. They rode slowly. Eleanor was concerned for Maria, making her dismount at the first sign of a slope. Dressed in her best, she took Maria to the Via Tornabuoni to drink afternoon tea at Doney's. She bought her chocolates in a red quilted box. She was all kindness.

Most of the time, though, she wanted to visit galleries, churches, monasteries – wherever there were paintings. Maria couldn't share her enthusiasm. So often what she saw seemed to her only gentler versions of the gaudy virgins, babes and angels she'd grown up with in Sicily and New York. Many, far too many, were of the Madonna and Child. Eleanor would stop before these, visibly moved.

'There's something – you see, it's so beautiful the love of mother for child.' She said it almost as if she were a mother, which she would be soon enough, which she *wanted to be*. Perhaps that was the strangest thing about those dreary outings: seeing Eleanor so full of joy, radiating a strength which seemed to come from happiness. It wasn't the Eleanor of Thackton-le-Moors, and for some reason that frightened her.

They went to call on Basil's friend, Father Grierson, who had recommended the pensione and was arranging a convent for Maria. Slight and balding, he had a distracted face and manner:

'Your brother, Miss Dennison . . . yes, yes, a dear friend.' He addressed his remarks to Eleanor, ignoring Maria. He spoke of the convent she would be going to. Sant'Agostino. He would arrange a preliminary visit, but in the meantime, he had had an idea, a suggestion only: 'If I may speak of it later, Miss Dennison?'

In the room where they sat was a large statue of the Sacred Heart. Christ, showing his bleeding heart, gazed at Maria.

Two days later they visited the Foundling Hospital. As they walked through the loggia, babies in swaddling clothes, circled as if by a deep blue sky, looked down on them. 'Andrea della Robbia, his work,' Eleanor explained, and as they passed into the courtyard, there was della Robbia again. The archangel Gabriel giving the good news to the Virgin Mary (yes, for some it was *good news*).

Capable-looking women dressed in white walked past carrying in their arms real babies. 'It is four hundred years we are doing this work,' said the nun escorting them: plump, bursting from her blue habit with the alarming headdress, a bird in flight, of the Sisters of St Vincent de Paul.

It had been Father Grierson's idea they should visit the Holy Innocents. 'A suggestion merely, Miss Dennison . . . I know you have plans made but this would have the advantage – the child would be Latin rather than Anglo-Saxon.'

Eleanor told Maria, 'We must of course go. Father Grierson has been to a lot of trouble. And after all, perhaps . . . who knows? But we mustn't forget the little one concerns the Graingers also.' Maria saw she was already distressed. And why not? Eleanor wanted this child, didn't she? It wasn't charity, her kindness.

Iron cribs swung from hooks in the ceiling. They stopped beside one. The baby, with flushed pointed face, mewed in half sleep. Round his neck, a small medallion. 'This little one, he is very new.' The baby's tongue poked out, his mouth made a sucking movement.

'How long do they stay with you?' Eleanor asked.

'Eight weeks only, then so long they are healthy we find them a nice family in the country, where they shall live till they are old enough for working. They are brought up, you see, into the family.'

Maria found her voice: 'What is on the medallion?'

'A number – and a letter. That corresponds, you see, to a name and address which only we know. All our babies when they are grown, they may come and ask who are their parents – if they wish.'

'If they wish,' Eleanor echoed.

'They are all loved,' the nun said suddenly. But Maria felt cold. Cold of the cloisters. She could hardly concentrate as they were shown around the dairy. The milk was sterilized and sealed in bottles. 'Scrupulously clean,' Eleanor remarked with approval and surprise.

The morning bath. On a huge table fitted in the centre with hot and cold water, naked babies lay kicking on the padded yellow oilcloth. Maria found this worse than the little swinging cribs. Nothing was said. The nuns, surely, thought it a visit by tourists: an English lady who has an interest in these matters, Father Grierson would have told them. Eleanor made no comment as they left. Maria found herself shaking.

'We can walk up here, I think,' Eleanor said. 'The Via della

Sapienza. We shall go to San Marco – Fra Angelico's frescoes. These you will love, Maria.'

San Marco. Here was yet more of the Virgin hearing her joyful news. Everywhere Madonnas of such beauty and serenity. And what colours. The reds, the golds. The blues, the greens. In the carrozza going back, it was Eleanor who spoke first. She had seemed preoccupied, but now, in a calm voice, she asked, 'Well, dear, what do you think?' And when Maria didn't answer, '*I* think it would be much better for you, and for the babe, if we kept to the arrangements we've made. That he or she will be brought up English . . .' her voice tailed away. 'Father Grierson was only suggesting an alternative. But in the end, as we've always said, it's what you want, Maria. What *you* think for the best.'

I don't think, Maria wanted to say, I pray that I shan't have to. Here today she had been forced to, a little. And to feel, a lot. Tears lay heavy and painful in her chest.

'I couldn't. It's not what I'd want at all . . . No, no. Please leave the arrangements just as they were.'

The days were passing. Everywhere now on the street corners and in the Mercato Nuovo were sheaves of irises gathered before the sun was up. At the pensione, she tried to avoid talking to the other guests. Especially she didn't want to answer questions. But mealtimes when they sat several at one long table were difficult. The last week twin boys arrived with their father before returning to Oxford for the new term. Handsome and self-assured, they made her think of Peter. Her sad anger with him rose in gobbets so that she would sit, fork poised over her mutton cutlet, hating him.

She longed for Eleanor's holiday to end. The faster time went the sooner it would all be over, the whole unknown terror of it. But perversely, when the day of her departure came, she wanted to cling to her. Take me back to Thackton, she cried inside, and *make it all right again*. Seeing the leather trunk and the gladstone standing in the hall, she was afraid.

'I shall write of course,' Eleanor said, taking Maria awkwardly in her arms, leaving a delicate scent of flowered cologne. 'And you know Father Grierson is always there.' Riding to the station with Maria, she handed her a small package. 'Open it when I have left.'

Inside was a brooch – gold filigree and garnets. Maria had seen it several times on Eleanor, worn with her high-necked blouses. Tears filled her eyes, for herself, for the child. She laid it carefully at the back of a drawer in her room. She was at the Convent Sant'Agostino now. She had gone there the same day that Eleanor left. When they had visited it the week before, Eleanor had been lavish in her praise of everything. 'I'm sure they will take good care of you, dear.'

And indeed the nuns seemed kind enough, although she was not so sure about the Superior, Sister Ignazio. But it was strange, and lonely. She was to learn fine embroidery during her waiting time. Although there were thirty or so girls learning these and other skills from the nuns, they all came in by day. She was the only girl living there.

The clean lines of the convent, the marble floors, smell of waxed furniture, laundered linen. Scrubbed wood. Piety. She was at Mass in the chapel every morning at seven. It was expected of her. Her room was a convent cell: hard, white-covered bed, small table and scrubbed wood chest of drawers. A crucifix hung above the bed and a brightly coloured, almost lipsticked portrait of Pope Benedict. She laid out on the bare wood photographs of Dick and Ida and Uncle Eric and all the family. Of Trimmer. After only two days she put them away again. She could not bear to think of her love for them. Of their love for her. All lost.

Sorrow and anger. Some days the anger was greater than the sorrow. So dark and deep was it that she could feel it like some black tarry substance, a lava. As if it would boil up, bursting forth suddenly: scorching, burning up not only her but all around her.

Now it was May and great white arum lilies stood around the altar, the painting of Christ risen. She stepped out of chapel most mornings to a high sun in a blue sky, the blue of Eleanor's much-loved frescoes. She breakfasted alone in her cell. Coffee, bitter, with boiled milk, the skin fragmented. Two hard rolls.

At eight o'clock the classes began. Until midday she embroidered with Sister Agata. Tiny, birdlike, Sister Agata's fingers flew. So did her tongue. But her temper wasn't distressing, for when she pulled impatiently at Maria's drawn thread spider with its uneven legs and too loose body, it was the bad quality of the spider she deplored, not its creator.

In the afternoons she often crept into her cell, falling at once into a heavy sleep. Sometimes she went with some of the girls either in the Cascine park where they would take out younger brothers and sisters, or to their homes. Most of the girls came from poor families. Their skills would bring in some money. Her most frequent companion was Fiorella, a thin girl, slightly stooped.

Three afternoons a week she gave English lessons. Once a fortnight she paid a duty visit to Father Grierson. This she dreaded. If there'd been a letter from Eleanor, she would read from it, so that she didn't have to look at him.

Another person she tried to avoid was the Superior, Sister Ignazio. Outside the chapel one day, she had asked Maria if she found it easy to talk to the convent chaplain, Father Bevacqua? Framed by the coif, her small pretty face, lightly lined, stared at Maria. 'You know all you have to do is to repent, don't you, that God *wants* to forgive you? You must be good and grateful here, and learn this useful trade –'

Maria said haughtily, from her pain and anger, 'I shall be going to London, to work in an office –'

'Is that so? A pity . . . City life . . . You don't want to get into trouble again, do you?'

'Seventy times seven – God keeps on forgiving,' Maria cried. 'He forgives, doesn't He?'

Sister Ignazio flushed. 'I don't like your way of speaking. A very different sort of Italian, aren't you? *Sicilians* . . . Pagans, all of you –'

Maria turned and ran away. The day after that encounter the child quickened. She thought at first it was a nervous stomach or that she had eaten too many *nespoli.* When later she realized it was the child, she became at once protective and frightened. Now there was no going back.

May was almost over. Fireflies appeared in the evenings and mosquitoes threatened. In the market and at the street corners, wild gladioli were for sale. Summer matting was laid at the convent.

One morning she woke to blackness. Deep, deep, as if she fell into a pit. At first she could not even think where she was. Then: I am in a convent cell in Florence . . .

She had been dreaming, of the Lion. This time he wore his kind face. Her family were all there too, even Minicu. Minicu had not died but stood beside her laughing, teasing. Za Rosetta asked her why the shame, the disgrace? But when she tried to explain, the Lion interrupted.

'It's all right,' he told Maria. 'We shall take care of you.' She said, 'But you know what I've done, what happened to me? The disgrace . . . If it's not all right in England, how can it be all right in Sicily?' But he only repeated patiently, throwing open his arms, welcoming her into them, 'We take care of our own. We shall take care of you, and of him –'

'Him? It could be a girl,' she said.

'Of him. The monster who did this.'

'Oh, but –' she began, then suddenly turned to Rocco and Gaetano. They wore their army uniform as in the picture they had sent. She felt such warmth in the dream, such security. 'I need you,' she told them all. 'I need you here. I'm not Tuscan, not *settentrionale*. Their ways are not my ways. I'm as strange here as ever I was in England . . .'

And then she woke. Almost at once the blackness descended. She felt it like a heavy pain all through the morning class. Tomorrow was her fortnightly visit to Father Grierson. I won't, she thought. I *can't*. Fiorella asked if she was going to the Cascine this afternoon. She was taking her little brothers and sisters, and the family mending.

'No, no,' Maria said, 'I'm not so good. I must rest. Since I got heavier. An ache –'

'Yes, my mother is the same. I understand.'

She told Sister Giuseppe to whom she had to report her comings and goings: 'I shall walk in the Cascine with Fiorella probably. It may well be I'll go to their house and help with the little ones. Their uncle will bring me back.'

Waiting in the hall of Santa Maria Novella station, she had a fit of terror. She felt faint too from lack of food: she hadn't been able to eat at midday. From a food cart she bought two rice balls coloured orange with tomato and spicy meat.

She carried with her only a black shawl, knotted and containing just a change of underclothes and a loose cotton dress. The idea had grown on her all morning: first during Mass, and then, more strongly, in class. *Their ways are not my ways.* All through embroidery, unpicking an unsuccessful *point de venise*, risking Sister Agata's temper, she planned. Quickly, desperately. Home. Sicily. Loved ones. There had never been America in between, or Yorkshire. *I want to go home.*

Her first problem was money. The nuns held a small sum for her, but there was no way to get at it. To pay for the journey she would have to sell something. When she went up to her cell at midday she saw, lying at the back of her drawer, the brooch Eleanor had given her.

Could she, was it not rejecting Eleanor? In the end she sold it to a small shop near the Ponte alla Carraia, on her way to the station. Sadness and guilt, seeing it glow in the dark wood of the counter. She had no means of knowing if she'd received a fair price.

She had left a note pinned to her pillow. 'Gone to visit my family for a little while. Then I shall be back. Please do not worry about me.' She had no time to word it better, nor to think of any hue and cry there might be. The great, the only thing was to be away. Home. Sicily.

Safely on the train, she was still frightened (what have I done, what am I doing?) She felt a sick hunger in spite of the rice balls and when the train stopped at Rome late in the night, she leaned out – she didn't dare alight – and bought a basket, more food than she could eat, and a quarter litre of chianti. She drank it hurriedly from the flask. For a litle while after, she dozed.

The train arrived in Naples in the small hours. She had not thought of that. She planned to take the day boat to Palermo. The station at Naples frightened her more than Florence. In the hall, a small man darted up to her. 'You're looking for a place to sleep? Sleep in the day too?' She shook him off. Another, in spite of her simple clothes, addressed her in English, French, German. She wouldn't answer. She wanted now only to be in Sicily. To be home.

She shivered in a waiting-room till it was time to go for the boat. Because she was afraid and tired, she took a cab to the quay. The boat was crowded. Livestock, children. She bought rolls and prosciutto, but her mouth even after coffee was too dry. I need wine, she thought, hoping to sleep the journey away.

Below deck it was hot and smelled. The water was calm but even the slight rocking made her feel queasy. Children ran everywhere. It was the first time for five years that she had heard the language of Sicily. Men played cards, muttering as they played.

She went back up. A group of men, women and children with tambourines were singing and dancing. They had several flasks of wine with them. She sat near, gazing at the water, her shawl of belongings on her lap. They were songs she knew but she did not join in. *Lu me Sceccu.* The crowd swayed as a young boy, his adam's apple working, imitated a cock crowing. A gipsy-like girl offered her some wine. She drank thirstily. Her world blurred a little. An elderly woman, arms crossed, sang the descant, sad and haunting, of *La Pampina di l'aliva*. She tried to think of herself as the rich returning emigrant: the *americana*, that figure to be admired. But in trying to blend into the landscape, she'd failed to look or feel the part. She was the *signora inglese*. I am wearing a wedding-ring, she thought.

As the boat neared the harbour, she longed and longed to see Rocco's face. Gaetano, Rosalia, her nephews and nieces . . . In Palermo it was too late in the day to make her way up to Monteleone. There was enough money from the brooch to pay for a hotel. She wondered in panic if she was even now being chased? She sat up in the night, heart beating, uncomfortable in the sagging bed, certain that she heard Father Grierson's voice. *They have sent him for me.* Later she heard a church clock strike two.

In the morning very early she made her way to where she could find a carrier going up to Monteleone. The sun was high in a fierce blue sky. As the cart rattled up the rough path, its wheels stirred up white dust. She felt the jolting excite the baby.

The carter was a small elderly man, who showed no curiosity. They talked little on the journey. Tall blue-flowered thistles stood by the roadside, pink-tipped daisies, huge dandelion clocks. She smelled borage and wild garlic. Great white boulders, dazzling in the sun, broke the landscape. For a while two small hawks hovered above them. Later, sheep grazed among some olive trees, herded together closely, their long goatlike necks hanging. The sounds, the scents – she might never have been away.

And then Monteleone came into view. Nothing had changed. Mangy, hungry grey cats darted past open doorways and down alleys. Hens wandered from house to street and back again, pecking hopefully or rising with an angry flutter of wings. The sun beat down on her bare head. Her ankles, from that first night up in the train, were swollen still. She had forgotten her sister's married name and would have to ask for Rosalia that had been Verzotto, then she remembered which had been her house: the second turning just near the square. The door was open. A small boy running out threw his arms round Maria's legs.

'Tiru, what are you doing?' A woman in a torn black skirt came out after him. Maria noticed at once she was pregnant, but at first didn't recognize her. This woman looked forty . . .

'Yes,' Rosalia said, 'yes?'

'I'm – it's Maria, your sister. Little Maria.'

Rosalia's face lit up momentarily. Then she looked doubtful. She frowned. 'From England – from '*Merica*?'

'England, from England,' Maria said, in a rush to get the lies over with: 'I'm married and visiting in Italy. I wanted – it seems silly – my husband had to go away on business . . .'

But Rosalia wasn't listening, she was smacking another child who crept from behind her skirt. She said distractedly, 'You know Rocco and Gaetano are back?'

'Yes.'

'They won't stay, of course. Who'd want to? They're lodging at the Randazzo's . . . Are you spending the night here?'

'A few days,' Maria said, 'I thought, a few days, to see the family.' She stretched out a hand to caress the child. 'How many?' she asked.

'Too many. Six, and this one.' She struck her belly with her fist. 'There's no end to it, is there? And he's proud of them, Nicu is. They always are. Men . . .' She lifted a pile of linen from the table. 'Get yourself a chair. You might as well stay around a little.' She said in a rough voice, 'You're that way too. Is your husband – your husband's pleased?'

'Of course,' Maria said. 'I have it in September.'

Rosalia muttered something to an older child who ran off. Suddenly Maria was surrounded by people. A few she recognized but many seemed total strangers. She was an object of curiosity. People wanted to know more than she could tell them. A young woman who could have been only a child when Maria left, said, 'Crucianu's daughter, don't you remember me?' They all wanted to talk of Mamma and Maria's life in New York. There was confusion: she hadn't come from 'Merica then? No, of course, she had been on that big boat . . .

'The boat that sank,' it was a wail almost. 'Terrible, terrible. We heard you had no Mamma. But adopted – you were fortunate to be adopted by a rich man. And now you are married. And a baby on the way.'

Yes, yes, a baby. Of course she was happy and proud. Only, where were Rocco and Gaetano? But they're coming, they're coming. They had fought in the war, did she know? Now they spoke of going back to 'Merica? Gaetano was with the wheelwright again. Rocco had some secret, some business work. Did she know Za Rosetta had died many, many Easters ago?

Then there they were standing before her. Rocco and Gaetano.

They looked older than in their photographs. Gaetano slighter, timid almost. He laughed nervously as he embraced her but Rocco hugged her so tightly she wondered if perhaps he hadn't noticed the baby. Standing back, he looked at her with pride, affection. 'You never said. Never wrote of your marriage. *Nothing*. And now you come – like this. But it's marvellous. How long can you be with us?' A flask of wine had appeared. 'Listen,' he said, 'Listen – tell me everything. Now. All about him, your husband, life in England, why you didn't write. Everything.'

The tissue of lies. She wove it ever more intricately. Whenever she could, she asked questions herself: 'What happened to this one, that one, the mother of old so and so?'

She was so tired by nightfall – wine, talk, heat of the day – she thought she might be ill. Rocco had found her a bed. She was to eat at Rosalia's, where he and Gaetano usually ate.

That evening she felt, though she was to stay only two nights, that Rosalia resented her. Maria was another mouth. The plate of steaming pasta and fennel: stealing from tomorrow's and tomorrow's food.

She had come empty-handed. Her own family and she had brought them no gifts. But the little money left from the brooch was needed for the journey back. If she were to be stranded between Sicily and Tuscany . . .

Rocco's appearance – not too smartly dressed, but very clean. He wore a belt with a large brass buckle showing a lion's head. She shuddered, remembering Don Cataldo. The lion with the heart of stone, and Minicu.

'The police,' Rosalia was saying, staring at her empty plate, 'these days always suspecting someone or something. They come up here, searching. Cattle gone, sheep gone, some persons missing – they should mind their own business down in the towns and let us alone. We only want to feed the little ones, how we do it is our affair.'

Her husband, Nicu: 'Your tongue. It's too long. Your sister here, she doesn't talk in that fashion.'

Supposing they come for me, Maria was thinking with horror: imagining Father Grierson, Sister Ignazio, making their hot sticky way up the mountains. Exposing her, telling *all* . . . Or worse, far worse, the carabinieri. She would be arrested, taken down to Palermo. To prison . . .

'Are these all your belongings?' Rocco asked, seeing the knotted shawl.

'All I wanted to bring,' she answered quickly. 'I didn't plan to come back the rich *americana*. I wanted just to slip in – as if I'd never been away.'

'Except that you have . . .' He pushed his hands out, shrugging his shoulders. 'We shall go back, of course. You know that?'

The second evening, her last, she and Rocco walked out together as the sun was going down, beyond the village to where the path twisted up towards the mountains. They sat on the ground by a clump of ancient olive trees, grey-green, their gnarled roots spreading. The warm air was heavy with the scent of sage. Gaetano was to have come too but he excused himself. 'He's courting,' Rocco told her. 'It's more or less arranged but he likes to spend time at the house. He'll take her to the States. He's discontented here, you see.'

Rocco too. 'Some things I don't speak of . . . But those who were not away fighting, they've taken everything. I name no names. But they've grown fat in our absence. And they don't wish to share.'

They talked about America, their very different experiences. 'We could have invited you to live with us after the boat sank. If you'd stayed with us in Detroit then maybe we wouldn't have become soldiers. And now you'd be American. Instead – look at you. You've done well, though.'

He seemed to want to confide in her yet without telling her very much. 'As I said, things here, they're not right. We resent – you understand? I've had some ideas how Monteleone, how to bring some prosperity – but without the help of others, if they won't share? Things aren't going the right way. They grow dangerous. You understand?'

'Rocco,' she said, 'what happened to the Lion?' She had walked past Don Cataldo's house, but, shutters fastened, it had a neglected air.

'I don't know,' he said, casually. 'Who cares?' He picked up a stone and threw it lightly. 'Dead. No, not dead . . . as good as. He had a fit, a stroke, a couple of years ago. A cousin nurses him. Why?

'I'm just curious . . . What about his family?'

'Gone. A long while back. The daughter who lived there, she's dead. The others . . . There are grandchildren, of course. But not here, not in Monteleone.'

She said suddenly, 'Does anyone ever speak of Minicu's disappearance?'

'I know nothing of that, Maruccia. Why should I? They found the body –'

She persisted, 'And no one's ever said they knew what happened?'

'It's never spoken of.'

She lowered her voice, as if the olive tree, so ancient, could tell tales. 'I want to tell you – what *I* know. That I shouldn't know. You see, I heard . . .' She stammered over the tale, living it again, her fear suddenly as real as it had been then. 'I think, you see, the Lion –'

His silence frightened her. He was breathing heavily, staring straight ahead. Then touching her shoulder: 'It's the first time you've spoken of this?' And when she nodded, 'Listen, never speak of it again. It isn't . . . *You should never have known this.*'

She wanted to ask then, 'Did you know?' But she was afraid. After a moment, though, he answered for her. 'I didn't know. But it's man's knowledge – not woman's. And as for a child. A *child* –' He spat on to the ground. 'But an order is an order. You understand me?'

She did. As if it were in her bones. I know, yet I do not know. (What wonder that, living in Tuscany, she should feel, their ways are not my ways?)

Morning, and time to leave. The blackness descended again, and with it a hopeless, helpless fear. Creeping back to the convent, facing the nuns, Father Grierson . . . If anyone had been sent from England!

Beneath a hot sky the stonecrop flamed gold, cow parsley, tall and flowery, ran rife. Rocco sat beside her in the cart. He had insisted on accompanying her to Palermo. Rocco, blood of her blood, and at the same time a stranger. Going down, they didn't speak much. Often she felt his gaze on her.

Sitting in a café on their way to the harbour: 'Your ticket for the boat?' He examined it, 'Don't they pay for you first class?' When she said hastily no, he said resentfully, 'You were first class on the *Lusitania*.'

'That was different –'

'Listen,' his voice was urgent, 'perhaps you don't want to go back? Something's wrong?' Suddenly persistent: 'You never talk of this man, your husband. You aren't proud of him, are you? Love, all that, perhaps not – but you don't think well of him, do you?'

116

She spoke from the blackness. 'It doesn't matter what he's like.'

'Was it a forced marriage?' She knew he meant, had her husband been chosen for her by the family? He did not mean the other thing at all. In later years she never knew what possessed her, why she should have suddenly burst out, the urge to confide unbearable.

'I'm not married. I don't have a fiancé, betrothed. Nothing. It's their son, the family who took me in. The younger one, Peter – the other would *never*. Peter, he . . . it was none of my doing.' She turned to look at him. His face was drained, hard. Both hands gripped the buckle of his belt. She stammered:

'I'm not wicked. I never, there wasn't –'

'*He did that*? He did that *to you*?'

She nodded dumbly. She had placed her hands over her belly. He asked in a harsh voice:

'What do they do about it, what are they doing?'

She told him about Eleanor, the convent, the plans. 'I'm going to be all right, you see. It's all been taken care of.'

'Let me go with you to Florence. I know where I can borrow money. I'll travel north with you –'

But she wouldn't allow it. 'All that – it would only make it worse.'

He made her promise to call on him if anything should go wrong. 'We go to 'Merica certainly – perhaps there is some way you can join us.' But she knew he knew that in that idea there was no future. 'Listen, I shall be thinking of you always. And I forget nothing. Your visit – and the other. I shall never forget . . .'

Very late the next night, she took a cab up to the convent. The gates were locked and she had to ring twice. But her reappearance was so important that Sister Ignazio was sent for. The portress, frightened, told Maria: 'There's been much trouble. The police, priests, telegrams . . .'

Later, she crept into her cell, an animal into its lair. In spite of the summer night she felt an autumnal cold. She lay awake shivering, waiting for yet dreading the morning. For she knew that now the prison gates were truly closed behind her.

9

Dick, looking down the agenda of the Board meeting, saw that they were scarcely half way. He felt he'd been all afternoon in the dark panelled room, shut in with Stanley Taylor's pipe: dirty, wet, foul-smelling.

Outside, it was summer. Inside, not. The sun could be glimpsed only faintly, shafting through the small leaded window. He saw that Dad was watching him. Carefully, to show that pain was the cause, he adjusted his leg. Uncle Fred Rowland said fussily, 'All right, are you? Not feeling seedy?'

No, not seedy. Just impatient. He could put his heart into the work itself, but never into the talk about it. How he hated all this necessary business . . . And the company he had to keep. Stanley's pipe. Uncle Fred with his slow ways. Great-uncle Arthur, who had taken now to snoring through part of the meetings. Dad would nudge him, and he would wake suddenly, bad-tempered, ready to argue the toss with anyone. What he hadn't heard while asleep had not been said.

'The price for Admiralty Mixture,' Dad was saying, 'it's way up. But it's to rule till the end of September.'

Bernard Thorpe asked: 'Anything there about Du Cros? They've instructed us to proceed with the same patterns . . .'

Summer. Maybe they thought he was restless, wanting to get away to Thackton? Last year, yes. But all he wanted now was to get over to Bradford. Since discovering the Adelphi Tea Rooms, he had taken any excuse to get there. He told Dad, 'If there's ever anything needed? I rather took to the place,' and Dad, mildly surprised said, 'Well . . . I'll let you know.'

But nothing happened. There remained only the weekends. He began to find excuses for not going to Moorgarth. It puzzled the family. They asked if he was getting like Mother. And what about Eulalia? He who'd been so keen, who'd loved Moorgarth the best of them all from childhood. Maria – was it because she wasn't there? Of course not, he'd said indignantly.

Dad asked once, 'You're not low-spirited about the leg? That sort of thing – it can get to you late.'

Dick snapped back, 'I never give it a thought. It's not spoiling my work, is it? Anyway it's war hero stuff, for what that's worth nowadays . . .' Already he'd noticed more and more of them on the streets now. The walking wounded, the disabled, fathers of families, placards on their chests: 'Six mouths to feed.' Uncomfortable reminder of a carnage less than two years ended. 'I'm fortunate,' he told Dad. 'A job, enough money, prospects . . . What's a gammy leg?'

'Good lad,' his father said. 'Good lad.'

He was a good lad, no doubt of that. But on his journeys to Bradford, he wished he weren't so good, that he was able to be wicked, a bit of a lad. In his dreams, he wasn't a lad at all but a merchant's son, hidden inside the Golden Lion, the lucky one of the brothers, certain to win the Princess. And when he had won her, he wiped the tears from her eyes and gave her hearth and home (he had seen already the house in Middlesbrough that he would make theirs).

He dreamed that she asked for his help: what she needed, she told him, was all of him. 'I need your body,' she said. In his dream he stood naked, but it seemed so natural. He gazed at himself, in the dream pointing ramrod up, hard, excited, full of longing and happiness and about to be fulfilled desire. 'I need you,' she said, not in her brisk voice but in a soft one he'd never heard before. She stood by the fire, the same fire which warmed his naked body. 'I need him, and you, for babies,' she said '*Our* babies. Oh, how I need and love you. You must have guessed, Dick.'

He kept having dreams like that. They were mostly happy, sometimes sad. Once she laughed at him. Oh, may that never happen in real life . . .

Uncle Arthur, after a loud snore, woke suddenly.

'The price of yellow brass, we've not had a price for yellow brass.'

'One and fourpence ha'penny,' Dad told him brusquely.

'If you said it, no one heard –'

'Bernard has it in the notes –' Dick could see his father's impatience, worse now than his own though for different reasons. Market metal prices. He scribbled some figures on his sheet of paper: 'Decorated Copper £95. Spelter £44 . . .'

Since Easter he'd managed to visit Bradford twice, the first time four weeks after the chance meeting: he had had to wait all that while to pluck up courage. When he arrived at the Tea Rooms about midday, it had been full of Saturday shoppers. She was serving a roast and two veg meal for one and sixpence. He sat down at a table where an elderly couple were already eating. He thought it was a table she would wait on. Mrs Ackroyd was sitting behind the till. He imagined she'd seen him and disapproved. He felt the most noticeable person in the room, to everyone but Gwen.

And then suddenly there she was. 'If it isn't our birdman again! They must keep you hard at it, having you travel for them Saturdays.' Pencil poised: 'What'll it be, then?'

'Roast beef, please. And a double of Yorkshire pudding if it's you've made it –' He spoke boldly. He saw the elderly couple register interest. He couldn't resist telling them something about Gwen, his voice, manner becoming more and more proprietary: '. . . So you can guess, all the boys were really fond of her . . .'

'Roses of No-Man's-Land, they called them,' the elderly man said. 'Wonderful, weren't they?'

But none more wonderful than *Gwen*. 'What about me coming round?' he asked her, when at last he saw his chance. 'After you close. Like last time.'

'Didn't you see the notice?' she laid his slice of apple pie in front of him. 'Closed at three-thirty today. Cousin Cuthbert from Australia, he's over on a visit. We're away to the station to meet him. Then a celebration meal, I shouldn't wonder. A bit of a family reunion.'

He could have wept with disappointment. She wasn't to know he'd come especially, it wasn't her fault, but now he wanted to say like a child, 'Can I come too?' Because of the dreams, perhaps, he saw himself already part of her life. At home in it. At home in *her*.

She must have caught some of his disappointment. 'If you're at a loose end before your train goes –' He thought she was going to say, 'Come with us,' but, 'If you've a long wait,' she went on, 'there's a good picture show at the Regent.'

'Oh, I'll be all right,' he said airily. 'It was only a thought.'

All the way from Middlesbrough to Bradford for two helpings of Yorkshire pudding, roast beef, cabbage, roast and mashed potatoes and apple pie. And of course a glimpse of, a few words with, her. At least she'd said, as he limped over to where she was serving to say goodbye: 'Next time you've to come this way, why don't you scribble a little note? This address will do – and we'll expect you. I could cook something special.'

'*All* your cooking's special –'

'I didn't make the Yorkshire pud today,' she said. She was laughing at him. 'But the apple pie, that was mine.'

He waited for two weeks, then wrote to her. It was mid-May now. He invented some story about a cousin (I can have cousins too). This time he would tell her the truth about his love and the dreams and everything. 'I'm free most of Sunday,' he wrote, 'if you are? I thought I'd stay on after I've seen him off.' (Oh, that mythical cousin.) 'What about a walk?'

She wrote to him – he realized he'd never seen her handwriting before except for the scrawls on her order pad. 'A walk in the fresh air would do me good. Come and eat with us first.'

He was surprised after her week's work she felt like cooking a proper meal. But she had done it all: lamb with fresh mint sauce, new peas, early potatoes, onion sauce, rhubarb fool and cream. He ate too much from greed, and to please her. Next time he would take them both to an hotel for a meal. A meal with wine, and liqueurs for both of them afterwards.

He wondered if she'd be impatient with his limp on the walk. Mrs Ackroyd didn't approve much of the idea. 'Gwen's used, aren't you, Gwen? to a nice sit-down with the *Referee* and the *Dispatch*. Considering she's on her feet all week –'

Gwen had just changed, and was telling Dick the route ('first we've to take the tram up to Shipley Glen . . .') when from her seat by the window, Mrs Ackroyd called gleefully: 'Rain. It's coming on to wet.' Within minutes the spotting had become a heavy downpour. He wasn't sure whether he should leave. He stood a while awkwardly, watching the rain splash on to the street below.

Gwen solved matters for him. 'We'll play Ludo – and wait for it stopping.' She got out the board. Mrs Ackroyd left her knitting and joined them. But the rain didn't stop. After Gwen had put the kettle on, he thought he must leave soon. They hadn't had their walk. He hadn't told her about his love and the dreams and everything.

'It's been a dull afternoon for you,' she said. 'I'm surprised you've not run home.'

'Did you want me to?' He wished Mrs Ackroyd weren't always

there, knitting and listening and breathing disapproval. 'Have I overstayed, then?'

'Daft,' she said, opening the cupboard for the teacups. 'It's good if you weren't bored. That's grand.'

'I have to be back again next month.' He thought of lying, saying that the foundry was expanding to Bradford.

Next time, he thought. Next time.

But on his June visit, he found himself further than ever from saying anything. Once again it was wet. Gwen and he joked about how he brought the rain with him. Mrs Ackroyd cheated at Snakes and Ladders, and he wondered if Gwen noticed. For most of the early afternoon her mother had been singing Cyril's praises. There seemed nothing he could not have done had he lived.

'They say they're crying out for folk with his mechanical savvy.'

Dick was angry, thinking it might upset Gwen. But apart from not answering, she took little notice.

When it was time to leave, they had not been alone together for even a minute. She came downstairs with him. It was too late to say anything now. At the front door, she lifted the latch.

'Look,' he said, 'Mrs Latimer, Miss Ackroyd, Gwen –' he blurted it out '– I love you. That's why, you see, why I came back, why I keep coming . . .'

'Get away,' she said, laughing but kindly, warm. He noticed she had flushed. 'Get away with you.' She gave him a sudden affectionate hug. 'You only think that, Dick. It's the nurse thing. That's all it is. I've seen –'

'No. I love you.'

'They all say that. Only they don't, not really. You just kept on longer than the others.' She clasped his hand in both of hers. 'You want to find a young lass. There's lots about. After the war and everything – there's no shortage, Dick.'

He wished now he hadn't said it. He longed for the time back to do it right. Her hand was on the latch again. He asked, 'Is it all right if I come back? I've not offended you?'

She laughed affectionately. His eyes cast down, he stared at the wrinkled leather on the bar of her grey shoe. 'You'll have to promise me something, Dick. That we'll hear no more of – what you just said. I'm nearly half as old again as you . . . Promise me.'

How could he? To promise that. Of course he couldn't. He

said, 'The first voice I heard, the first face I saw when I knew I was still alive, it was yours.'

'Yes,' she said. 'And that's bound to be special . . . But that's all it is.'

'No,' he said obstinately.

'Yes, Dick. You'd be surprised how many of the boys were in love with us. Officers, tommies, the lot. Angels, roses, princesses – we were all those . . . Of course you were different. Our only birdman. But it's the same thing.'

He turned his head away, prodding at the linoleum floor with his stick. He thought of saying, 'Is it because I'm a bit lame?' but knew that was unworthy. Even more, it was not true.

Stanley Taylor's voice broke into his thoughts.

'The way things are, I move that in future contracts'd be best made only for fixed quantities. Fixed periods too . . .'

Next time, he thought, *next time*. There must be some way to win her. Do I have to be a prince, then, to get a princess?

'. . . A block of a thousand pounds of eight per cent priority preference shares, issued just for that purpose.'

'This lad here, is he all right, then?' asked Uncle Arthur. 'Looks over the hills and far away to me . . .'

Eleanor, out walking, wheeling the wicker perambulator in the sharp October sunshine. Tomorrow Eric would come to Thackton for the weekend. It would be his first sight of his grandson. Going now in the direction of the village, she felt both pride, and great joy. She hoped to meet someone, to meet many people – so that she could make introductions. This child that had been her care for little more than a week, that was still news in the village. This beautiful child. Maria's child.

A week of such excitement and happiness. Behind her the journey through to Paris where Dulcie had met her. Before that, the parting with Maria. And Maria's parting with her child (such odd, fatigued indifference where Eleanor would have expected suffering. Was ready to *help* suffering . . .) After two days in Paris they were met by Basil in London. He had advised that it would be better not to try and prepare Mother. No telegrams from Florence or Paris or even London. 'Present her with a surprise. It will be easier.'

She wondered later whether he had been right. On a practical level there had been few problems. Dulcie had already arranged for clothes, bedding and so on to be at the ready. She had also engaged, secretly, a young girl who would come immediately as nurse. Amy Thackeray was the niece of Elsie, the housekeeper at Moorgarth, and had recently left a post as under-nursemaid in a Newcastle family. The timing was perfect.

Mother had been sitting downstairs at her desk when Eleanor's motor taxi drew up at the door.

'What, in God's name? Eleanor, what *have* you got there?'

'A baby, Mother, An Italian *bambino.*'

'Italian? Whose is it? Dear God, Eleanor –' her voice, cold, cutting '– are you mad?'

'Never more sane. And now, if you'll allow me, we're very tired from the journey.' A mistake to have told her nothing, perhaps. But revenge is so sweet, she thought.

'I always considered a visit to Italy unwise. You are not balanced enough to travel. And this second journey. So precipitate. You are unhinged . . .'

But then there had been the arrival of Amy, and a cart with all the equipment. Cot, bedding, rubber bath, wicker perambulator. Fresh milk, bottles. Eleanor was amazed at Dulcie's efficiency. Some milk was already boiled. Amy set to work at once. Small, neat, with dark hair plaited round her head, she had the complete assurance of one who comes from a large family: 'You do it like this . . . and this . . . Mam told us allus . . . He'll settle best if he's wrapped this way.'

Mother, outraged, waiting her moment, then making her way slowly upstairs to where Eleanor, alone now, sat in her room.

'Words fail me, Eleanor. *Have you gone mad?*'

'You asked me that already. No. I've made an impulsive but sensible decision. He's an orphan. I shall adopt him.'

'Dear God. *How* I am punished through my daughter.' She sat herself on the velvet chair beneath Titian's *Portrait of an English Gentleman.* 'Dear God, Eleanor.'

'I saw the baby in a Florentine orphanage. Nothing much is known of the parents. I made my arrangements out there.'

'*Your* arrangements. And to whose home have you brought this child?'

'Ours.'

'Mine, you mean –'

'No. Since we are to be so particular – *my* house.' She was surprised at the ease of it all. 'I think you forget the conditions of Father's will. My house, if I look after you – and I do. He did not stipulate I should not adopt a child.'

'You *are* out of your mind. Brazen. Hysterical –'

'I was never calmer.'

'Hysterical, my dear. Suffering perhaps from early middle age
. . . There is no question. This child must go to an orphanage.'

'He came from one, Mother.'

'Then he must go back to another. To the Sisters of Charity at
– where is it? Basil will know. Basil will deal with this – and
you.'

Her trump card. She waited now, calmly, to play it.

'Basil knows all about this, Mother.' She watched her mother's
face. 'And he thoroughly approves. It was his colleague in Florence who helped me make the arrangements.'

Mrs Dennison, showing only by a twitch of one cheek that she
was disconcerted, remarked: 'You did not think, any of you, to
let me know earlier about this invasion of our calm, ordered life?
The peace I can reasonably expect in my old age –'

'Oh, stuff and nonsense,' Eleanor said. 'You're not required
to *do* anything. I shall keep all that side of things well away. I
wired Dulcie – it was she arranged Amy.'

'I see. Miss Rowland is telegraphed, yet I am told nothing.'

'I knew how it would be if I did. What sort of greeting I should
get. That is the fact, you see.'

Her mother jabbed at the bedside rug with her stick.

'That is the fact, you see,' Eleanor repeated. 'Your Christian
charity, your vaunted Catholicism, where is it, that you cannot
take in a waif and stray? I was hungry and you gave Me to eat.
I was thirsty and you gave Me to drink.'

Her mother rose, with difficulty.

'How self-righteous you are, my dear. And how little you know
of life –'

I don't mind, Eleanor thought joyfully. I don't mind.

It had been not just her calmness that amazed Eleanor. It was
her happiness. It had welled up in her at first sight of the child.
To be as soon hidden when she saw Maria. Maria, standing by
the cot in the convent cell. Hair pinned severely back. Her
features lifeless, heavy. For Maria it couldn't be all right. Best
not to refer to the upset of June – the thoughtless escape to Sicily:
Maria seeming unable to imagine the worry she would cause.
And her own attempts, doomed, to get into Maria's head. I do
not know what it is like to be pregnant, to be from another
country, to be an orphan – to be Maria.

Sister Ignazio said, in front of Maria, that they had all forgiven her for the fright she had given them. 'It was a wicked thing to do, was it not, Maria?'

Eleanor had felt shame then because during that dreadful panic, exchanging of telegrams and telephone calls, there had been her own cold nugget of fear – that she was about to lose the child, *about to lose Eric.*

He was to be called Guy, she had explained to Maria.

'Your brother's memory. Is that how you honour it?' Mother had said that first evening, pursing her lips together as if in pain. 'What does Basil have to say? His brother's name for a little dago scrap?' But later when she asked, 'Who is to pay for all this help? His upbringing, his education? His *education*, Eleanor?' Eleanor had been able to say, proudly,

'All seen to. It is some of it to do with Basil. And the Jesuits.' Yes, that was it. The Jesuits . . .

Perfect child, sleeping peacefully through the stormy weather, autumn equinox, of his first days in Thackton. His cot in the room once set aside for Basil's visits, now the night nursery and facing out on to the long garden. The day nursery, formerly a guest room, faced the road and was to be barred so that he could watch the world in safety.

Dulcie had visited yesterday bringing with her an excited Jenny who knew Dulcie had been to Paris, who was part of the secret that an orphan was to be adopted – but who knew nothing of the real truth. (Eleanor, glad of this, wondered, did not perhaps too many people know already?) She had rushed delightedly to the cot. 'Isn't he absolutely – oh, how sweet! Those hands, and the tiny nails – I've never really *looked* at a baby before. Aunt Dulcie,' and she linked her arm round Dulcie's waist, 'darling Aunt Dulcie, did I look as sweet? You were there, do you remember did I look as sweet, as dinky as that?'

Jenny had left the room, when Dulcie said, 'Eric is so grateful – you can't know how much . . . It's Maria I worry for. Giving him up. *That* cannot have been easy –'

'She seemed to care less than I would have thought. She even said to me, "I don't want him, you know. He's yours. I'm really grateful you and Uncle Eric have arranged all this." '

'And you believed her? Oh, Eleanor . . .'

'How not? She's only sixteen. To have her life ruined, an outcast, a millstone round her neck. How could she have kept him?'

'I think, dearest,' Dulcie's voice was one of reproach, something so rare that Eleanor felt immediate shame. 'I think it's something I know a little of . . . Having travelled along the same road.'

'Of course. Of course.'

She took the turning now towards the river and the beech woods. As she walked along the narrow path, the sunlight, filtered through the trees, danced. Dense ivy clung to the oak, knotted greasy tree-roots spread out near the path. Scent of the trees: a solitary pine, dry, scaly-barked. Ash and oak seedlings springing up between the great shadowing trees.

For her, during this walk, the late autumn beauty was all part of her deep, unexpected happiness. A man child. She had always known it would be a man child. She looked down at him, deeply asleep, rocked by the rhythm of the pram, not heeding the bumpiness of the path. The rooks had begun their evening cawing and from not far away there was the sound of rushing water. When she reached the iron footbridge, with a small waterfall cascading below, she was afraid. The bridge was high, too high. She could not wheel the carriage over. (Pattern of things to come, never again to think only of herself, never again to be without fear. *Something could happen to him.*)

In the fields the other side of the bridge, cattle were lowing. Soon they would be called in. (And then I shall be back, she thought, and it will be his feeding time. His evening wash. I shall hold him, play with him. Talk to Amy. Know that already he knows me.)

A rustle of leaves behind her, and she heard before she saw, hurrying towards her: Eric.

'Eleanor dear, have I frightened you? I called at Park Villa –'

'Oh, but,' she began gauchely, colour flooding her face, 'you aren't expected till . . . It's only Thursday today.'

'I thought I'd arrive a day early and surprise my grandson – and you.'

'And me,' she said foolishly.

After he had looked a long while into the baby carriage: 'That's a grand lad we have there. We should be proud.' He fell into an easy step beside her. 'Shall I wheel the carriage?' When, laughing, she refused, he asked, 'How's it all going, how are you managing? Elsie said this evening, people about are quite curious. But there's no gossip, just interest and surprise – and I'll wager, from what she says, not a little admiration.'

She stumbled on an outspread root. He took her arm. 'My dear, be careful.' She was precious to him of course because of the child. He said now, again, 'Shall I wheel the carriage?' Her heart thumped as she felt the pressure of his arm. It seemed she was touching his side, where his heart beat. How easy it would be to say now, '*I love you.*'

'I wanted to tell you,' he said, 'how much as a family we appreciate what you are doing –'

'But I love it, I love him, I love . . .'

'Of course you do. But nevertheless – taking on at the very least twenty years of work and worry . . . We'll say no more. I just wanted you to know.' She felt the atmosphere tighten: 'I should ask you – how was Maria?'

She told him, much edited, her impressions.

'Ah, she'll be all right,' he said, as if brushing away a nuisance. 'The young. They soon forget.' But he did not sound convinced. They walked the way back, uneasily now. The sun was leaving the trees fast, the air growing damper. The scent of wet earth and tree bark was stronger. He asked:

'Did you think I was hard, then – on her?'

'A little hard. Yes.'

'Can't, couldn't help it. Women, girls, they should be – it's maybe dishonest, you might say hypocritical. But untouched, they should be untouched. Not leading lads on. I'd expected better of her – that's all.'

A little later: 'She should marry soon,' he said. 'That would be best for all concerned. A good marriage. The right person. Except what's right, I sometimes wonder?'

'The right person is the person you love,' Eleanor said, 'and who loves you.'

'Bonny. Bonny sentiments. You should have wed, Eleanor. Children of your own . . . Dick won't marry where he ought, I see that coming. Nothing's happening with the Carstairs lass. Nothing will, I fear . . . And his for the asking. Carstairs money behind him. He could go right to the top –'

'He may not wish to.'

'I did,' he said simply. Silence, then he went on, sharply almost, but sadly too:

'Married for money. Married, Eleanor, for enough capital to set myself up. And some standing, of course. The Rowlands, a family like the Carstairs, really. And the eldest daughter – not running after me like Nancy but not averse either. Maimie. No one else wanted her, you know. There'd been scarcely a nibble. Old man Rowland was quite crude. "I'd pay you, pay you to take her," he said. And I suppose, really, he did.'

She wondered, trembling, why she was being confided in. Oh, don't stop, she said inside. Tell me everything. You know you can tell me anything.

'But then we've to live always with what we've done, eh, Eleanor? Lie on the bed we've made. But you know what? This'll maybe shock you – I discovered there's no obligation at all to lie on it. At least not with the original occupant. The ways of the world . . . I shouldn't be telling you this. Do I shock you?'

'No, please go on. If it helps. You know that with me, anything you say . . . Everything is safe.'

'The ways of the world. The world is made for men, that's plain. But easy as we have it, we can go very wrong. Enough to say that in leaving the marriage bed, in straying from it, I didn't stray far enough.'

She said in a low voice, 'I know a little of this. Dulcie –'

'Dulcie, yes. I oughtn't . . . But if Dulcie's spoken. If anyone's to know – and of course Jenny mustn't – then I'm content enough it should be you.'

Guy half woke, making a fretful noise, small tongue darting between his lips. They were out of the woods now and on to the road. Where it wound upward to the village, a boy came towards them, rolling an iron hoop. He steered it deftly away from the perambulator. Eleanor said, 'One day he, Guy, is going to be a boy with a hoop.' She thought of all the days of future happiness.

'Ida will be over to see him tomorrow. Dick maybe next week.'

The confidences were over, the tone light-hearted now. She was smiling to herself as Amy, in white apron and blue dress, came down the drive to meet them. It seemed to her she was always smiling now. Such happiness – she could not help it spilling over. Even Mother could not take it from her. Mother had lost her power.

10

'What was it like at the office?' Ida asked. 'We're dying to know. I've been thinking about you. We both have.'

My first day in an office, Maria thought. An office: just one of the many things decided for her. In those dead days last winter after the baby and the return from Italy, she had been someone who did as she was told, went where she was sent.

She had been sent to Miss Pritchard's Secretarial College in London, just five minutes' walk from Gloucester Road Tube Station – handy geographically since she was to live with Ida, and Ida's friend Lettice. Both were training as teachers. She had thought it would be all right living with Ida, who would be kind, who would care about her without judging or criticizing. Lettice was a wartime friend. She and Ida had been WRAACs together in France in 1918.

'I've heard so much about you,' Lettice had said eagerly that first evening: cold dark November, nearly six months ago now. She had one eye larger than the other, and a pinkish nose. Precise wavy hair. Her high voice, after Ida's pleasant low tones, irritated Maria.

Now she said: 'I expect you'll want a wash. One gets so stuffy in the Tube.'

Perhaps I smell, Maria thought. Lettice was always washing, either her clothes or her person. Scrubbing away to keep that pristine neatness.

The office was a firm of leather importers in Holborn. Frognal and Harrison's. She had been sent by Miss Pritchard for interview within a few days of passing a Pitman test. 'Knowledge of Italian essential,' said the advertisement.

She was interviewed by a Mr Frognal. Aptly, his face reminded her of a frog. His eyes popped out obligingly. She felt some fear. Suppose they didn't take her? She had hated every day at Miss Pritchard's. Winter mornings in a room so cold her frozen hands missed the keys of the heavy old Underwood. Shorthand, with its hooks and strokes and twirlicues. In the end, painfully, tongue between her teeth, she had managed ninety words a minute.

At the college she hadn't made friends (why bother when she came home each evening to the almost suffocating care of Ida and Lettice?) She wondered if she would make them now? Miss Hailey, the senior typist, was a reminder that this was a firm of leather importers. Dark hair in a bun shone greasily above a skin tanned like hide. Her small mouth was disapproving, especially of Maria. The other typists, Betty and Gladys, had been together for five years, but seemed welcoming enough.

The flat was small. The best room was the sitting-room with its white balcony overlooking the street. The very small dining-room had in winter scarcely any daylight at all. Tonight, Maria felt she'd prefer just to hide in her own room and eat from a tray in bed. Sardines, cheese – something savoury and simple, on toast. But a meal (she could smell it), was all ready. Mrs Riley, who housekept for the previous tenants, after cleaning up each morning left them a simple meal to be reheated. She was reminded of the Pensione Cafferkey: the watery cabbage, the mutton stews, tasted to her of darkness and disaster.

'Come in and eat at once,' Lettice said. They sat, but only for a little. Food was for eating, Lettice said. Ida, who, legs wide apart before the fire at Moorgarth, would eat an enormous tea of scones and parkin and fat rascals dripping with butter (she would end as large as her mother), might have made more of it alone with Maria.

But they weren't alone. And it wouldn't be possible to criticize Lettice without hurting Ida. Often when Maria had gone to bed early, she would hear them laughing and talking in the sitting-room before disappearing to their bedroom. Theirs was the larger one, with a double bed and a view to the street below. Maria's looked out on to the backs of the houses. She thought she would prefer to have slept with Ida. It would have been like the old days at Moorgarth when Ida had been the consoler of nightmares (the *Lusy* torpedoed and she not rescued. Mamma lost. The Ricciardis . . .)

She wept alone at night, sometimes when she first went to bed, sometimes at two or three in the morning. Often a bad dream woke her. She would know then with dreadful finality that everything was as terrible as it seemed, that life would never become any better. What had been, was all there was. For they

– Uncle Eric, Eleanor, the nuns, Father Grierson, all of them, had taken her baby away.

My baby. *My son.*

When on that June evening the convent gates had clanged shut on her, she had thought nothing could ever be so bad again. Her despair: I must learn not to care, she had told herself. Yet her flight to Sicily: the nuns told her she had done it only because she didn't care. 'If you thought more for others. The unborn child too . . .'

'What *can* Miss Dennison have felt?' The deceptively gentle, dry voice of Father Grierson. She could not bear to talk to him at all. The nuns were pained and distant. She was to be watched all the time, for her own good, Sister Ignazio said. When she wished to visit Fiorella's family then both must show themselves to Sister Giuseppe and travel together.

Confession. At least she did not have to confess to Father Grierson. Since she spoke Italian she could go to the convent chaplain, Father Bevacqua. The nuns watched as she went up to the box. She had sinned dreadfully: ingratitude, selfishness, deceit. But the priest had been gentle, telling her that what mattered was did she regret the distress she'd caused?

Yes, yes, she thought, I regret. I regret everything. Being raped, giving in to everyone else's ideas, trying to escape because it is worse now that I am back. I regret telling Rocco, because he could have been proud of his sister, living and working in London.

The week after her return was the feast of St John the Baptist. The city, illuminated at night, could be seen from the higher windows of the convent. Fiorella's family took her to the Carraia Bridge to see the fireworks. But the flashes, sparks, streaming into the air, rising, falling, now alive, now dead – frightened her. She wanted to escape. When the first rocket went up, the baby lurched, drumming its legs against her belly. She felt nausea and lack of love, resentment at the intruder.

She seldom went out in the afternoons now. Instead she would sit in some cool part of the garden. Earlier, she'd avoided the Naples laurels with their odd-smelling white flowers. Now it was another plant whose clusters of small bell-shaped flowers resembled the daphne in Eleanor's garden. Its cloying scent brought on sickness and a special heavy sadness.

She was not often hungry now. On the feast of Saints Peter

and Paul they were served lamb and rosemary and she surprised herself by eating greedily. Then she saw her neighbour's plate, the fat on the side grown cold and white, and the nausea returned. The nuns served hard yellow peaches soaked in red wine, the flavour sour, astringent. Occasionally she craved these. Yet she must be eating enough, for she grew and, she supposed, the baby grew too.

She made odd friendships. Silvio, the big white Maremma sheepdog, convent watchdog, on his chain in the garden. In the afternoon she'd sit beside him, talking to him of Trimmer. He would allow her to ruffle his coat. She had seen him prowling at night, teeth yellow and fanged, ready for tearing.

And Arturo the gardener. He worked in the cool of the morning, trimming and tying back the lemon plants in the courtyard, tending the terracotta pots of magnolia. They greeted each other shyly always. He was a wizened old man who kept himself to himself. One afternoon she came in earlier than usual. He was sitting in the shade of a tree near the shed, a cloth bundle beside him. He offered her something at once, courteously. 'No, no,' she said, 'I've already eaten.' She was a little shocked. She had supposed that the nuns fed him.

'Ah no,' he said, 'why should they? I have always brought mine. Thirty-five years now.' A hunk of dry bread. A leather bottle with the pale fluid made from water poured over used grape skins. She felt ashamed of the meals she refused daily – and yet she craved his. Bitter. Simple. I could live like that. She asked what he ate in the evenings, feeling the sudden tug of memory, the child who had known hunger. Some pasta, he told her, very occasionally saltfish. No, never meat. How could they eat themselves what they might sell to buy wheat?

The weather grew still hotter. Watermelon stalls appeared in the street. Wedges of the pink-green flesh rested on vine leaves while thick discs of the fruit hung from the framework above. More vine leaves, covered by water, lay in an earthenware bowl with the coins for change.

In the heat she became more uncomfortable. The baby formed a great jutting shelf. Her ankles were swollen, her bar shoes cut. All through August, temperatures in the hundreds, she longed with a deep frightened longing for Thackton. October evenings by the fire, Dulcie reading or sewing, Elsie bringing in the tea tray, while outside the wind bent the heavy branches of the elder and rain lashed the last of the convolvulus in the hedgerow.

Never, never again. She felt the dry weight, hopeless. The air heavy, oppressive as before a storm.

And the storms came. In the middle of the night, the convent buildings illumined, unearthly. The next morning Arturo bemoaned the young chrysanthemums irreparably damaged in their pots.

She had a dream. So real was it, that in it she called out, 'This isn't a dream . . .' Summer, and she sat on a chair in the flagged yard of Moorgarth, alone. In the field behind her she heard Eulalia whinny, then the clatter of the gate. But she didn't look round. Perhaps because she knew. A lion, magnificent, tawny-maned, glittering as he was caught by the late afternoon sun, strolled into the yard. Half terrified, half happy, she thought to call someone from inside.

'Oh, lovely lion,' she said. '*Golden* lion . . .' But then the dream went all wrong, for she was back in the linen chest. Six years old again, covered in dust, she could hear outside the banging, the heavy breathing, prowling. And voices:

'They're asking about Minicu – I need to know.'

'Where's the body?'

'Ask the vultures –'

There was a scuffling sound. She froze with terror. She was too big for the chest: there was no room in it for a sixteen-year-old girl with child. A violent griping pain began in her belly. She knew she must get out, whatever the danger. I must be silent, must not scream. The pain grew and grew, and then died down. She must get out before it returned. 'I will, I will!' she cried, throwing her weight against the lid.

She burst into daylight, falling, it seemed, into her bed. Sunlight through the blinds. A single bell tolling for Mass.

She lay trembling, the terror of the dream still inside her. And then the pain returned, coming from her back, rising in a great wave so that she clenched her fingers, her teeth, pushed her bare toes against the iron bed end. Then it was gone again. She got up slowly and dressed. She thought: How stupid I am. *My time has come.*

All the rest of that day she lay in bed in the small hospital of San Damiano. The Franciscan nuns who ran it were gentle, matter of fact. They brought her fruit to suck. She floated in an ocean of pain, lying there with weary resignation as if she were forty not sixteen – as if generations of peasant stock had taken her over.

In the evening, the doctor came to see her. She had gone into labour a few weeks earlier than expected. 'It should be faster than this. A strong vigorous girl –'

She said, in an angry voice, 'It'll come when it's time.' Minutes later her body took over, the child took over. Her body pushed for her. Voices encouraged her, and yet she was alone. She had become all body, her misery forgotten as she fought.

A boy. Propelled, slithering bloodily into the summer evening. She lifted her head from the pillows, calling out, 'Let me – I want . . .' He was being swaddled now in a layer of red flannelette. She stretched out her arms to receive the bundle. The flesh was warm, soft through the sheet. His gaze, unfocused, unknowing, met hers.

The nun midwife said, 'Put him to the nipple now, at once. Then we shall soon have the rest out.' By that they meant the afterbirth. The mouth she had already looked on with such tenderness, fastened hungrily, knowingly. Love. Happiness. Tears of joy coursed down her face. A nun approached with a sponge, wiping her face, wanting to take the child. 'No, don't. A few moments . . . Leave him with me.'

She was scarcely sleepy afterwards. Lying still, in the middle of the night, the babe beside her now in his crib, she was lifted out of herself. *I have a son, and he loves me.* Joy suffused her. She was invincible. In this new world, *they* could not reach her.

Half way through the next day as she held the baby to her, he was sucking – Sister Andrea, the young nun in charge, told her, 'The Superior from your convent comes to see you today. They have wired, you know, to England.'

Oh, but how could she not have thought? England, Eleanor – my son, who is to be Eleanor's. He had lodged in her body only that Eleanor might have him when all the work and travail was over and the loving should begin. She began to weep silently, tears washing down her face.

'Women are often like this,' Sister Andrea said. 'When the convent have visited, you must promise to sleep. I think you don't sleep last night?'

'It isn't my child, you see.'

'How, not your child? You saw, there can't be a mix-up.'

'He isn't mine. He belongs to a person, people, in England –'

'Yes. Yes.' The nun reached out, stroking the baby's head. 'They told me that.'

Sister Ignazio was coldly congratulatory: 'God brings good out of evil.' She told Maria, 'Father Grierson has been in touch. You know the arrangements.'

The arrangements. Three weeks in hospital then back to Sant'Agostino, when after a few more weeks Eleanor would arrive, staying a fortnight while the baby was weaned, then travelling back via Paris. Maria was to follow a fortnight later, going straight to Ida's.

She thought: what if I were to run away again? Why shouldn't I take him to Monteleone, why not? But she knew that she would not.

Father Grierson came to see her. He scarcely looked at the child. 'Ah yes,' he said, 'ah yes,' clicking his fingers. Was it correct, he asked, that Miss Dennison would be visiting Rome first? But when he spoke of Eleanor's return to England, Maria saw black suddenly before her eyes. Eleanor's journey back, she thought, *with my son* – and she felt the familiar, always welcome pricking of her nipples, and then the rush of milk. Soon it soaked through the pads. The child whimpered beside her. Of course he knows. My son knows. As soon as the priest leaves I shall feed him and be happy and not think of the dark shadow that is Eleanor.

Never as happy again as those September days in the hospital. Never as happy again, she thought, gazing at his head nuzzled against her breast. Tiny fingers, starfish-like, clenching and unclenching with pleasure, dark eyes closed. The fragile head with its black down growing so thickly over the soft bones.

Never so happy again as sitting with Sister Andrea, the young nursing nun who had become her friend. They talked about everything but the inevitable parting, the fate of her child. They spoke of Sister Andrea's home in Emilia, her family, her love of nursing. It appeared she'd been given free time to sit with Maria: perhaps also she had been told to mention the dread subject, for on the last day she told Maria:

'We shan't meet again, I expect.'

Maria said sadly, 'No, I go to England, you know. Although perhaps in the next weeks I could bring him to see you.'

'Better not,' Sister Andrea said gently. 'You see, Maria, God has lent him to you, that's all. A loan, for a short time. You must think of it like that. However hard, however unjust.'

You don't understand, Maria thought, not wanting to hear any more. Knowing that the young nun said it only to console – what else in the kindness of her heart could she do? She could not alter the circumstances.

Eleanor arrived. Tired, flustered. There had been upsets in Rome. She had been given the wrong time for a papal audience and so missed it altogether. There had been rumours of malaria. And she was only just recovering from a low fever which had blighted the ten days of her visit.

She wanted at once to see the baby. 'Where is he? Oh, but he's beautiful, Maria. How clever you have been, dear.'

At first Maria didn't want her to touch the child. There was an awkwardness between them much worse than before Eleanor had left for England. It came up when the baptism was discussed. Father Grierson was to do it the next day. Maria didn't want to think about that, just as she didn't want to think about his name. She had not dared to name him herself. My son, she had thought only. My son.

'Our *bambino*, dear. An English name might be best, don't you think? Since he's to be brought up an Englishman.' She hesitated. 'Would you, should you mind, *Guy*? It is, or was rather, my brother's name. The one who died.'

'Yes, yes, of course. Sure,' Maria said. 'That's all right.' Guy, she thought. Who is he? How can he be Guy, this black-headed, brown-eyed child who is all mine?

Eleanor took her to more art galleries. Maria did not like to go far: 'In case he cries for me and I'm not there.' Gently Eleanor reminded her that she must wean him. She had tried not to think of that. It was enough that they were to be parted. Now it was explained to her that she must squeeze from her breasts enough milk for one and then two feeds a day, and this would be given in a bottle. Freshly boiled milk would be substituted gradually: asses' milk from the Via delle Bombarde to begin with. Her own milk would dry up.

How terrible, she thought, how terrible. Perhaps Eleanor should engage a wet nurse for the journey and the first few weeks? She hated the galleries, the museums now. Her breasts, heavy with milk, mocked her. She was aware of her sulkiness, her preoccupation, as Eleanor tried oh so patiently to draw her out. If it feels like this now, she thought, how will it be *then*?

The dreaded day came. A nurse would be travelling with Eleanor and the baby as far as Paris. Eleanor had taken Maria to meet the widow and daughter who would accompany her back to London in two weeks' time.

'Perhaps it might be best,' Eleanor told her now, 'if you said goodbye to Guy in his crib and then went out for a little walk. Feed him and bath him first and lay him down. And then when you come back, it will all be over.'

It will all be over . . . She bathed him, alone, the tears obstinately refusing to flow. Only the milk flowed – unwanted.

The last feed, from a bottle. She could not bear this, as she could not bear the pressure of her full breasts. *Why shouldn't we?* she asked, unbuttoning for the last time. Last night he had refused the bottle, spitting out the rubber teat. What is to be done, she thought, if he refuses his food, starves, wastes away?

He clung to her. She knew that he knew. When he'd finished, she changed him and wrapped him in the blue crochet shawl he would travel in. His hands were hidden now, hands that had plucked at her breast, tiny peeling fingernails. She held him in her arms. He smiled at her, cooing, expecting her smile in return. She could not.

Eleanor's voice. Eleanor's face. 'You must go now, dear.' Maria scarcely lifted her head. 'You've said goodbye?'

'I don't –' Maria began. Then 'Yes,' she said dully. She walked away from Eleanor, the room, the building, out into the street.

She dragged her feet up the steps of the nearby church. She sat on a stone bench at the side. From time to time she stuffed her knuckles into her mouth so that she didn't cry out. Some of the time the pain was so bad that she lost all sensation. Leaning forward, she rocked to and fro. Almost opposite her was a Pietà. Mourning mother, body of her dead grown son. She felt it inside her, as she had not been able to feel the joy of the Annunciation. If I should begin to cry out, to scream, I should never stop.

Out in the street again, the milk rushed in. She was already hard with it by the time she reached her cell. Eleanor and the baby were gone.

There were two weeks to fill in at the convent. Her embroidery must have been quite good since they asked her to demonstrate stitches to the new pupils. And all the while the unwanted milk came in, again and again, relentlessly. Her breasts beneath their binder were like wood. She could not sleep at night.

When the time came to leave she said goodbye to as few people as possible. She managed to avoid Sister Ignazio.

The widowed Mrs Foster-King and her daughter were kindness itself. 'We heard you hadn't been well, my dear.' Over dinner in the restaurant car she told them about life in America. They wanted an account of the sinking of the *Lusy*. She gave it as if speaking of another person. That is not, she thought, the worst thing that has happened to me.

The weather grew chill as they crossed France. When she emerged sick and shaky from the boat train at Victoria, an icy sleet was falling. Ida, with Lettice, was there to meet her.

The lilac was in bloom in the square below the Gloucester Road flat. Now it was truly spring. After supper, they sat with the window open on to the small balcony where primulas flowered in the boxes. Down in the street, a motor roared to a halt, a door slammed, then slammed again.

'What a noise,' Lettice said. 'Some people, really.'

Ida peered behind the lace curtain. 'It's Pip Carstairs. Good heavens. And that's Sybil with him –'

'Whoever or whatever is Pip?' Lettice asked.

'Oh, people from home. They're very big in Middlesbrough, the Carstairs.'

Maria went to the door.

'Can we come in?' Pip said. He was no longer the Scarlet Pimpernel but a big man soberly dressed in dinner jacket and black tie. Sybil, beside him, was wrapped in a white marabou cloak. Pearl globes hung from her ears.

'It's my idea,' she said, 'I was just dying to see you.'

When she had climbed the stairs, 'Ida Grainger,' she cried. 'Look, it's me, Sybil. I'm in *London*!'

'And so are a few million others,' Pip said. 'Some even live here, like Ida and Maria, and –?' Lettice, introduced, stood back a little, wary, seeming to appraise them both.

'Working women,' Pip said. 'It'll be suffrage next.'

'Oh, I get so jealous,' Sybil said. 'To live in London.'

'Sit down, do,' Ida said.

Lettice said: 'I'll put on the kettle for tea. Or boil up some coffee.'

Not tea, Pip said. Coffee, perhaps? They were on their way from a drinks party to a dinner in Princes Gate. 'Sybil wouldn't hear of our not looking in. She's in Town for a few days . . . I've an *exeat* from college – I can make up nights after term ends. Tomorrow I shall show her Oxford.'

Sybil had taken off the marabou to reveal a green silk chiffon dress, embroidered on front and sleeves with chain-stitched flowers. They sipped politely Lettice's remarkably awful coffee. (Neither Maria nor Ida could stop her re-using yesterday's grounds. 'Water's poured on to tea leaves twice,' she told them cuttingly, 'why not coffee?') Ida had found some ginger biscuits. Sybil ate three, one after the other, greedily.

Her brother said: 'Leave a bit of your schoolgirl appetite. There'll be six courses at least.'

'I'm always hungry,' Sybil said happily. 'You know me. I could eat a horse.' She sat beside Maria on the sagging brown leather sofa. It was difficult to recognize the schoolgirl of eighteen months ago. 'I'm staying with my aunt and uncle. In St John's Wood. They're dreadfully nice. You must meet them, Maria. I used just to write to them at Christmas, I didn't realize they were such fun. I'm having a wonderful time –'

'Even if she's only sixteen and a bit,' Pip said. 'Next year you can do everything properly.'

'Oh please, I can't wait,' Sybil said.

Maria saw Pip watching her as Sybil spoke. If she had cared about her appearance she would have minded being caught this evening, unkempt hair falling loose, her body lumpy in the sober beige jersey suit chosen for the office.

Sybil quizzed her about life as a working girl. 'Typing and doing Pitman's – it must be fearfully difficult.'

Pip asked her, 'Is a stenoggie's lot an 'appy one?'

Maria smiled.

'How extraordinary,' Lettice said when, after many promises from Sybil to keep in touch, they'd left. 'An industrial family, isn't it?' She was a Brigadier's daughter, and often made comments which were meant perhaps to rile Ida.

'Yes,' Ida said, collecting up the cups, 'as of course is ours.'

The room, the flat seemed suddenly empty. To Maria, sad at their going, they seemed to have brought with them not only reminders of home, but also a glitter and an excitement. Perhaps London had more to offer than stenography with Messrs Frognal and Harrison? And life with Ida and Lettice.

'Back to work,' Lettice said now, briskly. 'I was able to get the second of the Marshall books out, Ida, they'd been kept back on loan.' She turned to Maria, 'Now you're settled, why don't you take up some serious study? Improve yourself. So that you don't have to stay always in an office.'

Who cares? Maria thought. She yawned and said that she was ready for bed.

For a few days after she wondered if Sybil would perhaps write or call. She thought: I should like her for a friend. But when a letter arrived ten days later it was from Pip, not Sybil.

. . . My chatterbox sister, little monkey, has got permission to come up for college Commem. This year promises to be terrifically good fun and we wondered if you could be persuaded to join us? It would be very jolly if you could. I remember you as a good dancer – Marie Antoinette to my Pimpernel!! Sybil will be chaperoned by our aunt and uncle but this could include you, should the fair Ida be worried (she looked as if she might be, or rather her formidable friend did!) I hope I haven't left it too late . . . PS. Sybil says you absolutely must!

When she first read the letter, she thought: I don't want to. What business had she dancing? But then sometime in the morning, she thought: Why not? It would be an escape from London; Sybil was sweet and lively and Pip pleasant. Nostrils full of the dusty inky smell of the office: Yes, I shall go, she thought.

Ida was thrilled for her. 'All right for some,' Lettice said, 'I'd consider it rather a shocking dissipation.' Ida produced money which she said was from Uncle Eric, so that Maria could have a frock made. She chose pink silk with silver and pink beading and gathered side panels. A sudden rush of interest surprised her, as if there rose above her heavy, dead heart, something light, frothy, unexpected.

Taking leave from Frognal and Harrison's was going to be a problem. She wasn't getting on very well there. Because Uncle Eric had spent money on her training, she tried, but she wasn't really suited. Betty and Gladys were not deliberately unfriendly – it wasn't the *Lusy* again – but they had been together so long, looking conspiratorially across the oak desks, making faces behind Miss Hailey's back, that without meaning to, they excluded. They were always kind. 'Poor thing,' they would say when she came in with a cold. 'Poor thing,' when she couldn't read back her dictation. Betty gave her own valuable time to help, although she had no shorthand.

'I suppose it *could* read "something something of varying thickness". But then it could be "*un*varying" couldn't it?' The letter, once transcribed, had to be translated into Italian. After the first days there, she discovered that no one in the firm knew more than a few words of Italian, so she stopped bothering too much about the shorthand phrases and words she couldn't read back. It's probably this or that, she would tell herself before going on to the easy part: turning her version into Italian. Her figures were always correct. 'Yes,' Mr Frognal would say, running his eyes over the letter, 'yes, 187 was the quantity specified.' Neither he nor Mr Harrison ever admitted they didn't know Italian.

But before the letters were signed, Miss Hailey had to see them. Usually she found fault: the eraser had been rubbed too hard, or two keys had jammed making an ugly black mark.

She'd always known that sooner or later, they would catch up with her. It was Miss Hailey who brought her the message that Mr Frognal wished to see her *at once*. Her satisfied smile showed that she knew what it was about.

Mr Frognal told Maria, 'You must leave. As soon as possible. You are useless to us.'

'In what way haven't I given satisfaction?'

He took up a paper. 'Look at this reply, in English, please note, from Siena. They're angry about our querying . . .' He turned some pages. 'It appears they sent *what we asked for* on at least two occasions. It was you at fault. Either you don't know your Pitman or don't know Italian. Why not ask if you weren't certain?'

'I was certain,' Maria said doggedly.

There was money involved, he told her. She sensed he was angry with himself that something should have gone wrong so far down, at the humble end of the chain. 'You can stay the week out. Then take your skills elsewhere.'

The Commem Ball at Oxford was not long away. She had already lied to Ida, telling her time off was settled. She thought: Why not leave now? But she would have to get another post. In the *Morning Post* she saw that Swan and Edgar's, in Piccadilly Circus, required an assistant in their haberdashery department.

The woman who interviewed her, noting her lack of experience, noted also her expertise with embroidery. She was offered the post. 'I must give two weeks' notice,' she explained. She would begin on her return from Oxford. Miss Pritchard would supply a reference.

She put off telling Ida until the last moment. 'Oh dear,' Ida said, 'if you'd only asked me first. We didn't realize you were unhappy. I'll have to tell Dad. The training, you see –'

'There may be some embroidering involved, or advice about it,' Maria said offhandedly. (What did it matter, since Uncle Eric no longer loved her?) 'That training was paid for, too.'

'Oh dear, I didn't mean,' Ida said, distressed.

'Guess who's late!' cried Sybil, hurrying down the platform ahead of her uncle and aunt. A porter followed with their trunks. 'Aren't you too dreadfully excited?'

Maria had arranged to meet her and the Detheringtons at Paddington. The tickets were all bought, Sybil had said, which was as well because with only five minutes to go, there had been no sign of the party. They took their seats in first class. The remainder of the train appeared very crowded. Maria liked the Detheringtons at once. She, white-haired, energetic, with a low, warm voice. He, stooped, with a creased friendly face and a loud laugh.

The day had begun bleak and rainy. While Sybil read a magazine, Maria gazed at the countryside: I have been too long in London (Oh, Thackton, oh, Moorgarth). The damp could not hide the early summer beauty of green and white hedgerows, flower-strewn meadows, willow-lined streams.

Pip met them. She and Sybil were to stay not in a hotel but in Walton Crescent, his lodgings of the year before. They left their trunks and then went to tea at the Shamrock Rooms, after which Pip showed them round the Oxford Union. Sybil's voice, loud and excited: 'Is that your friend Bim? No, then where *is* he? Is that dreadfully handsome man the famous Hodders, I thought you said his legs were bandy?' In the debating hall, she rushed to seat herself in the President's chair. 'Oh, she's too much,' Pip said good-naturedly. Her uncle said he thought leading reins and a harness were indicated.

They dined with Pip at the Clarendon. The hotel was full of guests ready for the balls that evening. A friend of Pip's, also reading Engineering but at Wadham, invited them then and there to his college ball that night. 'Oh, oh,' Sybil exclaimed, her eyes lighting up, but her aunt and uncle would not hear of it. Two nights dancing till dawn – most of tomorrow would have to be wasted lying abed. Sybil drooped for a few moments with childish sulkiness. Maria wondered: What must it be like to want such a little something, so much? She did not dare even to look at what she wanted.

When they returned to Walton Crescent it was to undress by candlelight. In bed, Sybil outlined excited plans. 'I mean to have fun from now on, for ever after, all my life! We should be dancing now . . . I'm not too tired, I'd have loved it.'

Next morning, a walk up Boar's Hill and then lunch at the George. In the afternoon, punting down the river – she and Sybil and Pip, and Pip's friend Bim Chatterton. The girls lay back on cushions. Sybil's fingers ran through the water: 'This must be what heaven's like. No, heaven will be tonight, I think.' The leaning willows shadowed the river, sunlight danced. Soon they would be dancing too. Maria felt the pressure of others' excitement, happiness. Proud, secretive, she laughed and joked with them all, vigorous, hearty Pip, his agile, clownish friend Bim.

Water rats lifting their heads from the reeds. 'Ratty,' said Bim each time.

'They can't all be Ratty,' Pip said.

Sybil said, 'Didn't you love *Wind in the Willows*?'

A family of two small children and a baby picnicked in the meadows as they passed. Maria averted her eyes. When the pain came (and I thought it was gone, that like the Lion I had a heart of stone now), it felt not sharp, but dull, heavy, a crushing weight.

Coming back, they fooled, rocking dangerously the flat-bottomed boat. Bim twanged an imaginary banjo to *A Bachelor Gay* while Sybil jabbed at him with an oar. Pip, manœuvring the pole as best he could, sang vigorously.

Sybil's bright yellow frock for the ball was very fashionable, the sleeves all in one with the bodice and the silk under-petticoat shorter than the dress. The floating side panels were of gathered chiffon. The colour suited her vivacity. She had promised to tie Pip's tie for him. 'Nancy does it at home.' When they arrived, Bim's was, deliberately Maria thought, at an odd angle. 'I think I need Miss Carstairs's help . . .'

Others in the party at St John's were a White Russian, Dimitri Poliakoff. Miss Evans, a pert pretty girl with cold eyes, reminding Maria of Jenny in a rage. Hodders, he of the bandy legs, and his sister, a young war widow.

Downstairs, the marquee, striped in green and white, took up most of the Quad, while inside, mirrors placed at intervals made it appear even larger. Blue and white flowers, the college colours, were the only decoration.

'Lloyd George's daughter's here tonight,' Pip told them. 'Megan L. G. You must watch out.' Hodders said Clemenceau was to get an honorary degree at the Convocation tomorrow: 'I mean to catch a glimpse of the old Tiger.'

During the dance itself, the Detheringtons were with them only occasionally – the easiest of chaperones. Dimitri was very taken with Hodders's sister. Sybil, glowing, was being gazed at adoringly by Bim. He'd fallen, Pip confided in Maria, during Sybil's visit in May. 'He's already talking of being part of the family. Really we demobbed chaps, oughtn't we to be taking our pleasures more lightly? Sybil's only a child.'

The orchestra played the music from Barrie's *Mary Rose*. The mirrors in the marquee swayed as they danced, reflecting the yellows, the pinks, the emeralds of the evening frocks. Pip claimed Maria back again and again after she had danced with others. They walked twice among the huge dusky trees in the gardens, where two elaborately costumed men played the post horn as a signal to return for the dancing.

Towards morning, after a session of shimmying, she and Pip went through the archway and out on to the terrace. A great sweep of lawn with clumps of dark trees, chinese lanterns hanging from them. The oriel windows could just be made out in the grey stone of the building, and very faintly, the delicate colour of the wistaria.

He said, 'I thought the band was coming it a bit fast. I wonder how much scotch they've put away?' They stopped at the far end of the gardens. Roses, pinks and stocks scented the night air. 'Enjoying yourself?'

'Why not?' She smiled. 'Of course, thank you.'

'You're quiet, though. Dark. Mysterious. I remembered you as more lively.' Taking her hand in his ungloved one: 'I wonder, do you like me a little?'

'Yes,' she said politely. It had been a good evening. For any girl not crying deep inside for her child, this must be a night to remember. She said, 'I love dancing. Foxtrot, shimmy, tango . . . I feel better when I'm dancing.'

'Grizzly bear? Is that one you like? Sounds a bit as if . . . You haven't some secret illness, have you? Not hiding a dicky heart, or the unmentionable, consumption?' His voice throbbed. He had tight hold of her hand now. She didn't mind being touched like that. It was kindly, reassuring. 'I'm not talking about dancing actually, but about you and me. Me and you. I think you know what I mean? We could be a lot closer . . . When I come down, I've to spend a few weeks in this firm in Fenchurch Street – I'd like to see more of you then.'

'Well, yes, I guess . . . why not?'

His hand tightened again, uncomfortable now. 'What I want . . . I'd be very discreet. Oh, hang it, help me a little. You know what I mean. You will, won't you, Maria? I want you, a lot.'

But what was this? She felt violently sick. As if Peter stood beside her. The words were different, the voice kinder, but . . . Fear, disgust. The night-scented stock nauseated her. 'No,' she said. 'No, *no* . . . What have I done to suggest I'm that sort of a person?'

'Sort of a person. Maria sweet, really what funny language! Don't think I can't sense something when you dance. You're nothing like all these jolly, chaste girls here tonight. You're different. Not English for a start –'

'My family,' she said, 'my real family, the family I was born into . . . If my brothers heard you speak, I tell you straight – a knife. I come from a country where the family protects –' She had been going to say 'virginity'. Inside her the wounds began to open. My child. My child.

'French, Gay Paree, naughty,' he was saying. 'When I was in the trenches, the French girls weren't above –'

'I'm not a French girl. I'm Sicilian.'

'I see I've gone too far.' He released her hand. Music, toetapping tune, *Whispering*, floated out to them. 'Let's go in.'

For the remainder of the night, except for a slight awkwardness on his part, it might never have happened.

Up the river to breakfast, in the pale early sunlight. Pink silk dress limp now, satin shoes grass-stained. Feverish with excitement, Sybil sparkled still.

A few hours' rest, then the train back to London. Before they left, Pip said to her, 'When I'm in Town I'd like to take you to a show. Your gaolers allow that sort of thing?'

Three weeks later he took her to the Co-optimists in a party with his aunt and uncle. His behaviour was impeccable.

Silk-embroidered garment shields, dusting caps in floral muslin, elastic and rubber-gripped blouse-holders, Gem linen buttons. She had been an assistant at Swan and Edgar's for nearly six months. Soon it would be Christmas again: the second of Guy's life. She wondered, forlornly, if she would be allowed to send him a gift.

Whenever a letter came from Yorkshire, she would hint to Ida, 'Is there any news of Eleanor?' And Ida, who knew too well what she was asking, would answer, 'No. Nothing about Eleanor.'

For Christmas she had bought Ida a Cona coffee machine. An end to the boiled coffee grounds. She and Ida would be going up to Middlesbrough. But not of course to Moorgarth. Although they had insisted her exile from Thackton wasn't a punishment, she knew that it was. Peter had not been punished. This year she would be expected to face him. She tried not to think of that.

She heard that she was to help in Baby Linen for the Christmas rush. It did not turn out as bad as she feared: she did not see many children. The shoppers were mostly mothers, nannies or relations: ('Tell me, would this fit a *large* two-year-old?')

Four days before Christmas a letter came from Pip. She had heard nothing since their visit to the theatre. He wrote:

I still feel dreadfully sorry about what I said that evening at Commem. I must have been mad, misunderstanding signals. But since then although we've only met the once I've thought a lot about you. And us. And what I thought was – my prospects are good, very good. I'm nearly twenty-six and more than ready to settle down. It's just – I hadn't realized it. And the girl I'd like best to settle down with is you. If you'll have me, that is, after I've been so clumsy.

Could you think anyway about all this? I've put it all very badly, but I hope the answer will be yes. I've come not only to love you but to respect you too. I'm certain we could be very happy together. I like girls who are *different*. And you are, you know! You are in Middlesbrough over Xmas I hear. I shan't make a nuisance of myself, only do give a chap an answer soon . . .

She could think of little else all day. It was another trap. Another door about to clang, shutting her inside. She could eat nothing. That night she scarcely slept. I have to make a decision, she thought. The next morning she had a headache which was like an iron band around her forehead, steel knives at the back. Just before leaving for work, she had a row with Lettice.

Lettice said, 'Your room's in a mess. Mrs Riley says she can't do anything with it. The sooner you go –'

It was doubtful Mrs Riley had said anything of the kind. The room was not so bad, a little untidy only. But she had felt for a long time Lettice's resentment of her, and her prior link with Ida.

'I'll go, yes, I'll go. Soon enough.'

I shall marry Pip, she thought, and hold my head up and bother no one. Uncle Eric will be proud of me. Only, what do I tell Pip and the Carstairs family? The *truth*? She felt the iron band tighten as she hurried down the stairs for work.

In morning break she met one of the girls from the Lingerie department. They grumbled quietly together about tired feet and rude customers. Maria was thinking all the time: I have to decide, I have to decide. Now. Soon. She said, 'I've such a headache, it's worse than my feet.'

'It's all the people,' the girl said. 'Have you seen it in Toys and Games?'

Maria had. That evening the shop would be open till late. She wondered how, as the band tightened and tightened, she was to get through the remaining hours.

In the early afternoon a well-dressed woman came into Baby Linen, carrying a large child in her arms. A boy, Maria supposed, since he was dressed all in blue, with soft blue leather reins. The woman placed him on the carpet then sat down on the chair near the counter.

'Washing suits, with contrasting collars and cuffs. What have you got?'

'What age, madam?'

'It's for him. Fifteen months.' She flashed a smile on Maria. 'Isn't he advanced? He's been walking since ten months.'

She turned suddenly: '*Phyllis*, how splendid!' A woman wrapped in furs stood beside her. 'No, but look, I haven't seen you for simply ages. The motor brought Timmy and I up to Grandma in Chester Street. Nanny's not here.'

A fifteen-month-old baby, dark, agile, beautiful. The woman's hand, looped loosely round the reins, let them go. In a second the child was up. His mother, talking, had her back now to Maria.

'Look, Phyl, we *must* have tea . . . Grandma's Johnson can take Timmy back. Then you and I can meet at Gunter's –'

Maria had come round the counter. The child was toddling over to where a porcelain doll, dressed in organdie, sat on a cushion. He ran, then tripped, and fell.

Maria was there even before he opened his mouth to cry. She heard the mother say, 'Oh, Timmy!' But already she had him in her arms. The smell of his breath, his skin. His arms went round her neck. The taste of his tears as his mouth touched hers. She was fondling him, rocking him.

Dimly she heard his mother: 'All right, I'll take him.' She paid no attention. 'I'll take him now, thank you.' The tone was sharp.

She looked at this woman, this stranger. The iron band tightened.

'I said thank you. Look . . . That will do.'

'He's mine,' Maria said suddenly. Seeing all at once how it would be when he left her arms. Such a wave of pain and desolation swept over her that she thought she could not live.

I cannot, I cannot. She saw the mother come towards her, her face puzzled. Why puzzled? The child clung to her still. Woodenly, mechanically, she handed him over.

'Thank you. I forgive your little joke . . . Timmy come to Mummy. Naughty, running off.'

A wave of pain hit her. Worse this time. The blood rushed to her face. And then tears began to fall. She stood there, crimson, not caring. Caring too much. 'My child,' she cried, through the tears, '*give me my child*!' Her voice rose. A wail, primitive, piercing through the Baby Linen department.

There must be a way out of this pain. She beat the dark air in front of her, and wailed.

Sacru miu Gesù, Sacru miu Gesù. The walls of the department, of the shop, closed in on her.

II

All I want is to marry Gwen. When we are married, he would say over and over to himself – never, if we are married. Yet how far on was he? Already it was the spring of 1922, two years since he had found her again. How many times had he visited Bradford, how many times had he proposed? It had become almost a joke. 'I know what's coming,' she'd say. Or: 'A whole afternoon, and you haven't asked me yet.'

Deep in his heart he believed that he could wear her down if he only asked often enough. She gave reasons, he had to admit that. Always the same ones. She was older than him – why not find someone his own age? She had been married, for a fortnight, and it had been wonderful. Now she'd learned to live without. Then there was her mother.

'I'd take care of her,' he said. 'She'd live with us.'

'She and I, we manage,' Gwen said, 'but it'd be a different matter, you supporting Mother and me and possibly a child . . . And you said yourself, your father's got different ideas for you.'

That was the truth. It was only Dick who wanted the marriage. No one else was for it, not even Gwen. Certainly not his family. Although he had never said anything, his secret was out. All those visits to Bradford. At first there'd just been teasings. 'Dick's sweet on a Bradford lass. Who is she now, Dick?'

He told Aunt Dulcie about her.

'*You'd* like me to marry her, wouldn't you?'

'I just want you to be happy, Dick. To do what's best for you. And sometimes, that's not following your heart.'

He thought: 'It's more than heart. It's all of me. I'm nothing without Gwen. He fully believed that his life *could not begin* until she married him (why else all the flying, the dicing with death, being partly lame, if not for meeting Gwen in No. 4 General at Amiens?)

Dad said, one evening in March, 'Can I have a quiet word with you, son?' He took Dick into the empty dining-room, and poured him a whisky.

'You haven't thought yet of settling down, eh?'

'Well, eventually, yes . . . There's no hurry. You didn't marry young.'

'This woman of yours in Bradford. How seriously are you into this?'

'I don't know what you mean.' He felt angry, insulted.

'You do, well enough. Mrs Latimer, Gwen Latimer.'

'She's not my *woman*. Don't speak of her like that.'

'I made it my business to find out . . . Marriage is a serious matter. Too serious to be left to youngsters . . .'

'I'm twenty-three. It's none of it your affair –'

'On the contrary. By all accounts, you're quite gone on her. Have you done anything foolish?'

Angry, and not wanting to associate what Dad spoke of with Gwen, he pretended to be puzzled.

'I mean,' Dad said impatiently, 'have you promised her you'll wed her? That sort of thing –'

'I've asked her if we could be wed. I've asked, but she won't have me.'

'She will, she will. Hard to get, an old ploy. You should be man enough to recognize that one.'

'She's not that sort of girl, Dad. If you'd met her –'

'The fact is I haven't. But I'm older than you and I hope wiser. I'm just giving you advice . . . A bit long in the tooth, isn't she? Thirty if she's a day.'

'Thirty-four.' Anger, warm, powerless, grew in him. 'She's thirty-*four*. We can't choose when we're born –'

'No, but we can choose who we marry. When you're in your prime, she'll be in her late fifties – an old woman. You're prepared for that sort of thing?'

'Her age doesn't matter to me. I've thought about it. And it doesn't.'

'Difficult this next one, but let's not mince words. Social class . . . I've done well for myself, very well, and expect my children to do better. Not to go backwards, in other words.'

'Her husband was an officer,' Dick said, defensively. 'Cyril Latimer, he was a Captain –'

'Temporary gentleman. Yes? Let's be frank. She runs a café, doesn't she, does the waitressing herself? Come, Dick – I'd worry less if she were a little bit of fluff. I can't make head nor tail what the attraction is unless . . . I asked if you'd compromised her – but since you've not cheated the starter, there's time to get out.'

'I love her,' Dick said.

'You don't want to be too fussed about love. What guarantee have you it'll stay? Does she love you?'

Dick was caught unawares. He felt the question like a belly-blow.

'Ever had a woman? Well then, you'll know how it can all be separated. Sex. Love.'

'It's my business, all that. If you've nothing better to say –'

'I have. Had you thought of looking nearer home? Two years at least the little Carstairs girl's been sweet on you. Old Carstairs even joked with me about it at the Rotary Dinner last month. She'd make a good catch, would Nancy. Think on it.' Lifting the decanter, he filled Dick's glass. 'Of course, we'd Peter to get out of a fix two years ago –'

Dick said sarcastically, 'An unsuitable match?'

'Don't misunderstand me. Maria, I thought of as my daughter – I'd have had nothing against . . . It was age, Dick. They were two children only. Always quarrelling. What sort of a future there?'

'What sort of a future now?' Dick muttered, under his breath.

Perhaps because they had finished their talk with Maria, it was of her he thought now as he made his way, leg tired and dragging, up the stairs. Think, think dearly, of Maria. Maria, seldom spoken of now except in hushed tones. It had taken him some time to discover (he'd wanted to visit her) that she wasn't in an ordinary hospital, that it wasn't an ordinary illness.

When he had first been told of the child, and the plan and the elaborate arrangements, something in him had cried out – Don't . . . Yet when Dad had asked, 'What's *your* solution, then?' he'd faltered and stayed silent. There weren't better ideas – just different ones. They came to the same thing: that Maria would suffer and Peter be allowed to forget. He didn't believe it had been anything but Peter forcing himself on her. He would like to have called it rape. He hated this suggestion which Dad obviously believed, that they were two impulsive fools, that Maria had seduced, Peter had been weak. He would have liked to talk to her about it. But that had been forbidden.

And now this. A breakdown. A nervous breakdown. She had been already several months now in a Home in Kent. He had written to her half a dozen times. But no letter ever came from her, for him or for anyone. After a while he had given up.

When he had told Gwen in great confidence the story, she had been at once distressed for Maria. She said over and over, 'Poor lass, poor lass.' Then: 'I've never had a bairn but – mother love, after all it's deep inside, isn't it?' All he could think of then, and he had to bite his lips not to say it, was: 'You never had a child, but I could give you one. *Let me make you mother of my children.*'

'Marry me,' he said again that evening.

He had begun to have migraines. He supposed that was what they were. Flashing before the eyes and then the terrible waves of pain, a giant vice squeezing his head. Forced to stay away from work, vomiting in a darkened room, he felt certain they were something to do with the 'plane crash. He began to fear, the walls closing in on him, that his leg had not been the end of it. Perhaps his brain had been after all damaged? He would grow worse, lose his mind. Deranged, he would end his days cut off, prisoner of this pain.

He spoke to the family doctor, and was told heartily: 'Nothing wrong there, we'd have seen damage before if the fall had had anything to do with it. Eating properly? None of this hasty-bite-and-rush-out-gallivanting. Waterworks all right? Bowels? No toxins in the system . . . If you were a young woman I'd say, get married. But a young fellow like you – wild oats . . . No trouble there, I hope?'

In a way the doctor was right, or would have been if Dick had been a girl. He did need to marry – Gwen.

He went to see Maria, without getting permission or telling his family. He made the excuse of a visit to Ida in the south. We are not a family, he thought, who confide much in each other.

The Home was outside Ramsgate but in sight of the sea. He was directed into a great garden that seemed all laurel bushes and yews, dark and damp. It was a mild spring day and many of the patients were sitting outside. A frilly-capped nurse in white told him, 'We don't know whether she'll see you. Some days she won't speak at all. And when she does it isn't in English.'

Maria was sitting on a bench, alone, wearing a dark blue dress too large for her, on her feet carpet slippers.

He sat down beside her. 'It's Dick,' he said. For a long time she said nothing but continued to stare in front of her. 'I've come from Thackton.'

'I know,' she said suddenly.

'Is there anything I can get for you, or do for you, dear?'

'Dick,' she said dully, 'Dick.' Then again, 'Dick,' as if holding on to him. 'They took my son, you know. I've been in the dark since – I don't see very well –' She stumbled over the words.

He feared she might ask, 'How can I get him back?' But she had lapsed into silence again. He risked telling her: 'They love him and look after him well. He's very bonny now.'

'Good,' was all she said. Then: 'I want to speak of him, but no one will talk.'

'They say *you* won't talk.'

'Why should I? Why should I ever? It doesn't do any good, it frightens me. Dick, I'm frightened.'

'What of?' he asked anxiously. 'What of, dear?' But as suddenly as she'd opened out, she was silent again.

After a while she said, without looking at him, 'Pip Carstairs wants to marry me.'

A sick fantasy surely, Dick thought. To humour her, he asked, 'Is that so?'

'No, no. Of course not. It isn't true.'

'I'm your brother,' he began. 'Just remember that. If there's anything at all I can do. Ever. You've only to ask.' But he thought: If I am her brother, so is – or was – Peter. I should not have spoken.

But she seemed to take little notice of what he'd said. She did not speak again. His last glimpse of her was sitting on the bench, staring over at a small ornamental lake, with a piece of chipped Greek statuary to the right of it. Somewhere in the distance was the sea.

The summer passed slowly. In July, Nancy invited him to a dance at the Carstairs home. He made his leg an excuse to refuse. On Sundays in St Mary's Church, he would see her turn, pretending to brush fluff from her coat, stealing a glance at him from the family's front pew.

In August, Maria left the Home and went on holiday with Ida and Lettice, staying at a farmhouse near Truro. After a few weeks there was even a card from her. Except for some shakiness in the handwriting, it seemed to come from the old Maria.

Dad hadn't mentioned Gwen again even though it was apparent Dick was still seeing her. He had a new motorbike now, an Enfield 2-stroke. He was able to cut twenty minutes from the journey time to Bradford.

The Adelphi Tea Rooms were to be closed for decorating and

154

alterations. Gwen's cousin Stan was coming up to be foreman. Just as Dick had been jealous of the cousin from Australia, now he felt threatened by Cousin Stan. 'Do you love him?' he found himself asking. Then changed it hurriedly, 'I mean, you like him well enough?'

'Well enough,' she said. 'He's family. If you get on with someone, and they're family – that's good.'

'What'll you do when the café's shut?'

'I thought of taking Mother to the sea. Only she'll never go. She fancies herself the king pin, and nothing done right if she's not there to see it. She'll not trust Stan.'

'So then – *you* could go away?' A wonderful hope, and fear, possessed him. She must agree. Before, she'd always been too busy. It had been he, Dick, running to Bradford, snatching what time she found free for him. 'Could you come over to us? To Moorgarth. A real rest, and a change. North Riding instead of West Riding.' His hands were clammy with fear.

'I don't see why not. I'd like that, Dick.'

He took the time off. He didn't ask. Dad was away in Lancashire. In the days before, he worried about everything. He saw it all going wrong. She would be unhappy, or not able to get on with Elsie or Aunt Dulcie. She would find being with him all day too much and *she would end it all.*

Suppose something weren't right about her room? He nearly drove Elsie mad with his fussing. He didn't like the wording of the text that hung above the bed – that had hung there ever since he could remember. The washbasin had a small chip. 'It won't do,' he said. Elsie grumbled, saying that the chip hurt nobody and didn't even show if the bowl was turned. He solved the problem by substituting the blue jug and basin from his own room. The day of her arrival he gathered late yellow roses and massed them on the dresser. On the little round table near the window he placed the latest numbers of *The Queen* and *John Bull*, and two new novels: *Dodo* by E.F. Benson and *Pleasure* by Alec Waugh, which he'd bought for her before leaving Middlesbrough.

They would need a motor. He couldn't expect her to ride on the flapper bracket of his Enfield. He drove over to collect her: Aunt Dulcie thought it would be all right if he borrowed the Crossley.

Aunt Dulcie liked her. That was the first hurdle over. The next was Elsie. Her face broke into a smile and she nodded to herself in the way he knew spelled approval. Gwen said, in her matter of fact voice, 'If that's your baking on the range there, I can't wait to get sat down.'

During tea she told stories about her early days as a VAD. She made his aunt laugh, that fluffy abandoned laugh he so liked to hear. She loved Moorgarth. He showed her the fireplaces from the old house when it had been a silk mill, with the water in the beck used for milling. He told her about their right to have seven sheep wandering the moors. 'Dad used to say, "Seven Graingers – I reckon it comes to the same." ' Trimmer, so loved by Maria, sat beside her, his head on her knee.

She was to sleep in the double bed that was usually Ida and Jenny's. That first night, he lay awake, tense, thinking about her a few feet away. Once he got out and saw a light under her door. He pictured her with the candle lit, sitting up reading one of the novels. It was all he could do not to cross the landing and burst in, to say 'Will you marry me?' *Perhaps she would say yes*, and he would climb in beside her and she would draw them both down into the deep softness of the feather bed. His head would lie between her breasts and then his hands would seek, and she might hide, and he would seek, and . . . But he always stopped there, forced himself to stop.

I ask so little, he thought. He told himself the tale again of the Golden Lion. The hidden prince who must find the princess, who must *recognize* the princess. The voice, the face that had come out of the darkness when he didn't know if he was alive – he had recognized them. The Princess.

They visited Eleanor on a day when Mrs Dennison was out, although Dick would have liked to see Gwen do battle with her. He said as much to Eleanor.

'Gwen wouldn't be afraid. She's used to difficult customers in the tea-shop.' He said it defensively, to remind Eleanor that he knew Gwen wasn't top drawer and what did he care? And then felt ashamed when Eleanor took no notice, saying only, 'To be frank, she's not improving with old age –'

'The child, doesn't he keep her young?'

'No, Dick. He keeps *me* young.' And indeed she did look younger, softer, than the Eleanor he'd known as a boy, who had often seemed so fixed, even a little elderly.

He said now to Gwen, 'Miss Dennison and I – we spent a night together out on the moors, one bitterly cold January. Lost. We're fortunate to be alive.' Telling the story again now, remembering the bond there'd been, the close, almost intimate feeling that had persisted for weeks after, he wished that it could by some wild chance have been Gwen and he bedded down in a sheep hollow, ready to die in each other's arms.

I think of death too often. He cleared his throat which felt gritty, sore. He hoped he wasn't sickening for something.

Guy, just two years old, was brought downstairs by Amy. Sturdy, with a confident walk and Maria's heavy-lidded eyes, he stared at Gwen.

'I've brought you something,' she said. 'If you're Guy. Are you Guy?'

Clapping his hands, he said solemnly, 'I Guy. Guy come down, down.'

She opened her handbag and brought out a clockwork mouse, grey silky fur and a long tail. Eleanor commented that it looked almost too real. Guy gave squeals of pleasurable fear as it raced over the Indian carpet. My nephew, Dick thought. And Maria's child. When Guy had gone upstairs again, he said:

'The news of Maria's better. She sent us two picture-postcards of Fowey.'

It rained the next morning. He had a heavy cold. At least I don't have a migraine, he thought. Tomorrow was her last full day. He planned they would drive to the coast, only an hour away.

Next day he woke early to a blue sky with white trailing clouds. His head was blocked, his nose hurt and his throat was dry and scratchy still. But he was happy. He had determined the night before that he would be happy. Today was to be quite perfect for her.

Perfection ordered, perfection delivered. They drove in the Crossley through Lealholm, Glaisdale, Egton Bridge – much of the picturesque route the railway took. The river Esk, brown and swollen with rain, was running fast. There were glimpses of muddy track, ochre-coloured, glistening with the wet and running in channels. They came down into Robin Hood's Bay. The tide was out and they walked amongst the slippery flat scaurs and the rock pools. In the distance Ravenscar promontory pointed out to sea. Gwen had used to come here as a child. She showed him the cottage in St Martin's Lane where they had stayed.

The morning was almost over as they climbed back up the steep cobbled hill. Driving to Whitby, they ate an enormous lunch of fresh caught haddock and chips, and then blackcurrant pie and cream washed down with lots of tea, for the salty air had made them thirsty.

'It's good,' he said, 'but of course it's not like your cooking.'

'I'll soon be back. It says a lot for the good time I've been having, Dick, that I've not given it a thought –'

He nearly said, 'You need never go back to it.' But sensing the fragility of a perfect day – the risk of snatching at greater happiness and perhaps losing everything, he said:

'After all you've eaten, I'll bet you couldn't climb the hundred steps to St Mary's –'

'Of course I could.' Then suddenly serious: 'Dick dear, what are you talking about? With that leg . . .' He wished then he hadn't teased her because she became suddenly concerned. His cough too, he had a fit and couldn't stop. 'Are you all right?'

They watched the catch come in, strolling amongst the boats in the harbour. On the pier before that, she refused to have her fortune told. Dick didn't want to know his either. They bought sugar pebbles, pink rock for Elsie and bright pink and white false teeth for Cousin Stan.

He was reluctant to drive straight to Thackton, imagining the last evening sitting by the fire, sharing her with Aunt Dulcie.

'I'm going to turn off here,' he said as they came to the Goathland signpost. It was quiet in the village: sheep and half-grown lambs strolled about as they did in Thackton, but with more space. To either side and beyond stretched the moors. No green hillsides crisscrossed with fields, but an expanse of dark purple blending with the mauve and grey of the evening sky.

He took the turning for the Roman road. They left the motor and struck out along the muddy track through heather and sodden bracken, but when they reached the ford before the climb up to the Roman road, they saw it was in full spate and impossible to cross. They climbed up in the other direction, a grassy path to a beck, and sat on a rock above the water, shaded from the evening sun by an oak tree. Some of its leaves had turned and fallen. There was a small rowan, overshadowed by the oak, its berries scant and pale.

She was worried for him. 'It's not just your cold. That leg –'

He said gruffly, 'My leg doesn't stop me doing anything. Motorbike, car . . .' He thought: Don't spoil the day. His lameness, that he tried to forget, but that he could never wish away or how would he have met Gwen? 'There are others so much worse. Limbs missing, blind, or can't find work . . .'

The full beck beneath was partly a waterfall. The twisting, turning flow fell with such violence that droplets shot up, charged, clear, bright. They sat without speaking. He felt a sudden twist in his heart. The thought he'd been able to hide all day. She goes tomorrow.

He sneezed heavily. There were shooting pains in his head.

'It'd best not rain tomorrow. Rainy Bradford,' he said desperately, 'that'll be the next thing for you.'

'Dick dear,' she said, resting her head on her knees, then turning to look at him, 'I've been thinking. Dear, would you still like us to be wed?'

12

1926 and Sybil and Maria are going dancing. They are taking a
cab from their small house in Chelsea. Dancing has become a
way of life. Three or more times a week they are collected
by their escorts and whisked to the Savoy, the Piccadilly, the
Mayfair.

Maria thought it must have been in her legs, her arms, her
head, all her life. Now even before she was on the floor, as soon
as she heard the drums, the clarinet, the cornet, she would feel
her legs tingle. She could hardly wait to order the meal or sip a
drink. She wanted to dance, to feel that lightness of her body,
head tossing in time with the music, hands turned in, out or lying
lightly in her partner's. Twist of hips. Necklace swinging on
bead-encrusted bodice. *I wish I could shimmy like my sister Kate.*
Then, excited, to stop breathless for just a small drink held in
jangling braceleted hands.

Dancing at the Carstairs' Fancy Dress Ball (I don't want to
remember that), dancing with Pip and his Oxford friends that
June evening of 1921 . . . Pip was married now. He had three
children by his tall blonde rather horsey wife, Nessie. Sybil was
not too fond of her. Maria suspected jealousy.

Sybil and Maria belonged to each other in friendship. It had
been one of the unexpected good things to have happened since
her return to the everyday world from the darkness, stumbling
like a pit pony, half-blinded by the light of day. They'd been
living together for nearly four years now. She thought of Sybil
as having saved her life: remembering not that first visit with Pip
but a telephone call in the spring of 1923.

'I'm in London like I'd always promised! I want you to come
over *at once*, Maria.'

Maria had been six months out of The Laurels and was living
with Ida at a small flat in Sussex Gardens. Lettice had left to
teach in New Zealand. Ida had been insistent Maria lived with
her and be looked after, but she was out all day teaching.
Maria had little to do. She was meant to 'rest', and do a little

embroidery. Ida cosseted her: hot-water bottles, dainty suppers on a tray, breakfast in bed.

In the afternoons she went for long walks, always forgetting afterwards where she'd been, and from January she sat three mornings a week with a General's widow, Mrs Collinson, to whom she would read out her mail past and present, together with novels by Robert Hichens and Mrs Humphry Ward. Mrs Collinson showed no interest whatever in Maria, which was a mercy, as were the embroidery, the walks, the dainty meals – for without such a routine, however empty, she could see nothing but a return to The Laurels. She paid no visits to Middlesbrough. Thackton was, as ever, out of bounds. She did not attend Dick and Gwen's wedding in Bradford in the January of 1923 even though she was invited. Peter would surely have been there.

It could not go on for ever, though, this life with Ida, although often it seemed that it would. No one suggested she should work again. She had no money and needed none, except an allowance for clothes in which she wasn't at all interested. She was empty of everything – feeling, caring, excitement, malice, even sorrow. But not anger. She met it in her dreams as she scrambled up mountainsides, slipping, sliding, pulling at bare earth with her fingernails, or fighting for breath under the weight of green foaming seas, hurtling from towers to see the unforgiving earth rush to meet her. Dreams as fearful as any at The Laurels. But here was no white-coated attendant at her bedside, only large Ida wrapped in maroon corded dressing-gown saying, 'Shall I make you some cocoa, dear?'

And then Sybil had telephoned.

'. . . I want you to come over *at once*. I'm with Aunt and Uncle Detherington in St John's Wood . . .'

'I'll get a cab and come right round,' she said, treating the invitation as a summons – a welcome summons.

'Wonderful,' cried Sybil. 'And look, come absolutely at once. Dinner's in an hour, an hour and a half at the most.'

Ida was at that moment steaming Maria an egg custard. 'Isn't it a bit short notice?' she asked amiably. 'And are your clothes in order?'

But except for a faint whiff of anti-moth herbs, her best fur-trimmed coat was all right and there was a grey silk dress with a red cravat which would do. She realized even as she hurriedly dressed, how unaccustomed this was. (*Maria doesn't go anywhere. She has been very ill.*)

At the red brick house with its green leafy garden and its view on to Regent's Park, Sybil rushed to greet her. It was as if there'd been no years in between.

'You angel . . . I thought it's silly to suppose that because we haven't heard from you, it means you don't want to hear from us. And me.' As they stood in the long drawing-room sipping dry martinis, she told Maria, 'I'm here for at least six months. Isn't it wonderful?'

It must have been wonderful because by the end of the evening after a delicious meal at the Georgian dining table, waited on by a white-gloved butler (who Sybil said afterwards was making enormous eyes at Maria), she had almost persuaded Maria to come there and live. 'Darling, we could have such *fun* together –'

Fun. Strange used-up word of the past. People who had not loved and lost had fun.

'I guess – I'd have to see about it.' She felt a pang for Ida, and fears for herself (*how would I manage*?)

But she found over the next few days new strengths in herself. Writing carefully to Uncle Eric (after all, he had arranged that Ida should watch over her. Perhaps he wouldn't allow it? She was not only dependent on him but under twenty-one still). Telling Ida. She loved and admired Ida for the easy, jolly way she took it. (Perhaps it had been so with Lettice: 'Oh well done – off you go! Send me a picture of a kangaroo, or is that Australia?')

Ida's main concern had been money. 'Do they expect to be paid, dear? Because if so, Dad . . .'

A clutch of cold fear that the gate so suddenly thrown open might now be shut. She said shakily, 'They want me as a companion for Sybil,' and Ida said, 'Oh – a sort of paid post then, really. That's all right.' But Maria didn't dare to mention any of this to Sybil for the first few weeks. When at last she did, she threw the question carelessly:

'Oughtn't I to do something? Embroidery? Six months, you see, it's a long time to be a guest . . .'

'Oh, but I hope it's going to be longer than six months!' Sybil cried. 'At the very least until one of us gets married. After all, we're having such fun.'

And they were. She and Sybil, exploring London in the way she should perhaps have done in 1920, if she'd been whole. On top of an omnibus, taking a boat up the Thames, gawping at the

Crown Jewels, but above all shopping, though not necessarily to buy. Marshall and Snelgrove's, Debenham and Freebody's, Harrods, were at first sufficient delight (they did not go to Swan and Edgar's). From department stores they moved to dress shops. Sybil, dripping fox furs, would try on models; Maria was the friend who gave advice. Nothing suited, they needed time to think it over. Occasionally, playacting, Maria would feel back in the shoes of the little Sicilian–American girl who had been equipped so smartly for the voyage of the *Lusy*.

At dinner at least once a week there would be a young man or two purposely invited. Afterwards, a letter or a telephone call, a party or even a dance either in London or the country. Maria began to go out, to take an interest in clothes again. Her petticoats, shortened, were crêpe-de-chine now, not calico.

In early August Aunt and Uncle went to their villa in Provence, taking Sybil and Maria. For nearly two months Maria gave herself up to sun and scents: lavender, thyme, sage, fennel – reminding her of faraway days in Monteleone. She ate goat's cheese, huge golden peaches, the first of the purple figs.

After the first three weeks they were joined by a young, newly married couple, Dodie and Clive Gilmour. Sybil and Maria were at once at home with them. They often sat up late after Aunt and Uncle had gone in to bed, breathing in the lavender-filled, flowery dusk, playing cards and drinking. Talking. Dodie never tired of hearing about Maria's Sicilian and American past. ('My dear, all that before you were twelve. Your life since then must have seemed very ordinary . . .') When after a fortnight they left to go back to their new home, a small house in Chelsea ('the excitement of it!'), Maria and Sybil felt they had made new London friends. And so it proved. Soon there were invitations to dinner and, as autumn turned to winter, parties and more parties, visits to clubs, even night clubs. Several times Sybil and Maria slept over, because at four in the morning it seemed easier.

Then just after Christmas, Sybil became restless as if suddenly they'd done everything, seen everybody. Maria felt the same. It wasn't Aunt and Uncle, who were kindness itself. Perhaps it was because although the days of chaperones were over, they knew an eye was kept on them that was still fairly strict. ('Do we know him?' was Aunt's phrase when a young man introduced himself who had not been through the usual hoops of dinner, afternoon tea, or some other approved entree.)

It was Dodie who came up with the idea, her smart shingled

hair clinging shiny to her scalp, pretty chiselled features sparkling, 'I think you should live with us for a while. *Both* of you . . . Clive and I would simply adore it.'

'A thorough good idea,' Uncle said surprisingly. 'Though we shall miss you like anything.'

Maria wasn't sure. She feared that Dodie would all too soon become pregnant and then she would have to live in a house with a baby. *I could not.* But if Sybil moved out, she could hardly stay alone with the Detheringtons, however fond they seemed of her. She would have to leave.

Sybil mentioned money tactfully. 'Mummy says if I go, we shall have to pay something – even though they *seem* to have lots of dibs –'

'I'll have to work again,' Maria said. 'I can't ask Uncle Eric . . .'

'Flowers,' Sybil said. 'Or hats. Some fearfully smart people have flower or hat shops these days. I read in *The Tatler* only the other day . . . I forget her name.'

But before anything could be done about it, there was Jenny's wedding, to Archie Douglas, twenty-two-year-old son and heir of a Canadian firm, over in England for a year to work at the foundry. It had taken six months for them to fall in love, another three to become engaged. Now his year was up: they would sail for Vancouver after a honeymoon in Scotland. At first some of the family had thought it too hurried and Jenny at nineteen too young. But Aunt Maimie trumpeted her satisfaction. The Douglas family were people of standing.

For Maria it wasn't a happy occasion. Although the wedding was in Middlesbrough, she found it difficult not to think of Thackton since Eleanor was one of the guests. Maria avoided her. Peter also, although that was more difficult. She heard he was doing well at Durham. Taller, heavier, sulkily handsome, favouring his mother's family still, he stood in his morning coat and grey striped trousers, three young girls listening to him admiringly. Her hate was slow and deep.

She looked at Jenny's excited little face framed in Brussels lace above the white georgette, Jenny hanging on Archie's arm and gazing up adoringly, and thought: She is running away. She knows she is escaping. It has always been wrong for Jenny. Running along behind the others, 'wait for me', never ousting Peter of his place as Benjamin. And then I came. I was the last straw.

Aunt Dulcie wept during the ceremony and again during the

feast that followed. They were not tears of happiness. She said to Maria in a bright little voice, 'She's awfully young. And to go so far away . . .'

A week after the wedding, walking along Dover Street with Sybil, she saw a notice on the door of a dress shop. An assistant wanted: 'Some experience necessary. Smart appearance and good manner essential.' Fortunately it was not a shop they had been to for trying on frocks. Leaving Sybil on a gilt sofa reading a magazine, she was shown at once into a small room, with frocks hanging from a rail and boxes toppling in the corner. The manageress – 'I'm Mrs Goldman, dear' – sat behind a table desk covered entirely by invoices, letters, brochures and fabric samples. She talked with an adenoidal but refined Cockney accent, asking Maria directly:

'You're not English, are you, dear? No, I thought not . . . Mr Goldman is from a Polish family, and my dad was from Calabria. He married a nice young lady from Balham.' She fiddled with the heavy garnet brooch at her throat. 'You speak Italian? We have a good little bunch of girls working here, but all from London. I'd enjoy it ever so if I could speak my dad's language.'

Maria would never have guessed the Italian blood. In looks, Mrs Goldman must have favoured her mother. She was more like a bird than anything, with sharp little features and brown hair turning grey. 'Now I'll take you to meet the others.' She walked carefully as if her feet hurt. 'It's being on them all day – ever such aching legs.'

A tall girl with buck teeth and a high colour came rushing up. 'Here is Miss Collins.' But Miss Collins was already pressing her mouth to Mrs Goldman's ear. 'Lady Staveacre . . . in the first cubicle.'

Mrs Goldman placed a hand on Maria's wrist. 'Wait there, dearie.'

Maria sat down beside Sybil, pulling an encouraging face at Sybil's questioning one. 'Tell you later,' she said quickly. Miss Collins remained standing: 'Excuse me, but are you clients?' Sybil told her no.

'You're ever so smart,' the girl said. 'I thought . . . You see, Miss Gina has the 'flu and I'm here alone. I'm Vera, by the way.'

After Lady Staveacre in a flutter of promises and assurances had been shown to her motor, Mrs Goldman took Maria back into her office.

'It sounds the most fearful hard work,' Sybil said later. 'And our social life. Our dancing . . .'

'Yes,' Maria said, mimicking Mrs Goldman: ' "Ever such aching legs" . . . I expect, though, I'll manage.'

She didn't see it as a choice, really. She had walked down the street, seen the post, and been offered it. It was meant. And – she would be independent of Uncle Eric.

So began a way of life. Except that she could no longer go to tea dances, it wasn't unlike the other. Finish work at six-thirty, hurry back to Chelsea. A hot bath, a milky drink and into her black crêpe-de-chine, her gold sequinned tunic, her grey silk tiered. Dodie's maid, O'Connor, doing her hair for her. At eight-thirty, a ring at the door, and their escorts for the evening. Then dance, dance, dance . . . Two nights a week perhaps an early night, in bed with supper on a tray by eight. As a way of life it left little time to think. Dancing was the anodyne, her work, something to get up for in the morning.

In the shop, Vera and she spent their lunch-hour together always. Vera was seventeen and her ambition was to get married. Clothes were the answer. The more elaborate the frock, the more irresistible to Vera. She was too scared to borrow overnight from the shop, but since she could buy at cost, she was always saving towards a frock which by the time she could pay for it was no longer fashionable.

The other assistant, known always as Miss Gina, was a niece of Mrs Goldman's. She was rather superior, and liked to ask Maria questions about her life outside the shop. 'Been dancing again, I suppose? Which hotel this time?' Her voice was nasal and penetrating, and could often be heard admonishing customers.

Mrs Goldman, who fussed herself regularly into a state of near-collapse, was seldom in her office. It was as disordered as when she'd first seen it. 'Ever such a muddle, dearie,' she told Maria one day. 'Keeping books and everything, I don't know how ever . . .' One day Mr Goldman appeared, shut himself in there and then yelled for his wife. 'Norina, Norina!' Fortunately there were no customers. 'This you call *in order* . . . If this place last one week more, you are clever.'

Maria liked dealing with the customers. When one was being particularly difficult, Mrs Goldman sent for her. Her days were often made up of small comforts, small goals. Today I shall sell four dresses, tonight I shall dance at the Savoy. When she looked really forward into the future, she closed her eyes and wished it away. One day, Sybil would marry, Dodie and Clive would have a houseful of children . . .

As yet, after nearly four years of marriage there were none, although she knew there had been at least two miscarriages. When she went on Sundays to Mass at the Oratory, Dodie would whisper, 'Say a prayer, darling, to your Virgin or whatever, that we get a little one soon.'

Maria, who hadn't told Sybil about Peter or the baby, and didn't intend to, found the easy way she confided her superficial day-to-day feelings passed for sharing secrets. Sybil told Maria that she did want to get married – but not yet.

'I can understand in the war, people rushing – but it's different now. *We* know what tomorrow's going to be like. Giving Cook her orders for the day, planning a little dinner-party for next month . . . If I married too soon, I know I'd have a sickener for it all. In fact, it might drive me potty.'

She'd ask Maria, 'What's your ideal?' Hers was: 'Fair, with a bushy blond moustache and great strong hands with hair growing on the backs. Not too young – he must have been in the war, perhaps with a decoration . . .' Once or twice they'd met someone who fitted this picture. But he was never recognized by Sybil.

Maria did not have an ideal. Either awake or asleep, nobody perfect came before her eyes. But to keep Sybil quiet, she invented 'a slight man with auburn hair and a freckled face, who owned a castle in Scotland'.

Their partners changed often. If one became at all serious, Sybil would say, 'Oh, So-and-So is beginning to *pine*,' and suddenly she and Maria would be no longer available. Sybil's favourite saying was, 'I won't say I will but I won't say I won't . . .' She was sometimes 'a little bit naughty' as she called it. Maria – never. She was on guard even as she danced. All her animation, her passion, went into the rhythm. She too received, and refused, proposals of marriage.

In the world outside dancing and the shop, she had news sometimes from America. Gaetano, who had remained behind when Rocco returned at the end of 1920, had been arrested last year in a clean-up by Prefect Mori, appointed by Mussolini to stamp out banditry. (My own brother.) As far as she knew, he was in prison still. Rocco was in New York. He hadn't returned to Detroit. He wasn't a good correspondent and wrote only once a year. Often her letters were returned from an out of date address. She knew he'd been working as a waiter at first. Lately she thought he was something to do with bootlegging and Prohibition. Reading between the lines, she suspected him of being as well off as he'd ever been.

The Graingers weren't too often in touch now. Ida wrote at Christmas and Easter, as did Aunt Dulcie. Dick was the most constant. He and Gwen often invited her to stay but she would not go up there if it could be avoided. (Her thoughts winged always to Thackton: Guy no longer a baby – what did he look like, think, feel like? My son.)

Jenny had just had a second son, Gordon. The first, James, had been named after his war hero uncle. At his birth Uncle Eric had thrown a party. Champagne corks hit the ceiling, the absent mother and son were toasted again and again. The first (official) Grainger grandson. For two days after she heard, Maria wept inside.

Tonight, she and Sybil were dancing at the Dubarry. It had not been open very long. Friday was extension night when there was a licence until two in the morning. It looked fresh, smart, glittering: there were a lot of mirrors, glass flashing like ice. Round the walls were coloured silhouettes of men and women in eighteenth-century costume. An advertisement (referring she supposed to the types of music played) said, 'If Madame Dubarry had known about Al Coleman and his Band, how hot, how sweet her nights would have been.'

They were seated at their table, waiting for Manhattans, Maria for lemonade. The band played *Gimme a little kiss, will ya?* She was to remember ever afterwards what she was wearing: a black frock with a three-tiered skirt and a gold-sequinned top; Sybil, in blue tulle with silver-sequinned bodice.

Their partners were Jack Grindlay and Felix Dutton, both of them long-time escorts, the only two to survive the Sybil–Maria edict against becoming serious. Jack had only last year proposed to Maria – he intended to try again, he told her. Felix, slight and dapper, had hopes of Sybil which Maria knew to be unfounded.

She glanced over to the bandstand. Velvet banners hid the metal struts of the music stands. Two sax players, two trumpets and a trombone. Two fiddles. Al himself played cornet, badly, blowing a few notes before leading the band into a new number. The pianist was a pale young man, already balding, cadaverous. Sybil last time had found him rather romantic.

Not waiting to give an order for food, she and Jack got up to dance. The band played *Dinah*. Her feet in new gold satin shoes seemed to fly. I love dancing, alas that I don't love Jack. She saw Sybil and Felix come out on to the floor. From behind her the vocal began.

'. . . *Dinah, is there anyone finer, in the state of Carolina?*' Oh, but she wanted suddenly to stop. It was as if she recognized the voice. '*Dinah, with her Dixie eyes blazin'* . . .' As they came nearer the stand she saw it was one of the fiddle-players out front. He wasn't very tall, her height only perhaps. Thick black hair, shiny, brushed back, some colour in his cheeks and in his singing such joy, such happiness. How much he's loving it, was her first thought. His voice was velvet, silk. He sang without a megaphone in a light baritone which carried well enough. His arms held out, hands open, as if to offer his music. '*If there is and you know her, show her to me* . . .'

One girl, a tall blonde with an even taller escort, fox-trotting almost alongside Maria, gave him a sidelong glance, trying to catch his eye as he sang. The smile he gave her in return, bestowed on her (for it was a gift, it would be if I were to have it), was so personal, so intimate. The sudden lighting-up of a dark room, blazing of the sun.

Afterwards she could never remember if it had been sight or sound set her heart beating. That furious drumming, portent of danger, the same dizzy sweat that was part of the terror in her dreams (shall I always suffer from them?). Dreams that were as much the fabric of her nights, as were the events that had caused them. And now to feel like that again . . . Back at the table she sat down almost too hastily, falling on to her chair, reaching for her glass. 'Water, if someone could – is there any water?'

What to do with such sudden, such strong feelings? Now the terror had subsided and she felt ordinary again – no, not ordinary, for something had happened. (A dance band singer who may or may not be very good, who flashes smiles on passing girls – why should that be so different, so special?)

She turned to Jack. 'Ask the waiter, would you, who he is?'

'Who who is, Minnie?'

'Oh,' she said casually, 'the fiddle-player on the right, the one who sings.'

'Righty-ho.' But he looked puzzled.

She said, 'It's just, I'm sure I've seen him somewhere before.'

The waiter, redraping the napkin on his arm, leaned forward to hear Jack's question. 'I'll enquire, sir.'

And back with the answer: 'A Mr Sabrini, sir. Eddie Sabrini. He's just with Mr Coleman for the evening.'

Jack said, turning to Maria, 'Does that mean anything?'

'No,' she said hastily, 'no. Thanks. It doesn't.'

But now Eddie was singing again. *'I've grown so lonesome, thinking of you.'*

Felix said, 'He's not bad, you know. He seems good as a sentimental singer *and* a hot one, often these chaps can't do both. Diction good. Modern phrasing and rhythmic effect.' She knew Felix fancied himself as a connoisseur. She hung on every word. 'No, he's good. I'm not surprised you asked about him.'

She wondered how she got through the rest of the evening. Excited, elated, happy and unhappy by turns. How could a heart pound through a whole evening and go unnoticed? She smoked more than usual, waving the mother-of-pearl holder, puffing coolly, but not soothed at all.

Back at the house, it was a relief to tell Sybil. Going up to their rooms, yawning, about to sit on one of their beds and dissect the evening:

'You look . . . I don't know,' Sybil said.

'I'm in love, I think,' Maria said.

If she had hoped that telling Sybil would exorcize the devils, she was mistaken. They consumed her. She willed the stormy feelings to vanish. She danced the next week at the Dubarry. He wasn't there. They had different escorts and she asked one of them to find out about Eddie. He did. Eddie Sabrini was touring in France.

Oh well. So that was that. She'd willed the excitement to go and it went, a little. But in its place came a longing, overwhelming, for Thackton. And Guy. It was as if in allowing in all this excitement about a dance band singer (for heaven's sake, she told herself, a *dance band singer*), she had lowered her guard. She longed now for Thackton, as once in Florence she had longed for Monteleone.

She longed despairingly. Then, just about the time of Guy's birthday, Sybil decided to go north for a few weeks. Maria was owed some holiday. She told Sybil she'd come up with her.

She stayed with the Carstairs although she went over to see Dick and Gwen, also Uncle Eric, and Ida, teaching in Newcastle now but home on holiday. Peter, thank God, was on business in

Belgium. On the Sunday Pip and his family came over. She felt her manner slip, oh so easily, into a sort of languid sophistication. Yet inside, she felt awkward with him. Her memories, his proposal that she had never formally refused.

The last day but one she left the house before breakfast, writing a note for Sybil. ('I have to see some friends for the day, and must make an early start . . .') All the time in the train to Thackton, she rehearsed what she would say. They, Eleanor, must let her see Guy if only for a few moments.

It was a dull muggy day, threatening rain. She carried an umbrella. As she walked up from the station, the memories swept over her. (Once I was happy here.) Nothing seemed to have changed. The long stretch of road up to the Thackton turning, green hedgerow, white convolvulus twisting through it, tight green and red berries on the brambles. Left now past the grey stone houses, the terraced cottages. The tinkling of the sweetshop door as two young children went in.

And Park Villa. White-painted gate, stiff handle. Yellow roses and red begonias in the front garden, a maid she didn't know answering the door. The familiar smell of the house. The Japanese umbrella stand in the porch.

'Only Mrs Dennison's at home, miss.' The maid showed her in.

A voice from a deep chair over by the window: 'Maria! I glimpsed your arrival, my dear. Eleanor will be back any moment, if she doesn't dawdle.'

Maria looked around the room for some sign of *him*. There was nothing.

'Forgive my not moving. I am almost completely crippled now.'

The voice went on: 'And what do you do with yourself these days? A dress shop? I had not heard, but still . . . And no marriage yet?'

'No. Nothing. Not at the moment.'

She was trembling, feeling a little sick. She opened her handbag and felt for the ivory cigarette-holder. But she could not smoke here. She thought: I have only to ask about him: 'How is he – that little Italian boy you adopted?' But the words, somewhere in her throat, were stifled. She prayed silently, *Sacru miu Gesù*, make *her* mention him.

'My son Basil – did you ever meet him? I am so proud. He has just been made Monsignor. He has a Roman appointment, you know.'

It wanted only a little courage to say, 'I've never seen the child, can I meet him?' (The promise I made. They *forced* me.)

'And you are still a good Catholic, my dear?' The question took her by surprise. She had forgotten Mrs Dennison's manner. 'I often think – and I wish my daughter would put it into practice – that it's whether we have charity in our hearts, that determines the reality of our Faith, not mere Church attendance.'

Just then the tea came. Because of Mrs Dennison's hands, clawlike now, Maria did the pouring. As she fiddled with the sugar tongs: ('How many, Mrs Dennison?') she heard the front door bell. Oh, let it be *him*. But there was no childish voice, only a measured tread going upstairs.

'. . . Ida Grainger. So competent. If a daughter is to remain unmarried one should be blessed with such a one . . .'

Eleanor came in. The blood rushed to Maria's face. She saw Eleanor had coloured too.

Mrs Dennison said: 'Look at our delightful surprise. We have been entertaining each other in your absence, Eleanor.'

And then began a stiff little tea-party. News exchanged all over again, Eleanor criticized for whatever she had been doing that afternoon. All Maria wanted was to be alone with her, but Mrs Dennison couldn't move.

'How smart you are,' Eleanor said. Her voice sounded uncertain. It was not friendly. 'Are you able to buy models from the shop?'

Mrs Dennison asked, 'How is the child, Eleanor?'

'Comfortable,' Eleanor said shortly. Then as Maria's second cup of tea lay filming, 'There is something I must show Maria, Mother. If you would excuse us.'

She led Maria to the morning-room. There, bounded by yellow looped curtains, was the familiar view: the railway line cutting through the moors, the moors up behind, a dingy mauve under lowering clouds. Eleanor shut the door, her hand staying on the knob as if Maria might want to escape. Her face was grave.

'What's the meaning of this? *Why are you here?*' Then as if to shame her, 'Oh, *Maria.*'

'I want to see him. Let me see him.'

'But dear, you know what we –'

'Where is he? I want – *Please* let me. Once, only once.'

'He's ill in bed.'

'Let me – what's he got, is he *dying*?'

'Keep calm, dear.' The ghost of a smile hovered. 'He has

172

German measles. Nasty but not dangerous. He's sleeping now.'

'Can't I just open the door, have a little look?'

Eleanor shook her head. There were tears in her eyes. 'No, Maria. No. You see, dear . . . You know you mustn't, ought not. You must not come here.' She barred the door still. 'I thought you'd got over all that.' Her voice was nervous: 'You're not going to be – ill again? You're all right?'

Anger, despair. It was all she could do not to shake Eleanor till her teeth rattled. She has it all, she has *him*. She has *my child*.

'No, of course not,' she said in a forced voice. 'Everything is wonderful. Syb and I . . . I just wanted to see Thackton again and while I was here I thought . . .'

Eleanor said, her manner kind, calm, 'Is there any . . . do you have a beau? Do you think – are you moving perhaps towards marriage?'

'Your mother kindly asked me that . . . No. No one special, thank you.' Standing sullenly over by the window, it was as if she were back in Florence, with all the guilt of her flight to Sicily. 'And now, I'd better go. I must say goodbye to your mother –'

'Maria,' Eleanor said, 'don't try again, will you? It wouldn't be good for him. For either of you. He thinks . . . He's quite happy, you see.'

As she saw Maria out, she seemed as if about to embrace her. But there was perhaps too much of the past. Maria would like to have killed her.

I am wicked, she thought, angry tears blinding her. There was a heavy cutting pain in her breasts, as if knives turned in them. It had begun to rain. She had left her umbrella in the Japanese stand.

There was a scene at the dress shop. An oversize client, Mrs Gamble-Ericson, was having words about a letter not answered.

Her voice raised: 'It was registered. I know it was received.' Picking up a blue crêpe-de-chine tunic, waving it into the alarmed face of Mrs Goldman. The shop was otherwise empty. Miss Gina slipped into the small rest room at the back. Vera watched open-mouthed. Maria felt strangely cheered.

'Do *not* expect to see my custom again. Or me. Mr Gamble-Ericson will be in touch . . . My solicitor . . .'

Maria comforted a distraught Mrs Goldman. ('How does this happen when I work so hard, I work all day, and look!') She went into her office, Maria's arm round her shoulders. She pushed at the toppling pile of papers. 'It's here somewhere, but what do they mean me to do – papers like that . . . Harry will kill me when he hears.'

'Would you let me have a little look through? I used to work in an office –'

She spent the rest of that day at the desk. By six o'clock, it had begun to make sense. 'If you get in a typewriter,' she said, 'I could see to it all. A few days a week.'

On Tuesdays and Thursdays, she and Vera took their lunch-hour early, from twelve to one. They went to the nearest ABC. She had grown used to Vera's company. On the days when she wasn't quite herself, it didn't matter, for Vera scarcely noticed. It wasn't even necessary to lie to her.

October now. The weather had turned suddenly cold. They couldn't wait to get into the warm fug of the café.

Vera said: 'I thought if I didn't have a poached egg, but just two buns and a pot of tea, it could go towards the dress – I might get it in about six months.'

'But, Vera, the winter'll be over by then. And it isn't a frock you can wear in the summer.'

'I know. But it's just . . . I *have* to have it.'

The waitress was there. 'Two teas, one poached egg, and two Bath buns,' Maria said.

A girl's voice, almost a drawl, asked: 'Keeping this chair warm for anyone?'

'No. It's yours.' The girl – woman really, Maria thought – sat down heavily. She blew her nose, then yawned, hand over mouth only as she finished. 'Oh God,' she said wearily. She looked over to where a waitress was piling plates on to a tray: 'Buck up, *do*.'

'A pot of tea,' she ordered a minute later. 'Very strong. And buttered toast. Something I can face at this godforsaken hour.'

She was a heavy, almost voluptuous girl. Her thick blonde bob was partly covered by her white velvet beret. A Clara Bow mouth, in deep red, but made up hurriedly, Maria guessed. She wore a pale yellow coat with an enormous fur collar, which she unfastened, but kept on.

Vera's and Maria's orders arrived. The girl had lit a cigarette. She tapped a manicured hand on the table: 'Like maggots coming out of Stilton – I wish they'd hurry.'

Maria poured some tea, then pushed over the cup. 'Go on, your need's greater.'

'No. Thanks all the same.' She crushed out her cigarette. Then as Maria put her knife to the egg, and the dark yolk spread over the toast: 'Forgive me if I heave. Food. My God.'

Just then her own pot of tea arrived, together with the two rounds of toast. She fell upon the tea eagerly. Then, taking out her cigarettes again, she sat sulkily, blowing smoke rings. Both Vera and Maria felt unable to continue their chatter.

Perhaps she noticed, for she said suddenly, 'Don't let me cast a blight just because my day doesn't begin till afternoon . . . You're working girls?'

'Yes,' Vera said.

'I was in an office once, what a life – I was never so glad to see the back of anywhere, and specially the old dragon who had charge of us. Common as cat shit and twice as nasty.'

'Fancy that,' Vera said. Maria asked her, 'Do you work now?'

'Dance hostess. The clubs. Much more like it. The pickings . . . Well, anything's possible.' She flicked ash on to her plate of toast. 'Where do you two work?'

Maria told her about the dress shop. Her imitation of Norina Goldman even raised a smile, although Vera looked shocked and tittered.

The girl had taken off her coat. She was quite forthcoming and told them about her brother who tested planes for De Havilland's. She even asked them their names.

'I'm Queenie, by the way, Queenie Johnson – or Sabrini, if you prefer. It doesn't matter, take your choice.'

Maria was astonished by the sudden pounding of her heart. She asked: 'Are you any relation of Eddie Sabrini? He sings with a dance band –'

'Eddie? I should just think so. He's my husband.'

'I'm sorry,' Maria said, 'I –'

'Why be sorry?' Queenie asked, drawing on her cigarette. 'Do you want him? Take him if you'd like him. I don't want him.'

1927, and in the spring she saw that Eddie was back, the resident singer now with Al Coleman at the Dubarry. Apparently he had been in Austria for six months with Max Schmitt's band, then three months in Holland.

She had not forgotten him (although after the encounter with Queenie she would like to have), but had pushed him to the recesses of her mind. She joked when Sybil mentioned him and made her promise never to say anything to their escorts about her crush. Jack, Felix, Bonzo, Dennis, they must not know. Sybil, she had told about the meeting with Queenie, and how Queenie had said, 'Just go up to him, give him the eye. All the girls do that.' (Vera had been shocked. 'What a thing to say!') And they had laughed it off. Maria had not felt like laughing. A married man, she had thought, a door clanging shut in her mind. A married man.

Maria, the good girl. She had become the prop of Mrs Goldman's life. She not only dealt with all the letters now, but opened them as they came. Made the decisions. Paid bills and settled accounts. 'Call me Norina, dearie,' Mrs Goldman said. She consulted Maria now on stock as well as special orders. She passed on expertise, made Maria choose from designs, from swatches, showed her small points about cut and flair. 'This afternoon frock now – what would you make it up in? Georgette? Yes, good, what weight, dearie?'

Mr Goldman ('Call him Harry, dearie') came in one day and gave her a lesson in accounting. She remembered some from Miss Pritchard. For a while he visited regularly. He was full of praise for the new arrangements. ('And she says she was no good in an office! You come and work for me any day.') But she loved best still to handle the frocks. The fabrics. They stocked a few hats now, cloches, and laid one or two in the window as suggested accompaniments.

In June Jack Grindlay celebrated his twenty-fifth birthday. He was still an escort, although it wasn't clear whether it was Maria or Sybil he hoped to snare now. Off the dance floor, neither of them wanted him. They made up a party at the Dubarry. She wore a black frock with a three-tier skirt and a vest insert of silver from the shop; Sybil, bright pink crêpe-de-chine with a dipping hemline.

The Dubarry which had become very popular was crowded. Al Coleman played *Sunny Disposish*. Sybil said, 'I'd just adore it if the Pragger Wagger came in . . .' She and Maria had seen the Prince of Wales at the Embassy. He seemed to love Charlestoning as much as they did.

They were an hour or two into the evening, but with still a table or two reserved and not taken up, when Maria saw Queenie cross the floor. Grey silk frock, gold-sequinned, a yellow gardenia high on her right shoulder. Leading her in was a silver-haired, high-nosed and very tall man.

Dennis murmured: 'A face I recognize there. See it in the City daily. I'll take a sunny bet that's not his wife . . .'

Maria, about to say to Sybil, 'That's her – that's Queenie,' thought suddenly better of it. She said to Dennis, 'Dance hostess, I should think. She has that look . . .'

'How do you know these things?' Felix asked affectionately. But Maria had turned to look over at the band.

'Ain't she sweet,' Al Coleman played. He blew badly a few bars on his cornet. Eddie had laid down his violin, and was getting up to sing.

'Ain't she sweet, see her walking down the street, now I ask you very confidentially . . .' He had gone quite white. His voice carried still, was clear. But the smile had gone, from his face and from his voice.

'. . . that's what keeps me up at night, that's why I can't eat a bite.'

She watched his hands. Instead of the open gesture, they were clawed almost.

She wondered if Queenie would recognize her. She hoped not. Sitting at the table, she imagined herself, glass in hand, walking out on the floor, cracking it across that golden head, that Clara Bow mouth. In defence of Eddie. (*'Take him if you'd like him. I don't want him.'*) A little later, dancing with Felix, shaking vigorously to *Crazy Words, Crazy Tune*, she came for a moment close to her. Queenie, smiling at her partner, looked through Maria.

She spoke to Sybil in the Ladies' Room. She said nothing about Queenie. She said only, 'What about doing something really daring? Have you a pencil?' Sybil had her little gold notebook. 'You like the pianist, don't you? What about asking him and Eddie Sabrini to come up to the house? Dodie won't mind – she'll be fascinated.'

'Just for a lark?'

'Just for a lark.'

It was she wrote the note. ('Hurry up,' Sybil said, 'the men will think we've been flushed away.') She wrote: 'Two girls think you, and the pianist, are quite marvellous. We'd adore to talk to you. Maria, MAY 6089.'

'It sounds rather naughty,' Sybil said, 'but nice. Do you think it's all right?'

'I've given the shop phone. I'll be able to explain.'

Red Lips Kiss my Blues away. The small rotund banjo-player plucked at the strings. 'Everything's hotsy totsy now,' Jack said. Eddie came forward to sing. Maria, dancing with Felix, waited till they were near the bandstand. She hesitated, disengaged herself to take out a handkerchief. She thrust out her arm – she'd never been so near him before – in a second the scrap of paper was in his hand.

'All right?' Sybil's eyes signalled.

She picked up the receiver in Norina's office. 'Yes, it's Maria speaking.'

His voice. A slight London accent. She wanted to say: I saw your wife upset you the other night, behave like a cow, taunting you with another man. Tell me to kill her and I'll do it. 'Yes, it's Maria here. Look, I'd better explain . . .'

She didn't know what he might have thought, but she told him straightaway that 'two girls' meant Sybil and her, and an invitation to tea. 'The people we live with don't dance often, but they'd love to meet you.'

He had tried to call on Sunday, he said. He hadn't realized she'd given her work number. The pianist was called Roy and he'd love to come too.

She felt sick with desire and anticipation for the remainder of that week. What is happening to me? She couldn't tell Sybil. She had to make a joke of it. 'You're still a bit sweet on him?' Sybil said. 'Pity he's not free. We'll have to find out if this Roy is.'

It was an afternoon of surprising innocence. The naughtiness of it all which had so excited Sybil seemed quite missing. Clive was not there, but Dodie and her mother who was visiting joined the party. Sunday afternoon tea.

Eddie wanting to know first of all, was Maria Italian? Surely with such a name, and those looks . . . Yes indeed she was, Sybil told them. Maria explaining yet again about Sicily, the States, the *Lusy*, Middlesbrough.

Roy was very shy. He lived with his widowed mother in Hammersmith. Yes, he'd always wanted to play for a living, ever since he'd heard the Original Dixieland just after the war. He'd played since he couldn't remember when. 'They say I climbed on the piano stool, trapped my fingers in the piano lid, and never looked back.'

Eddie told them about himself. Yes, he was Italian, and of course he spoke it at home but English was natural to him. He was born in the Abruzzi but came over here when he was two.

He had an older brother and two younger sisters. His parents ran a restaurant in Soho.

Yes, it was a busy life. Into the small hours always. Rehearsals in the daytime, perhaps a recording session morning or afternoon.

'What about playing our piano?' Dodie asked Roy. And could Eddie sing a number or two?

Of course they'd love to. 'This new one,' Eddie said, 'it's only just got words. *When Day is Done* – it was a German number called *Madonna* when I was in Vienna.' They played and sang *No Foolin'*, and *I left my sugar standing in the rain*. Roy played a solo, *Flapperette*.

Dodie asked for *The Whichness of the Whatness of the Whereness of the Who*. Eddie flung up his hands in hopelessness. 'The Astaires? *Stop Flirting*? No, can't recall that –'

Maria wore her best afternoon frock – bois de rose georgette, embroidered with silk in a Renaissance design. When she passed Eddie his cup, her hand trembled.

Sybil asked for *Ain't she sweet*. Maria, remembering Queenie's entrance, his distress, didn't want it. But she had forgotten perhaps his delight, his joy, in singing. For him, it was as if the song had not had associations before, and did not again now.

This time he sang directly at her, to her. Of her, perhaps.

'Ain't she sweet, see her walking down the street, now I ask you very confidentially . . .'

'Ain't *he* sweet?' Sybil said afterwards, of Roy. 'I'm sure he's consumptive, though. His mother must be dreadfully worried.'

'Maria, you're wanted on the telephone . . .'

'Listen, Maria, Eddie Sabrini here, remember me? Maria – crazy words, crazy tune, but I want very much to see you.'

She said, 'Why don't you come to tea again, and if Roy's free –'

'I've got a home too. A flat. I'm not with my parents. Why don't you –'

She cut him off. Meaning to say, 'You're married. So – no.' Instead she said, 'When shall we meet?'

'You've come to kiss my blues away?' he asked, showing her into the flat. (Maria, the good girl, visiting a married man, alone, in the afternoon.) She had left the shop early. Time off willingly given by a grateful Norina.

Inside the flat, she found herself looking at once for signs of

Queenie. He was showing her to the sofa, insisting she sat down. He seemed restless: moving off into the kitchen, coming back, fetching her an ashtray, offering her a cigarette. As he leaned forward to light it for her, she felt faint. He was for the moment so near she could smell his skin, see the light beading of sweat. He touched her arm fleetingly as he put away the lighter. 'Let's drink some tea.'

'I could make it,' she said.

'No, no. I do that very well. I boil the water, English style.'

He was gone again.

She walked round the room. It was simply furnished but rather cluttered, probably to fit the upright piano which stood in one corner near the window. On a small table just behind the door, so that she would have missed it as she came in, was a jam-jar of flowers in front of a photograph. Queenie, smiling, in white lace and embroidered chiffon, flowers on her brow. Eddie smiling too, proud, happy, handsome. Half a head shorter.

She heard his step behind her. The colour rushed to her face. She said, 'You don't hide it, do you?'

'What?' He looked uneasy.

'About being married –'

He shrugged his shoulders. 'It's no secret . . . That photograph, that's happy days. I let it remind me – why not?'

She wanted to say that it was like a shrine. That somewhere there must have been worship – before the disillusionment. He took her arm, led her to the sofa. It was all she could do then not to turn and fling herself into his arms. I should never have come, she thought. I shall never get out of here. All these years of buried longings – buried so deep I almost believed they were not for me. And now I burn. I am burning.

'I could do with that tea,' she said, stubbing out her cigarette.

'Queenie, she's called, isn't she?' she said, as he brought in the tea. 'Queenie Johnson, she used to be. Is that right?'

He was amazed, almost letting the tray drop. He sat down heavily beside her on the sofa. 'What else have you been asking around?'

'Nothing. We've – I've met her, you see. The girl I work with . . .' And she told the story of meeting Queenie in the ABC ('*Take him if you'd like him. I don't want him*'), but not what she had said.

'But that's . . . All right, OK, so what did you think of her?' He asked it, half bitterly, half eagerly.

'She's a good-looker, isn't she?'

The ball was in his court now. But, she thought, I didn't come here to talk about Queenie.

He astounded her then – as he wouldn't in the years to come. Easy tears came into his eyes.

'I sang for her, all that summer. 1925. All my songs were for her, you know.'

'Tell me about it.'

He wanted to. Of course he wanted to.

A love story. All Queenie had wanted was to be with him forever. 'She said that. She said that.' Queenie was English, of course. Her family came from Streatham, her father worked in a bank, they were very respectable. Queenie's work worried them. '*I* thought when I first saw her –' his voice trembled '– she was an angel straight out of heaven – even though it was in a club I met her. Smoke and noise. But that's my world anyway . . . I couldn't rest till . . . I wanted her so. To marry her. Sweet, she was so sweet to me. You don't know how sweet. I brought her home – we close Sunday evening, have the family meal. Poppa thought her an angel. Momma said never trust a blonde. She didn't like her – but who's going to be good enough for her son? A girl's got to learn that from her husband's mother, hasn't she?'

As he spoke, his hand stroked her hair, just to where it was cut low on the neck. She ached with longing.

'Twenty-two, she wanted to settle down, she said. "You'll give me babies and a home to come back to," I said. Momma and Poppa . . . we all got together. A real family wedding, Catholic of course. She said she didn't mind that, she even went and saw a priest and made these promises. That day in the church – it was the happiest day of my life.'

'What went wrong – or don't you want to talk about it?'

By now he was crying. She saw that he must cry easily. Sitting there, she trembled, tea left untouched. Listening to his love for someone else, as he wept and kissed the back of her neck – she was back on the dance floor: Eddie, first seen, first heard, waking the long sleeping ghost.

'We went to live with Momma and Poppa . . . I thought she'd soon have a baby and we'd move out. I got this work in Italy, a singing spot, six weeks. She wouldn't come along. She didn't

want to see Italy. I thought it was home-loving, a baby, all that
. . . She didn't write. Then I get back – and what happens? She's
back at work. All those men paying for her smiles and Jesus
Christ knows what else besides. And she's fought with Momma
and moved out. I have to look for her – my own wife. Oh mister,
oh sister . . . I've to go around *asking*. Then I find her and what
the hell, I get us this place but she won't come back. "I never
wanted sitting at home," she said. "I was mad . . ." I say, "I
don't want that. I want a *home*. I want a *wife*. I want *babies*."
But no. Her new life, her old life, it's too good . . . Now, just
look what I have. I have fun. Nice little girls come to call . . .
But I want that girl in the photograph. I want my wife. I want
Queenie. . . .'

She knew if she touched him in return, touched him to console,
then she was lost.

'Your cigarette's gone out.' He took it from her, 'I'll light it
again.' He put it in his mouth. His mood had changed. From
looking desperate; dejected, he became suddenly jaunty. 'You'll
see I don't care,' he said. Keeping her cigarette in his mouth, he
walked over to the piano, strummed a few chords.

She came and stood beside him. 'My cigarette,' she said. He
took it out, put it back in her holder. He reached for some sheet
music, 'Know this?'

'I can't believe that you're in love with me . . .'

She stood well away from the piano. Made as if ready to
go.

'Talk to me again,' he said. 'Tell me why you're here?'

'I'm a flirt,' she said. Falling into his arms. (Oh, good girl
Maria.)

He took her over to the sofa. Led her over to the sofa. And
then it was, it was . . . 'No,' she told him, '*No*, I don't, I don't
do that –'

'Is it because I'm married? I told you I –'

'No. No. I don't. I didn't come for. I have to stop, Oh
God . . .'

'I'll take care of all that, I don't give you babies –'

It was she weeping now. 'No, no . . . let me alone. I'm sorry.
I didn't . . .'

The sudden mood change again. He was shaking. Angry,
surely. 'I have to sing, that always makes me better. Listen to
this, and then – you go home.'

He sang, with all the patter, *That's my hap hap happiness.*

Time to go. I must leave now, and forget I ever came here. Forget *him*.

'When am I going to see you again?'

'Now you're asking!' She shrugged her shoulders. More the flirt than she meant.

'I'll take you down.' He helped her on with her coat. Her body, still on fire, trembled. A fine tremor. They went down the stairs together.

Outside a fine drizzle had begun. She had no umbrella. (Oh Eleanor, oh Thackton.) As they stood in the hallway, he said:

'I'll whistle you a cab. I don't want to have to sing, *I left my sugar standing in the rain* . . .'

'He's nice, Sybil. I've been to tea with him. The marriage is over really. She's left him completely. I might see him again, it'd be rather naughty.'

'Naughty but nice, M.'

How much to tell Sybil? She said nothing very much in the end. (All those years of talking. How very little she had ever really said.)

Above all, I can't tell of how I felt this afternoon. Of my deep terror. Yes, deep – because that's where Peter went. I am not just a good girl misbehaving – but a frightened one too. Not frightened of that, because with him how could it be anything but happiness? Frightened of myself – shan't I fall into the deep pit of my nightmares: those months at The Laurels. My nightmares that if ever I should *be myself* . . . Everything is mixed up. The Lion, the linen chest, Minicu, the *Lusy*, Peter, and *my child*. I must never let go. Never, never, unleash the demons.

'Eddie here. Eddie Sabrini. Remember? When am I going to see you, Maria?'

'Eddie speaking. Listen to this, Maria. *I can't believe that you're in love with me* . . . I want to sing that for you, Maria.'

'It's Eddie here, Eddie Sabrini. Would you like to see some records cut? I could fix . . .'

'Eddie again, Maria. I've been gigging around or I'd have called before. Maria, *When am I going to see you?*'

When am I going to see you, when am I going to see you, when, when, when . . .

*

She had become indispensable at the shop, or rather in the office. Norina couldn't praise her enough. Harry Goldman called still, but now only to approve. He patted her on the head, rumpled her bobbed hair. They involved her more and more not just in the selling and the paperwork, but in the decisions too. When Miss Gina left to get married in October, Maria took her place as second in command.

Autumn turning into winter, and she was meeting Eddie again. Why not, after all? Visits to his flat, Sunday outings sometimes. And every day deeper in love. She thought she'd lived to dance, now she lived to see Eddie, to be kissed by Eddie, fondled by Eddie. But not to be happy. She said no always to his pleadings. No, no, no.

She burned so. She read once of persons who spontaneously burst into flames. She could imagine sometimes that she walked in flames, burning herself out, dry to ashes with longing, longing, desire desire desire for Eddie.

He tried. How he tried.

'I love you so much. You love me a little bit, don't you? You do, you do . . . so why not? *Why not, Maria?* Such a lovely name. Maria, Maria, Maria . . . You want to come home and meet my family? Why don't you? They'll like you. They don't mind, they know I have to see some girls some time . . . Maria, come and hear me sing – this dance at the Fascist Club. Maria, Maria, *Maria* . . .'

No, Eddie. No, no, no.

In the spring Sybil went up to Yorkshire for the wedding of her widowed sister, Molly. She was to be one of the six bridesmaids. Ida, at thirty-two, was another. It was to be a very big affair. The Graingers were of course invited and that included Maria. But she did not want to go, and made the presentation of a new collection at the shop an excuse.

Sybil said she would make a small holiday of it. 'At least ten days, darling.' She would be back, though, in time for an engagement dinner-dance for friends of Clive and Dodie's.

But after almost a fortnight there was no news of her, except for a newspaper cutting of the wedding. The day before the party, irritated rather than worried, Maria thought of telephoning, but did not. Late that night a wire arrived.

SORRY NOT BACK STOP SOMETHINGS HAPPENED STOP ALL WELL LOVE SYB

Next day she had just got in from the shop when the last post brought a letter. The fat envelope in Sybil's generous writing fell onto the mat.

Dearest dearest Maria,

Aren't I terrible, not coming back like I promised? I hope you got the wire and weren't too extraordinarily puzzled. I thought afterwards "Something's happened" might be rather frightening but – well, it's not like that. Wait for it, dearest Minnie. You're not the only person in love, you know.

I'm in love, in love, in love! Absolutely head over heels, upside down, inside out, can't tell my right from my left, can't see straight, can't *anything* – the pen just slips about on the paper. Can you read a word, darling? Darling Minnie. 'I'm just wild about Peter, and he's just wild about me –' Isn't that how the song goes? Darling, isn't it just too marvellous, wonderful, all anyone ever could have dreamed of? *And* you and I are going to be sort of sisters. Because yes, Peter and I are not just terribly in love, we're actually *engaged*! You'd never think anything could happen so quickly. Mummy and Daddy don't know what's hit them – they say they don't know what's hit us either! And as for the Grainger parents, they're stunned as well. (Hardly anyone's been told except the families concerned – and you, darling. So keep it under your hat. Just for now.) We plan to be married very soon, though. I think it could even be this summer . . .

Three days later she became Eddie's mistress.

13

'You're a dago,' Miller said. 'You're a dago, so, Dennison.' He gave Guy a jab in the stomach with his fist. 'Dago Dennison.'

Guy lashed out with his foot, kicking Miller first on the knee, then a second time higher up, near the hip bone. Miller screamed, 'He'll kill me. Get Dennison off me.'

Akester, one of the prefects, came behind Guy, pinning his arms to his body. 'Steady. You'll do him an injury.'

Guy wriggling, cried, 'I want to kill him –'

Akester tried to calm him while Miller continued to scream like a stuck pig. Two boys went in search of authority and found Brother Damian working not far away in the rose-garden.

Miller said between sobs, 'Please, Brother, I only asked Dennison about some homework and did a bit of play boxing – and he upped and kicked me here . . .' He clutched his privates.

Brother Damian wrenched Guy away from Akester. 'I'll deal with this little lad.' He tweaked Guy's ear roughly. 'Here. Just wait till I tell what you were up to. And you with your uncle a Jesuit. Glory be to God.'

Held up by his collar, dragging his feet, Guy struggled still. 'No you don't, young fellow-me-lad.'

'I want to go home,' Guy yelled, 'I'll make them send me, I want to go back to Yorkshire, I don't like Derbyshire, I don't like any of you, I hate Miller, I hate –'

'It isn't one devil you have, it's five hundred,' Brother Damian said, puffing and panting. Delivering him to the Headmaster's door.

Guy Thomas Dennison of Park Villa, Thackton-le-Moors, North Riding, Yorkshire, England, The World. Age eight years and one month. Adopted (I know I'm adopted, because I'm Italian and Aunt Eleanor isn't married). I was all right until they sent me here. I never wanted to go to school but when I told Amy I was going to run away, she burst into tears. She made me promise I wouldn't. So I shan't.

*

He wore black shiny wellingtons which were new and gave him blisters. He swung on the barred gate of Park Villa, watching the world go by. He had always done that, promising not to go down to the village without permission.

It was leaning over the gate, he first saw a drunken man. One of the Irishmen over for the haymaking: he came past Park Villa dancing, lurching from one side of the road to the other, singing *Take me home again, Kathleen*, loudly. Guy was so impressed he gave an imitation when he went indoors. Grandma Dennison said it was disgusting. Aunt Eleanor wasn't cross but she took him aside and explained about getting drunk. Amy thought it the funniest thing ever. 'That's Paddy Burns,' she said, laughing till the tears ran, 'Paddy's over every year. It's hay money he'll have been supping . . .'

Sometimes Guy went along the road to Moorgarth with his bowling hoop, to see Uncle Dick and Aunt Gwen. The hoop was a very fine one and had belonged to Uncle Dick.

Both the night and day nursery had bars at the window. In the daytime he could watch the road outside but on summer evenings, in bed far too early, he could gaze down the long narrow garden and out at the fields beyond, and then the moorland stretching up to the long flat top of Thackton Rigg. The railway line came in between. He watched the smoke curl up as the train left Thackton, chuffing past the window on its way to Whitby. If he pulled back the curtains after dark, he could pick out the lights of the station.

In winter he fell asleep watching the shadows from the fire-guard. When he had earache, Amy brought up a cotton bag full of warm salt to lay on it. For a cough there was hot syrup from elderberries he'd helped pick that very autumn. There was always a lamp turned down low: Aunt Eleanor said she knew what it was to be frightened at night.

Aunt Eleanor had rescued him when his real parents died. He loved her. And Amy. And sometimes Grandma Dennison (he liked to watch her frizz the front of her hair with curling tongs, and the smell of singeing paper as the tongs were laid down). He loved some of the Graingers. Uncle Dick for instance (I call him Uncle though he's no relation) and Aunt Ida who laughed a lot. Uncle Peter couldn't be bothered with him, and wasn't there often anyway. Old Mr Grainger ragged him and was very jolly.

And then there was Uncle Basil. When he visited, Guy sat on

his knee which was not very comfortable and recited answers to catechism questions. But when he asked his own questions ('What does covet mean, is it hitting somebody's wife? What is adultery?') the answer was always: 'We shall see, in a little.'

'If Heaven's in the sky,' he asked, 'when you go down and down why isn't Hell in Australia? *Is* Hell in Australia?'

In summer when the bluebells came out in the woods he picked a bunch for Amy and put them in a bloater paste jar. They went to the seaside. Long afternoons on Whitby sands. They made him wear squelchy rubber paddling shoes that he managed to lose on an outing to Robin Hood's Bay. He kept sea anemones from the rock pools in a bucket.

Uncle Dick and Aunt Gwen took him on picnics. As well as toys from his own childhood, Uncle Dick brought him books. There was the story of the Golden Lion. Guy wanted to know where you could buy a lion like that, a magic lion who was friendly. Not long after that he'd found Leo under the Christmas tree: tawny, very soft, with a furry coat and whiskers. He had been six then and still needed the night lamp. He grew much braver after he had Leo to protect him. He never went anywhere without him. Amy and Aunt Eleanor had packed up Leo to go to St Boniface's with him.

The year he got Leo was the same one he asked for a puppy. But his birthday and then Christmas had been and gone, and still no puppy. Aunt Eleanor explained that although he lived at home and had lessons from a tutor, one day he would have to go away. And then how would the dog manage? 'Better not, darling.'

But one day just before the next Christmas, Amy took him as usual to see her family. There were black lurcher puppies at the farm. When he saw them, he picked one out and wouldn't let it go. Amy protested, 'I don't know whatever they'll say,' but he only clasped the puppy tighter. The farmer's wife said, 'Let him, now, we're looking for good homes.'

That was how he'd got Greta. He missed her terribly now. She'd not grown very big and was a little bow-legged, but she trotted around after him, black and impudent with short smooth ears. She had been eleven months old when he went away to St Boniface's.

He got two black marks for the episode with Miller. It was his own fault, for boasting about being Italian. He'd wanted to have something those first few miserable days, when everyone seemed to have rich and clever fathers and beautiful mothers. 'Anyway, I'm Italian,' he'd said when asked for the umpteenth time what his father did (and why his skin looked as if he'd been in the sun all winter). '*And* I'm adopted,' he boasted. After that they wouldn't let him alone. 'This is a school for English people,' Utley told him, 'unless you're Scotch or Irish.' Packard-Smith asked if his father sold ice-cream. 'Does your pater have an ice-cream cart?'

Father Dominic made it worse by telling the Catechism class, 'Dennison is the nephew of Father Basil Dennison SJ, the prominent apologist. We're very privileged. Hands up anyone who knows what an apologist is?' Packard-Smith told Guy after, 'You're an apologist too – 'cos you're going to have to apologize for being Italian . . .' Straightway, he had had a fight with Packard-Smith and bloodied his nose. That meant four black marks.

'What shall we do with you?' Father Clement asked sadly. 'You fight for the sake of fighting.'

It was true. He seemed to have been fighting ever since he'd arrived. St Boniface's. A good Catholic prep school. He would have to be here five years until he was old enough to go to a Jesuit school, which Uncle Basil would arrange.

From the first day it was terrible. He'd never seen a dormitory before – there were four of them for the fifty boys. He was in the largest. Matron was quite kind but brisk and hurried. She had unpacked Leo and then his clothes for the night: blue striped pyjamas and fawn wool dressing-gown from Daniel Neal's, bought on an expedition to London, his first (the Zoo, the Tower of London, Buckingham Palace, tea at Rumpelmeyer's).

Then one of the boys had noticed Leo. No one else had a soft toy. It had been too late then to hide him. Besides, he wanted him most terribly. The fur of Leo's coat was soft, although there were scratchy places where Guy had spilt Ovaltine and it had dried and spoilt the fabric. The second-year boys mocked. 'It's got mange, your lion,' one of them said. The others joined in: '*And* bad breath and runny eyes and a snotty nose.' A tall boy called Pilkington snatched up Leo and sniffed him. 'Phew, he's farted. Pouf . . . don't get near, chaps.'

The school lavatories were inside a courtyard. They queued up before breakfast, and again at break. Brother John Bosco kept a register: 'Were your bowels open today?' As each boy said yes, he ticked his name. The third day Guy wasn't able. No amount of straining. And the same next morning. 'Please, Brother, I couldn't . . .' Seeing a cross beside his name. No one else had crosses, every other boy had bowels that opened and shut to order. Brother John Bosco told Guy, 'Won't we have to do something about that?'

'Something' was a grey powder mixed up with jam. It worked very quickly. Then all through Greek class it wanted to work again. He was doubled with cramp and had to rush out. When he crept back to his desk, he heard the dry voice of Father Laurence.

'Back with us, Dennison? I'm edified to see the ablative affected you so strongly . . . The past participle for *ferre* now, please.'

Next time he had a grey powder he was late for two lessons (bent double in the lavatories), and got a *tardus*. It was a month before he discovered that the other boys lied.

His homesickness was worst in the mornings, choking him through the breakfast of mushy tomatoes and curled-up bacon. The over-boiled sulphurous egg, the strong tea. At break there was milk from the home farm, thick cream above, watery blue below.

By the end of the first month he was in trouble again, the seat of his short grey trousers split – he didn't know how or why. But Matron was angry with him. And even angrier when she saw that he had worn down already the backs of his elastic-sided black shoes. 'The other boys don't . . .'

The weather grew colder. The bread at break, thinly spread with rancid butter, was stale. A few of the boys prised open the circular coal fire in the recreation hall and tried to toast their bread. Some older boys made Guy do theirs. The excitement and sizzling and mess brought over Brother John Bosco – Guy got into trouble. Another bad mark. (One more and the headmaster would send for him again.)

After the midday meal each day there was a precious half-hour when they could read in the library, or make models, or just sit. There were three easy chairs near the fire and there was always a rush for these, but Guy preferred to lie on the floor. Sometimes he imagined that Greta lay beside him, and his arm would go out and round her neck. Then, feeling a fool, he would hastily put it back. Lying on his stomach, he read Sapper and forgot for half an hour that he was unhappy. And Italian.

*

Eleanor had known she would miss Guy, but not how much. She tried to make provision with good works, and art interests. She spent as much time as possible with Dulcie, tied up these days with a home for the deaf and dumb not far from Middlesbrough.

She could talk to Dulcie about missing Guy. Dulcie knew what it was to be an unacknowledged mother (so alas, must Maria, but she must not think of that – cruel to be kind, cruel to be kind). They spoke sometimes of the reaction of the village to his adoption. Dulcie said:

'They think us, and you too, rather odd still. Yet their hearts are big enough – those Belgians in the next village, a whole community of them in the Great War.' But two families adopting an Italian child (even though one was almost American), and that the two should never meet – 'Miss Maria, she's never this way, not since she went to London. *She'd* be pleased and all, to see a little boy from Italy.' Someone even said, 'You can see he's Italian – he's that like Miss Maria.'

Dulcie never thought it odd if Eleanor talked endlessly of Guy, what he was and would be. 'He'll surely be somebody, surely.'

Dulcie, laughing, said, 'Of course he's wonderful. In spite of being half a Grainger.'

'But that's *why* he's so wonderful.' She said it so casually Dulcie could have thought nothing. But she knew yet again that it was the Eric in him, the fourth part of Eric, that she loved.

It was an excuse, with Guy gone, for Mother to make barbs yet again about a missed vocation. Basil the Jesuit, successful. Eleanor whom no man would look at, who would like to have been a nun.

Eleanor ignored it all. Nor was she put out by the inevitable awkward questions. When, before Guy left for St Boniface's, Mother asked, 'Who is to *pay* for all this? His upbringing, Eleanor, his education?' she had been able to reply proudly, 'It has all been seen to – it has been taken care of by Basil. And the Jesuits.' Yes, that was it. The Jesuits. For she and Basil had thought of all the answers, approved of later by Eric. United with her brother over this, she found herself beginning even to like him.

The Jesuits. She left Mother to exclaim at their generosity:

'Perhaps *Guy* will have a vocation,' she said.

Eleanor went over twice to Middlesbrough to stay with Dulcie.

Although to be so near Eric, living in the same house, would not do – it was too rich. She marvelled at how Dulcie did it. They seemed to her almost like brother and sister. She knew that he slept separately from Maimie and had done for years now, but he and Dulcie? She had been afraid of her fantasies, although Dulcie, while they were in Paris with the baby, had told her in a burst of candour:

'We never did – after Jenny. It had all been too terrible, you see. And yet I stay on. You must think that odd. But we both wanted it. And it is not so bad . . .'

I could never, Eleanor thought, imagining the joy and the pain of seeing each day the beloved at the breakfast table, of sleeping under the same roof. And I am here only a week . . . Each night of her stay just before she fell asleep, her spirit (no, not her body, not her body) went wandering in search of his room. She had seen that room, and the dressing-room with its scents of Hungary Water and hair pomade and leather. In fantasy, she hovered above him and around him, blessed him, protected him. Each night she tried to send her hungry body to sleep before her soul. My soul, my body – those two distinct halves.

A letter came.

> Dear Aunt Eleanor,
>   It is very cold here there is frost on the dorm windows inside, last week I was two days in the san with a bad ear. Some oldar boys have a lot of tuck can you send some appels? and some peppercake and toffee if you can spare it. I am quiet good at conkers. The days till I get home are only 42 now, From your loving nephew, Guy Dennison.

She wept when she read it.

Unhappy Guy. Happy Dick, father of two little girls. Happy that Christmas of 1929 (the world in recession, the Wall Street crash not two months old), happy even though the foundry was feeling the cold winds, happy married to Gwen, now expecting another child. It would be a son, he was certain.

Happy Dick, even with a leg which ached in damp weather, and at other times too. He had long since ceased to rail against it. If he hadn't fallen from that 'plane, he'd never have met, would have lived in a world without Gwen. But without Gwen – there was no world.

Happy even though old Mrs Ackroyd lived with them. She'd proved much less difficult than he had thought. Reconciled to Dick, contented and with plenty of interests – a great organizer of bazaars, a doting grandmother.

Sitting by the fire, he read the day's mail. From Canada, Jenny's neat writing – and photographs of Jim and Gordon, five and three, in swimming costume beside the lake. That was their log cabin in the background. They really hoped to come over next year but with the slump Archie's firm hadn't been that good. She'd asked Aunt Dulcie to visit – 'it would do her good' – but so far there was no sign of it.

A thin wail under the window. *Once in royal David's city . . .* Soon the front door bell would ring of the house he had bought for Gwen, the very house he had earmarked for her all those years ago.

Voices. 'Look at me, Daddy, I'm the fairy queen!'

'Well, well now – shall we put you on the top of the tree, Betty?'

'My crown's a bit torn, I want you to mend it, Daddy, Daddy, mend it *now*.'

Betty, plump and red-faced, just six, and in fancy dress. The same outfit she'd worn last Christmas as a butterfly. Now, seams let out, hem lengthened and wings removed. White net, buckram, wire, silver sequins, a wand with a star, and a crown. How ridiculous she looked with her fat little body and her red cheeks, feet turned out at nearly a quarter to three. Ridiculous – and lovable. Bossy Betty. Gwen had been like that, old Mrs Ackroyd told him. 'Those two lads, her brothers – pulling them to school, pushing them home again.' It was Jan who very soon would make the perfect fairy, with her red-gold hair, her tiny bones, her pert but gentle face.

By the fire in his house slippers. Yes, Gwen warmed his slippers. 'It doesn't take a second,' she told him, 'and at least I know you'll come home, don't I?' He could never understand that: how she could imagine his gaze might stray. 'I don't want Nancy to get you . . .'

'If I'd wanted Nancy, I'd have had her, wouldn't I?' he'd say, his arms tight about her. His nose (cold like a dog's she said, these winter nights) buried in her shoulder, then down, down between her breasts – not against skin, but against warm flannel. 'Off with that,' he'd say, and '*You* can take it off,' she'd say. And so, the unbuttoning and twisting and pulling, Gwen pretending to shiver – but Gwen was always warm, always. And then his fingers would be on flesh, warm flesh, touching, loving oh so much while all the time his mouth was kissing, kissing, thinking all the time: I can hardly wait. Gwen, Gwen!

And now they'd made another baby. A son.

14

'*Ooh that kiss,*' Eddie sang.

Maria said, 'You'll disturb the neighbours –'

'*Ooh that kiss . . . What is love but a helping of angel cake* – I know what I'd like a helping of . . .'

'Hush.'

'They went to the seaside. I saw them go off . . . *What is love but the kisses you give and take?*'

'We're respectable now, darling. Keep your voice down, and sing that sort of thing indoors.'

'What? When they can hear the greatest crooner of 1932 for free, serenading bella Maria . . . You told me off, darling. *Was that the human thing to do?*'

'If you talk in songs once more . . . That's all you are, Eddie Sabrini, one great big sheet of popular music – and I love you.'

'Talking of sheets, Maria, let's go inside –'

A sultry August night. They were sitting in their small back garden, eating and drinking at a table under a plane tree. The weather had been growing stickier for days. In the stifling air, the leaves were still, the candle flames barely flickered.

'*Ooh that kiss* . . . come on up, come on up to bed. Bed, bed, bed. Come on up, Mrs Sabrini . . . Bedtime.'

Mrs Sabrini. *Mr and Mrs Eddie Sabrini.* Married at Easter, after more than four years of loving and waiting. The happiest day of my life.

Her body had been happy and perhaps her soul. Even though they had been unable to marry in church. Certainly she'd never worried again. From the days of Sybil's news, from the first days and weeks of giving herself to Eddie, nothing else had mattered. Neither religion, nor convention. It seemed for a while that before Eddie there'd been nothing. Her past: she thought, I'm able for the first time to put all of it behind me. No, not burying or hiding anything. It's as if the world is washed clean, so that, *bad girl as I am*, I am good. I know that it is good, good to love Eddie.

A new life had begun almost at once after Sybil's letter. In the weeks that followed Sybil had scarcely returned to London, wanting just to stay up in Yorkshire, making preparations for, counting the days till her wedding.

And I had to attend it, she thought now. I almost took the coward's way out, of illness. But I went, and perhaps because I carried Eddie in my heart and, although Eleanor was there, we did not speak of Guy – it was all right. I was even polite to Peter. That handsome man, twelve years older, charming, able (forget that I hate him). 'We're all going to be such friends!' Sybil cried, and perhaps it will be so, for I have not told her – and no one else will. Certainly Peter has not.

Her love for Eddie, his for her, made all things possible that before . . . How soon had she known that Queenie was uncrowned? The photograph went from the shrine, succeeded that summer by a framed snapshot of – yes, Maria. Maria on the pier at Brighton, in a pale green linen frock with horizontal tucks and a spotted silk tie.

She was well dressed always, because she'd been happy to stay on with Norina. Norina and Harry needed her. She was an important part of the concern, more and more responsibility falling on her shoulders. And then after Sybil's marriage, and the much better pay she was receiving (so that she had been able to ask Uncle Eric to cancel her allowance), why continue to live with Clive and Dodie? Why not defy convention and live with Eddie?

Over twenty-six, and not married. They thought in Yorkshire that she had made a career for herself but that one day perhaps, she would find someone suitable. At her age, she was no longer a worry and a responsibility. She had been gradually cutting herself off for years. Now with Eddie as her lover – oh, happy word – she did it almost completely. When Sybil (who, although shocked, knew the truth) managed a shopping trip to London, she would see her. But that was her only sight of the family now. Better like this, better.

To begin with, she had not had to think of Queenie much at all (Queen Hotbot, Eddie called her rudely), since Eddie made love only to her – or so she hoped, believed. And he sang only for her. *Just when I least expected it, I found you* . . . When he recorded that last year, 'I sang it for you,' he said.

She met his family. Momma and Poppa and his sisters Rita and Connie. Eddie took her to Sunday evening supper in the closed restaurant two weeks after they'd begun sleeping together. Mrs Sabrini threw her arms about Maria.

'A good Italian girl, Italian, Sicilian . . . good girl, good for Eddie.' They wanted to tell Maria, couldn't wait to tell her, that they'd warned Eddie. 'She wasn't a good girl, Queenie. "Don't do it, Eddie," I say. "You'll be sorry." But no. "Momma, I *love* her –" And then he's a good boy and he marries in church, and now what? He can't . . . You're a good Catholic girl, Maria. You understand. The stupid boy . . . But eh, eh, perhaps Queenie she walks over a bridge, she walks into the sea, makes a mistake eh? And then . . .'

But she had never wished Queenie ill. It was too frightening. If she had let her thoughts run . . .

A way of life. A new way of life. Making love in the afternoons, making love at three in the morning (keeping different, self-chosen hours at Norina's, coming in when she pleased), and always Eddie's body – and her body that had been waiting all the while for his. Eddie of the flicking tongue, the warm hands that probed and touched, the hardness, the softness, her own yielding. Heavy-breasted again, but not with pain, only with longing satisfied.

Outrageous Eddie, lying in bed (singing to the tune of *Ain't she sweet?*), '*Tell me where, tell me where, you've seen one, just like that . . .*' (but he was right to be proud of it). '*I repeat, don't you think he's kind of neat? Ain't he nice? Look him over once or twice . . .*'

But then of course in the end it wasn't enough. Not when she began to reflect, when his parents made comments, when she looked into the glass of the future. Eddie, who'd wanted a home and babies and domesticity in the evenings. And she?

They spoke of it – Eddie's fear that he was stopping her from marrying someone more suitable. 'Hey, you don't want a crooner.'

'Yes, I do, I want *this* crooner –'

'Someone free – and rich and smart and all that.'

'But you're going to be rich and famous! As if I cared, as if I cared – But you *are* . . .'

He was of course going to be famous. The records might say only 'with vocal refrain', but the vocal cords that filled the grooves could easily be recognized. And were. Women loved him. But not like I love him, she thought.

All those songs. And new ones always being added: it seemed the band could play and he could sing, any number, any request. He told her that some singers wrote the words on a card cupped in the palm of their hand. He didn't need to. Along with that joyousness went an easy, reliable memory. She would go through his songs with him if they were together and he had no rehearsal or recording session. Sometimes they would be songs from American shows which, although forbidden, the band would play and the dancers enjoy (when discovery was likely, at a secret signal the band would change quickly to another number).

Darling Eddie. 'Flamin' Mamie, you don't want a crooner.' Oh yes she did. But as the months passed, and the years – already nearly three – it wasn't enough. Then towards the end of 1930, Eddie was under contract for a six months' tour of India. As his wife she could have gone with him, as his mistress – no. The six months of his absence were for her terrible. She stalked London like a ghost. She met Sybil down for a Christmas shopping spree, and confided in her. She said, 'When he comes back, I'm going to say we must marry. We must forget we're a good Catholic girl and boy. He must divorce Queenie – or else I think it will have to end.'

But how could it? It must not end.

. . . *If you're heading for a sunny honeymoon, learn to croon* . . . Eddie back again, strangely (or not so strangely) had the same thought. He'd lived only to be back with her. Roy, who'd been on the tour too, thinner and even more cadaverous now, had been Eddie's keeper. He said Eddie had been impossible – crying for Maria when he should have been sleeping. 'You're a couple of noddles . . .'

Queenie, seldom seen these days, but by hearsay doing very well – a kept woman possibly – must be asked. She said no. She was fine as she was. And who knew, if he continued becoming so successful, she might not enjoy some reflected glory? Little Eddie Sabrini's missus. Why not?

'*Flamin' Mamie*,' he said, and sang (one of the first numbers he had ever recorded, in 1926). Maria said, 'To think she once offered you me.' ('*Take him if you'd like him* . . .')

Eddie pleaded. Queenie refused, became more obstinate. Maria in a sudden fit of religious guilt, said that it was the Virgin

Mary trying to stop them excommunicating themselves. When that mood passed, she said angrily:

'Divorce *her*. You've got enough grounds . . .' But Eddie wouldn't. Maria objected:

'Why do you have to be a gentleman, an English gentleman? That's all it is.' It was she now became ruthless, desperate.

'Italian, English – I'm still the gentleman. I can't.'

Then happened something Maria had quite forgotten to pray for. The oh, so obvious. Queenie met someone rich, and eligible and free and mad to marry her. He was American, from Kentucky. She wanted a divorce, very soon, and cleanly and neatly. With her as innocent party.

Eddie went to Brighton, not on a day trip this time, but for a night at a hotel. The chambermaid bringing in early morning tea found him tucked up with a small volatile blonde – Maria never asked and didn't want to know more.

A painful six weeks after the decree when she pretended scarcely to know him, six weeks without being in touch, six weeks without touch – although nothing beside the six months' separation the year before, it frightened her.

They left the flat and rented a small house in Chelsea. It was a register office wedding. Their honeymoon was postponed because of Eddie's engagements. A big family party was held the week after the wedding. The Sabrini clan welcomed her. 'God understands,' her new mother-in-law said. 'He knows Eddie he needs a good woman – for babies.'

She was Mrs Eddie Sabrini. Lying beside Eddie now, blessed, if not by God then by the state. Mrs Sabrini, wife and (soon, please God, soon) mother.

'I'm so happy, so happy.' Eddie's tongue, Eddie's fingers. His voice in her ear. 'Let's make a baby . . .'

It wasn't going to go wrong – ever.

15

New York,
7th November 1935

Dear Dick,

I was so happy to get a letter from you. Such a welcoming one too. You always were a good friend. And now you deserve to have one back with all the news.

New York, New York – it's still a dream. I know we had the crossing to get used but it isn't enough, not when you get the grand welcome and excitement we've had. All the difficulties with the Musicians' Union got sorted out (seemed crazy when we've got all these wonderful US players over in England) and Al was cleared to play with Eddie as his vocalist. We'd hoped Roy was coming too – he plays wonderful stride, I'm sure he'd have been a success. He's married now, his wife Aileen's lovely, and he'd have been good for Eddie. But he's sick, it's really worrying, they think it's TB.

Eddie's been a success from the word Go. Now he's singing at the Rainbow Room! If you haven't heard of it, it's *the* place here for eating and hoofing. It's in Radio City (which is huge and covers four whole blocks) on the top floor of the RCA building, really high up as only things can be in this skyscraper city. 'Sixty-five stories nearer the stars,' is the slogan. He's on every night except Sunday, nine to three, and of course a broadcast's included in that. I'm so proud of him. He was asked twice for *I cover the waterfront*, they liked his version so much. Lots of rehearsing for which they get paid, so everything's all right. In fact altogether, *everything's all right!*

Before I go any further I must just say something about Sybil and Peter coming here later this month. I gather they're going to make a trip of it while they're over, and see some of the rest of the States. But it all sounds like a good idea, because if the proposition is to be made seriously to the Allison Corporation, then it's best done in person. I only wish, Dick,

I wasn't reminded of Uncle Eric (and me!) on the *Lusy*. I think that's just a fatalistic streak – the bit of me that's more East than West. Maybe. That Arab strain we're supposed to have in the Western part of Sicily.

We'll be touring the States ourselves with the band, but not before January or February at the earliest. Canada too, so maybe we'll see Jenny.

Anyway it will be lovely showing Sybil everything. No, as you said, I can't be quite at ease, *even after fifteen years*, with Peter. If I could choose about his coming over, I'd say rather not.

I've seen a lot of my brother, of course. Rocco is fine. Although Prohibition got repealed after the Volstead Act last year, he's still doing all right (he had two speakeasies, or speaks). There are things about the American way of life which really suit him and are to his advantage. He's not married alas, though I think there may be a girlfriend. He's not saying!

It's funny to be back somewhere you lived so long ago – I went with Rocco to see the Ricciardis' old house. I'd remembered it maybe the size of Buckingham Palace – and there it was just a pleasant largish house with a stoop in an area that's grown a lot less smart, I think. None of the family is in New York now.

Much braver, Dick, was to go back where Mamma and I had lived before. It brought back such memories. Coffee roasting and cooking smells and baking – and all those faces that are the faces of my childhood before 'Merica. Frightening poverty.

Dear Dick, how I ramble on. You are my good friend. I know the family don't really approve. Maria wed to a divorced man (it was hard for Eleanor not to be shocked, she's such a religious person), but I know you wish me happiness. You always were a firm friend to me. And, Dick, I'm happy that you're so happy. My fondest love to Gwen . . .

Sybil in her blue georgette wool coat with the silver fox collar, glossy-lipped, smelling of *L'Heure Bleue*. So happy Sybil, spreading her things about the room. 'Stay with me, while I change.' Flinging lacy camisoles, petticoats, hand-embroidered cami-knickers, silk stockings.

'You'll eat with us, darling? There's a grill room at the hotel or we could have had something sent up . . . Any chance of seeing Eddie?' Sybil charged with excitement. More excitement in the air than warranted even by her arrival in New York.

'Peter's downstairs, drinking with . . . Can't remember his name – the manufacturer he has to see first. Darling, it's going to be a wonderful trip – Daddy's given me so much to spend. I'm still shamelessly spoilt . . .' Sitting at the dressing-table in a silk kimono, head hanging forward as she brushed her shiny black hair.

'We are going to see Eddie, though? Lots of people on the boat coming over, English, they were quite impressed I was semi-related . . . He was doing so awfully well before – and now it's good here too.' She looked in the glass. 'But he's still . . . like you said that time in Town – he's still straying?'

'Still straying, Syb.' She said it edgily, sitting curled up on the bed. 'And I mind desperately. It never gets any better. He doesn't even *mean* it. It's so casual – just someone admiring him, showing they're available – And then, it's a short step . . . But if just looking at him does things to me, why shouldn't he be irresistible to others? Perhaps – if I could just give him a child.'

Sybil said suddenly, 'Maria darling, I should have said. I think, we think – it's almost certain *I'm* in the family way –'

'Syb, darling. Oh, but I'm so glad!'

'And we'd almost given up. Something with my tubes they said in the spring . . . We nearly didn't come on this trip, because it's – well, it's about two months. I'm sure it's not a false alarm. And I'm feeling wonderful, not queasy at all. Wonderful.'

Her silk stockings were on now. She slipped into shoes of bronze kid. 'It's not public yet of course. Keep it under your hat.'

'Syb, it's for *you* to keep it – inside you. Do be careful, darling.'

Rattling on, prattling on, to mask the shock and the envy. I who've shown that I can bear a child *by that same man* – and now? I seem to be barren. Peter, father of Sybil's child. Perhaps we shall all play Happy Families?

'I thought you might be upset, Maria darling, with your not . . .'

'Oh, one day,' she said carelessly. 'It could be my lucky month any time.'

'You haven't been to a doctor again?'

'Oh yes. A specialist. But there's nothing wrong . . . And he terribly wants babies. He'd love a photo in *Melody Maker* of the two of us, with about five little ones – or six or whatever, as long as it's more than Bing Crosby. He's a family man at heart – whatever his strayings. The rest isn't important.'

Sybil disappeared to wash. When she came back, reaching into the wardrobe, she asked, 'Are we going to meet this brother of yours? Rocco. He sounds so glamorous. And not married? I should have brought Nancy over. What a hope! Thirty-six now, darling, and still dreaming of Dick, who of course adores, but *adores* Gwen . . . No more babies there, I fear. That miscarriage four years ago, stillbirth rather, that was a boy. But you knew that?'

She stood there in pale yellow satin: low square neckline, crystal beaded straps. Maria said: 'Darling, you look quite gorgeous.'

'Making the most of this slinky figure while I still have it. I'll bet Peter barely notices. Terrible man . . .'

'I'm the guy you give your goodnight kisses to – remember me? Wasn't I good? No, tell me, you listened in – I was good, wasn't I? The applause, you could . . . I'll bet that made the waves crackle . . . There were all these dames afterwards – some really gorgeous . . .'

'So what happened? I waited up. Don't tell me – they all fell on you, undressed you and forced you –'

'Hey, hey . . . I came straight back to you. Who else'd I want? You're proud of me, aren't you? Say you thought I was good.'

'Eddie, you were wonderful –'

'Let's call room service, I need a bottle of wine, let's celebrate. Crosby, Vallee, Austin – forget them, Eddie's the best. Come over here on the sofa, put your wrap on . . . I'm the guy you give your goodnight kisses to – remember me?'

Two nights later he sang for her (she knew it was for her), '*I don't know, what would happen to me, if anything happened to you.*' There were tears in his eyes.

What to make of her brother? Blood of her blood. Over fifteen years since they'd met. She carried in her the picture of him as he'd said goodbye that time in Palermo, in the days when she had only wanted to die. Before the baby, before Guy. She had somehow expected him to be the same. As if the picture, frozen, were to be suddenly reanimated – so that from the quay at Palermo, he turned now and walked towards her.

It was a forty-three-year-old man who met her in the hotel

foyer. Grey camel-hair coat slung over shoulders, expensive shoes, mirror-shining. And then close up when they'd kissed, the star sapphire cufflinks. Beautifully kept hands. Hat off, the hair not even beginning to recede, grey at the sides but as thick and curly as ever. A fine figure of a man. But not married. ('Of course there are dames . . .')

They talked in Sicilian, rapidly. As if she had never talked anything else. And yet, apart from dreams, from moments of terror, she had put it aside at the age of eleven.

Not taking her to his apartment at first. Taking her to El Morocco. The table alone cost twenty-five dollars. Dollar bills, folds of dollar bills. Saying to the waiter, 'Listen, this is my kid sister, what do you think, isn't she gorgeous?' They went to the Rainbow Room. She wore her new crimson organza frock and danced with him, and led the applause when Eddie sang *Everything I have is yours*.

'Of course, the women love him,' she told Rocco.

'He loves them?' Rocco asked.

'Sometimes,' she said, laughing it off.

Rocco said, 'Maria – you want him taught a lesson? If you want that – just say the word.'

'No,' she said. 'No. Don't touch Eddie. Ever.'

But he'd already changed the subject.

She had to do it right, get it right. She was his little sister. He made a fuss of her, and later a fuss of Eddie too. On Sundays when Eddie was free he took them out a few times.

She wondered sometimes how he made his money. He had been lucky to get back to the States before the quota was imposed. She knew bootlegging had been the main source of his riches to begin with. Then his speaks. 'A lot of people knew Rocco's.' It had been expensive, she realized, paying the police. Now he must be making money in other ways.

Although he made a fuss of her, he didn't introduce her to his friends. Yet he seemed to know many people, of all sorts. He was OK. 'There ain't nobody gonna call me a greaseball,' he told Eddie, 'they don't call me a Wop neither . . .'

His English, which he spoke when Eddie was there, wasn't that good. But he never used that odd vocabulary, neither Sicilian nor Italian, which she could just remember from before. ('Olivetta' for elevated railroad, 'cotta' for coat). He spoke English as if he'd been around some time.

*

'Rocco here, Eddie, Maria, listen – I wanna ask you all to supper, what you say next Sunday, we'll go maybe Jack Dempsey's – I dunno, listen I'll find somewhere real good, the Graingers they like fish? You think you can make it? Listen, I'll call again tomorrow – you clear it with them. Maybe I bring a dame, maybe not.'

Peter asked, 'What's your line of business, Mr Verzotto?'

'Business,' Rocco said, 'sure I'm in business. All sorts. Real estate maybe . . .' He had hold of the menu, pointing to it. 'Listen, you peoples is going to choose. Anything you want. You choose.'

The restaurant was crowded. Maria was glad it hadn't been one with singing waiters. Although Sybil, who'd never heard of such things had been intrigued, Maria said they were rather awful. 'It's fun the first time, perhaps.' The place Rocco had chosen, Grazzano's, was smart, elegant and no more noisy than to be expected. The tables were well spaced. White cloths, sparkling glass and silver. A piano in the corner played, just audibly, numbers from *Top Hat*.

Sybil, in coral crêpe-de-chine, glowed with her secret.

Peter, sitting opposite her. A fine figure of a man in his early thirties. The moustache he had grown suited him. He radiated health, open air, cleanliness, gleaming white shirt front. Proud of himself, of the firm, of Sybil, no doubt of the child to be. Perhaps it was that news which had aroused bitterness in Maria. *He gave me my only child, who was taken away from me. Now he triumphs in the latter day. A father again. While I . . .* Sitting there, she felt a slow burning wave of hate, such as she had not felt for years, against him.

She could see him appraising Rocco. A little in awe, a little impressed against himself? But thinking too – 'Wop, isn't that what they call them? Just a Wop who knows how to go where the money is.' Helping himself now, choosing from the antipasto trolley, loading his plate up. A man of large appetites. *Hateful. Forget that he is Uncle Eric's son, Dick's brother, Sybil's husband. My despoiler. Am I meant to forget? Why should fifteen years make me forget, when Guy walks and talks and I cannot see him?*

Now, talking to Rocco, he was disclaiming any knowledge about drink. 'No, you choose, old chap. I'll not quarrel with your choice. And my wife here, Sybil'd maybe prefer something sweet . . .' He leaning back slightly in his chair. Rocco had asked him, in his turn, something about his business.

'Very good. It's been more than worth my while, the trip already. Not just the leads I've followed up. But others. I had a couple of 'phone calls yesterday – quite out of the blue. *Could* be very interesting.'

They talked about the sightseeing trip to follow. 'We're really excited about that. Too bad that Eddie's touring isn't going to coincide with any of ours –'

'Too bad he can't be here tonight,' Sybil said.

'He's free Sundays, I can't fix Sunday,' Rocco said. 'Sure, I miss Eddie.'

They were eating lobster when Peter asked Rocco, 'How long now since you left Italy?'

'Sicily? Fifteen now – but I'm in the States before, I'm there in Detroit eight years. Then I'm that kind of dumbo goes back to fight. Crazy, I do crazy things –'

'You'll not know much of Mussolini, then? Fascism – after your time?'

'Musso. I spit in his face. My brother he's in prison five maybe six years – he didn't do nothing. Musso sends this guy Mori, he says, "Mori, you're in charge of police – you just take them all in." Guys who hadn't done nothing – six in our village . . .'

But Peter had grown bored with that topic. Perhaps he did not want to hear about persecution, rounding up of small-town offenders. For Maria it was an unwelcome reminder of the world of Minicu, of the linen chest. Of promises, threats, revenge, executions – and secrets. Who knew what Gaetano had been up to? And Rocco too, before he left? He had got out in time.

Fascism – she winced at that. Thinking of Eddie, singing at their dances, doing cabaret at their dinners, photographed with his family, props of the London Fascist Club. ('It's the way for Momma and Poppa to get in, get on. Family first – and it's best to be in good with the Government when I sing over there.') She backed out of accompanying him, feigning illness, only going with reluctance.

Peter wanted to talk about Prohibition, about the Depression. Trying to ask questions in such a way as to show his superiority along with his ignorance.

'We had it – not on your scale, but we had it all right. Reflected in every business. It was the suddenness shook us all. Crash, bang. Bubbles have to burst – we had one in our school books, the South Sea Bubble. But bubbles don't make such a din . . . The people you knew, did a lot go broke?'

'They didn't went broke,' Rocco said, 'they went crazy. Like you pay five thousand bucks, that's stock and then it's down and it's maybe two hundred. Me, I got property – Maria's told you. Like two leases, I sell them eight times what I paid. And I got a speak – So no peoples has any dough but in my business, they got it, they wanna spend it . . .'

Sybil, leaning over, talking in a low, laughing voice to Maria. 'You know what happened today . . . A shopping expedition, Dick's children. I have to look out something for Pip and Nessie. Macy's – it's like a fairy tale. Christmas in the air already . . .'

Peter was saying, 'Well, Prohibition – after repeal, apart from having a wonderful Christmas, I expect coppersmiths were very much back in trade. Overtime, I shouldn't wonder.'

'There you go, darling,' Sybil said. 'Anything to do with metals,' she said, 'that's his first thought.'

Rocco was busy with the menu again. 'You choose ice-cream. Any ice-cream you want. You like cake? Here they have real cassata. Siciliana. You like chocolate, something with chocolate?'

'Peter – my husband, he's a sweet tooth, weakness for chocolate –'

They were half way through their ices and cake when a waiter came to their table. He spoke to Rocco, then turned to Peter. 'Excuse me, sir. You Mr *Grainger*, sir? A call for you.'

'Right,' Peter rose lazily, wiping his moustache with his napkin. 'No peace for the wicked – or for the business man. They've found me even here.' Maria felt annoyed by his obvious self-satisfaction.

'So long for the moment. When I come back I'll have perhaps – who knows, clinched the deal . . .'

She watched him walk out. Threading his way past the tables. She was glad suddenly to be just the three of them.

Peter's chocolate gâteau had been almost finished. It lay, fork in cream, waiting. Rocco pressed Maria and Sybil to eat some fruit. 'Peaches, grapes, they get them Florida, they gotta be good.' But they wouldn't. They ordered just black coffee. And liqueurs. He persuaded them to liqueurs. 'Your husband what's he gonna have? Maybe a brandy, we'll get brandy . . .'

'I'll need to leave soon,' Maria said. 'When Peter gets back. I counted on listening to Eddie.'

'Eddie sings Fridays –'

'This is recorded. It's a commercial. Not Colgate, but something like. It's this evening.'

'Peter's a long time,' Sybil said apologetically. 'I know him when he gets talking like that. But all the same . . . a dinner guest . . .'

Rocco said, 'Maybe he fixes a meeting tomorrow. Maybe he got talking.'

The coffee came. The liqueurs. Maria took out her fob watch. Checked it against the restaurant clock.

'It's *too* bad of him,' Sybil said, petulantly now. 'And when you need to get to your broadcast, Maria.'

When did annoyance, irritation, anger even, turn to worry, apprehension?

'Listen,' Rocco said. 'I'll go ask.' He crossed the room, spoke to the head waiter. When he came back, he said, 'He don't know nothing.'

'If he went in the Gents . . .' Sybil suggested. 'Perhaps he got ill in there?'

'If he got sick, they find him. I said, "You go look there, the washroom's where you look." '

Maria said, 'Had he drunk much? He didn't seem . . . Just well wined, dined, but OK –'

A waiter came across again, speaking first rapidly to Rocco, in Italian. Rocco said, 'He says he ain't nowhere in the building.' The waiter repeated to them all. 'We look everywhere. The signor walked out for fresh air –'

'Nonsense,' Sybil said sharply. 'He's not . . .' She crumpled suddenly. '*Find him*,' she said, half tearfully, half in anger. 'Find my husband at once.'

'Listen,' Rocco said consolingly. 'Listen, we look. We do our best. I'm worried, Maria here, she's worried – we do our best. Maybe we call your hotel?'

'Yes,' Sybil said, her voice rising, the beginnings of hysteria. Maria, never remembering her like this, thought it was the baby. 'Ring the hotel now. *Now*, do you hear? Room 276. Grainger. Room 276.'

By now, people at the other tables were beginning to look over to where the smartly dressed Englishwoman was pulling at her evening bag. She had pushed over her cup of coffee. It ran crazily into the white tablecloth. She began to cry noisily.

Maria, an arm around her, tried to comfort her. She wanted to tell Rocco, 'Sybil's having a baby. Be gentle.'

Rocco was doing his best, that she could see. He at least kept calm. 'It's gonna be OK. You see. We go back to the hotel. Maybe we're back – he's there.'

'Why?' Sybil cried, 'Why should he be there? What ever does he want to go off for anyway? That's not like my husband, not like Peter. He doesn't just disappear. He says where he's going.' She bit and tore at her handkerchief. 'He walked out of the door for a minute's fresh air – and under a motor. He's run over. I know he's run over –'

Rocco was getting the check, paying up. 'Hush,' Maria said to her. 'It'll be some simple explanation. You'll be laughing soon. You can tell him off. It's got to be simple. People don't just disappear into thin air.'

They spoke to the doorman on the way out. Rocco had spoken to him already. He was little help.

'. . . OK, mebbe it's him? I dunno. He was stood with a guy. They was talking . . . I never see the guy before. They sound like they're doing business. Mebbe they stepped outside. I dunno – I don't listen peoples talking business.'

Rocco whistled a cab and they went all three straight to the hotel. Nothing. No Peter. No message. Maria rang her own hotel, both to leave a message for Eddie and to make sure there was nothing there.

It was now, surely, a matter for the police. Maria, waiting in the hotel bedroom with Sybil, was full of sinister fears, haunted by a sense of *déjà vu*. Rocco insisted on staying. 'If you like, I sit downstairs. I'm in the foyer when we get news.'

The hours passed. At first the police had not been as helpful as Sybil, or Maria, would have wished. She could see, perhaps reasonably enough, their belief that he might just have disappeared for a night out. 'He'll be home with the milk, you wait.' They asked had there been any words, a quarrel at all? 'I tell the cops,' Rocco said, ' "This is a party, we're all friends, we're *happy*, for Chrissake." '

Meanwhile a Missing Persons bulletin had gone out. Sybil said, between bursts of crying, 'If we could only find out who 'phoned him. And if it *was* him – who he was speaking to outside.'

But of course no one knew. The restaurant had known nothing, why should anyone else? Sybil insisted on calling, at three in the morning, both of the firms which Peter had come over to talk to.

For one of them she was able to get the private residence of the chairman. She seemed past caring, didn't mind the angry, sleepy reply.

Eddie had joined them just before that. Rocco insisted still on remaining. Eddie seemed more frightened even than Maria, sweaty with apprehension. For once he didn't mention his evening's work, or his broadcast.

And all the while Sybil, sobbing, crying over and over:

'I want him back, where's my husband? What's happened to him? *I want to know . . .*'

She would not have wanted to know. Most of the following days were spent making sure she learned only what could not be kept from her. That he was dead.

New York City Police records told a different tale. A tale of finding 'at about 4 a.m. on 20th November 1935, in a garbage can, near Grand Central Building in 46th Street and Park Avenue, the body of Peter Grainger, male, white, British citizen, of Yorkshire England. Cause of death: gunshot wounds of left chest and neck. Body subsequently mutilated. Genitalia removed and placed in mouth.'

PART TWO

1939–1961

I

'Extraordinary,' Eleanor said, sitting in the dining-room of Park Villa, a dish of grouse surrounded by game chips and watercress before her, waiting to be carved, 'I was at the dentist's yesterday, leafing through this magazine. There must have been every trivial topic – excitement about Paris collections, even suggestions, believe it or not, for *1940* holidays abroad. But not one mention of the world crisis. Nero and fiddling, really . . . 1914 of course was different. We hadn't had it hanging over us for months on end.'

Eleanor, and her dinner guests, Dick, Gwen – and Maria. On a warm Thursday evening in the second half of August.

'Oh people know it's coming, all right,' Dick said. 'It's not been much of a Peace anyway. And God knows what's to come. Remember Lloyd George after the last do? "If this war is not the last war, the next war will leave Europe in ashes . . ."'

Gwen said, 'Dick's had his war. It's when I see these youngsters . . .'

Guy, Eleanor thought. As she thought every day now, and had done for nearly a year. Every day since Munich. (Guy, safe now, walking in France and Spain with an Oxford friend. Planning to visit his great school chum, Andrew, now in the Navy and stationed in Gibraltar.)

Be calm.

'Dick dear, perhaps you would pour out the claret?'

'As the only man present, of course, Eleanor.'

Gwen said, 'Jenny, her eldest. Her Jim. If it goes on any length of time, she'll have worries.'

Eleanor asked, 'Have you thought any more about sending Betty or Jan to Canada?'

'Betty's sixteen,' Gwen said, 'you'd never get her to go. Even if we'd want it. And Jan – she'd not want to be away from us. No, we reckon to stay on in Middlesbrough as a family. Face the worst together.'

Dick said, 'But young Peter's off. That's certain. Sybil's taking him and maybe staying on herself. Which should work quite well. A lad needs his mother. Dad even approved, which surprised me . . . Although there've been times since the tragedy when it's seemed young Peter's more of a Carstairs than a Grainger. This way he'd be with our family. After all, he is the heir.'

No, Eleanor thought. Guy is. And Eric knows it. Dick knows it too, of course. It is Maria's presence at the dinner table makes the awkwardness. Peter's firstborn, she said to herself. And put away the thought of dead Peter.

But all this talk of sons and heirs, apart from Maria's feelings, couldn't be good for Gwen. Losing her last like that. A six-months still-birth. He would have been nine by now. Too late perhaps to have tried again, if they'd had the heart?

Maria was talking. Her low, warm voice: 'You were saying about the Paris collections – but in their own way some of the dressmakers have entered into the spirit. At the risk of sounding like Eleanor's magazine – there are some really quite witty and apt names for the colour shades this season. Envy green, rage red, blackout . . . It's one way of coping, I suppose.'

'What style of clothes are they, Maria?'

Oh Gwen, who cares nothing for fashion, wearing tonight her serviceable dark red satin, four years old at least. Maria in a dinner dress of black silk crêpe, with black patent leather belt.

To have Maria here at all is strange. The last time she was in Thackton was that dreadful day she turned up, suddenly, asking to see Guy. Thirteen years ago, and how many changes since. Not least, Eddie Sabrini. Maria, sadly marrying outside the Church. (But back again now, with the death of Eddie's first wife in a car crash.) I should have been shocked by it all but was only saddened. I had so wished her married. I had so wished a child for her.

And now here she sits, at my table, with my guests, Dick and Gwen. We have not asked any one else to make up the numbers. We prefer just to be ourselves. Family (for that is how I think of us.)

And as a family we have seen too many deaths this last decade. Maimie Grainger three years ago. A liver complaint. Dulcie a devoted nurse. I wondered afterwards what the position would be *vis à vis* Eric. But she has taken the Rowland inheritance – she came into Maimie's share – and begun at last to enjoy herself. Although she hasn't visited Canada. ('I wouldn't trust myself, dearest.') Now she is away on a P & O cruise to the Azores. We shan't see her till early September. Her third cruise this year. Perhaps she will meet a husband. Who knows? Although it's too late for me (perhaps it always was?), for someone like Dulcie it is *never* too late.

Mother. How sad that I was glad when she went. Eighty-five and unpleasant to the last. I waited for twinges of conscience. But none came. I searched my heart for one good thing she had done or said for or to me. None.

But oh, the worst of all, the year before Maimie went (and was her illness precipitated by it?), the terrible death of Peter. Even now I don't trust myself to think about it . . . Dick rushing over there on the *Queen Mary*. The fear that Sybil, in a state of shock for so long, would lose the child – all she had left of Peter. The details that we never learned (and that I did not wish to know). A savage death. Peter obviously mistaken for some other person, in a gangland killing – gone wrong. Everything shrouded in a veil not only of horror but of mystery. Eric made enough fuss both sides of the Atlantic, but to no avail. All investigations came to a dead end. The police, swearing they had done all they could. (No one ever traced that mysterious telephone call.) Didn't he perhaps step out for fresh air – and get mistaken for someone else? (And yet, how very un-American he must have looked.)

She had felt safe to invite Maria tonight. For Maria to be in Thackton at all was a great step forward. It had been, as ever, Dick's idea. Dick and Gwen with whom she so often stayed in Middlesbrough. Now they had brought her over with them. Eddie was in Holland, at the Kurhaus in Scheveningen, after six weeks at Butlin's in Filey. Maria for some reason had not wanted to join him abroad and had proposed herself to Gwen and Dick. No Uncle Eric at Thackton, he was fishing in Scotland, Guy safely abroad – it was all right.

The grouse were finished. Summer pudding now, from home grown raspberries, served on the gold lustre dish bought for her by Guy, as a thank-you for the Grand Tour of 1937.

And what an adventure that had been. Eleanor, Basil, Guy. An odd trio. Eight weeks abroad. She had worried in Florence that he might want to make investigations about his origins, imagining him disappearing off on his own, perhaps visiting orphanages. But 'Which orphanage?' he had asked only, and that quite casually. 'It's gone now,' she said, pointing in the direction of some new buildings. She wondered if she should say it had been burned down, records destroyed . . . Eight weeks abroad: France, Switzerland, down through Italy – the Naples area for a fortnight – but stopping short of Sicily. Basil's decision. But she had gone along with it, and Guy had not commented.

Greta, his little black lurcher, had died while they were touring. She had not been sorry to see her go – badly disciplined as she was, stealing food, leaping on to visitors' laps. Yet so much loved, his cherished companion in holidays from St Boniface's. Homesick, unhappy little boy: if it hadn't been for Basil's firmness and, she supposed, Eric's (the Graingers after all were paying), she would have removed him – to where?

Maria was saying, 'I see there've been changes at the sweet shop. I know it's a long time but –'

Eleanor said, 'Old Mrs Armthwaite? She decided to go and live with her son in Goathland – after all, she's over eighty . . . Some townees as they call them have bought the place. They're from the Midlands and wanted to be safe from the bombing. They seem kind enough. But of course it isn't the same.'

'The old order changeth,' Dick said.

Eleanor said, 'I shall be taking evacuees. A mother and child. There's room here. The villages around will all turn up trumps, as they did with the Belgians in the last war.'

Summer pudding was succeeded by a savoury, Dick's favourite, Scotch woodcock. Mounds of scrambled egg topped with anchovies. Dick attacked his.

Outside, two sharp rings of the bell.

'It's all right,' she said. 'Mrs Brown will see to it.'

'A fine time to call,' Dick said. 'Ten o'clock. You've maybe got wardens seeing about light-proofed windows already. There's some can't wait to be in charge over lesser mortals.'

Then the door opened. Oh happiness, (oh complications). There, travel-stained, tweed jacket rubbed at elbows, flannels muddy – but smiling, was Guy.

'What a surprise! What are *you* doing here?'

'Just being a sensible chap. Hurrying back to England. I should have wired but I got on a boat in a rush, and then raced over to King's Cross to get the afternoon train. But it's rather *nice* surprising you all . . . Hallo, Gwen, hallo, Dick. And – Maria, is it? Mrs Sabrini. Maria. Everyone's always talking about you, and yet we've never met. A fellow Italian . . . Anyway, how do you do? You're very charming . . .'

Eleanor, asking him hurriedly now, if everything had gone all right. And Guy shaking his head: 'Aunt Eleanor, it wasn't a patch on our Grand Tour, or last year's trip. To begin with I couldn't get on with my fellow hiker –'

'But Andy – you managed to see him?'

'Oh, that was a great success. He almost fired me to join the Wavy Navy. I shall have to join something, soon enough.'

'Come and join us,' Dick said. 'We're eating well.'

'Oh, look, Scotch woodcock. Any for me? Just let me have a quick wash and brush up and I'll scoff all the leftovers. Grouse? I'm game . . .'

Sacru miu Gesù, that this should happen. The one thing they all of them wished to avoid. (And yet so obvious, with a war scare. He's not the only one to cut short a holiday.)

So this is Guy. So this is my son. Of course I've seen photographs – by accident and by design. It would have been impossible to hide them from me totally. Groups of family and friends, in Dick and Gwen's album. Guy at every age (at the age when, trembling, I stood here in Park Villa and *begged* for a glimpse of him). But none of that prepares me, has prepared me, for Guy in the flesh. My son in the flesh.

He is not so very tall, but not small either. And his hair grows thick but is already receding a little – that is Uncle Eric. He has something of a Verzotto face. Large brown heavy-lidded eyes – there is no doubt he looks more Italian than English. Yet his manner – Ah, this is terrible, that we should meet like this, that *he doesn't know*. Soon we shall be making small talk about the world of dance music. 'What's it like being married to a famous crooner?' he will ask. And I will say . . .

I don't want to think about all that life. Eddie and his infidelities. And his love for me, in spite of all. Eddie, whose career has never been right since he left America. Upset, running scared, when none of it had anything to do with him. He should have stayed where he was doing well. Over here, things have never really picked up again.

But just to think of Eddie and me in New York is to bring it all back. Those terrible, terrible days. Sitting with Syb in the hospital, willing her not to lose the child. Hearing the details from the police and keeping them to myself. Waiting for Dick, dear Dick, to arrive.

I didn't want to see Rocco, to have anything to do with him.

217

I did not want to know what I knew. But we had still to see each other. I could say nothing. He said nothing. His only comment – I remember we were going up in the elevator together. He wasn't looking at me. He said in Sicilian, 'Listen, Maria, I don't know anything about a baby, no one tells Rocco about a baby, eh?' Then was silent. Yet he could not have been more generous, more helpful. It was he who paid for everything – Sybil's hospital stay, the room a bower of flowers – it was he who organized the funeral as discreetly as possible. But I knew what I knew . . . And wished I did not.

My terrible guilt. Guilt that I shall always carry (yet another secret I must keep to myself). Guilt that came over me that day when I went to see about Sybil's passage back to England. Altering her steamship ticket, arranging for her to return with Dick.

The Cunard building in Broadway. That great hall with its domed ceiling, its maps of their sea routes for decoration: and in the centre, sea gods in clouds of foam, dolphins, cherubs. (Myself, in the dining-room of the *Lusy.* I gaze up at the cherubs on the ceiling, while the band plays *The Blue Danube.* Soon, very soon the *Lusy* will sink. Mamma will die. And all the Ricciardis. Uncle Eric will save me.)

Standing there, amidst reminders of Cunard liners, reminders of the *Lusy,* I was overcome with terror – and certain of my guilt. How I hated Peter. Had I not hated and hated him, with a slow burning rage? I knew I was guilty, as surely as Rocco. That saying of my childhood – 'Revenge is a dish best eaten cold.' Without my hate, could it ever have happened?

And now, Guy, Peter's son, sitting opposite me. Glass of claret, plate of summer pudding. Raspberries, their juice running dark red like blood.

A war to come. Guy in it, and perhaps lost. *How can I lose what I never had?* Has he not been lost to *me* since Florence? And yet, *sacru miu Gesù,* a war. He may go to his grave and never know he was mine.

'. . . *Anyway, how do you do? You're very charming . . .*'

2

The train stopped. A porter called out, 'Thackton-le-Moors, Thackton-le-Moors.' Three women in green uniform were standing on the platform. Miss Fairlie, the teacher, came by with her list, 'It's out here for you two,' she said to Helen and Billy.

The label pinned to Helen's coat was in indelible ink, in case it rained and her name was washed away. Helen Connors – as if she didn't know her own name. Like a parcel being posted. But it was because she might be hurt by bombs and not be able to speak. Bombs were the reason too, why they'd had to rehearse *every* morning this week, behaving just like the real thing (kissing Mam goodbye five times – oh, it had been terrible), so that the Germans wouldn't know which day they were moving.

There was a coach outside. One of the women said to Helen kindly, 'Not far, dear. Just up the hill to the school hall.' It seemed the train had run late and everything was now behind. The hall was full of people besides the ladies in green, who were the WVS, the Women's Voluntary Service.

They were handed round mugs of tea and there were trays of buns with currants sticking out. When a woman carrying one came by, Helen stood on tip toe and whispered, 'Our Billy's dirtied hisself,' but the lady only said, 'The toilet's are over there, dear.'

She couldn't take him in the girls', and she couldn't go in the boys'. In the end she went in the girls' and stood with her foot against the door which didn't lock. Billy was crying. She cleaned him up as best she could, stuffing his pants down behind the pipe together with his trousers. She made him put on his spare pair.

When she got back, a WVS lady was calling out names.

'Mr and Mrs Phillips would like a nice little boy, who'd like to go with Mr and Mrs Phillips? Over here – a nice little boy . . .'

A tall grey-haired lady with a long, heavy but kindly face stood not far from Helen and Billy. The WVS lady said, 'Miss Dennison is a Roman Catholic. And she would like –'

Dear Our Lady, Helen prayed, Please let her like *us*.

'. . . a mother and child. Is there a Catholic mother and child to live with Miss Dennison, at Park Villa?'

Yes, there was: a woman Helen had seen smoking on the train, whose small boy kept rubbing his chocolate-covered face against his mother's dress.

Gradually more and more children were collected and taken away. The hall grew emptier and emptier. Helen knew that often they were being turned down simply because there were two of them. Then the dreadful moment came when no one was left, just one lady in green – and Helen and Billy. She could smell Billy. He had started to snivel. She smacked his hand, 'Our Billy, don't.'

Then she wished she hadn't. How could she? When she'd promised Mam she'd love and look after him, *whatever*. She wanted to cry herself too now. This last week had been the most terrible she'd known. *There was going to be a war*, and she might never see Mam again. It felt now like the whole of her life, not just a week, since she'd sat on the bench at St Aidan's, and listened to Father Casey.

Father Casey, with his long black cassock and his shiny bald head, standing in the middle of the classroom:

'Your mammies and daddies will have told you why you're at school on a Saturday. The President of Poland and Mr Roosevelt have appealed to Herr Hitler to find some way of avoiding this dreadful war. Meantime we must be prepared, so I've come together with your teachers to tell you about the rehearsal on Monday for Evacuation. You will be told what to bring, what to wear . . . Then after that, we shall with Almighty God's blessing, do a normal day's lessons.'

It was hot and stuffy in the classroom even though two of the windows at the back had been opened. Smelly too. Dried ink and chalk and the brown paper that covered their exercise books. And people: Ronnie Tibbs on the same bench, was always blowing off. The silent ones were worst. If she said anything, 'It's *you*,' he'd tell her. Then he'd whisper to the row behind, 'Helen Connors farted again.'

The room was divided in two by blackboards. On the other side were the eight-year-olds and upwards – the Big Wans. Helen was in the five to sevens. Three rows in front, she could see her brother Billy. They'd let him start school early, because of Mam being ill and their having to live with Auntie Winnie and Uncle

Arnold. Father Casey had been really kind, Mam said. Except that they hadn't reckoned with Billy not being dry. Wet every night and much worse since Mam came out of hospital, wet at school every day.

'Miss Creedon will tell you about packed food,' Father Casey said. 'Enough for two meals, and *do not forget your gasmasks.* We shall write out our own labels this afternoon and thank Almighty God for a day well spent.'

Long, long hot day. She yawned all afternoon. Billy had his hands between his legs – she was afraid the priest would notice and say something dreadful about him touching himself. She knew he wanted to wet. She willed him, 'Billy put your hand up,' But nothing happened, so she called out, 'Please, Father, Billy Connors wants to leave the room.' The others laughed and she went red. Ronnie Tibbs blew off. He smelled of cabbage both ends. She was glad he wasn't her brother.

There were just the two of them, Helen and Billy. And Mam, of course. Her dad – she couldn't remember. He'd been a steeplejack and died in an accident. When Mam was brought the news, it made Billy be born early. She thought she remembered Dad at the top of a very high building, in some town she didn't know. Standing and waving his arms about. But Mam said that couldn't be. The other memory was sad because there was so little of it. A door slammed, there were footsteps, someone said, 'It's her dad's in.' She ran to the arms of someone with scratchy clothes and a red friendly face. And then – nothing.

Until last year she'd at least had Mam. Until the illness. TB they called it – in her mind it joined with RI and PT. Auntie Winnie never spoke of Mam's TB. She called it always 'Your Mam's complaint', which puzzled Helen. Complaining meant making a fuss and that was the one thing Mam never did. 'I'm sorry, pet,' she'd say to Helen, 'I'm a nuisance to everyone with me blasted cough.'

Her cousins were all older. Frank was sixteen and had already gone to sea. Alan and Leslie, eleven and thirteen. Valerie was ten and though she went to the Elementary School down the road, Mam explained that she hadn't been given everything she should ('God kept some back, you see'), so she didn't always understand when she was spoken to. Helen had to share a bed with her. There was a real crush in the flat, which was a two-bedroomed council one. Auntie and Uncle had one room. In the other there was a double bed for Alan and Leslie and a truckle-bed which Helen and Valerie were squashed into. Billy was meant to be the third in Alan and Leslie's bed but because he wet, he had a mattress made up underneath. It was terribly cramped – you could see the springs sagging right down when Alan and Leslie jumped in.

And then just two days ago, Mam had been turned out of the hospital because they'd need the beds when the war started. So it was back to her sleeping in the living-room, only now she was in bed for most of the time, and Auntie said it was really embarrassing when visitors called, having to explain that an invalid was behind the cardboard screen Dr Atkinson had got for them.

'When will you get better, Mam?' She didn't like to keep asking, especially as Mam seemed to be getting worse. She had this horrible little dish she had to spit into. Even though it was kept covered up, sometimes Helen saw into it. 'Don't,' Mam said, 'don't look. I can't help it, you see. If it wasn't for you and Billy . . . I'm just a nuisance to everyone. I wish God would take me, I do, Helen.' Helen asked, 'If He taked you, will that make you better?' 'Of course,' Mam said.

Mam didn't eat much, although sometimes she would say she was hungry. 'I could eat a carthorse,' she'd say, but then when Helen had asked Auntie, and brought her a plate of bacon scraps or some nice black pudding, after perhaps only two mouthfuls she'd say she'd no space for anything, and Alan or Leslie could have it. But Auntie said none of the family was to eat anything Mam had touched. Mam had her own glass, knife, fork, spoon and plate. To Helen it was all a frightening fuss, especially as half the time the family didn't use knives and forks at all. Meals were often just bread and marge or a bit of bacon dripping, or send out for a chip supper, with fish if they were lucky. When they did sit down to eat, the tablecloth was the *Northern Echo* or the *News of the World*.

Mam had always used red and white check cloths which she boiled up in the copper on washday. In those days, when Helen and Billy still lived with Mam, because Mam worked there'd been enough to give Helen some pocket money. Now there was none. Mam whispered, 'You understand – I've to ask Winnie for everything I need. And what the Council gives, that's for her. It's only right, when she's taken us in.'

Of course it was right. Except that once upon a time she had had one whole penny every Saturday. It bought her a Milky Way bar which, if she ate it sliced up, lasted as much as four days. Sometimes she spent it on misshapen sweets sold cheap: liquorice wrongly twisted, sugar mice without heads, a flattened Palm Toffee bar. She longed for sweets now with a dreadful longing.

'And now,' Father Casey was saying, 'let us finish with a Hail Mary. Hands together, please. *Hail Mary, full of grace . . .*'

She had said her night prayers and was trying to sleep. As she lay there, a train hurtled by. The whole building shook. Perhaps this was what the raids would be like?

Dear Our Lady, don't let there be a war. She prayed to Our Lady because she was RC. Roman Catholic. Alan and Leslie called her and Mam 'Roman Candles' (they didn't call Billy anything except 'Pisspot' – he wasn't just rotting the mattress, they said, but the floorboards too: in the morning, they held their noses before jumping out of bed). She didn't have Sunday school like Valerie, but two evenings a week after school. There had been extra teaching this summer because of making her First Confession and Communion. She had a lot of Catechism to learn.

'Helen Connors, what is Grace?' (*Who* is Grace? she'd thought. Grace Swarbrick was in the same class, and had impetigo and nits worse than Helen's. And ringworm and all her hair shaved off last summer.)

Helen went to Mass each Sunday, because she'd promised Mam when Mam was taken into hospital that she'd go whatever. She quite liked it once she was there. No Alan and Leslie to tease her, no Valerie to throw tantrums, no tellings-off. Afterwards she always visited the statue of Our Lady in the little chapel. It was surrounded by a circle of flickering candles. They cost a halfpenny or a penny depending on the size. Helen had no money for one unless she kept back her collection penny, but she always lit one for Mam to get better *soon*, and hoped no one would see and tell on her. Our Lady had long dark hair to her shoulders, roses in her cheeks, a half-smile on her face, and a long white dress which flowed over her body, with a pale blue sash. Mary, Queen of Heaven, standing with her arms open as if to love and hug all the world.

Sometimes she took a bottle with her to fill with holy water for the pink china stoup which hung by Mam's makeshift bed. They splashed themselves with it night and morning. But the most precious water was the Lourdes water Father Casey had given Mam. (If you couldn't go to Lourdes, you could use the water, and you might still be cured.)

It had been a horrid day at school. The only thing she was good at was sums. Fifty-four divide by six, eighty-one divide by nine. Her hand shot up. But writing out the sums was difficult – the nib was scratchy and split open, leaving great blobs of black ink. She was always spoiling her copybook too. Father Casey, when he inspected, held hers up: 'Here's someone should be ashamed . . .' Two pages of proverbs to practise joined-up letters: 'The fox may grow grey but never good. Life is not all beer and skittles . . .'

Another train hurtled by. She was certain Mam must be lying awake. She wanted to go to her but had promised not to. Billy whimpered in his sleep. Leslie snored steadily. Other noises too, and smells. Valerie beside her was damp with sweat.

A rattling sound: the last tram clanking its way to the terminus. Soon it would pass the gasworks, then the stretch of canal where dead rats floated bellies upwards. She counted the parish church clock: ten, eleven, twelve. She knew she would never sleep.

She got out of bed. Quietly – warm feet on the gritty linoleum, hand ever so gently on the door knob.

'Mam, Mam – it's me, I heard you cough. Mam, can I come in?'

It was all right, after Mam had protested and told her off ('Whatever will Winnie say?') She sat on the floor beside the camp bed, pulling her skimpy nightgown over her knees. The screen was folded back at night, and Mam had a nightlight in a saucer. It had a peculiar smell – something to do with her medicine.

'Can I turn big light on? Mam, can I do yer medicine for you?'

Mam's voice was thin and croaky, and trying to be angry. 'Helen, pet, you oughtn't – why didn't you fetch your coat in with you, pet?'

'But it's hot – that's why I couldn't sleep. Mam, Father Casey says we're to be *vackies* . . . But we'll not have to go, say we'll not have to, Mam.' Her voice came out like crying. She *was* crying. It was all terrible. Perhaps on Monday when they had the practice, it would turn out to be the real thing and they'd all go – without saying goodbye.

'What if I don't go, Mam? What'd they do if I don't go, Mam?'

'Pet, we've all to do as we're told –'

Mam was coughing and coughing. Helen thought she'd never

stop. There was the bitter-sweet smell of Mam's medicine, and then the disinfectant smell that Alan and Leslie were rude about.

'Where'll they send us? They've not said where they'll send us –'

'They'll have it arranged, pet. You'll be somewhere nice, with cows and sheep and green grass –'

'I don't want cows and sheep, silly daft things. I want you, Mam, why can't you come too? You'll come and see us, promise, Mam?'

'Pet, I can't promise – not when I'm so poorly, like. I'll write. Winnie'll help me. Or one of the lads.'

'They're away too. They're going with their school.'

'I forgot. Well, I forgot,' Mam said in a small voice. And then she too was crying.

'Mam, I'd like to sing for you, *Someday my prince will come*. I do it really well, don't I? Only it'd wake up Auntie. And, and . . .' She had her arms tight round Mam. She could hardly bear the boniness of Mam's shoulders, jagged points through the thin nightie.

'Now you must go back, pet . . .'

The train was very crowded. Alan and Leslie's school had joined the same party. Most of the children had their parents to wave them off, and hug them tight before the train left. Helen and Billy had had what was left of Uncle and Auntie's love, which wasn't much. Mam had spoken of coming to the station but Auntie Winnie had said angrily, 'And if you give yourself a turn, who's to look after you, Evelyn? Answer that now.'

Billy pulled at her best brown coat, his face pinched and white. She whispered gently, 'Billy, you want the lav?' but he shook his head. She knew he was upset like she was, but there was nothing to do about it. It wasn't the sort of pain that crying helped.

There was a lot of running about and horse play, though St Aidan's was very well behaved. Father Casey saw to that. There was one little girl in a blue coat with a velvet collar and a velvet-covered hair slide to match. She was clutching a soft toy, a Bambi deer, with lovely big eyes and white spots dusted on its back. She looked all the time as if she had a bad pong under her nose. Helen christened her Ermintrude after the heroine in a story they'd had read to them.

A lot of people were eating: pieces of orange peel lay under the seats and their smell was mixed with the sooty train smell. Helen stopped Billy from opening their parcel. What'd they do if their sandwiches were gone and they were still miles away?

Both her and Billy's belongings had fitted into one small suitcase. Their gasmasks were in cardboard boxes. When they'd practised with them at school, there was the smell and taste of rubber and the misting up of the celluloid eyeshield, but worst of all the rude noise it made every time you breathed out. The Big Wans got the giggles but Helen was ashamed and wanted it to stop.

They would be for ever in the train. Still, no one knew where they were going. Miss Creedon and Miss Fairlie came round the carriages to see they were all right. Out in the corridor some boys sang *The Lambeth Walk*. Helen waited each time for the OY! Yesterday she'd sung *Little Sir Echo* for Mam as a goodbye present. Her voice was really good, Mam said, but Alan and Leslie put their hands over their ears. They said it was like an air raid siren.

The train, blowing steam, whistling, rushed into a tunnel. Darkness suddenly. Helen's arms went round Billy. From the corner seat came high-pitched screams: Ermintrude. When at last they came out blinking into daylight, she was still screaming, her face all scrunched up. The velvety Bambi on the floor with the orange peel. Miss Fairlie rushed in and even though Ermintrude wasn't a St Aidan's child, she slapped her face hard. The noise stopped at once.

The food was all gone and Helen and Billy panting with thirst (she'd finished their water bottle), when the train stopped and a porter called out, 'Middlesbrough, Middlesbrough!' Motor-coaches were waiting for some of them. She caught a glimpse of Alan and Leslie going off.

They changed trains now. Ermintrude, clutching Bambi, was one of those in the new one, which was small and without a corridor. Helen knew at once that Billy should have gone to the lav. 'You can't now,' she hissed. He whispered that he wanted Number Two. 'You *can't*.'

The view out of the window was nothing like home. Great hills covered in purple, green fields, woods. The train kept stopping. Each time a group would be called out. It was after the third or fourth station that Billy had his accident. Helen thought she would die of shame. Oh dear Our Lady help us, the smell was dreadful. The two boys sitting near, she knew they knew. In the end one of them spoke up. 'He's messed his pants, dirty beggar.'

In the empty school hall the WVS lady, who was called Mrs Carter, said, 'Helen is it?' peering down at the label. 'Helen then, and Billy, come with me.'

Outside, they crossed the road, then after a little stopped at a shop, its window full of sweets in tall jars. Helen thought: She's going to buy us a bit of toffee or something. She pulled at the lady's sleeve: 'Our Billy likes jelly babies, and I'm not fussed.'

Behind the counter was a small woman with tight corkscrew curls, an upturned nose and large spectacles. When she saw the WVS lady, she put her hand to her mouth.

'Oh my, we never come down, did we? Father's away to Doncaster for supplies. It went right out of my mind –'

'You said you'd take in a child, Mrs Bolton. Here's little Helen Connors. But Helen must stay with her brother.'

Mrs Bolton, leaning over the counter, picked up a Mars Bar and handed it to Helen. 'There you are, love . . . I expect we can, Mrs Carter. We've the room spare.'

Mrs Carter explained about being RC, but it didn't seem to matter. 'I'm used to those,' Mrs Bolton said, 'I'd a sister turned.'

'A sweet shop, isn't that nice now?' Mrs Carter said to Helen. 'The others will be envious.' She checked then that Helen had her stamped postcard, ready to write to Mam her new address. 'You can write, dear?'

'I'll help her,' Mrs Bolton said, her mouth full of liquorice allsorts. She had just passed some to Billy.

'Our Billy doesn't eat them ones,' Helen said. 'Thanks, missus.'

'Auntie Hilda, love. You've to call me Auntie Hilda. And now, let's shut up the shop, and make ourselves a nice tea.'

At first it was all right. Or would have been if she hadn't been homesick and worried about Mam. Every day she hoped for a card or letter, but in the end when one came – with Mam's 'capitals' writing on it because she'd never learned joined-up – it only said that Mam missed her and Billy a lot and was glad they were with nice kind people.

The first evening Auntie Hilda had given them a big meat tea. The next day the same, and the next. The table groaned with food. Oatmeal porridge with thick cream, bacon, eggs, fresh new bread, roast lamb with mint sauce, apple pie, gingerbread parkin, curd tart, treacle tart, griddle scones dripping with butter. Cream and more cream. She had never in her life seen so much food, let alone *eaten* it.

And it wasn't just Auntie Hilda feeding them up. Mr Bolton (Uncle Jack she was to call him) told Helen she was 'very small for seven years old', and needed a bit of fat on her bones. He himself was plump like his wife and had a small sticking-out stomach. He squeezed her hard to him, which she didn't much like, and breathed tobacco on her.

She saw some of the other vackies when school started a week or so later. There must have been some mix-up because she could see no one from St Aidan's. From what she heard, some vackies hadn't been nearly so lucky. One girl said she'd had a little saucer of cold baked beans to her tea, with the rest of the family eating thick slices of ham. Another had no furniture in her room, and her clothes on a nail which she had had to put up herself. Helen had a lovely little wardrobe with transfers of Snow White and the Dwarfs which Uncle Jack had stuck on for her. She'd hardly any clothes to put in it, but Auntie Hilda was taking her into Whitby to buy some.

Ermintrude was very unhappy. Her real name was Audrey, Helen learned. She cried almost every day, and when not doing that, she would stamp her foot and look haughty. She said the work in class was too easy. One day she had hysterics just like when the train had gone through the tunnel. This time she had cold water thrown on her. Another time the Vicar came into the schoolroom and he and the teacher pointed to Ermintrude and spoke in hushed voices.

Helen asked her one day, 'How's Bambi? Why don't you fetch him to school?' But Ermintrude just stared hard at Helen and said, 'Mind your own business, you horrid little girl.'

School would have been all right if it hadn't been for the crowding, all the desks pushed much too close together, and the difficulties between the vackies and the village children. Helen didn't really know any of them and would like to have belonged to the village group.

As well as all the food, there were the sweets. Auntie Hilda and Uncle Jack both said, 'Help yourselves, love.' Helen had to keep a rein on Billy who didn't know when to stop. To begin with, Helen ate and ate. She seemed to have endless space to fill. Whenever the pain began about wanting Mam, she would cram her mouth full of nut toffees and chew and chew it all away.

Uncle Jack encouraged her. 'Puppies need to be nice and podgy. Eat up.' But she never got any fatter. The village boys, in and out of school, called her 'Skinny-stick'. 'Skinny-stick, skinny-stick!' they would shout during sliding games, sliding into her deliberately when she stood with a group of the other girls.

Auntie Hilda said how they'd always wanted children but God hadn't sent any. She cuddled Billy a lot and called him 'lollipop', and 'peppermint candy', so that he became quite cocky sometimes. Like Helen, he was allowed as many sweets as he wanted. But it was her task to clean him up, both ends – Auntie Hilda made that clear the first days. 'If you did it at home, love, you can do it here. We don't want any mess, do we?' There was a young girl called Doreen who came in to do the washing: she had to see to the sheets each day.

Billy was filling out. Auntie Hilda complimented him on being 'a bonny boy – if only he didn't wet . . .' But after tea and before bed he'd drink cup after cup of Eiffel Tower lemonade, stirring it as he drank, the bright yellow grains still undissolved. Helen felt saturated in shame for him. She never thought if she loved him. He was just Billy. She looked after him, but it was for Mam she did it.

She tried not to worry about Mam but it was difficult. No news could mean anything, but oh, how she wanted to know if Mam was stronger, and what the hospital had said. Above all, she wanted to *see* Mam.

On Saturdays now she sometimes helped Uncle Jack in the shop while Auntie Hilda went to have her hair done, in tight corkscrew curls. Then they'd have a fish tea and she and Billy would go up to bed while Uncle and Auntie listened downstairs to the wireless.

Nothing much seemed to be happening with the war. No bombs falling on big cities. Every night she prayed, Our Father, Hail Mary, Glory Be. She'd have liked her First Communion rosary she'd left behind, but didn't want to ask Mam for it. She knelt beside her bed in the warm room above the shop. 'Dear Our Lady, make me a good lass and Billy dry and make Mam well again and send me a Bambi like Ermintrude's.'

She half woke. Saturday night. She felt a hand on her shoulder. It was Auntie Hilda in her blue dressing-gown, her hair net on, holding a torch. Helen blinked.

'Up with you. Get up and come along. Father wants to speak to you.'

'What's that?' she asked sleepily.

'I told him – how naughty you've been.'

'But I haven't, I never did,' she said, sitting up now.

'That's as may be. Quick now. He's something to say to you.'

'I want to go to sleep. It's bedtime.'

'And after all we've done for you . . . Come along. Up with you.'

She followed Auntie Hilda. In the bedroom, the lights were on over both their beds. Uncle was sitting up in striped green pyjamas. 'Well,' he said. 'Come over here, lass.'

'What have I done?' she asked. 'You'll not say what I've done.'

'It's not what folk do,' Auntie said, 'it's what they are. You're a naughty girl, Father says.'

'That's right,' Uncle said. 'Naughty. And what happens to naughty girls, eh?' He smiled at her. She didn't answer. Auntie said, 'They get smacked, don't they?'

'That's right,' Uncle said. 'Lie down like a good lass. Lie on Mother's bed, there.'

She climbed up fearfully. Puzzled. Afraid. Perhaps it was a dream. I'm in the middle of a bad dream.

'No, on your tummy, love. It's your bum gets smacked. Where's the hairbrush, Mother?'

'Don't,' she said into the pillow. 'I didn't – I never did –'

'Hush, will you,' Auntie said sharply. 'You do what you're told.'

She lay there shaking in her thin nightgown, though the room with its electric bar fire was quite warm. Auntie held the brush. It came down, bristles up, on to her flesh. She heard Uncle say twice, 'That's right, aye, well done.'

And then it was over. She felt Auntie's hand then on the back of her head. 'Lie still. No moving now, lass.'

She pressed her head into the pillow, biting her cheek by mistake. She spoke up:

'Can I have my bum covered, then?'

'Hush,' Auntie said irritably.

'I weren't naughty. I cleaned Billy up. And I never cheeked.'

'Don't back answer, you'll put Father off –'

Uncle was still in bed. She thought she heard Auntie climbing in too. They were making a great noise. She wondered if Uncle was going to have a coughing attack. All that groaning and Auntie saying, 'Quick now, while it's up.' She remembered about coughs and mucky stuff. Mucky stuff – you had to get mucky stuff up. But then the groaning and grunting was more like someone in pain. She supposed Auntie was looking after him – but if they'd to send for the doctor and she was found in here with her bum uncovered? Saliva filled her mouth. *I don't want to be sick.* Please Our Lady Jesus Mary Joseph. There'd be dribble stains on the pink pillow as it was.

Auntie's hand on her head again. 'Back to bed with you, lass.' She heard the bedside light go off. The room was almost dark, just the light of Auntie's torch. 'You were a good lass, taking your punishment like that.'

Her legs were all shaky. 'But what did I do, I never –'

'And what's more,' Auntie was saying, 'we've never to speak of this, eh? To *any folk*. You got that? You know about secrets. It's best a secret . . .'

Our Lady, Jesus, oh Mam, as if I'd tell . . . I'd be ashamed, she thought. And anyway, hadn't Father Casey told them they were going to new Mams and Dads that Almighty God had chosen for them? You *had* to do what they said.

But as she crept back into bed, she shivered uncontrollably. After a few moments she began to cry. Oh Mam, Mam. Mam who was ill and might need Helen. But not now, tonight, as much as Helen needed her.

Sunday morning. And there was Miss Dennison in the car with her evacuee Rosie, waiting to take her and Billy over to Egton to church. Auntie her usual bustling self, making a fuss about Helen fasting ('It's not right, going out on an empty stomach'), slipping a Milky Way into her pocket to eat on the way back. Last night might never have happened. *Except it did.*

The brown church. Candles burning. She had money to light one for Mam. The priest, and words she couldn't understand. *Introibo ad altarem Dei.* Going up to the Communion rail with Miss Dennison, sticking her tongue out, hoping there'd be no dribble. Remembering her face pressed into the pillow, her mouth filling and oozing, bitter, frightened.

As she watched Miss Dennison, with her pale kind face, she wanted to tell her – but how could she with Rosie there? And anyway mightn't Miss Dennison think *she'd made it up*? Worst of all, she might tell Auntie Hilda and give away that Helen had talked. And then, what then?

Auntie Hilda took her into Whitby and bought her a kilt, red and green tartan, hanging from a white bodice. Like one that Ermintrude wore. 'That's for being a good girl,' she said.

The weather had changed. The ice-cold school milk, sucked through a straw from the bottle, sent shafts of pain through the roof of her mouth. Cold raw mornings, going out full of porridge and bacon and fried bread but still cold inside, wondering if this Saturday if would happen again. Coming out of school, she would meet often a misty damp in the darkening sky. Beneath lowering clouds, the moors looked strange and frightening.

At school Billy clung to her. She didn't seem able to move without him at her elbow. It was difficult to tell if he was unhappy – he never talked of Mam, or of home at all. She wanted to be angry but couldn't because of Mam and her promise. Auntie Hilda and Uncle Jack didn't even like her telling him off for drinking at night or for eating too many sweets. 'You're too hard on the little lad . . . And the other thing – he can't help it, can he?'

Auntie told him to fill his pockets with sweeties before school. 'There's no sense in going hungry . . .' But he kept them all to himself. You could see his pockets bulging with wrapped toffees and shiny glacier mints. The older boys would rob him of them, holding him down, and dipping their hands in, pulling out the lining to his pockets. Then she'd hear him cry, 'Our Helen, they've took my goodies –' A thin screech, 'Our Helen!' Tears running down his sticky face. And there'd be nothing to do but to rush in, all flying fists. Defending Billy. Sometimes there'd be such a fight that it took Miss Garner, the teacher, to come in and stop it. Because she didn't know who'd started it, Helen would get punished along with the others.

She couldn't tell on them, though. Just as she couldn't tell on Auntie and Uncle. Oh, how she wanted to tell *someone*. She had come to dread Saturdays so, especially as she never knew before she went to bed if it was going to happen. Once there were three Saturdays in a row without it. She thought perhaps it was all over. Only it wasn't. The next time it was worse. Auntie hit harder. She said Uncle had told her to. 'He needs it,' she explained, 'he says I've to give you a real clout, so as he can hear – don't you, Father?'

Only three weeks to Christmas now. Some of the children had been visited by their families several times already. Helen hadn't expected that. Mam couldn't travel. Now a lot of them simply stopped being vackies and went home. Ermintrude had already left. Instead the Vicar had two little girls who'd been unhappy at their first billet. Helen wished he'd offered to take her and Billy – but a Vicar couldn't take RC children.

The war was still quite quiet. Miss Dennison called it the Bore War, and Auntie Hilda the Phoney War. Helen wrote home and asked if she could come for Christmas, or best of all, could she come home for good? Auntie Winnie wrote back saying Mam wasn't well enough to write anything, even printing, and as for her and Uncle Arnold, they'd Alan and Leslie and Valerie to visit, and couldn't hardly be in two places at once. 'So no more talking about coming back, Mr Hitler has plenty up his sleeve, your best where you are . . .'

She tried to be brave. Two weeks before Christmas she was told to write to Santa Claus, telling him what she wanted. She wrote: 'A Bambi to cuddle. A party frock.' She felt wicked. Who had money for that sort of thing and what ever would Mam say? Auntie Hilda read the letter before it was sealed up. 'Well, there's no harm in asking,' she said.

Miss Dennison's adopted son, Guy, went in the car with them to church on Christmas morning. It was the first time she'd met him and she was shy and tongue-tied. He admired her kilt and asked her if she liked living in a sweet shop. 'When I was your age – it'd have been absolute heaven.' She muttered something. She felt sick and dumb. He was very kind and wore a warm brown coat and soft leather gloves with cuffs. For a prayer book he had a missal like Miss Dennison's.

Miss Dennison gave her a rosary for Christmas. Pink beads which felt lovely as they ran through her fingers. 'It's been blessed by the Pope, dear. So you must take great care of it.'

Auntie Hilda and Uncle Jack did their best and she knew she ought to be grateful. Billy cried a lot. 'Can't we go back to Mam, our Helen, why can't we?' He cheered up on Christmas Day itself. Under the tree for him there was a real Hornby engine with two carriages, a tunnel and set of rails.

Bambi was there, underneath several thicknesses of brown paper. She wanted to cry when she saw him. She could not stop stroking the velvet coat with its lovely dusty spots. The sweet expression in his eyes. Uncle Jack said wasn't she going to look at her big present? It was a dress of pink organdie, with silver thread on the bodice and a petticoat to go with it.

She wore it for a Christmas party at Miss Dennison's. Billy had a stomach upset and couldn't go. All the vackies left in

Thackton were there. The house was very warm and welcoming and there was a large tea with buns and animal biscuits and red jelly and farm cream whipped. But because the next day was Saturday, she felt all the time a little sick. Party games. *Oranges and lemons . . . and here comes the chopper to chop off your head.* She got the shakes, she couldn't help it, she knew the chopper would come down on her.

Perhaps she really could tell Miss Dennison this time? She thought: I've just to tell her it's bad, that it's something *bad*. She even had a chance, and didn't take it. It was when she went upstairs to the lavatory after tea. As she came out, there was Miss Dennison in the doorway of a room.

'Helen dear – what a lovely dress! Are you enjoying yourself?'

'Yes, thank you, Miss Dennison.' She hesitated. But it was too difficult. She said, 'Is that room where you sleep, Miss?'

Miss Dennison smiled. 'Do you care for paintings? Come in and see, if you'd like –'

The room was very simple with a plain dark bedcover and a bedside table with books on it and her slippers lying neatly side by side underneath. You could hardly see the walls for pictures. She'd like to have stayed a long time looking at them. 'There's Our Lady!' she exclaimed. 'That one there – it's Her with the Angel, we had that one at St Aidan's . . . I think Our Lady's the most beautiful person in the world after Mam.'

'How is your mother?' Miss Dennison asked. 'I always remember her in my prayers, Helen.' They walked down the stairs together. Helen thought: I'll tell her *now*. But how to say it? The seconds passed and she hadn't.

They were back in the big downstairs room, for Hunt the Thimble. She knew now she never would.

Saturday night. And there was Auntie Hilda waking her.

'You're to come to Father.'

When she followed the torch sleepily, the bedside light was on as usual and there was Uncle Jack sitting up in his pyjamas. Auntie Hilda whispered, 'Did you wash last night? All over?' Helen tried to remember, fighting off the dizzy sleepiness. Auntie persisted, 'All over, you washed all over? Properly?' Helen nodded her head.

She thought at first she wasn't going to be smacked because instead of telling her to lie down, Auntie said, 'Come over to Father. He wants to see –' She gave Helen a little push. 'Show

Father you've washed down below. He wants to see if you're, you know – clean.'

'No,' Helen said, 'I can't – I mean, I've not to show people. Mam said. It's not nice, is it?' She began to cry.

Auntie smacked the side of her head. 'That's the only language you understand, you and your dirty little brother. Nice, don't talk *nice* to us. Do you think the mess he makes is *nice*, eh? Is it then?'

Helen was choked with tears, 'Well, I won't – I can't –' Auntie hit her again.

Uncle Jack spoke then. His voice was kind. 'Come on, little lass. Up with your nightie.'

She didn't struggle when Auntie lifted it for her – but she thought she would die of shame. She shut her eyes as Auntie parted the lips down below. She felt the shivers coming on. 'Still, now . . .'

'Lie down, there's a good lass.' She didn't open her eyes as she was pushed over to the bed. Her nightdress was still ruckled up. She didn't dare to pull it down, waiting as she was for the smacking. But tonight it didn't happen. Instead the creaking and the groaning and grunting began at once. 'Get it over with,' she heard Auntie say, 'come on now, get it over with.' A little while later and she was shivering her way back to bed.

Next morning she felt so dreadful she was scarcely able to answer Miss Dennison's questions on the way to Mass. In the afternoon, up in her room, she wrote a letter. She didn't want it to go to Mam in case it upset her, so she addressed it to Auntie Winnie. It felt like crying inside, when she wrote the words down:

'They make me do things I don't like, *bad* things, so let me come back please Antie Winnie, I cant stay hear . . .'

She stole an envelope and stamp from Auntie Hilda's desk and posted it on the way to school on Monday.

She waited anxiously for an answer. Perhaps they'd say yes? Perhaps they'd even come and fetch her home. Then suddenly she'd be sick with worry because they mightn't understand or believe, and if they wrote to Auntie Hilda . . .

The answer came after two and a half weeks.

'If its work they want from you I dont blame them, billet money there paid, its not much, we have to pay now, just having one of your moods, all your other letters was cheery wasn't they – maybe theres too many sweets for your good, we dont want your mam worried so be a good girl and dont you write again till you can write cheery – Valeries not any trouble . . .' When she'd read it, Helen tore it into little bits and stuffed it in a sweetie bag. She felt as if a door had slammed somewhere. Tight shut.

The weather stayed cold. At school they sat in a circle round the stove to get what warmth they could. The cobwebs on the ceiling fluttered in the heat from the stove. The lights had to be on all day. She thought she might always be cold, always miserable.

There were a few nice times, like when Miss Foster came to give the singing lesson. After they'd practised *The Ash Grove* and *The British Grenadiers*, she would suggest a sing-song. She could play any tune by ear. They sang *Roll out the Barrel* and *Little Sir Echo* and *Wish Me Luck*. Helen sang loudly, standing as near the piano as she could get. Miss Foster told her: 'You've got a good sense of rhythm.' Suddenly Helen would feel sad, remembering how she'd used to sing for Mam.

She worried about Mam. She wrote to Aunt Winnie and asked why couldn't Mam write? Was she back in the hospital? She'd heard nothing now since Mam's Christmas card. But Aunt Winnie didn't answer.

The Saturday nights went on. In the daytime Auntie Hilda and Uncle Jack were so kind that sometimes she told herself – she almost believed it – that they were *different people* on Saturday nights. Like in some of the fairy tales – they weren't really Auntie Hilda and Uncle Jack but wicked spirits that got into their bodies at midnight. She tried to think of that the next time the hairbrush came down. They're different people.

March, and still winter. In the middle of the month there was heavy snow. One Friday afternoon Auntie Hilda was waiting to meet them as they came from school. She told Billy to go right upstairs and play with his Hornby engine. Then she took Helen into the small room at the back of the shop.

'Get sat, love,' she said, pointing to the chair by the fire. She stayed standing up. 'I'm sorry to be the one to tell you this, love, but your auntie and uncle, they've wrote . . .'

Dear Our Lady, please say they've sent for us. 'Is it – have we to go back? Can we go back?'

'They've wrote – what they've said is, you see . . . Your Mam, she's passed over like.'

Passed over. Moved to another place?

'Over where, Auntie?'

'Passed over,' Auntie Hilda repeated. 'Passed *on* . . . She's not with us any more.'

'Is it a hospital in another country, then?'

'Dead. Your Mam's dead.' She said it abruptly now, embarrassed. Her voice was sharp, like a knife cutting.

Helen didn't try to answer. She just sat on by the fire, feeling cold and dizzy. A feeling like creepy-crawlies in her hair. Giant shivers.

'You've understood then, love? I didn't want . . . It's difficult for us, that we've to tell you.' When Helen still didn't speak, she said, 'You know you've always a home here, love.'

'Can I see her? I want to see –'

'They said not. Your auntie . . . You've to stay here and not upset yourself with funerals. Your priest has written to you, Father Casey, is it? It's a nice letter.' She rustled the paper. 'Will I read it you?'

But Helen couldn't answer. The pain in her heart was choking her.

'Don't feel badly, love. You'd not want her to suffer, would you? And your priest . . . It says here she went easy.'

A great heavy stone settled in her heart.

'Who's to tell our Billy?' she asked.

She couldn't remember anything about the rest of the day. At bedtime, she took Billy into her bed and didn't bother if he wet or not. They clung together. Billy woke up before she'd gone to sleep at all. He banged his fists on her back. 'I want Mam, our Helen, I want Mam.'

Everyone was kind, very kind. Auntie Hilda and Uncle Jack couldn't fuss over them enough. At school even the boys were careful: no one called her 'skinny-stick' or 'daftie', or Billy 'a dirty bucket'. On Sunday, Miss Dennison said, 'I'm so sorry, Helen dear,' taking her in her arms. Hugging her a little stiffly.

Perhaps it was to try and cheer her that Auntie and Uncle suggested she serve in the shop. Before she'd occasionally helped Uncle Jack, handing out Fry's chocolate cream or Cadbury's Filled from under the glass cover. Now they showed her how to weigh out and how to use the till. 'You're a smart little lass. Quick with figures. We'll have you running the place yet. Then Father can retire and I'll put my feet up –'

'But I shan't be living here that long,' Helen said.

'Where are you off to, then?'

'To my family. We'll go when, when –' She broke off. When? Auntie Winnie hadn't said anything about sending for them.

Perhaps when the war ended? But it showed no signs of that.

She knew the French were all right because they had built a Magic Line with tunnels to keep the Germans off. People laughed about the German line. In school they sang with Miss Foster, *We're gonna hang out the washing on the Siegfried Line.*

'Mr Hitler's missed the boat now,' Auntie Hilda said. 'He should've got on with it, oughtn't he?'

Spring came at last. The first days of warm weather. Perhaps Auntie and Uncle thought they'd been kind long enough, but the bad things started again. One dread Saturday night – woken from a deep sleep, not sure where she was. Frightened. Then sick with recognition of it all.

This time it was worse. She wasn't asked to show anything – not that. But the smacking was twice as hard, with a stick now, not a hairbrush. She thought afterwards: If I've ever to undress at school . . .

She couldn't see how anything was going to come right now. No one talked about what was going to happen to them. 'When the war's over,' they said. But the news was beginning to be bad now. Norway and Denmark had been invaded. And even if she and Billy went back, it wouldn't be home. Auntie Winnie and Uncle Arnold didn't care for them, she knew that. Oh, Mam, she cried inside, why did you have to die? Any Saturday night now, until the war was over, that stick might come down on her, and then the awful things afterwards.

Once or twice now when Auntie beat her, she'd let herself be angry as well as frightened. It hurt so terribly. 'Ungrateful,' Auntie said to her, 'making a fuss like that. And if you tell folk of it, there'll be worse things. We might have to cut Billy's . . . cut off his little, you know. *Don't you dare tell a soul.*'

She had to get through the days. She had a ritual at bedtime. She lay on her right always, Bambi tucked under her left arm. In her right hand she held the pink rosary. Then she prayed for Mam. Miss Dennison had had a Mass said specially for her. Helen heard the name read out. '. . . for the repose of the soul of Evelyn Connors . . .'

It was the month of May. The whole feeling about the war had changed. 'Waiting for Mr Hitler,' they said now. Their teacher, Miss Garner, showed them a map with all the countries the Germans had conquered. The boys at school boasted of what they'd do to the Germans when they came to England. Helen knew she would just be frightened. She seemed to be frightened all the time now. Miss Garner asked her several times if anything was the matter. 'You're missing your Mam, aren't you, love?'

Once when she'd been beaten really quite hard and it hurt her to sit down, Auntie said, 'I wonder why ever that should be?' Helen knew then for certain that she and Uncle Jack were different people . . . *Oh, Mam, come and take me away. Take me to Heaven with you . . .*

She helped a lot in the shop now. Twice she'd been left on her own, which in a way she rather liked. She was good with the till and it was nice to make people happy. She had to stand on a stool to serve, and climb up the steps to get down the glass jars.

The weather was very warm now and she wore the summer dresses which Auntie Hilda had bought her in Whitby, together with real leather sandals. It was June, and the sun shone in a cloudless blue sky. 'Waiting for Mr Hitler.' She heard that all foreigners were to be hidden away in case they took the Germans' side in an invasion. After church Miss Dennison was talking about it. 'I fear for several friends,' Helen heard her say. 'Particularly a certain crooner.'

She didn't know what got into Auntie Hilda that next Saturday. Perhaps they were more worried than they said about Hitler, because the stick came down really hard. She stifled her cries into the pillow. Oh, but she couldn't bear it. She twisted her arm round, put out a hand to stop the stick – only instead down it came on her hand.

Auntie was really angry. 'Stop mucking about – how many times have I to tell you? You know it's for your good, *don't you*? You'd not want your mother in Heaven to know you made a fuss about a bit of chastisement –'

She cried into the pillow, 'Leave my mam out of this –'

Uncle Jack said suddenly, 'Send her back. I can't be doing . . . Get rid of the lass.'

'Off with you, then. To bed. I don't know what he's about . . .' As Helen stumbled out, she could hear their voices raised in argument. *I don't want to know anything more.* She curled up in the bed. If she could never wake up . . . The idea was wonderful suddenly. If she could *die* and go to be with Mam. I could ask Our Lady to come for me . . . Then she thought of Billy. It was too much. Was he to come with her? She'd promised Mam she'd look after him. Oh, *I just want to die.*

The next day her hand was swollen, and very sore. 'You had an accident with that,' Auntie said, looking at the brown and

239

black patches. 'That got caught in the door, I shouldn't wonder.'

'Please, Miss, my hand got caught in the door,' she said on Monday. Miss Garner put witch hazel on it and told her to be more careful in the future.

On Tuesday after school, Uncle asked her to mind the shop for an hour. He and Auntie were donating some prizes for a whist drive. They took Billy with them.

At first it was very quiet. Two Mars Bars and a quarter of jelly babies only. She sat on the stool and shut her eyes and said the prayer about dying and going to Heaven. *Our Lady, come for me soon.*

The bell tinkled as the door opened. She looked up and couldn't believe what she saw. For there was Our Lady. Just as she would look if the statue came to life. A lady with dark wavy hair and olive skin, in a white dress with floating panels and a thin blue sash. It was Her face too.

'Hello,' Our Lady said, 'I need some sweets for presents. Could I have a half of nut toffee, a quarter of humbugs – and a box of Pomfret cakes? Can you manage all that?'

'Yes,' Helen whispered. She was frightened as well as happy.

'You're very young to be minding the shop –' Our Lady said.

'I know how to, though – and I can work the till. I do it often, when they're out.'

Our Lady frowned as Helen began shovelling toffee on to the scales: 'What did you do to your hand?'

'I shut it in a door.'

'It looks nasty. Are you taking care of it?' Her voice was so gentle. Deep, and warm. Just as she had always thought Our Lady would sound.

She burst into tears.

'Darling,' said Our Lady, 'darling, what's the matter?'

'Nothing.'

'Well, something's wrong. Tell me. Tell me what's the matter . . .'

'It's what they do to me. I haven't to say –'

'What mustn't you say, darling?' Our Lady opened her hands wide.

'Oh, help me, help me!' Helen cried, lifting the counter flap, knocking over the jar of toffee. 'And take me to Heaven with you.'

In a moment she was round the other side and in Our Lady's arms.

3

'Well, what do you know,' Gwen said, turning over towards Dick as his arm came round her, 'Betty joining up like that. Only the nineteens *have* to, but I knew she would.'

They were proud of Betty, that summer of 1941. Bossy Betty (she never seemed to mind the name), in the Women's Army now, in the ATS.

Saturday, with an early morning sun filtering through the thin summer curtains. A weekend visit to Thackton. He and Gwen in the old double bed against the wall. The bed that had been Dad and Mother's. Memories . . . Mother, nightcap, little spectacles, sitting up reading. Dad, on the same side as Dick slept now, against the window, turned away from her. Arm up as if to shield himself. Heavily asleep.

'Gone six o'clock,' he said now, 'and not a sound. Usually Helen's about, dealing with little Billy.'

'She did well, Maria, taking on those two –'

'They could hardly have been separated, not after what Helen'd been through. Hanging'd be too good for them, that couple . . . Anyway the thing is, it's a success.'

It certainly was. Dad, having finally decided at seventy-five to retire to Moorgarth, was loving it. With young Peter in Canada with Sybil, and the other grandchildren grown big, the arrival of these two meant he could start again. Every day he thought up new treats for them, allowing a now lively and confident Helen to get away with real cheek.

Maria had been in Thackton since last June when, during the invasion scare, Eddie had been interned as an enemy alien. In the autumn he had been deported to Australia. It had been Dick's idea, after the internment, to invite her to Moorgarth. A month or so's visit to recover from the upset, the distress caused by his arrest.

'You and she always got on well. Now, let bygones be bygones,' he had said to Dad. To Eleanor too. It would be quite safe after all – Guy, who had just joined up, would not be in Thackton. (No one now could undo that meeting in August of 1939.) So the twenty-year-old ban had been lifted. Then, within three days of her arrival, the pathetic encounter in the sweet shop. Neither Maria, nor anyone, had thought of her going back after that. It had seemed so obvious, so natural, so approved of by Eric, that Helen and Billy should stay with her here, at Moorgarth. She had wound up everything, every interest in London, had joined the local WVS, had become a busy countrywoman, and foster mother. How she loved the mothering . . . Maria the childless. No – Maria robbed of her child by *us*. (We did it. Dad, Eleanor, Peter, all of us.)

There were not so many people to use Moorgarth these days. Red-haired Jan came always with Dick and Gwen, but this time was away with a schoolfriend, youth-hostelling in Swaledale. Ida, seldom seen now, was teaching in Northumberland. Dulcie, sixty-two now but looking only fifty, was in London, working in a nursing home in Wimpole Street, and seeming very happy. She had said, 'I could stay up here with your father. But then, you see – after all these years . . .' She had not expanded on this. Letters came regularly from Jenny and from Sybil, who with young Peter had been nearly two years in Canada now. Jim, Jenny's eldest, wanted only to be old enough to join the Air Force. Jenny and Sybil were doing Red Cross work.

And as ever, there was his own happiness. He felt often that he shouldn't have it. Not now, during a war. And yet it was there: underground stream, running through his life. Times like this morning – Gwen lying in his arms, the smell of her skin between hair and shoulder where the neck of her nightdress ended. Sensibly dressed Gwen, with her long-wearing nightclothes, flannel for winter, dimity for summer. Move a little, and feel her thigh against his. Change position again. Gwen, Gwen, Gwen. Whenever he was deep inside her, he would cry out or mutter into her skin – not too loud, the family were not to hear – '*My princess.*'

Perfect happiness, almost. Gwen did too much, was overtired – part of the reason he'd insisted on this weekend away. She was mother to Jan, wife to him and how many other things besides? Her war work as a nurse. So capable was she, it seemed the hospital wouldn't run without her. Too much time on her feet, and then working nights. That was the reason for the backache, that dragging pain inside which she mentioned occasionally. There was a cough too which had persisted now right from the winter. (Hadn't she had an uncle or – someone with TB? Words of old Mrs Ackroyd came back to him.) But perhaps, as Gwen suggested, it was still the Change. That could go on a long time.

Reaching across her now: 'Pass me a cigarette, love.' First cigarette of the morning. Oh bliss.

'You smoke too much,' she said as the flame from the lighter shot high.

'I don't cough. I've puffed going on thirty years now. But I don't cough – unlike some.'

Her answer was to cough suddenly, a spasm.

'What did I say, then? You might take that to Dr Appleyard when we're back – just so I don't have to worry. And mention the backache at the same time.'

'He'll only tell me to do less.'

'Do less, then.' He hissed smoke in spirals. 'That'd be good.'

She said, laughing fondly, 'What'd be good for *you*'d be cigarette rationing – except you'd get extra, of course. Buy your way out . . . Mrs Bamford at the hospital knows lots of women who'll sell their clothing coupons. They haven't the money to use them. That's your Fair Shares for Everyone country.'

'Are we buying any?'

'We're just like the next person . . . Yes. Betty's all right, ATS uniform and plenty left over for mufti, but Jan's that unsure age . . . When I let her get shoes, she got some frightful peeptoes that didn't fit. They can't afford mistakes on coupons, and that's hard. She's a real clothes-horse –'

'Dulcie, Aunt Dulcie she gets it from. Not from Mother.' His cigarette was finished. He leaned across her to stub it out. Instead of turning back, he remained on top of her.

'Get away. I was going to make us some tea.'

'I'll let you then, when I've had my way.'

'Oh, you,' she said, laughing, arms round his neck. 'You with your loving. Never have enough, do you? You'd best get on with it, then. Folk are stirring.'

There was the sound of Helen passing on the landing, going down the stairs, singing *'I've got sixpence, jolly jolly sixpence,'* in her funny little voice.

Maria, woken by Helen, felt something almost like contentment. Back in Thackton, back at Moorgarth again. Her new, her busy country life, a year old now.

And that meant a year since they had come for Eddie. I was sick, physically sick, with losing Eddie. Even though lately we had had such difficulty in getting on. Worst of all, since America. Nothing went right after America. And the most terrible thing of all, the thing I don't think about (and there's so much of my life I don't think about, *cannot* think about), Peter's death. My secret. (And Rocco's? No wonder perhaps that I can seldom write to Rocco.)

Eddie, the philanderer, the ever ready. I could not become used to it. I never shall. My own fierce loyalty. If anyone else should criticize him . . . Eddie, for whom I would have died. How to *live*, though, with that passionate rage which couldn't bear him to look at others? Looking as if he wanted to touch (I know he does, I know he does). To know was one thing, to see it another. (That early summer of '39 on tour . . .)

And his career? Gone now, of course. But before internment, what to make of it? He was flattered, of course, with these new holiday camps, that he was asked for the first season. Good, good. But then the war began. The theatres and cinemas closed. There was nothing. It seemed no one wanted him. That same Eddie who played the Rainbow Room in '35.

Then the shock of last summer. 1940. The Fall of France, Dunkirk, the invasion scare. But worst of all, for me, when they came for Eddie. Bitterness all dissolved in that moment. My outrage that they should do this. I forgot, did I not, that I was angry with him? The day before there'd been a blistering row. That woman, half as good as me (yes, I dare to say it), badly made up, loose flesh, poor complexion, bad teeth. But younger. Younger by nearly ten years. And crazy about him. Like that one at Christmas: nineteen or twenty, mouth opening vacantly on pearly white teeth, 'Oh, you do sing marvellously.' In uniform by day, but wearing Schiaparelli by night. Shades of his earlier conquests: he can never forget that Harry Roy married the daughter of the Rajah of Sarawak. Princess Pearl. Perhaps he wishes he'd never tied the knot with me, then he could think himself in line for Princess Margaret Rose in eight or nine years' time. After all, he'll only be fifty or so then. And still so charming.

The thoughts tasted bitter. Remembering them was bitter too. She had had them that very day they came for him. She had even spoken some of them.

And then, the knock at the door. The tenth of June, 1940. The police: 'He's to come with us.' Formal identification. 'Eduardo Sabrini, 37 years old, born in Chieti, Italy. Dance band crooner. Member of the Fascio.'

Yes, yes, of course. But a token membership only. Everyone knew that. It had been to do with his parents, more of a social club than anything. He, they, didn't know the first thing about it all, didn't even care about politics.

'Well, you're going to care now, sonnie.'

Enemy alien. *Enemy alien*. What a label to put on careless, harmless (to his adopted country at least) easygoing, happy Eddie. She didn't want to remember how he'd crumpled. His incredulous expression, face becoming soft, unbelieving. The ready tears – that should belong only to the songs he sung, to his love-making.

'I'm glad Poppa's not alive to see this . . .'

And then suddenly he'd rounded on her. 'Why not you?' he'd asked.

'Why not my wife?' he'd said to the policeman. Yes, in his distress he had even stooped so low.

'We've our orders. A list. It says nothing here about Mrs Sabrini.'

'Well, it ought. She's the real thing, she's *Sicilian*. You should be afraid of her. What she can do to you. She has the evil eye sometimes.'

Had he meant to make them laugh? Had he laughed himself? She had felt bitter, at him, at them: the police, rifling through Eddie's wardrobe, chest of drawers, suitcases. And very frightened.

They were bad days after that. His first weeks up in Lancashire, at Warth Mills, when she'd heard nothing from him – and only learned later by indirect means of the conditions. The fastidious Eddie: rats and filth everywhere, cold water only, boards in place of mattresses. Then his time on the Isle of Man – never a great letter-writer, he had still managed the two short pages allowed a week. But much of it was censored and because of the backlog, so late in arriving that he was already on his way to Australia. Now, she had to believe that he was making something of life in a camp. He was certainly singing again.

Apart from the distress of it all, those first few days, her body had wept for him. And wept for him still. It had been then she had made the decision to come up to Yorkshire: going first to Middlesbrough, to stay with Dick and Gwen. The kindness of those two – a weekend had been spent discussing what she should do. 'For the time being, go to Thackton,' Dick had said. 'To Moorgarth.' Yes, Eric was there. Retired. But Dick would arrange it all. Betty and Jan would be along later to spend August there. Gwen couldn't leave her hospital work. But for Maria, it was time to be friends with Eric again.

Hot June days. The invasion threat over us still. Myself, dressing up for a garden fête at a house near Lealholm: white shantung frock with the floating panels – bought for last summer's tour. Stopping off at the sweet shop for Uncle Eric's favourites, and humbugs for Elsie. And then, that extraordinary . . . A child behind the counter. Skinny little waif. Scabby, with an ugly voice and bad teeth. Nothing like my own child. Nor the child of my dreams. So why? Unless it was that I'd been waiting, without knowing it, all this time. So that I noticed – what? The hand. That small bruised hand. And then the flood of tears, the frightened howl. And bit by bit, the whole sad story.

I was the Virgin Mary. In my white frock and blue sash, I was Our Lady. I still don't know whether to laugh or cry. (And God and the real Virgin Mary, do They laugh or cry at people's cruelty?) I made enough fuss. With Eric, with Eleanor Dennison. Police threats. Mr and Mrs Bolton: their incredulous denials, their accusations of the child. *But I knew.* Never for a moment did I think it a fantasy.

I believed her. So now here she is, under my care. Just as, twenty-five years ago, I was under Eric's. Full circle.

Our Lady, indeed. Mother too, for I began so soon after to think of adoption – of them both of course. The money, that must be thought of later. And their dreadful aunt and uncle – not cruel like the Boltons, but uncaring – they couldn't wait for me to take Helen and Billy off their hands. ('Said that, did she? She always was a little storyteller. The father was Irish, you know.')

The little brother. What can I say of Billy? What I do for Helen I must do for him. He too is pathetic, but not attractively so.

Helen still believes, I think, sometimes, that I'm the Virgin Mary – in disguise. Her worship of me is almost embarrassing.

'If your name's Maria, that's Her name too, isn't it? *Mary*, mother of God.'

Oh, how I long and long for Eddie.

The railings in front of the Graingers' old house, and Dick and Gwen's too, had been taken down as scrap metal for the war effort. The fronts looked strange – like mouth with teeth missing. Coming back at night, Dick would think: How incomplete home looks. Twice, in the dark, he had walked right past.

But tonight in the autumn light he was watching out. Hurrying home. Worried as ever about Gwen. He had thought she looked tired this morning. She was on a day shift just now, and she'd promised that if she felt no better she'd go to bed when she came in.

It was Jan's night for Red Cross. The wireless could be heard in the kitchen so Gwen must still be up. He went through. She was standing, beating mixture in a bowl.

Kissing her, he asked: 'Why not sit to do that, love?'

'Daft. When did I ever sit?' With great care, she broke an egg into a cup and then into the mixture, 'Jan's birthday cake. I've been saving margarine, and eggs. I want it to be special, a birthday to remember . . .'

He pushed the kitchen stool against her legs. 'Are you wanting your backache better or not?'

She had visited Dr Appleyard in the summer, as promised. She'd told Dick then, 'He says what can you expect at my age, and with a war on. I've to cut down a little. That's all. It's not serious.'

He had tried to make her rest. And for a while she'd gone along with him. But soon it was rushing about as before. It had seemed to him too that she was getting thin. He wanted her to sit down and be waited on. Be a princess.

He hung up his coat, changed his shoes, went to the letter-box in the hall. A pile of bills, circulars, several items which ought to have gone to the Foundry and an already opened letter from Betty. He read that first.

'She's happy,' he said, sitting at the kitchen table. 'Happy as a sandboy.'

'That's a daft way of talking. Sandboy! Did you see – she's getting leave? Not in time for Jan's party, though.'

He opened one of the bills, then another. The third one he stared at, puzzled.

'What's this? When did you see a consultant?'

'It's a lot, is it? I'd –'

'Five hundred, a thousand, ten thousand, I wouldn't give a damn. No – Why a consultant? Why did you see him? You've said nothing –'

'I forgot. When I was at Dr Appleyard's . . . there were some X-rays, you see. He just wanted someone else to look me over. I mean, we always go privately – I didn't think –'

He said angrily, pushing the letters aside, 'Stop it about the money . . . I want to know *what he said*. And why you didn't tell me.'

She shrugged her shoulders, still beating the cake. 'Nothing to tell. Isn't that why I forgot?'

'Did he say everything was all right, then?'

'He said there was nothing we'd to do – that's right.' She tipped in some flour, stirring it gently.

'Very good then, if everything's so all right, how is it you don't feel well? Don't *look* well. And with winter coming on. Not even a tonic. Nothing prescribed.'

'Hush now, while I turn out the mixture –'

'I'm too quiet, too often. You promised to go to the doctor.'

'And I went.'

'You didn't think I might want to know there'd been a consultant called in?'

'I'm sorry,' she said, wearily. 'Is that enough?'

Irritable with anxiety, 'It'll have to be,' he said. 'Except –'

'Just give over about it all. Be a love.' She sounded, for Gwen, cross, anxious. Only extreme fatigue would make her short with him in that manner.

The lined cake tin lay ready on the kitchen table. She'd finished folding the flour into the mixture. She turned, and as she did so, tripped over the leg of the stool he'd placed behind her. The Pyrex bowl fell. On the stone floor, fragments of glass, dollops of cake mixture.

'Drat,' she cried, 'Drat that stool. Oh, Jan's cake, her *birthday* –' She slumped into a kitchen chair, arms on the table, head down, heaving with sobs.

'Hush, love. It's only a cake.' His arms were about her. 'Bob knows someone . . . we can get the stuff tomorrow. What's wrong with a black market cake?'

Still she sobbed.

'Love. For you to cry over a daft bit of cake mixture . . . It's not life and death. I'll clear it, and no more said.'

When she looked up and reached for a handkerchief, scrubbing at her eyes, he was struck suddenly by something in her expression. He saw for the first time since he'd known her – a Gwen afraid.

'Something's up. You've not told me something.'

She looked away.

'Had it to do with the consultant, Parry? Did he say something – anything I ought to know?'

'I'd meant . . . When I was sent on to see him, love, I said nothing to you – because, why scare you? Then after I'd been, it seemed . . . why two people miserable?'

'*What did he say?*'

'Not like me, is it, not speaking plainly?' She put out a hand. He clasped it tight. Too tightly. 'You see, love, because of the X-rays – he'd to examine me. You don't want medical terms, Dick . . . But inside, a great mass. From the ovary. And then the liver. That's the bad bit, the liver. It's in there –'

'*It?*'

'A growth. It's gone to the liver. But there's nothing we've to do. He said that – nothing can be done.'

'And you kept that from *me* –'

'They're not ones for straight talk, Dick. I'd not have been told either, except I know too much. I asked him directly.'

She was silent for a moment, then she said, 'Do you – guess, from all that? Or have I to say?'

Although his hand clasping hers was firm, his body had begun to shake. A pain, a jerking in his bad leg. 'Did he give any sort of let-out? I mean . . . it's as bad as that?'

'Yes. No hope. Not with something that size. Gone that far.' She turned to him, 'Don't be saying now, how if I'd gone earlier . . . He said not. The cough, it could have been anything. Nothing neglected. It's just – this dratted sort, in the ovaries, no warnings really . . . I'd have told you later, of course. It was just – oh, why, love, before I need?'

He knew he could say no more. He wanted to ask, most of all he wanted to ask the dreaded question – How long do you think? *How much time?* But he knew he couldn't. Perhaps she did not know herself. All that was known was the sentence.

He was afraid he wouldn't be able even to stand up. He whom she would need as a support in the days to come.

'I can't live without you,' he opened his mouth to say. 'I can't –' he began. Then stopped himself.

'Can't what?' she said brightly. Standing up, all businesslike. Rough, busy, caring Gwen. Gwen, rumpling the hair of the birdman who'd called her princess. 'It's me to clear this mess up, I can see . . . And mind you get those illegal ingredients quick. If there's no cake by Friday . . .'

When at last he stood up, dragging his aching leg, he felt the ground trembling beneath him. A world without Gwen? Without Gwen, he thought, there is no world.

249

4

Guy at Park Villa, on leave for a fortnight. What Eleanor wanted more than anything these wartime days: Guy home with her, and safe. (Better not to think that soon, too soon, he would be sent overseas.) A cold April day and Guy arriving, tired but smart as paint in his uniform. Changing at once into grey flannels, Clydella shirt, the blue pullover she'd knitted him at Christmas. Feet up, smoking, drinking the Glenfiddich she'd hoarded for him, leafing through a pile of magazines.

Later, he'd go out for a drink, be off to spend the day in York, ring up a girl or two, perhaps a dinner-dance. But mostly he would just be man about the house again. 'My nephew, Guy.'

His being there made even the evacuees all right. Rosie, Malcolm, and baby Kevin. The home offered in 1939 to a Catholic mother and child, and now regretted. Rosie's army husband had been overseas from early in the war, and was now out East. Nevertheless she'd had a second baby. Eleanor had been too embarrassed to ask any questions and Rosie had said nothing. Kevin, eighteen months now, trailing a bunched often smelly napkin peeping out from torn rubber pants. 'Can't get rubber for love nor money,' Rosie said. She thought very well of Guy, putting curlers in the day before his arrival and filing her nails in the kitchen, leaving the shavings in the cutlery drawer. Guy took just enough notice to make it worth her while ('Flattery costs nothing,' he told Eleanor. 'I don't expect it's much of a life.').

His visit, an oasis. She could put aside the trivial worries that nowadays took up so much of life. Coal soon to be rationed, electricity, paraffin. She thought with dread of the cold winters to come, and to come. Although the war had taken a turn for the better, with the Americans our Allies now, it was a long way from over.

Guy. Why should he be spared over any other mother's son? (His namesake, fighting in a far less worthy cause, had not been, nor his uncle, James.) All her life, all her love for Eric, all her lifetime's dreams, everything – all invested in Guy.

It would have been a perfect time, this fortnight together, if it hadn't been for Maria's request. Plea, rather. Maria, at Moorgarth for the duration, looking after Eric, caring for Helen. Billy too, until last Christmas when there'd been the surely welcome appearance of Cousin Fred, a relative on their father's side, over from South Africa to fight, and married to a Scots girl last year. They were willing and eager to have the boy.

Maria's strange plea. And why now? After all these years? *Let sleeping dogs lie*, Eleanor had thought. 'My parents are dead,' Guy told everyone. And it was true enough – of Peter. Did he really need to know the rest?

Three weeks ago now and Maria coming to see her. For once not in WVS green, but elegant in navy blue wool dress and striped jacket, high heeled brogues. A sailor type hat.

'I've thought,' she said. 'I want you to tell Guy. I want him to know.'

'Is that wise, dear?'

'Please. He must know.' She looked directly at Eleanor. 'If something happens, were to happen to him. Peter's gone. Uncle Eric's an old man –'

'Is Eric to know or not? What are your wishes?' Eleanor spoke coldly, feeling already a chill around her. That *she* was to do the deed, that it would be up to her.

'I'll tell him, if needs be . . . But the other – telling Guy, it oughtn't to come from me. I'd ask Dick to do it, but with Gwen so ill – with Gwen dying, I couldn't.'

'I am to tell Guy, then?' It would be difficult, terrible. She would not do it. Why me? she thought.

'Why not? Who else?' Maria asked, her voice sharp.

'It's just that it's so . . . Dear, it will be very difficult –'

'He's not mine!' Maria cried. It was the voice of the sixteen-year-old in Florence. 'He's not mine,' she repeated angrily. 'You took him. Brought him up as your own. A twenty-one-year-old deceived man. His chances . . . when he goes overseas, he could die not knowing –'

'Hasn't he enough,' she tried to say it gently, 'with possibly going into battle? Do you want him to go off in turmoil too? How can this revelation be anything but a terrible upset?'

'I want him to know.'

That was to be the gist of it, her argument, over the next half-hour as Eleanor talked, suggesting this, that compromise. Coming back always to the obstinate: *'I want him to know.'*

Nothing for it but to agree. She saw it as a punishment. For what? What had she done wrong?

'It's the price,' Maria said suddenly. 'For what you took.'

'You're very hard.'

Punishment perhaps because I did it all for Eric? That we two who could be joined together in no other way, might for ever be linked through this child. And now Maria, who was robbed, exacts her price.

'He may well want to see you about it,' she said coldly.

'Or he may not. He may want nothing to do with me. I'll take the risk.'

The days were passing. Only four left now. And the deed not done. She could not have believed herself so cowardly. Each morning she woke and determined that today would be the day. Not of course at breakfast, she must not spoil his morning. And never at a mealtime. Afternoons were too precious and as evening drew on, how could she threaten his night's rest? There never will be a right time, she thought. She was afraid to meet Maria when out. Afraid Maria would call on her.

She thought of it as she worked in the garden planting onions, chives. Summer spinach. She found a sheltered spot to lay out some tomato plants. If the weather would warm up, spring really come. If I could only *tell* Guy.

She blamed the chill weather for the heavy cold and cough he had caught. (How to tell him while he snuffled?) The next night he coughed without ceasing. She herself hardly slept at all. In the morning he was having difficulty with his breathing. A rasping sound. She told him he must stay in bed, and lit a fire in his room.

'I'm getting Dr McIntosh,' she said.

'It'll pass,' he said, 'don't make a fuss. Right as rain tomorrow. And I've to go back anyway.'

'I'll call him,' she insisted, thinking already of the reassurance he would provide: young earnest Scot, freckle-faced, endlessly patient with Malcolm's recurrent ear infections, Kevin's summer diarrhœa.

It was just after one when she opened the door to a large bulky man with a shock of white hair, and carrying a worn medical bag.

'Miss Dennison? Well now, and where's the invalid? Armed forces, I hear –'

'Yes, yes. My nephew.'

He was some time upstairs. When he came out of the bedroom she was waiting on the landing.

He said, 'No question of the laddie going back to camp. It'll be a wee while. I'll write a note – It's a nasty chest infection. He mustn't leave the house at all.'

They went downstairs, he puffing heavily. At the bottom he turned.

'Now,' he said, 'perhaps you'll tell me why when you opened the door just now, you looked as if you'd seen a ghost?'

'I didn't –'

'Och, yes.'

'Well, it was only . . . The receptionist said Dr McIntosh would come –' She heard her voice, pedantic, fussy.

'But I *am* Dr McIntosh.' He smiled, putting out a hand, covering hers. 'Dr McIntosh, senior.'

'You might have said.' But she had not meant to be rude. She added hurriedly, 'I'll get you some coffee, such as it is – Or tea?'

'Tea, please. Strong, if you can spare it –' There was a clattering suddenly from the kitchen.

'What's that noise now? Your patient needs quiet.'

'Evacuees. I took in a mother and small child. They were amongst the few who didn't go back during the Phoney War. She had another last year.' She lowered her voice. 'A different father, I'm afraid –'

'Is it a tin drum the wee one's banging?'

'Two tin drums. I thought seriously of giving them to salvage.'

'Well, they'll not do the laddie upstairs any good. Could you not ask for quiet just now?'

In the drawing-room he sat down heavily, still out of breath. She feared for a moment that he needed help. Physician, heal thyself. He was an alarming colour. She asked:

'Are you all right?'

'Never better. Nothing like getting back into harness.' While he drank his tea, 'I'm here for the duration,' he explained, 'Young Alistair joined up a week ago – on the understanding I'd come down from Stirling and take over.'

It appeared he'd been out of medicine only a few years. 'The Lord smote me a mighty blow, in the shape of a heart attack. Too bad to ignore. It was my own lassie, she's a nurse, talked me into retirement. At only fifty-eight. There never was a more reluctant one . . . But here I am back – one of that happy breed who in spite of the worry and the heartbreak, are managing to enjoy their war.'

It was his third visit. Guy was improving fast. She said, from the foot of the stairs, waiting for him to come down, 'He's not really my nephew, you know. Guy – he's no relation. No relation at all.'

'Is that so?'

She made tea for them both. Rosie was in the kitchen with Malcolm, who was rolling tins of food down a chute made from one of Eleanor's trays. She said with concealed impatience, 'If the tins get dented, they don't keep.'

'Let him be,' Rosie said, 'he's not troubling you, and any road, there's not much keeping anything these days, is there?'

Back in the drawing-room, the fire had hardly begun to draw. She put down the tray and rubbed her chapped hands.

Dr McIntosh said: 'The laddie's maybe no relation, but he certainly thinks of you as his aunt.'

'Oh, he knows I'm not. But it makes an easy fiction . . . He's been given some sort of story – that he's adopted and of Italian origin. And that I brought him back from Tuscany in 1920, as a baby. He thinks he has no parents.'

'*Thinks?*' Dr McIntosh wiped his moustache. 'Does he have some, then?'

She said impetuously, almost at the same moment as she had the idea:

'I'd like you to tell him. It's the most tremendous cheek, to ask you. But I thought, as a doctor . . . You see, I think he should know the truth.'

'Och, of course,' he said. 'Of course I will. There's just one wee problem.'

'Yes?' Her voice shook. She was trembling. What have I done? Asking a stranger . . . She imagined Guy leaving his bed, coming down. Hearing her betray him.

'The truth. I don't know it myself.'

Relief made her speak lightly. 'Oh, stupid. How stupid of me!'

'Don't apologize. It's understandable.' He was looking closely at her. He said, 'When you spoke just then, you seemed so young. A lass again – ready to break hearts. You must have been very fine-looking.'

She reacted badly to the flattery, sensing a wrong note where there was none. She suddenly had no idea where to put her hands: strong, capable, would-be artistic hands, fluttering now around her face. 'Oh, I don't think –'

'Well, I do . . . And –' he took up his teacup '– the fact is now, I'm still waiting. For the truth. If I'm to talk to the lad –'

She took a deep breath, and began.

(What am I doing? What have I done?) Telling him haltingly, going back and back. Maria. Florence. Eric. How she had wanted to help the family in their trouble. What Maria had suffered.

'Poor wee lassie . . . But it was a lot to do,' he said, 'what you took on. A lifetime's work.'

She had told him everything – except her love for Eric (how could she speak of that?) He asked now, 'The killing. The murder. Did anyone hang – go to the chair?'

'No. The police, they weren't able to find anything. It was thought . . . He was mistaken for someone else, they were sure. A gangland killing . . .'

'But the laddie knows what happened?'

'Yes. But no details. I myself only know what I was told.'

She looked across at his kindly face. Impossible to know if this was the right thing. And yet insist as Maria might, she could not have done it herself. *Could not.*

I am my mother's son. The words, meaningless. Each one like a banging of a drum. I am my mother's son. Furious drumming, part of his rage. He walked fast, away from the village. When he stopped to cough, bent over at the roadside, he noticed for the first time that the sun was shining.

I am my mother's son. He had no idea of what he would do or say, and had known only that he must get out of the house at once. Go and confront her. *My mother.* He felt a great rush of sickness, coming up in waves then to where his head raged. Heat of the April sun. Heat of his rage. Rage, rage, rage.

The gate of Moorgarth was open. Coming round into the yard, he could see Maria at the window. She was peeling potatoes. He banged on the door. When she came to answer, drying her hands on her overall, he said,

'I want to speak to you. *Now.*'

She looked at him. She knows, he thought. She knows that I know. He pushed past her rudely. As if someone else acted. She must have been a little afraid of him perhaps, for she went back immediately to the sink. She picked up the knife. Not looking at him, her head bent.

More breathless, tireder than he'd realized – it was his first day up – he sat down at the table.

'Well, right, look – are we alone?'

'Yes, we're alone,' she said. 'Helen's with Eric – they've gone after bluebells and then to tea with the Vicar.' She recited the news almost. Impersonal information.

'Look,' he began again. He thumped the inside of his wrists on the table. Painfully. He wanted to say, 'Help me, help me.' But the anger boiled, bubbled. Grew more desperate. 'Well. Bloody hell – *well* . . .'

'She's told you?'

'No –'

Maria appeared puzzled. 'Then – what?'

He stood up. He felt stronger suddenly. Seeing her leaning over the sink, he thought she looked for all the world like a peasant woman. She *was* a peasant woman. He could hardly bear to look at her. Instead he said:

'I couldn't, can't bear to speak to Aunt Eleanor. Can't look her in the face . . . Bloody hell. Does it matter? Does it really matter?'

'Yes. Because *I* couldn't do it. Couldn't tell you. And Dick –'

At the far side of the room, the telephone went. 'I'll get it,' he said irritably – shouting down the receiver, 'Yes, yes. Who is it?' He told her: 'For you.'

He heard her, warm, polite, efficient.

'. . . tell them I've arranged a collection . . . It'd be best to use mine – either here or take it down to the depot . . .'

This woman whom he didn't want to acknowledge, who had begun life in poverty (Sicily, America, Yorkshire, London, fashionable dress shop, wife of a famous crooner), she is a peasant peeling vegetables.

Coming away from the 'phone, she lifted a lid of the Aga and put on the kettle.

'I don't want anything,' he said. 'Don't make me cups of tea or other nonsense.'

'It's for me,' she said.

'You'll need something stronger than tea when I've said what I want to say –'

'*Sacru miu Gesù,*' she said under her breath. He wished she would speak to him, answer him, *fight*. He could sense her unease, as if she'd gone right within herself. She had her back to him again, she was protected.

A stab in the back. She needs a stab in the back.

'I'll tell you who told me. No, not Aunt Eleanor . . . An elderly Scotch doctor. Can you imagine? I'll never get over this . . . The whole bloody lot of you. And you the worst . . . This doctor, she asked *him* to tell me. A stranger by my bedside – breaking my world into pieces. "Och," he says, "it'll take you a wee while to settle this in your mind –" A wee while . . . If I could've crowned him –'

'I wanted you to know,' she said slowly. 'If you don't come back from the war, I didn't want you to die, deceived.'

'Isn't that rich? "Dead! And never called me Mother!" Cheap melodrama.' He laughed, dry, bitter. '"Dead, and never called me Mother!"'

'You're very English,' she said.

'My father was English, so what's the surprise? And of course that's my *grandfather*, gone picking bluebells with orphan Annie. They're very good, very good, the Graingers, at taking in waifs and strays. Look what they did for you. Look what *you* did for them –'

'How much did they tell you, Guy?'

'More than I wanted to hear.' He paced the kitchen. Kicked against a tin pail filled with eggs in waterglass. 'I don't want any of the disgusting details . . . Listening, are you? That effing doctor said, "Two young folk, an accident, we're all human." OK. But *why was I deceived*?'

'You were always going to be told. You would have been, before you married.' Her voice was harsh, dry.

'I should hope so, I should bloody well *hope* so.'

'I'm sorry –'

'What – for having me, or for not telling me?' He banged the pail again. '"Give it time to sink in," the medico said . . . I don't want it to sink in. I want to throw it up, vomit it away. Sick, I'm *sick* with this news. Can't you get that into your thick peasant head?' He was terrified by his anger. Burning him. Burning her.

'You'd better go,' she said. 'You've said all you need to say.'

He banged his fist again on the table, sending the cups rattling. On the Aga the kettle sent out clouds of steam. She crossed over and removed it.

'Get your tea. Get your bloody tea.' Even as he said it, he wanted suddenly to throw his arms about her. *I am my mother's son.*

And as soon the moment was gone. 'I need a walk, I'm going

to walk. That's the English in me. Walk it off. Walk as far as the pub. Wait till they're open, see if it's their day for beer.'

His heart thumped painfully. The storm still raged in his head. 'I hope I die. I hope I'm killed – soon.'

'I never meant –' she began. 'I did, like all the other times, what I thought was best. I –'

'Well, you did wrong. Then. Now. *All the bloody time.*'

He turned to go. As he neared the door, lifted the latch, she said:

'I suffered. I suffered too.'

'I don't want to hear.'

He heard instead – his banging of the door, the latch not fastening. Outside the farmhouse, he crossed to the grassy hollow, nettle-covered, near to the gate. There, coughing, half crying, he was violently sick.

Avoiding Eleanor, that evening in his room he wrote to his schoolfriend Andy, in the Navy still. They had not met since the summer of 1939.

. . . When this reaches you on the high seas, I'll be back in camp. Have had to overstay leave because of lung trouble. If you're surprised to get such a screed from me when I've been such a rotten correspondent lately, the truth is I've received the most terrible body blow. All of this in *utmost confidence* – (Just you, me and the Censor) but I have discovered who my real parents are. And they were *not* a couple of impoverished Tuscans. I don't want to say very much here except that my father was English, and was killed in America seven or eight years ago. My mother's of Sicilian origin, English by adoption. And they got the family doctor to tell me.

In the past when I quizzed my aunt (aunt indeed!) she always said she only knew what she'd been told. 'The nuns said very little.'

I've been round to the house where my *mother* – yes, I've got to keep writing the word – is living here in the village, and had a blazing row. Blistering. Row mostly on my side. I felt pretty ropey after and still do. There's no one about I can unburden myself on to, so that's why you're getting this Epistle to the Mariner. Unburden – that's about it. I've got to be fair, that's the English bit of me (and that's something I'm trying to take in, when all these years I thought myself English by adoption, education, traits acquired by rubbing themselves off on me), I know they didn't tell me, but would I really have wanted to know earlier? Did I really want the priests telling me? Did it really matter *who* told me? The medico was a decent cove, making the best of a bad job. My aunt could never have done it. She shies from intimacy like a well-bred, nervous horse. She has always been at all times quite wonderful, and I love her, and get exasperated by her.

I feel sick with shock, the most horrible fantasies. Every few minutes another wild idea. Example – if my real mother had had a daughter (she's married but without children) and I'd met the daughter and we'd fallen in love – then what? Greek tragedy, Andy, simple Greek tragedy.

Hang it, lots has been lost and nothing as far as I can see has been gained. Just someone I knew a little already and rather liked, I now hate. And I can't help it.

I feel I could *use* a woman just now. Punish one, Andy. Remember that stage you and I went through at school, of a truly fierce purity. We thought St Aloysius (that creep) rather fine. And we were going to remain pure always. Not monks, but holy in the world – Hardest thing of all, they used to tell us. And then remember how we went the other way. I don't think we thought about anything else but girls and IT for that whole term. But the one thing we never felt then with all our extremes, I feel now – and that's disgust. It's as if when they told about these things, then underneath, what they were really trying to tell us was – oh God, brute beasts, disgusting acts, women – tainted vessels. I'm terrain that's been ploughed up. Earth turned over, broken up, and the worms all underneath.

And what do worms and earth (and freshly turned soil) tell you? Men have died and worms have eaten them, but not for love. *Nor* because they've learned the truth about their parents. It's terrible to say this but I feel now the best thing that could happen to me is that I should go out soon, and be killed.

This letter's awfully morbid. (Too morbid for the Censor – have you read this far, sir?) But I feel better for talking to you. As ever. How innocent we were when we tired the sun with talking. I hope we haven't sent him down the sky for ever.

Yours,
Guy

5

Helen brought in the teatray and set it down. She put two logs on the fire. Outside the sky was grey, darkening already. A north-east wind blew icily – more like March than early April. It was the third day of her holidays.

'Shall I pour your tea, Uncle Eric?' She placed a table napkin on his knees.

'They've made a real little homemaker of you, have the convent. Is it yours, the chocolate cake?'

'Yes, and there aren't any cocoa lumps . . . But you have to have bread and marge first. Do you want honey on it?' She treated him like a child sometimes.

He asked, 'Still top of the class in arithmetic?'

She nodded proudly. 'We do problems now. About trains and bath water –'

She was happy at the convent in Harrogate, though she'd have preferred to be a weekly boarder. But petrol was rationed and the train journey too awkward. Billy was happy too, with Cousin Fred and his wife Auntie Janet. Cousin Fred was stationed still in Dundee, but might be sent overseas. He was someone she couldn't remember at all, though when he came over to Thackton to collect Billy, he promised her that they'd met when she was four. Seeing him there at Moorgarth, Helen's only thought had been, what a good thing it was Billy didn't wet and mess any more.

Before eating, she crossed over to the record case. 'Shall I play the gramophone a bit? There's Deanna Durbin that Maria bought me. Or some of Eddie's records.' She thought of that voice which came only out of the black Decca box now, never the wireless. She couldn't associate it with the photograph by Maria's bed. The two never came together.

'Not for me,' he said, 'I'd as soon sit and talk to you, ducky.'

From the very first she'd been at ease with Uncle Eric. Maria had worried. Helen had overheard her saying, '. . . I wonder if she won't be afraid of all men, all older men, now, after that.'

She thought Helen might not want to call Uncle Eric 'uncle'. She thought of everything. But 'No,' Helen had said, 'I want him to be my Uncle Eric.'

Maria was her mother. Eddie, when the war was over, would be her stepfather. Mam's death, three years ago now, was a buried sadness. A dull ache on cold days, a heartache coming on suddenly when she least expected it. She prayed for Mam after Communion and at Benediction, saying for her Miss Dennison's pink rosary. Mam was in heaven and happy. And safe inside Helen's head too, in memories.

Uncle Eric was an old man but he loved to walk, and the two of them went off here, there, everywhere. It was she who couldn't keep up. Walking, talking – he loved to talk to Helen. When Dick and his family came over, he showed Helen off to them. 'My new niece.' Dick had laughed, throwing his arm round his wife's shoulders (he was always touching her). 'Another Maria then'

But there was no Gwen now. She had died just before Christmas. Jan had come to stay with Maria and her grandfather. Helen had wanted to tell her she knew how it felt, but couldn't. Jan was almost a grown-up. So she just said, 'I offered up a Mass for your mother,' and Jan, red-rimmed eyes, looking a bit surprised, had said, 'Oh, thank you very much.' Politely.

It had been Gwen who had been so especially kind the first summer when Helen was settling in at Moorgarth. July and August 1940: bringing over from Middlesbrough, books, dolls, gramophone records, even a dolls' house. 'Our girls have grown out of them. You enjoy them, love.' There were boys' adventure books, fairy tales, girls' school stories. She hadn't been too good at reading then so Maria had read to her in the evenings. Our Lady, in a white satin dressing-gown with swansdown round the collar, and blue satin slippers.

In one of the fairy books, someone had coloured in all the black and white pictures. Maria read *The Golden Lion*.

'. . . *the Princess took the lion into her own room . . . She was just beginning to doze when she heard a voice, "O lovely Princess, if you only knew what I have gone through to find you." The Princess jumped out of bed screaming, "The lion! the lion!" but her friends thought it was a nightmare, and did not trouble themselves. "O lovely Princess!" continued the voice, "fear nothing! I am the son of a rich merchant, and desire above all things to have you for my wife . . ."*'

'What tunes had the lion inside?'

'Tunes from Sicily, where I come from, where the story comes from.'

'Sing me some –'

'Another day. If I can remember. It's a long time, you see.'

'Who did the colouring, can I colour the ones that aren't?'

'Dick did. It was already coloured when I read it, after I'd been rescued from the sea.'

'Tell me again about being rescued.'

How could she ever tire of Maria's tales? They had bits left out, though – things Maria wasn't telling. 'Everyone has secrets, Helen.'

'Grown folk even?'

'Ah, grown-ups most of all, Helen.'

Maria did so much for her. At the end of a day's work she sewed Helen trousers, summer shorts, blouses from her own old frocks. Next month they would be spending a week by the sea together in Wales.

'Will I pour you more tea, Uncle Eric?'

'Yes, please. You're very dear to me, Helen love.'

'That's all right.' She didn't know what to say when he made remarks like that, which was more and more often now. She loved them.

'If you really liked the cake, why don't you have another slice?'

'And spoil my supper?' Often when he was speaking, his eyes sparkled, so that he didn't look old any more. When they went out walking together at the beginning, he had held her hand. Now she held his. Then he would be safe.

'Know who you remind me of – I've said it before, haven't I?'

'Maria,' she said. 'You are a daftie –'

'Don't cheek me,' he said in mock anger. Then:

'She was a clever girl, was Maria. Running that business – sound head on her shoulders. There's many a man could do with her head. And that ice-cream fellow she married, all charm and little else, he's had cause to thank her. If he'd had the handling of the brass he made, there'd be nothing now.'

She thought he was probably talking to himself, which he often did now. She'd come into the room and he'd be in the middle of an imaginary conversation. 'Well, I said, if copper doesn't pick up . . .'

'I'll go out and feed the hens,' she said, 'then when I come in, we'll put the news on.'

'North Africa,' he said. 'Tunisia. News of Guy.'

'There was a letter,' she said. 'Miss Dennison read me bits. She's sending it over for you.'

She prayed for Guy every night. He had been several months fighting in Africa now. Miss Dennison's face on Sundays was anxious and careworn.

'Good,' he said, 'good. I worry about the lad.'

The kitchen with the Aga was warm, but outside the east wind blew icily. She hadn't on a heavy enough coat and shivered as she carried out the mash. She couldn't wait to be in again by the fire with Uncle Eric. Soon Maria would be back and the two of them would cook supper together. Afterwards they were all three going to a sing-song in the village hall.

'Hey, I'm back, here I am.' She put her head round the door. 'Shall I put the wireless on?'

He was sitting in his chair, quite, quite still.

'Uncle Eric,' she said, 'Uncle Eric, wake up.'

But he must be awake. He was looking at her. And so strangely. So strangely. She knew that he could see her.

They looked at each other. 'Talk to me,' she said. 'Talk to me. What is it, Uncle Eric?'

She put out a hand to touch him. His hand grasped hers. She said, 'Oh Uncle Eric. You can understand me, can you understand me?'

His silence terrified her. And his eyes, asking her some question she couldn't answer.

'Uncle Eric, please. Oh, Uncle Eric,' she took hold of his other hand and kneeled down beside him. 'Uncle Eric, don't worry about anything, you're going to be all right. I'll get someone to help . . .'

Without putting on her coat, she ran all the way to Park Villa. Banging on the door – she wasn't calm now, but shaking, sobbing. She clutched at Miss Dennison.

'Come quickly, help us – something awful is wrong with Uncle Eric.'

For Maria, the greatest shock at the funeral was Dick's appearance, even though it had been only a few days since she had seen him – when he'd come hurrying over, too late, to see his father for the last time.

It seemed to her standing by the open grave in the April sunshine that hardly any time, hardly enough time, had passed since Gwen's death. Gwen who had been buried in Bradford on a grey-skied, bare-branched November day. Today in Thackton, apple trees had burst into blossom in the corner of the churchyard, but Dick looked as cold as on that November day. Leaning on his stick, he stood beside Eleanor, the dark shadowing of his eyes more marked. Dulcie, up from London, on his other side.

Eric, victim of a stroke, had lingered less than twenty-four hours. Dr McIntosh, summoned by Eleanor, had arrived within minutes. A vigil had been kept all night. But he had died just after dawn, of a further massive stroke.

Death, death. Echoes and echoes. Dead on the sea bed, Mamma and the Ricciardis. Za Rosetta, dead. Zu Orazio, dead. Minicu. Why did death, thoughts of death – hark back always to Minicu?

'Where is Minicu?'

'Ask the vultures –' Seven-year-old self, hidden in the linen chest. Listening with beating heart. 'The Lion has a heart of stone.'

Where is Uncle Eric? I have just seen him go, oak-coffined, into the earth.

He had wished to be buried in Thackton. Great-Uncle Arthur, Uncle Fred, Stanley Taylor, Bob Hardcastle and others from the foundry had all come over from Middlesbrough, travelling with Dick. Helen stood beside Maria, wearing her convent uniform and hat. Some persons had not approved of her attending. ('It's enough upset she found him, without she's to see him buried, poor little lass.') But Helen had told her: 'I want to say goodbye to him.' As the coffin was lowered into the earth, she held Maria's hand. Her eyes were tight shut.

Death – and Guy. Oh, terrible scene of a year ago. Guy, the beloved, shouting hatred and shock and pain at her. And she, full of pain herself, unable to answer. (Why did I want him to know, could I not have left it? She remembered Eleanor's reluctance, their decision to say nothing to Eric.)

Had the revelation, the knowledge, taken root in him since? He had seen it as, yes, terrible, but had he seen also that now he had a mother, not just an aunt by adoption but a true blood mother?

Perhaps after (if there was for him an after) something would be possible for the two of them. Some compromise, something *English*. Yes, it would be English, that part of him which would allow them to know each other, be sometimes together – and never to mention the truth.

Secrets. So many secrets. She imagined suddenly some world where they would not have been needed. Peter confessing, being forgiven. Herself, cared for, comforted, and after nine months brought to term of a boy. Some other world or time, where no child was ill-begotten. Love-child – a beautiful expression . . . But Guy could never have been a love-child. Only a loved child.

Victories in North Africa. Progress of the Eighth Army. Tunisia falling to the Allies. But in all that someone had to be killed. Oh, let it not be him, *Sacru miu Gesù*, let it not be him. Blessed Virgin whose Son was taken from Thee this Easter season, *bring me back my son* . . .

6

Dick could see that at least two members of the Board wanted to hurry on the agenda, to reach as soon as possible the provisions of his father's will. Bob Hardcastle was visibly impatient, jogging his knee against the table. Old Stanley Taylor pulled noisily at the edge of the agenda sheet.

Dick's fingers, lying on the open Minutes Book, trembled. He pressed down the heel of his hand firmly, licked his dry lips and gave as lucidly as possible a report of his visit the week before to Rolls-Royce. Uncle Fred explained at length about the purchase of half a dozen turret lathes, a single electric motor and shafting and a Gisholt combination valve. 'Purchased . . . let's see, the twenty-second February, and already in use.' Then Bernard Thorpe was re-elected auditor, proposed by Dick, seconded by Stanley.

I should have had a drink, Dick thought. A small one. Three hours, without a drop. I *need* whisky. That's the damnable thing. Now, no chance of any until this is over. And it will take time. Good God, it'll take time. Although the point's not debatable, they will try.

He was right. Bob was the most angry, as if in waiting for the other items to be cleared he had built up a greater head of steam. Dick thought tiredly: We should have begun with all this, got it over. I should have stuck to my guns.

Here it was now: Dad's bequest. Request. Bob was the first away:

'There's no question, no question. I'll not mince my words. Stanley and I –' He broke off. Then loud with indignation: 'There's never been a woman on this board –'

'My mother,' Dick said. 'There's a precedent –'

'Maimie Grainger . . . You know well that was on paper, lad. I've – we've no objection to paper women. They don't talk, do they? They've no voice. I'll speak plainly. We'll not have it. And if it's to go to the vote –'

'It's not a voting matter exactly,' Dick said, an edge to his voice. 'I thought I'd explained. It's set out in the memorandum. Dad owned the company. Now I own it. And the conditions of his will are quite clear. Mrs Sabrini is to sit on the board and *to have a voice*. Those were Dad's words.'

'Look here, lad –' Bob said.

Irritated and thirsty (if only he had slipped his flask in his coat pocket), Dick interrupted him:

'Don't give me "lad". I'm a man of forty-five.'

'Ninety-five, Dick, and I'd still not care . . . We don't want a woman on the board.'

He tried again. 'She was after all Dad's protégée. More than that – he adopted her legally –'

'I don't care *whose* lass she is. Herr Hitler's, Winnie Churchill's, we don't want her. Don't want any women having their daft say, standing up here, telling us what's to be done.'

As soon as Bob had finished, Stanley composed his heavy face. His expression was sorrowful, mildly reproachful.

'Your brother, your late brother – what would Peter have said if he'd been here today? I'm surprised at you, Dick. But you always were . . . Special treatment. There was a soft spot for her, wasn't there? A Wop, a bloody Wop –'

'Take that back, *now*. Take it back, at once –' Dick waited, hands shaking. But Stanley gave only a shrug of his shoulders, smiling a half-hearted apology. I must have a drink, Dick thought. Nothing less than whisky could calm this alarming faintness, nausea. Bowels turned to water. Trembling. If he were to lift a hand against Stanley?

'Water,' he said, 'pass the carafe, please.'

'There's a war on –' Uncle Fred said (wanting, as ever, peace), trying to distract. 'And what do I find, eh? New suit, best cloth – and then their wretched regulations. Look at this waistcoat now – no hole allowed for a watch chain.'

'There's a war on,' Bob said. 'All the more reason, with our lads away, to have someone knows what's what –'

Uncle Fred said, 'She's a clever lass, is Mrs Sabrini.'

Bob turned on him. 'Where's the proof of it? Working in a shop in London, marrying an Eyetie crooner – I've not seen it. Bed and board . . . There's one place for women, and it's not on the board.'

Dick thought: He is not going to, he will not dare.

'It's in bed,' Stanley said, laughing loudly, willing the others to join in. A man among men.

Bob banged his fist on the table delightedly. 'I never – you can't give out *I* said it –'

The dull ache in Dick's leg, constant companion now, turned slowly, relentlessly into pain, gnawing from ankle to calf, then up to his thigh. He changed position restlessly in an attempt to ease it. Finally he rummaged in his pocket for the tablets. 'The water,' he said, 'could you pass the carafe again?'

'O Death in life, the days that are no more . . .' He read poetry now. At night. The nights were so long. Without whisky they would be even longer.

The whisky. How long would it last? He could not manage on a ration. Perhaps one bottle in a couple of months, if he could get it. Although maybe it would not be so difficult. The same source as cigarettes. Black market contacts. Under the counter. Payments in kind that he could make. A year ago he would have been ashamed. But now, his need was so great. If he could not light up first thing in the morning, have a small drink, how was he to get even as far as the Works?

Dad's cellar, when the house in Linthorpe Road had been sold up. All that whisky. 'I'd quite forgot,' Dad had said before moving to Moorgarth. 'But if there's a scarcity we'll not go short.' And they had not. Most of it had gone to Dick – barely touched while Gwen was alive, but broken into in those first terrible weeks, when he had drunk several tots each night-time, knowing that after perhaps three pages, unseen, of a novel, he would be asleep (forget that forlorn waking in the small hours, the struggle for sleep which at five or six came too late).

It wasn't just the lonely double bed. He'd tried for a time sleeping in Betty's room, until a war worker had been billeted on them. An iron-faced spinster with greasy stiff curls, and smelling unpleasantly of mothballs, she could not have been offered his and Gwen's room. So he had gone back. He slept always in his half of the bed, as if she were still there – waking in the morning always to an empty pillow, and cold realization.

Another day to be lived through. Jan, off to school, kissing him first, 'See you later, Dad?' squeezing his hand tightly. Never saying very much. They didn't talk about Gwen's death. In the autumn, when she was eighteen, Jan would leave to nurse. They spoke in roundabout phrases: 'Now there's just you and me . . .' or 'it's been hard since November . . .' Never the name 'Gwen'.

Not even Mummy or Mother. Nothing. Horribly, this never mentioning her only reinforced her absence. But he could not alter anything, could not be the first. It had come to seem impossible, for Jan apparently as much as for him.

He thought Betty was courting, and was glad for her. A French Canadian she had met just before her mother's death. Her letters were full of him.

He could spend some time at Moorgarth, which after all belonged to him now. There was space, he would be more than welcome. And Maria would look after him. But he did not want to go anywhere. Least of all there. It was full of memories, and all of them happy.

Two deaths in six months. It had been too much. And Dad's death had affected him as Mother's had not. (He had never been close to her, she had not been proud of him. When she had not been grumbling, she had been scaremongering.)

And now today, this upset over Maria.

Dad had thought so well of Maria and her business head – how well she had managed Eddie's affairs, and the dress shop. Peasant virtues, Maria had told Dick: thrift, caution, husbanding of resources. 'Don't look to me for any lucky gambles, or flair . . .' But it was because of this Dad had wanted her on the Board. The display of bad manners this afternoon – it would blow over. Possibly she wouldn't interest herself too much, although it was probable she'd want to fulfil Dad's wishes. She had loved him very much.

His own work at the foundry: 'There's a war on,' and for a while, stretches of an hour here or there, the pain would be dulled, because he had to think so furiously of other matters. But although he could lose himself for a little, none of it meant anything to him now. He did not suppose that, generally, he was a success. The Honours list would never have his name, he was unlikely to be Mayor or even on the Council. He did not care enough. He'd always done a day's work as honourably as he knew how, and then come home to Betty and Jan – and Gwen. If that wasn't success, why care? Why worry, when they were so happy?

Back home now there was a meal to face. Jan was away in the Lakes with a schoolfriend. The billetee was working late. As he came in, Mrs Scriven, the housekeeper, was preparing to leave. The wireless was blaring. *'It's a hap hap happy day . . .'* She had made him some vegetable soup to be reheated. There was a plate of sandwiches under a glass cover. He poured himself a whisky and sat down in the chair opposite Gwen's.

Time passed. Nine o'clock. Ten. Eleven. Soon it would be all right to go up to bed.

'O that 'twere possible, After long grief and pain
To find the arms of my true love, Round me once again.'

He prayed each night not to wake in the morning. His leg hurt more than for many years. Perhaps something had gone wrong. But a bad leg would not release him, a bad leg only became worse. Death would not come so easily.

7

They heard about the Italian surrender on the evening of September 8th. Guy had just joined General Clark's Fifth Army in Sicily as part of 10 British Corps. They were to invade the Italian mainland early the next morning. For a few stupid moments he thought: Now we shan't have to go.

Operation Avalanche. They were bound for the sandy beaches around Salerno: their aim, to fight their way as quickly as possible up to Naples. Guy had visited Salerno on his 1937 Grand Tour. Accompanied by Aunt Eleanor and her brother Basil, he'd stayed two nights at the Montestalla Hotel. He remembered little – narrow medieval alleys, some tree-lined squares, and always, up behind, the mountains.

Quarter to four in the morning. They were crammed together in the assault craft. Guy, and Randall Furness (lieutenant in another platoon and discovered to have read Italian at Cambridge while Guy did the same at Oxford) and Miller – that same Miller he'd hated so at St Boniface's and who had now turned up suddenly in his unit.

'Just what you'd expect of the Wops,' he was saying. 'Jacking it in like that. If we're to have them as allies now, God help us.'

Randall said, 'They'll be an occupied country now like half of Europe – though when I heard, I thought, Christ, we needn't go in after all. Then I remembered Jerry –'

'Ditto,' Guy said. 'Spirit thinks its willing, but the old unconscious lies in wait.'

'The Krauts'll be the ones lying in wait,' Miller said, 'don't worry.'

Earlier he'd said, 'Dennison. Not sure I'd have recognized you – but the name clinched it.'

Guy had thought: I've no trouble remembering that face, that voice. Fighting Miller.

He had said, 'Miller, yes. St Boniface. '28, '29. Frankly I hated your guts.' He remembered his frightening anger, fists in face, *wishing Miller dead.* Here now was this pale, small-eyed, spotty young man.

'If I remember rightly,' Miller said, 'I ragged you and you went for me. And got a black mark –'

Tired memories. A lifetime away. 'St Boniface. Ghastly place . . .'

'Perhaps I was a bit rough,' Miller said, piggy-eyed, 'but I was right about Italians. General, of course – not particular, Dennison. Pretty poor lot.'

The engines throbbed, the boat throbbed, rising and falling on the waves. How to tell fear from seasickness? All around him his men, some cheerfully, some miserably, threw up their insides. Vomit covered their boots. 'In this campaign, don't ask who's got guts,' Randall said sardonically. 'Some are busy losing theirs the old-fashioned way.'

Guy, kitted out: trousers, one pair long, tropical; shirt, one tropical; one cap, service dress; one pair boots and gaiters. His stomach heaved to the rhythm of the craft. The sea shook with the huge naval shells fired by the destroyer's escorts. The air shook. He was sweaty with nerves.

As the churned up sea sent water over the bows of the craft, he shut his eyes, and thought of death. Six months now since the sea had claimed Andy. Gone down with his ship. Nevermore, Guy had thought, nevermore. Andy, the only person he had been able to write to after that doctor had told him about Maria, in that innocent world of eighteen months ago (Guy the soldier, who had never heard a shot fired in anger). Later that summer he had spent a week at Andy's home, both of them on leave, before Andy changed ships.

Andy's little sister had been there – not so little now. 'Sh, sh, here comes Sheila,' the family said. So neat, so fair, so English. Seen last in 1939 on her way back to convent school: navy blue mackintosh, gym tunic and striped tie, blue velour hat with elastic band, lisle stockings and navy lace-ups.

And here she was again, but grown up now. Sh sh Sheila. Quiet but vivacious. About to join up, to become a WAAF. They went riding together on his last morning while Andy slept in. He asked her then if she would write to him.

They kissed, Sheila leaning against a tree. Their horses were tethered. Her lips had been very sweet. He did not dare to think of touching her body. Sh sh Sheila, not for touching. His hands, so warm, so ready to explore, to satisfy, mustn't be allowed their freedom. He held them pressed hard against the grainy tree trunk.

'I've never had a boyfriend,' she said. 'Not one that counted – There was this man at the Young Farmers . . .' She giggled. 'I go sometimes to dances at the RAF base. But it's always someone different brings me home. Safety in numbers, the school chaplain used to say.'

And so they had begun to write to each other. She proved a chatty, warm, spontaneous companion on paper. She wrote not as she talked, but much, much better. Words she would never have spoken glided easily from pen to paper. That she loved him, he felt certain. The words, unspoken, were there loud and clear in those letters from her heart. Tiny writing, even smaller when reduced to an airgraph, crowded the page. She surprised him. He suspected she surprised herself.

They met only once again before he left for Tunisia. She had been stationed in Lincolnshire. An awkward meeting: two days that had gone too quickly. Holding hands in a cinema. The long closed-mouth kiss. She smelled, and tasted, of lily of the valley and soap. 'Your kisses are wonderful,' she told him. 'Like I said in the last letter – I have them in my dreams. Honestly.' Ah, my dear, he thought. And is that all?

'I feel like someone in a film. They kiss like that, don't they? Like us?' Sh sh Sheila, in her neat sky blue uniform with the lace-up shoes and the peaked-cap – almost the convent girl again.

And then Andy was lost. It was she who had written to tell him. She had told Guy she wanted to cry in his arms. How happy Andy would be, she said, that they had each other.

He carried her letters about. Her photograph. Last thing at night, he thought of her. So if it wasn't love it was something very like it. Sh sh Sheila. 'Pray for me,' she had said. Her sudden little pieties: in her letters, an account of how many decades of the rosary she'd managed after camp lights out – interspersed with memories of his kisses.

In her latest she had written, 'There's a special sort of kissing – one of the girls said something I didn't understand, but it's to do with *souls*. I'm sure you'll know – or could find out. Whatever it is I expect we'll want to do it . . .' And another time: 'I think honestly, Guy, *everything* is all right in Time of War whatever the priests say. The nuns told us if you die in battle you go straight to Heaven – a complete plenary indulgence, isn't that *marvellous*?'

'This place is lonely but very beautiful,' she wrote from the far north of Scotland. 'I have lots of time to think of all the things I love about you, Guy.'

Love. Yes, she had used that word. He thought perhaps he also had used it once or twice. He did not regret it. And yet he felt always as if, having seen a door open somewhere, he'd gone through it in curiosity, only to hear it slam behind him. Why? After all, it had been *he* who'd said, 'When the war's over we'll do this, that . . .' He had not mentioned marriage, but the notion was there for anyone to see. For Sheila to see.

As the craft drew nearer to the coast, the mountains reared blue-black in the early morning light. In marching order, they stood to. Seeing his men, their misery and their seasickness put aside, he prayed, 'God, don't take too many of them.'

And then suddenly it was as if giant electric lights . . . The scene was illuminated. German searchlights. A waiting enemy, just as Miller had said. The screaming and whining of mortars, and the white foam as they exploded around the assault crafts. Then a massive jolt forward as the craft hit the beach.

Confusion of battle. Staggering, pushing forward, stumbling in the waist-high water. Bullets whipping the air, whipping up the loose sand. Shrapnel whizzing by. And the noise: great 8 mm shells screaming their way, overhead – aimed at the armada out at sea.

I am my mother's son. He fell. Then he was up again and running forward. Now down again, and crawling. And always the noise and confusion. Light-headed still with fatigue and seasickness. Pressing forward . . . There was Randall, alive still. How long to survive? Shall I see nightfall? Heat of the early morning sun. Heat of battle. Helmeted warrior, the sweat trickling down his face, his neck.

Fighting, still only a few hundred yards from the water. And now a concerted attack by the waiting Germans. An armoured car coming towards them and as they crouched, turning its gun on them.

More troops landing. The beach crowded with jeeps, trucks, ambulances. A jeep in flames. Sea spray and sand, blasted on to everything.

Rubble, smoke. Above them now, a brilliant blue sky. *I am my mother's son.* Why had he ever thought that wrong? What mattered was to stay alive. Today. And tomorrow. And tomorrow. I love her, he thought. Behind them was the crowded sea, crowded still with ships. Aimed at the fleet, the shells screamed over their heads.

Later that day, slowly, they made their way inland through an area of low trees and thick vines, under a blazing sun. Day's end – and he was still alive. The third night, he slept in a real bed in a deserted farmhouse. The bedside drawer was full of black-bordered burial cards: photographs, tender inscriptions – grand-fathers, grandmothers, uncles, babies . . . The worn bedlinen was embroidered and lovingly darned. Someone's home. He thought of Maria.

I am my mother's son. Probably he could live with the revel-ations. He had after all, almost died with them.

Ten days later they went behind the lines to rest, a few miles south of Salerno. There were orchards laden with fruit. The weather stayed extremely hot.

They lay on their backs, arms for pillows, gazing up at the sky. Miller, Randall, and Fletcher and Young, two others from Guy's outfit. Discarded apple cores lay about them. Fletcher munched.

'Redder than a drunk's nose, this apple,' he said, 'but the texture's wrong. Mealy. Give me Beauty of Bath, green and pink and misshapen.'

'At least they're free, available, and don't come out of a tin –' Randall said.

'Like Miller hopes the popsies will be when we get to Napoli. Free and available, that is.'

'Clap hands, clap hands – I wouldn't really,' Young said. 'Even a Boy Scout might be unlucky . . .'

'How can you tell good-time girls from *good* girls?'

'Good girls won't be available,' Miller said. 'Anyway, ask Dennison here. Dennison knows something about it. He's Ital-ian.'

'Done a recce, have you, Dennison?' Fletcher asked.

'Not exactly. A visit in '37 as a stripling. Accompanied by a maiden aunt and a Jesuit priest.'

'Really – no escaping at night? No secret assignations?'

'Not a thing. A good boy.'

'He still is,' Miller said. But not unkindly.

Randall said, 'Do we honestly need floosies this moment? Peace, no guns, rest. Enough surely . . . God knows it'll start up again soon enough.'

Fletcher whistled, *When the lights go on again all over the world.* 'Damned tune. Had it on the brain all day.'

'When we get to Naples,' Young said, 'there's Capri to see. Capriot excitements –'

' *'Twas on the Isle of Capri that I met her,*' sang Miller. His singing voice was nasal. He quizzed Guy, 'Did the maiden aunt and the Jesuit take you there?'

'They did, actually.'

'. . . *Now it's goodbye to the isle of Capri* . . . I only remember the last line. And the first. Sung in the most revolting manner, I recall – all sentiment – by Eddie Sabrini. Dance band crooners, don't they make you want to spit?'

'I used to rather like him,' Guy said.

I am my mother's son. (He wished now suddenly, passionately, that he might not die violently as had his father.)

'Eyetie, wasn't he, with a name like that?' said Miller. 'He'll have been put behind bars for sure. Ever hear his records now?'

8

Every Friday evening now, Eleanor gave supper to Dr McIntosh. She had been doing it since just after Eric's death, eight months ago. She had visited his surgery because she couldn't sleep ('An old family friend . . . a great shock . . .') 'Do you eat properly?' he'd asked, 'it's very important for morale.' Eleanor said that of course she did. Her housekeeper had left to work in a factory, and she now cooked for herself and usually for Rosie.

'Then you'll eat better than I do, on black Friday.' He explained how his housekeeper always visited her old aunt on Fridays. The replacement she had found: 'She's a widow lady. I pity her good husband when he was with her – a cast-iron stomach he must have had. Och, it's an experience, and I've not the courage to say, "Away with ye, I'll do it myself."'

'Let *me* invite you,' she'd said, 'come and have a good meal at Park Villa this very Friday.' She pressed him to accept, seeing selfishly in the effort of entertaining him a distraction from the pain, the vacuum that Eric's death had left.

Now, in the December of 1943, she no longer worried so much about Guy – in Naples, where he'd been seconded together with his friend Randall Furness, making use of their Italian. There was much to be done there, she could not imagine it an easy posting, and although the British and Americans held the city there was danger still from German bombs. But because he was not fighting up through Italy, she relaxed a little. Yet since Eric's death, her days and nights were anxiety-filled. Of course he was elderly, of course she had known he might at any time die – but that it should have been so sudden. To have seen him for the last time like that. Oh, Eric, she had thought over and over, if you had *known* how much I loved you. (Eric, who had loved Dulcie, but who had not married her when he was free.)

In Heaven there was no marriage or giving in marriage. She and he would meet again there. But she could not wait – it was *now* she wanted to see him. The short distance from Park Villa to Moorgarth, that was as far away as she could bear. Their talks together over the years about Guy and his future. The gratitude, spoken and unspoken, for what she had done for this, his first grandson . . . Realizing he had gone for ever, she found herself night after night sleepless yet exhausted. As long as he lived, had she not hoped that in the end? (No, she told herself, *I did not.*)

And so, although beginning as distraction from sorrow, the first meal she had cooked had been so to Dr McIntosh's liking, had given so much pleasure, that she had asked him again. Before long it had become a ritual. With the wartime dispensation from abstinence for Catholics, she was able to save and cook him the best of her meat ration. Vegetables from the garden, home-bottled fruit, honey from her bees.

They talked. And talked. Gradually she heard his life-story, from babyhood in Stirling through school, medical school, happy marriage, widowhood, and heart attack . . . He talked easily about himself. She could not.

The fifth Christmas of the war approached. About ten days before, she had the idea of having her hair permanently waved. Or rather Maria had. Maria, whose thick black hair, winged now with grey, went easily into any style, looking at Eleanor's bun (first put up in 1903 and never altered since, except perhaps to grow more severe), had said, 'Why not a perm, Eleanor? Had you ever thought of a perm?'

Eleanor argued with her. Such an irrevocable step – and if she didn't like the result? But looking quickly in the glass that evening (she never lingered), she had 'seen' suddenly a halo of curls and wondered, perhaps?

'Dear Guy,' she wrote, 'your old aunt is about to have her hair *permed*! Having managed to miss Marcel waves, bobs, shingles, etc., after all these years I am about to be dashing. Shall I send you a photograph? I go into Whitby on Thursday morning to have it done . . .'

She sat in the cubicle, fastened to the permanent wave machine, worrying about frying. She was scarcely over the shock of seeing her fine grey-brown hair lying like a mat at her feet. The girl who cut it talked non-stop about her fiancé who was due home on leave that weekend – and about Bevin Boys, the conscripts who were to be sent down the mines instead of into the Forces.

She was amazed and shocked by her appearance when, rinsed, washed, set and dried, she was confronted by a head of tight curls. Whether it suited or not, she could not reconcile the change. For the first time in many years now, she thought: What would Mother say?

Outside was a damp, gloomy day, an icy wind blowing off the North Sea as she walked along the harbour towards the station. Unusually she was not wearing a hat because she had not wanted to flatten the new curls.

Back at Park Villa there was the usual disorder and mess. Rosie had a third baby now. Before Eleanor had been able to make any comment about this fresh, third pregnancy, Rosie had told her that this time it was her husband's. 'He visited – that time you was away two nights. They flew him in. Special flight . . .'

'From Burma?' she had said. 'Oh, Rosie . . .'

About her hair, Rosie said only, 'Had it cut off, did you?' She was preoccupied because she had mislaid their sweet coupons. 'You've not moved them anywhere, Miss D?' She slapped Malcolm about the legs when he tried to look for them in her purse. The new baby yelled. 'Remember you promised to take us to the Toy Exchange.'

In the afternoon she forked over one of the flowerbeds, even though she felt chilled still. Next morning she woke with the beginnings of a cold, which she ignored. Today was the day for entertaining Dr McIntosh. She had managed to get some oxtail. She was standing over the stove stirring it, when she fainted.

Or almost. Feeling bad, she turned, caught at the kitchen table and stumbled into a chair. There she blacked out. She was alone. Rosie and family were not due back for another hour.

She was pretty sure that she had a temperature. Cold, hot, sweaty and shivering now, she telephoned the surgery and left a message with the receptionist: she was sorry but due to unforeseen circumstances she must cancel that evening's invitation.

'Wait, Doctor'll speak to you,' the receptionist said. 'No, no,' she said.

She lay shivering in bed. The warmth she had made ready for the evening did not extend to her bedroom. She was too weak to carry back upstairs the electric fire she'd taken to make the dining-room warm for him.

Two or three minutes after Rosie and the children returned, he was at the house. He came straight upstairs.

'What's all this, now?'

'I didn't send for you,' she said.

'Och, but I can read between the lines. What would you do me out of a meal for unless you ailed?'

He took his thermometer out of its case and shook it. 'There's some very nasty 'flu about. You didn't see the King has it? You've good company . . . Your temperature, now. Keep this under your tongue a wee while.'

She could not speak with the thermometer in. She remembered suddenly her hair.

He held the thermometer up to the light. 'A hundred and three . . . as I thought.' Then:

'You've done away with your crowning glory –'

'I felt like a change. It's been forty years in a bun.'

'I say it only to praise. You suit curls.'

She said, 'Your supper. I so wanted to give you a good meal –'

'And I looked forward to it. What was I to have?'

She told him. 'Doesn't that make a man's mouth water? I had a nice bottle all ready. A patient's cellar . . . I'll take that oxtail away with me if Rosie likes to put it in a dish . . . But no getting up tomorrow. You hear me? It's to be taken seriously, this 'flu. If I tell you there's more than seven hundred dead, will you believe me and not take risks?'

'Yes,' she said humbly, feeling weak as a baby. She thought she'd never been so glad to see his bulky form – fine white moustache, head of white hair – come lumbering into the room.

'And in the meanwhile, what are we to do with you? Rosie can't . . . I know just the wee lassie I can send up.'

It turned out to be a second cousin of Amy's. Helen, just home for the holidays, came to help as well.

He visited her next day, and every day following. The next Friday was Christmas Eve. On the Wednesday, she asked him, 'What about Christmas Dinner?'

She was certain that some family would have asked him, and surprised when he said not. She herself would be going up to Moorgarth where Dick would join Maria and Helen. Rosie and her brood were already bespoke to a family in Thackton with a great many small children.

'Then you'll eat here?'

'I will indeed.'

She made excuses to Maria. For the meal she was able to get a chicken, and roasted it with all the trimmings and her own homegrown celery and carrots. A real plum pudding from one of Sybil and Jenny's food parcels, and rum butter.

Bright sunshine in the morning on her return from Mass. At one o'clock she sat down to wait. At two o'clock she put everything back in the oven. At three o'clock she listened to the King's speech on the kitchen wireless. After that, she rang his house. The housekeeper was there.

'Doctor rushed out at midday – but I've an address he can be found. Are you poorly?'

'Don't bother,' she said. She shut the door on the warm dining-room with its candles and holly. Feeling flat, and hungry, for she had not wanted to eat alone, she sat down with a book and picked at a slice of Christmas cake. At five o'clock Rosie returned with the children. She didn't notice that Eleanor had not eaten.

At six o'clock he appeared.

'What can I say?'

'I kept it hot,' she said. 'Only . . .'

'Ten miles away,' he said, 'and no telephone . . . They'd ridden over to fetch me. A great hurry. There was no leaving the old man. But he's safe now – and I'm hungry. Cups of tea is what I've had all day.' He brought out of his pocket a bottle. 'Montrachet '27. Didn't I promise you something?'

He was very repentant. She was surprised how good the food tasted still, although kept hot several hours. Two electric fires had brought the room to a fine heat. The wine relaxed her, and her tongue.

Now he was telling her off. 'There – Dr McIntosh again. Didn't I tell you *Ian*?' She was at ease, and could see that he was too. Even though deafening sounds came at intervals from upstairs. Kevin shouting, 'No, our Mam, no!' The concentrated wail of the new baby.

'Is that the wee one fathered by the Holy Ghost? He has a fine pair of lungs . . .?'

They could laugh together over Rosie's mishaps, and she was able to tell him her good news, heard only yesterday, that if no fresh raids came in the North, Rosie might be returning home to live with relatives.

'And Alistair?' she asked as usual. She always asked about his son. 'Any news?'

'Still in Kashmir – I'd an airgraph Thursday. He's so taken with India, perhaps he'll not come back. I mean, he's not married, there's nothing to tie him here. And I've looked after his practice well, have I not?'

'Are you sure you're not overdoing it? You came out of enforced retirement – your health didn't allow . . . Why should it be all right now?'

'Never happier, never fitter. Puffing a little now and then, but och, I said I was having a good war, didn't I?'

She knew as they sat there, eating crystallized figs from Jenny's food parcel, that she could never have borne to sit at Maria's table – in Eric's absence. He would have been there, his ghost sat opposite, his voice filling the air. ('Eleanor, I insist on pulling the wishbone with Eleanor . . . the only one who won't cheat. Eleanor . . .') Oh, how I loved you, Eric.

The brandy which followed her fourth glass of wine filled her with a warm glow. She remembered then that she had felt the glow already with the second glass of Montrachet. Her head floated delightfully.

'I think I may be a little – tiddly,' she said.

'Och now, that's good. Let your hair down the once . . .' He stopped, then chuckled. 'Too late for that, is it not?'

'I wish I'd had it cut years ago,' she said. 'The sense of freedom. It's wonderful.'

'I feel now you're not used to freedom, as you call it. It's not just enough to be a brave lassie – no, don't protest, for you are – but there was your mother, wasn't there? You told me something of her once. And I've seen her picture. I know fine the sort of woman.'

She reached out to push the brandy towards him. Her fingers grown thick misjudged and the decanter almost toppled.

'Oh dear. I really am tiddly –'

As he righted it, he said, 'And I mustn't be. I could get another call again yet. So, I'll not indulge further.' He sighed comfortably: 'And when I think now what I could drink in my student days –'

The clock struck nine. Sturdy grandfather clock which once Father, the retired General Dennison, had wound every week. Its sound came from far away, advancing, receding. She put her hand to her head, then touched her glass. 'Oh dear,' she said, 'I think I'd better leave this.'

He was looking at her. He placed his big hands palms down on the table. 'I wonder,' he said, 'are you too tiddly now to answer a serious question?'

At once she was alarmed. He looked so grave.

'Och, I seem to have frightened you into sobriety –'

'No, no. It was only . . .'
'I was wondering just now – would you marry me, Eleanor?'

Lying awake, with only the bedside lamp, gazing at the ceiling. How often in the past had she seen Eric's face, appearing unbidden (*for*bidden) in the shadows cast by the light? And then later, when she was half asleep, there he would be in her arms. Oh, the wickedness of it. My hopeless, hopeless love for Eric.

And yet not hopeless. For without it, would she ever have adopted Maria and Peter's child? And that had been the right thing to do. For everyone. If she had had nothing else, she had had Eric's precious gratitude. All those years of living on so little, but that little had been enough.

Or had it? Surprised by happiness (would she ever see Ian's face on the ceiling?), I am to be a married woman, she thought.

9

It was not the Naples he remembered, this Naples of 1943. For a start it smelled different. In 1938, with Aunt Eleanor and Basil, although the stench of the sewers had come up in the heat, there had been also the smell of freshly roasted coffee, roasting food, mouth-watering dishes cooking in the trattorie, or served on the food stalls.

Now, everywhere, a smell of burnt wood, of decay, bitter, acrid. The peculiar smell of a city in disarray. Smell of panic, disease, desperation. Buildings that before, although slums, had smelled alive, now were full of the curious suffocating odour of powdered plaster. Crumbled yellow stone ruins blocked the streets as they tried to pass.

Apart from army vehicles there were few motors. Carriages brought out after years of storage, were drawn by worn-out horses. Intensive air raids by the Allies had made everyday life a nightmare of hazards and shortages. Because there was now no proper water supply, typhus lurked always. Electricity failure, trams abandoned in their tracks and systematically ransacked, stripped of anything that could be sold or exchanged. And what could not, these days?

Above all, it was a hungry city. Hunger governing every action, making the physically weak, weaker and more desperate. And yet ingenious. Hungry, but still with wits enough to beg, borrow, steal. He remembered from school his reading about the Irish famine. Not so hungry as that. He saw no walking skeletons. But all the same, they did not look well, these Neapolitans.

The harbour, when they had entered Naples last month, had been a ruin. Girders twisted and tangled with broken cranes, standing out against the skyline like some surrealist pen and ink drawing. In the harbour itself, sunken ships, chained to each other by the retreating Germans, made formidable obstructions. They had driven in past derelict factories, ruined tenement slums. Electric wires looped and useless. Craters in the streets, pitfalls for the unwary.

It hadn't been the entry into Naples they had pictured. Randall said, 'From my reading of history, plus of course a few flicks, Hollywood historical, I imagined we'd come in like one of those South American heroes, flags flying everywhere, lots of the old brass bands, and hundreds of dusky-haired beauties, flowers between their teeth – throwing them from the balcony –'

'Their teeth?' asked Guy.

'Silly bugger. No, flowers. Tossing luscious blooms and calling out seductive come hithers.'

'You've listened to Bizet's *Carmen* once too often –'

Later Randall said, 'We came in the wrong end, it appears. No Neapolitan would have expected conquerors entering from the south of the city like that. It's up by the Royal Palace our beauties should have thrown their blooms and called their invites.'

'We got the calls, even if they weren't invites,' Guy said. '*Vivono gli Alleati, America,* even *Inghilterra.* They know which is the right side now. And it's not as if we didn't get kissed.'

'And clawed at. All that hysteria, weeping and wailing. You're an emotional race, you Southern Italians –'

'When did I last weep or wail, Randall, old chap? And these are Neapolitans, not Sicilians, anyway. Just completely different.'

A good-natured exchange. Randall, the person he saw the most of these days, since they had been left behind in the city. Because they were together so much, he had let slip the truth about himself. What do I care now? he had thought after that first, final moment of reconciliation in battle, of acceptance, when death had become suddenly real. When it had seemed more important to have a mother than to be righteous.

Everywhere in Naples, the barrel organs, playing mournfully. Wheezing the familiar *Funiculi, funicula,* or *Vieni sul mar,* which at first he didn't recognize.

'*Two lovely black eyes,*' sang Randall. '*Oh, what a surprise* . . . A great whiff of the English music hall . . . Thought I'd heard it somewhere before.'

A block of apartments in the Carmine district had been requisitioned for British troops. It had been made sketchily comfortable: the men were to write letters, read, play cards, and for this there were some chairs and tables. Most of the furniture was pushed to the sides, the valuable and the ordinary rammed crazily together. Books, china ornaments, clocks, paintings, were piled more or less carefully. But it worried Guy – whose business it wasn't. The carpet had been rolled up: from the reverse side he could see its quality. He was afraid of looting, the easy slipping into the pocket of some small valuable.

He was just leaving when he heard a commotion on the stairs. A man's voice, a girl's. 'No, but we have to be let in, it must be allowed.'

'No,' the sergeant was saying, 'No. Not even if you speak our lingo. Army property. Shoo . . . Back. Back. Where you came from.'

Guy stepped out on to the landing. Where the marble stairs turned a group of three could be seen looking up. Protesting. Arguing. A tall thin man with a moustache, in a worn suit, a cigarette in one hand, the other round the waist of a girl. With them a swarthy man, short, dark, with a wrinkled forehead. Both men appeared in their early thirties.

Guy walked towards them. 'Look, can I help? I've some authority here –'

The thin man said at once: 'I speak for my friend, this is his home.'

'Heard *that* one before,' the sergeant muttered. All three tried now to get past. The swarthy man came first. As the sergeant tried to restrain him, the other two made a dash, past Guy.

'I'll deal with this,' he told the sergeant.

The thin man, ash falling from his strong-smelling cigarette, said to Guy:

'Permit us in to prove it – wait, I show you . . . Permit my friend Gianni –' He turned, saying in Italian, 'Laura darling, you explain . . .' Then to Guy, 'She has good English, you see.'

'Speak Italian, please,' Guy said rapidly. 'There's no problem.' He signalled that the man they called Gianni should come in too.

He smiled at the girl, Laura. She did not smile back, although she appeared to accept his smile. Her face was pale, thin-skinned, the forehead high, the black hair springing back from it was coiled in a bun. The expression on her face was mildly surprised. In some ways it was a haughty face. Her voice when she spoke was cool. He knew that were he to touch her skin, hand, bare arm, it would be cool. Chill even. The body outlined beneath the skimpy red dress was thin, like that of her companion. (Lover? he wondered. Husband? He saw no ring, but that would be sold or pawned.) Looking down, he saw her feet. Elegant, arched, shod in fine, very old and worn, once expensive and now very old-fashioned shoes.

Inside the main room, the men, twiddling the knobs of a radio, let out a blast of Glen Miller.

Gianni told Guy, 'I brought my friends because they speak English and could help me. But now it's not necessary. I show you quickly, prove to you this is where I should live. My mother and two sisters and younger brother – they're in the country. We evacuated. I was prisoner. I know it's all bombed round here, but this *is* our home, truly. Let me find a directory . . .'

The thin man was searching amongst a pile of books. Gianni turned. 'Hey, Tomaso, see there – that's an album. Family photographs. Here –' he looked at Guy '– wait and I'll show you. Tomaso was looking for books with the family name, but this is better. Look . . .'

He opened the silver clasp of the red leather album, turning rapidly the early pages. Triumphantly he showed Guy. Gianni in hunting costume, in a sailor suit, in army uniform. Family groups, anxious mother and proud, whiskered father . . .

Already to Guy it seemed enough. He was about to say, 'Point taken, case proved,' when with an excitable yell of triumph, Gianni showed him a family party: Christmas, New Year, a saint's day perhaps, but taken in the very room they stood in now. The pattern of silk hangings could be seen, the same distinctive frieze. A party, full glasses to their lips. Still excited, he pointed to a dark girl, sixteen, seventeen, perhaps. 'And there *she* is! So beautiful – Hey, Tomaso, there is your beloved Laura. So terrible you aren't there also – but . . .'

Laura looked away from the picture of herself when very young. But Tomaso, moved by it, his arm round her shoulders now, kissed her ear. Gianni said, 'My friend is not long back. You understand? The family, all the family are so excited. But he has his home. And I want mine. You understand?'

Gianni's family were moved back later that week. Gianni was excitedly grateful for Guy's help – without it, he said, he and his mother and family would have been forced to squat in bombed-out ruins somewhere. It had been so important to get back to Naples after four years of war, of which only a few months had been on the right side. 'If only you'd waited a little we could have got a Resistance together. We could have seen the Germans off Italian soil. I think you didn't know what feelings there are, of the right sort . . .'

Guy wanted to ask, 'And your friend, and his sweetheart or wife?' He managed only, 'Was your friend in the fighting?'

'Yes, yes. Tomaso. Of course he wasn't in that picture, at that party, he had already gone to the war . . . Laura, only a young girl then . . .'

He asked, 'How old is her – is Tomaso?'

'Tomaso – oh, thirty-eight perhaps. He looks younger, I think. But Laura is eighteen, nineteen, I forget . . . Tomaso and Laura Varelli,' he said.

Beautiful month of October. The rain which had fallen earlier had changed the scorched drab soil to green. The air was clear. The sun still shone. That winter was in the wings was difficult to believe yet.

He went to call on Gianni, who was out. His family seemed embarrassed by the visit. He wondered why he had come. All that day he had been sickening for a fever, which began that evening. While he lay ill with threatened malaria, Laura's face haunted him. When he was hot, delirious perhaps, he thought of her cool skin. He would have liked to touch it, and be cold himself.

But Mepacrine and fly spray and the rest paid off. It was not malaria. Nor was it typhus. But gradually it distracted him. When he grew better, he had almost forgotten her.

He received an airgraph, (the address written, he thought, by his mother). The sender, Helen Connors. It was a chatty letter with an air of doing good, pen and ink equivalent of knitting for the troops:

. . . The convent adopted a ship early last term and we each had to write to a sailor, I was quite lucky. Mine is called Bert and he was at Barnardoes, he doesn't remember his dad but he had a lovely mam once, so he says we both know all about that, he wants to meet me after the war. Gabrielle's a boarder and she said she was homesick and her sailor Jimmy said he was homesick *and* seasick. Are you homesick? Were you seasick? I've written four letters this week to boys on Active Service . . .

He put it away with a smile, slipping it unthinkingly into the same bundle, fat bundle, of Sheila's airgraphs. There had been three to read when his fever had lowered enough. In his billet on the waterfront, her photograph smiled back at him, wholesome, pure, loving, trusting.

What happy times we'll have when you get back, which I *know you will*, darling . . . The novena I did when you went in at Salerno, it was answered, wasn't it? I ask Andy in my prayers to watch over you, darling. (I'm sure that he does anyway!)

Eleanor wrote too of course, the most faithful of correspondents. She wrote of her busy life, her worries. Dick (my *uncle*, he thought), was still not making a recovery from his wife's death. Eric's death had not helped. It was thought possibly he was drinking too much.

Of all the people she gave news of she seemed studiously to avoid his mother. She spoke of Dr McIntosh (forget, forget, that session of revelation. The storm of feeling after). He came to supper every week. She gave an account of her search for delicacies to feed him with. Talk of rations, clothing coupons. It was the most wonderful autumn for blackberries . . .

In Naples they heard that at last the electricity supply was to be switched on. But information had been received, false as it turned out, that switching on would set off specially laid mines all over the city. Jeeps rushed round the streets, while loudspeakers instructed the whole population to evacuate. Nothing happened, and sometime in the afternoon over a million people made their way back home.

Waiting to return, up on the high ground, he looked down on Naples. From up there he could not see the chaos and the grime. Could not smell it. Washed clean, a city of gardens, cupolas, towers . . . He wondered then if Palermo looked anything like this? In his fantasies, uninfluenced by photographs or paintings, it did. (In 1937 they need only have travelled a little further, he and Eleanor and Basil, to reach Sicily. Or would that perhaps have meant danger for their secret?)

November came. The autumn sunlight grew thinner, chiller. There were warm days still but it was more often cold, appearing more so perhaps, because of the shadow over everything.

By the end of the month some restaurants were open – all of them off the main streets and in theory out of bounds, but in practice not. He and Randall ate at several, but mainly at a small one called Zi' Lucia's.

The atmosphere, the company, the sights and sounds, and the drink certainly, were all better than the black market food served. He would not have chosen chicken if offered. It was unlikely to be rabbit, almost certain to be cat.

One chill evening, eating there, Randall said, 'Remember reading about the Franco-Prussian War? Siege of Paris and all that? Delicacies like *ragoût* of rat. Why not *ragoût* of rat now?'

'Hundreds of reasons,' Guy said, 'and all of them guaranteed to put you off your meal . . . Didn't they eat the contents of the Zoo? Jumbo and so on?'

A brazier a few feet from them was burning some strong disinfectant – part of the war against typhus – bringing tears to the eyes and fits of coughing. Somehow the cooking smells, the brazier, the disinfectant and the sewers by the entrance all retained their separate pungencies.

A couple of boys, aged eight or nine at the most, ragged, barefoot, ran among the tables, thrusting out a desperate grubby hand when passing Guy and Randall. When tearing his roll Randall dropped a crust, it was snatched up and eaten. A little girl carried a deformed baby, his head larger than hers, eyes gummed together, mouth drooling. She had no hands free, so thrust him towards Guy. 'Yankee?' she asked. The proprietor shooed her away with his apron.

'That looks very queer fish,' Randall said, pointing his fork at Guy's plate.

'Safer perhaps than your shellfish. I fill myself up with pasta. It suits me. And the pretty good Chianti puts a different complexion on it all.'

'As does the violin,' Randall said.

A small and haggard man had struck up a spirited version of *Il Bacio*. He swayed his way through the tables.

'I hope he won't sing,' Guy began, looking a little over his shoulder in the direction of the violinist. At a table where some while before there had been two US officers, a couple were sitting, a flask of Chianti on the table between them. Laura and Tomaso.

'Christ,' he said to Randall, 'I know them. That business at the apartment in the Carmine last month . . .'

Tomaso had his hand over Laura's.

Randall said: 'Quite a girl – if somewhat haughty. But stylish. A good-looker. *He* seems to think so too.'

Guy said, 'They haven't seen us – me . . .'

'Go over and speak to them,' Randall said. 'I shan't steal your fish –'

He walked over. The violinist was at their table, scratching at the final passage of *Angel's Serenade*. Tomaso, looking up, smiling at Guy, dismissed the violinist with a gesture.

'So, we meet again . . . You never called on Gianni? We are often there.'

Beneath Laura's shabby coat he could see heavy ruby-coloured velvet. A frock that must once have been both fashionable and expensive. This time he was afforded half a smile. He asked:

'Everything all right for you both? No problems?'

'Only the problems everyone has . . . We are lucky that we have our home, and that we don't have to share it with too many . . . That is your friend with you?'

'I'll bring him over,' Guy said. He introduced Randall. 'Captain Randall Furness . . . Signor Tomaso Varelli . . . his wife, Laura –'

Tomaso flung up his hands. 'But what's this? *Wife?*'

Guy coloured.

'Please, not wife, *daughter*,' Tomaso said. 'No, no, listen, it's a compliment – that I look so young –'

Laura said smoothly, 'Or that I look so old?'

'No, no – that he should think us married. I am thirty-eight – she, my darling little daughter, is nineteen. So you guessed, I married *very* young, and see how young it's kept me. I pass for thirty . . .'

Guy talked round it politely to cover his embarrassment, an embarrassment not felt by the delighted, amused Tomaso.

'A drink. You'll drink with us? Before we eat – after we eat?' But Guy and Randall had to get back. 'Look, here is the address. You must promise to visit us. What day can you come? Tomorrow, Wednesday, Thursday? . . . That's settled then, we receive you Thursday . . .'

He did not dare to look at Laura. Why? he asked himself. He was certain that as they spoke, she was not looking at him.

The night of the visit. 'Do you really want me tagging along?' Randall asked.

'What do you mean – tagging along? For God's sake.'

'Because you think the daughter a smasher – and you're smitten.'

'Randall, I have a girl. A fiancée almost. I don't know how you dare –'

'Don't know how *you* dare, but you do. Look, visiting them isn't going to stop you leading a monk's life – if that's what you want . . . But you were moaning only the other day about not meeting the natives. OK? Now those same natives urge you to call on them, and hey presto, you have scruples. You're next door to mad.'

'You started it, saying I was smitten . . .'

'I was ragging. We're not at school . . . But OK, I'll come.'

The Varelli apartment was in what had once been a good address. Now, more families lived there than had ever been intended. The courtyard was shabby, with dying plants, chipped and broken statuary. A concierge watched them balefully as they made for the stairs.

Inside it was a pleasant surprise. Not wonderful, but better than they had hoped. Antiques, vases, chairs, porcelain, china. (One air raid, a bit of bad luck, he thought, and all these will go.) The elaborate coverings for the electric wiring were of faded torn silk, pale yellow.

In one corner of the high-ceilinged room in a tapestry chair, an army issue blanket tucked round her legs, was a woman of perhaps forty. Prettily faded but recognizably Laura's mother. The skin was unhealthily dark and dried, the eyes sunken, yellow-tinged. Her voice came as if from a distance. She held out her hand. It was not cold as he expected, but dry and weak.

'Mother. Mother, as you see, is an invalid.'

Coffee had been prepared. There were some small, rather dusty cakes. He had brought with him a Hershey bar from one of the American's K rations. He watched fascinated as Laura broke it into pieces, laying them in a majolica dish. He could almost see the saliva behind her dry lips. Her eyes were fixed with desire. She offered him a piece.

'No, no. It's a gift. Eat it after we're gone.'

She protested, looking directly now at him. 'Please. You are our guests.'

'Eat it after we've left. It'll go further that way.'

She gave a little shrug, then looked away from him with a dismissive gesture.

'You're all so kind,' the mother said in a faint voice. 'The English have always been kind.'

Laura looked at her coldly. The skin underneath her fine dark eyes was a little swollen in a way he'd noticed often these days of hunger. He felt ashamed of his own well-nourished self. (However little he liked the sausages, the mash, the duff, the copious badly cooked vegetables, he was not in want.)

'Beloved,' said Laura's mother to her husband, 'the smoke. The smell of the smoke.'

Tomaso put aside his strong-smelling black market cigarette. He told Guy and Randall:

'These are not Italian, of course, but what can you expect? You excuse me? A man must smoke what he can obtain, what is to be found.'

He paid his wife exaggerated attention but in a manner Guy found odd, for it was the exaggerated attention a stranger might receive. Sometimes as he fussed around her, his eyes would suddenly seek out Laura's. She would give him a small signal of approval.

He and Randall were asked about themselves. They spoke of university – Tomaso had been at the university here, Philosophy, you understand, nothing very practical. It didn't fit me for business, or the army. But, you see, it's been all right. The secret is to forget the deep thoughts. I should have learned to speak good English. I think now, with forty almost here, it's too late. I don't have that flexibility.

'You're lazy,' Laura said.

Guy, remembering their first meeting, asked her, where did her excellent English come from?

'You could guess, you can guess – an English governess. Of course.'

Her mother murmured, 'Mamma. Dear Mamma . . .'

Tomaso said, 'It was her grandmother's idea, obsession – Her baptism gift. Formally, in writing. The finding, upkeep, delivery, of an English governess . . .'

'Miss Travers,' Laura said. 'We called her *La traversa* – to her face in the end . . . She was rather nice.'

'*So* nice, the English,' Signora Varelli said. 'My mother was a true anglophile. A friend of the Duchessa Sermoneta . . . a visit to England with her . . . in our Roman days.'

'My wife is from Rome,' Tomaso explained. 'A large, energetic family –' (but look at her now, he seemed to say). 'So it's strange, you see . . . Such a small family as this. Before, two aunts and a cousin lived with us. But the last of them died this spring.'

'Better,' his wife said, 'better for Eugenio to die. He would have been condemned to a chair – even his bed. Who could wish that on anyone?'

There was an awkward pause. Laura said she would ring for more coffee. What would they drink? Randall and Guy must say frankly what they thought of the wine. 'We aren't at all easily hurt. It's fine if you criticize. Then we can obtain better for you another time.'

Later they drank Strega. Tomaso said, 'You've studied a lot of our literature? Laura here is very well read. She would wish to have gone to university. Now, we don't know what will happen.'

Guy asked her, 'What do you like, who do you read?'

'Oh,' she said, tilting her head back, 'Leopardi, Dante, of course. That sort of thing. The usual.'

'Cor!' exclaimed Randall, outside the apartment. 'What's to be made of all that? Pathetic mother, beautiful daughter, absurdly youthful father. The scenario is – He can scarcely be bothered with his wife (though her family may have been occasionally useful), but his daughter reminds him of what he once loved about her, so he dotes on her and she on him. For the real thing, he's got lots of lady friends, one lady friend? . . . None of the family gets enough to eat – I'd recognize that skin texture anywhere. In fact no different from thousands of their fellows, except they still have a roof and all those possessions, which doubtless they've started selling to eke out. Am I right?'

'Masterly,' Guy said. 'If one cared a tinker's curse for any of them.' He yawned ostentatiously.

'Not so smitten, then?' Randall asked. 'I'm not sure Signorina Laura mightn't sound rather splendid, declaiming Dante. And very desirable.'

'Who's smitten?' Guy asked, laughing.

'Anyway – do we go back?'

'We go back.'

Darling Sheila,

Thank you for all your letters! Three arrived at once, and now I think I'm up to date with all your news. Will try and make you up to date with mine. Not a great deal happens here except we are very busy trying to keep law and order, which doesn't leave much time for social life, of which there isn't much anyway. I'm with my own sort most of the time, or Americans. We meet very few Neapolitans except in the course of work. I can see this letter is going to be very dull. I wish you were here to talk to. And touch. Actually, Randall and I did call on a family yesterday and were entertained. I'd helped a friend of theirs over some business about an apartment . . .

Unexpected work cropped up on the day of the next visit, and they had to postpone it. By the time the rearranged day arrived, Randall was ill in hospital with severe hepatitis.

Guy went alone. It was to be the first of many visits. He tried never to come empty-handed. Neither his rations nor pay allowed him much in the way of extravagance, but usually he could manage to scrounge a little something. A single egg, some bread, a rabbit (at least he hoped it was – its head had not the roundness of a cat's skull). They were always pathetically grateful.

The evenings took on a pattern. Sometimes Tomaso was out and would come in only as Guy was leaving. Cigarette dangling, smiling, eager: 'How is my darling?' A kiss for Laura. Other times he would be there with Gianni and his family or some other friend. Then there would be much laughing and talking, with no concessions made to Guy's pure Italian – rapid cross-fire, exchanges, allusions over his head. Once Laura, noticing, beckoned him through to the dining-room. It was also a sort of library. Book-lined. There she took down a volume of Leopardi. 'Why don't we read together? Choose your favourite.'

Alla sua Donna. He read:

> *Cara beltà che amore*
> *Lunge m'inspiri . . .*

And she, from *L'Infinito*:

> *. . . Così tra questa*
> *Immensità s'annega il pensier mio . . .*

He found her voice very beautiful. And told her so. He said it gallantly, lightly.

'So – I can continue then?' She half-smiled in acknowledgement, and went on reading.

She told him, 'You read well yourself. And speak well . . . You have that *lingua toscana in bocca romana*, which some call perfect –'

He was flattered. He and Randall, bracketed at first together for their excellent Italian, learned in the course of study and visits to Italy. He had told Laura something of his story – enough only to explain his connections with Italy. The Tuscan orphan, Aunt Eleanor's determination that he should speak as nearly as he would have done had his mother taught him. (My mother, he thought. *My mother.*)

Sometimes there was music. The gramophone with its great brass horn stood in the drawing-room, together with a cabinet of elderly records. The tone was crude and made a poor rendering of Artie Shaw's *'Who's Excited?'* brought by Randall one day at Tomaso's request. The voices of Rosetta Pampanini, Tito Schipa, Gigli, sawed the air thinly. Signora Varelli sighed from her chair, remembering mournfully her uncle on her father's side, whose voice was so beautiful and who had studied with Fernando de Lucia – but who had not been allowed to make singing his career. Her thin hand lifted the wine glass to her lips.

Christmas approached. Randall, recovered, came to visit also. But by February he had a romance of his own, and other things to do with his time.

In January the happy news had come from England – Aunt Eleanor to be married. And to that same doctor, who three years ago had shattered his life. Now when he heard, he was simply happy for her. Amazed, but happy. They were to live in Scotland as soon as the war was over. Since there could be no children, she was not worried by his being a non-Catholic. They were very well suited, she said. 'If only you could come to our wedding! We shall be married in the spring.'

Spring 1944. He wondered afterwards that he did not see what was happening. To him – if not to Laura.

He was with her in the library when the raid began. It was very sudden. There had been a short one during an earlier visit, when he had been able to get them into the shelter. It had taken time to get her mother down. He had had to carry her.

Now there was no time. This fearful rattling, booming, thunderous shaking. He had his arms about Laura. She felt, not soft and yielding, but hard with terror. He put his hands over her hair, drew her head to him. It was buried in his chest. He pushed both of them against the wall. The noise was deafening. We are in battle again, he thought. In battle. But here he could do nothing. He thought suddenly, a blindingly beautiful thought: *We shall die together.* We shall die in each other's arms.

They were covered in a thick white dust. The building rocked. The world rocked. Kissing her, passionately, again and again, longest of dusty kisses, their juices mixing. Her mouth was not cool. As they clung together: We are alive, he thought. And shall remain so.

E quindi uscimmo a riveder le stelle.

And thence we came out to see the stars again.

He tried late that night to write to Sheila. He hadn't done it the evening before when he should have. His letter had all the excitement of a school exercise. He saw that it read like one. There was no account in it of a raid. Earlier, he had had an account of the eruption of Vesùvius to give her. Tonight it seemed he had nothing. He could only write the truth, or rubbish.

He looked at her photograph. I can only hurt her. He felt pain at the pain he was about to inflict. Yet how could he know there was no turning back? He could have hoped this new love was only a passing passion, a flirtation even.

However strong, may it only be *passing*. (Randall did not take his seriously – and he had no girl back in England.) Oh Sh sh Sheila. Where in this world, this new world, do you belong?

10

Dick, in the winter of '44. It was getting no better. He sometimes thought it never would be.

The face that stared back at him in the mornings – if he could have avoided that. To shave blind. But not possible. Looking at himself: the drawn, gaunt face, the eyeballs tinged yellow, the skin dull. The whole topped by white hair becoming sparse now. And yet before he had not been even tinged with grey. It had appeared if not overnight, then in those first weeks after the funeral. Just as the blood seemed to have left his body, so had the black seeped from his hair.

Lately the face in the glass had begun to frighten him. Once shaved, he would think: I don't have to see it again today. I can forget about it. Until the next morning.

Everyday life must go on. The foundry – no trouble there. Busy with wartime orders. He could still put in a good day's work and no one be any the wiser – so long as he could drink.

Drink. Drink made the little he must accomplish, possible. Not tolerable, but possible. He wished only that he and drink were not so securely wedded. Other people knew, of course. He didn't deceive himself. But as long as work went well, what did it matter that his life was that of an automaton? Get up, wash, shave, force down breakfast to give himself the right to the first, life-saving tot of whisky. Throughout the day, fuelling himself. Always sober, serious. So reliable that even Stanley Taylor could not fault him. He moved like clockwork – and with as much life in him.

There was no trouble now with the rest of the Board. Maria was accepted. Had that been his doing? He scarcely remembered. Only the dull memory of the pain of that meeting, when they had fought Dad's wishes, mocked Maria, and he had defended her. Now it was different. She had surprised them not only by her active interest, sitting in on every meeting, but in following up matters. As if she hadn't enough with her busy life in Thackton.

Drink. How he'd once despised those who couldn't live without. It had been different in his flying days. Hard drinking the norm (who amongst them hadn't felt the need? It seemed to have made little difference to their chances). Once he had feared the Orange Death. Now he feared life.

He despised the shambling figures: glazed eyes, trembling hands (he saw with wonder and detachment, his own hand, steady still – unless he waited too long for the next dose), the dribbling, the incontinent, the sick. Vomiting. Perhaps DT. Some terrible end. But *an end*.

He could wish to slip into death. I haven't even the courage, he thought, to do it for myself. Was he to let drink do it for him?

He didn't want to hear how much he had to live for. He wanted only to live for Gwen.

He should wish to live for Betty and Jan. Betty was a married woman now. Wife of a French Canadian army officer, Jean-Fernand. Her future after the war would be in Montreal, but in the meantime she was blissfully happy, appearing to boss Jean-Fernand about, which he accepted – only to do exactly as he pleased. 'He really is a wild man – I live in fear of my life,' she said happily. He had wanted her to be happy. But – Betty happy, and no Gwen there to see it. His thoughts, stuck in a groove, ran the same way always.

Jan, the nurse – how Gwen would have loved that too. Working in a naval hospital at Southampton. Betty and Jan cared, of course. Their care shamed him and drove him to deceit. He would have hated either of them, home on leave, to see the empty bottles, or any evidence of his dependence. But they had not noticed. No one, thank God, had noticed.

Maria on the 'phone. 'You're coming then, Dick? Christmas Eve – you'll need to arrive fiveish. Helen has some sort of surprise planned. Eleanor won't be there. She's celebrating being Mrs McIntosh alone with her Ian . . . Dick, you will come? Fiveish, Friday? Be there.'

He was.

Thackton, so much loved Thackton. Dark icy road from the station, the dripping hedgerow, the long dark line of moorland, gaunt dim shapes of the houses with their blacked-out windows like shut eyes. Knowing every inch of the way to Moorgarth: the nettle-covered hollow before the gate, the trickling of the cattle trough, the exact creak of the gate.

Moorgarth. Mine, he thought sadly as he limped into the

courtyard. Hand on the farmhouse latch. Once he had thought: Gwen and I, Darby and Joan, this is where we'll retire.

Helen threw her arms about him. 'We've been waiting for you. Look what I've cooked.'

It was a strange dish. Pasta. Helen's friend's mother, brought up in Italy, had made it. 'After all, flour isn't rationed. She makes all these lovely shapes and squares. This is cannelloni. We got her the chicken to put in – she's made it for all of us for Christmas. Maria only helped with the sauce.'

Maria said, 'I never learned anything. We just chased whatever tastes I remember . . . the best one can do without olive oil. Bottled tomatoes from our stores. Basil from Mrs Outhwaite's herb garden. See what you can do?'

See what you can do, he thought.

Christmas, and in spite of the armies bogged down in the Ardennes, almost certainly the last one of the War. Sprigs of holly, evergreens, Dad's photo decorated by Helen. Red polyanthus in a vase. Jasmine. Pink and blue hyacinths.

'Heard from Jenny?'

'And Sybil. Jenny sent some photographs. Jim expects to be sent to Europe any day now. Gordon's a dab hand at chemistry still and says he wants to be a surgeon . . . Sybil's fine and says young Peter's become a very keen boxer.'

With the meal, a toast to Eddie. 'May he be with us, next Christmas.'

They sat around the wireless, Dick fortified by whisky. The King's speech. He spoke of prisoners of war and the separation of families as one of the great trials of war. 'Eddie,' Helen said in a proprietary whisper, taking Maria's hand, squeezing it.

'You're the man of the house today, Uncle Dick,' she said.

Good food, warmth, affection.

'The reason the mince pies are so bursting with mince is Jenny. She and Sybil sent lots of dried fruit. Hardly any carrots needed this year . . .'

'What news of Guy?'

'Still in Naples, of course. He seems to be in love with it. That's the impression Eleanor has from his letters.'

'I wrote to Guy, twice,' Helen said in an injured tone, 'but he never answered.'

He would stay only one more day. The weather was bright but with a frost – the flagstones and the tops of the gates shimmered

300

with it. He went for a walk by himself at midday, whisky flask tucked in his greatcoat. The sun had melted the frost. After lunch, Helen went over to Park Villa where Eleanor was giving a tea-party. 'You're going to rest that leg, Uncle Dick,' she said before she left.

Maria said, 'She fussed like that over Eric. It was good.'

'You're all right, aren't you?' he said. 'I always mean to ask. You have Helen, and a busy wartime life . . .'

'Yes, I suppose so. At least I'm not the Virgin Mary any more.'

'You're all right. I do see that.'

'*You* aren't,' she said suddenly, severely. Sitting down the other side of the fire.

He didn't answer.

'Are you?'

'I get along –'

'You're drinking – you drink, don't you?'

'I like a drink, yes. I suppose I rely on it a bit.' He felt uncomfortably hot. The logs from the fire seemed to move towards him.

'You don't rely on it, Dick – you bloody *depend* on it.'

'I depend on it,' he said. He spoke like a child. He waited then till she should say something else. He felt at once both cornered, and immensely relieved.

'And you think no one's noticed?'

'A few,' he said. 'Maybe. "Old Grainger's hitting the bottle a bit," that sort of thing.' He cleared his throat. 'My work's all right. Bloody dependent, you say. Bloody difficult to get the stuff – But it's the same dose. Doesn't go up . . .'

'It can't be doing your liver any good.'

'Does that matter so much?'

'A great deal – to all of us here. But especially Betty and Jan . . . Pushing yourself into infirm old age or expensive illness, I don't know what. Selfish, stupid idiot. Whatever in heaven's name would Gwen think?'

Her voice was harsh. He was appalled. In the silence that followed, without warning tears coursed down his cheeks. Salt tears, running now into his mouth. When had he last wept?

'Forgive me,' she said.

'Why should I? You're right. I don't want to hear it, but you're right.'

'Forgive me then –'

'What have you done, ever, that I – or any of our family – should need to forgive you?'

He looked up. She threw a log on to the fire, kicked it. The welt of her jumper had ridden up, and she pulled it down. 'You know well enough. You know the old history. I ask you just to forgive my frankness. What I've just told you needed saying.'

He reached for and lit a cigarette, offering her one first. He drew on his hungrily. Feeling the salt tears dry.

'I'm going to make us some tea,' she said. She disappeared into the kitchen. While she was gone, he reached for the whisky flask secreted in his briefcase. Warm soothing fire. Travelling down his throat. Cleansing, numbing fire.

When she came back she said at once, pouring out his tea, 'Do you want to put whisky in?' He shook his head. 'You haven't got over Gwen at all, have you?' she said.

'No. But people expect . . . Others –'

'Some things you never get over, Dick. Sure, that sounds depressing. It is. But it's better than your load of guilt just because you can't.'

'Yes,' he said, stubbing out his cigarette. Lighting another.

She paused. 'I'm going to tell you something. It's a bad time to come out with it, it won't cheer you, I don't even see what good it can do, except – the Grainger family – haven't there been too many secrets?'

'Tell me.'

'It's about Peter, and me . . . Peter didn't seduce me, he raped me.'

'My God,' he said.

'I'm not asking if you believe me. I know you do. I wish to God I'd spoken then . . . I ought to have protested. To have fought. But my background . . . I think now . . . it seemed natural to suffer then.'

'Peter. Getting away scot free. My God, how you must hate us . . .'

'No . . . I hated *him* for a long while. But – he didn't get away scot free. You can't say that of someone who died as he did. That death was very horrible. And Sybil, what *she's* suffered.'

'I wish you'd fought back. I'd –'

'If I'd pointed a finger at him, protested my innocence – My word against his . . . Who's to say I'd have been believed?'

'I'd have believed you, if I'd been asked . . . All I got was . . .

I was just told what was happening – the secret, that I was to be part of.'

'The wrong he did – I don't know which was the greater, the rape or the lies afterwards. The lies were just my reputation, the other was myself, my heart – all that loving and losing a child. I lost Guy . . . And when I wanted him to know the truth, I couldn't tell him myself. I had to get it done for me . . . And now I think he hates me. There were some terrible words spoken. They haven't really been unspoken since. If he'd *died*, been killed . . .'

He didn't want to interrupt. She went on: 'I don't know why I tell you, except that – You've always thought Peter better than you. Handsomer, cleverer – I don't know. Isn't that so? Peter wasn't the best, Dick. *You* were – Dear, dear Dick. Don't misunderstand me when I say I love you . . . I love you for qualities I can't put a name to. And don't misunderstand this either – but in some other world, if things had been different, we could have loved each other.'

All the might-have-been revealed itself, hid itself again, in those few moments of filling a teacup, laying another log, lighting a cigarette.

'And so you're going to get Eddie back?' he said, in an ordinary tone, almost normal. 'It can't be long now.'

'They'll probably intern him over here first. I don't know the plans. But it'll be difficult enough, God knows. His career. Adjustments to ordinary life. What he makes of Helen . . . Where we'll go, what we'll do. That all lies ahead.'

'You love him a lot, don't you?'

'More than I need, more than I want to. He's in my blood, Dick.'

'What's bad about that?'

'What's bad? Dear Dick. If loving him was enough. Eddie isn't your slippers by the fire husband. His eye has always roved. And I've always known it. He's inside every pretty girl who's willing . . . Forgive the crudity –'

'I'm sorry,' he said. A tide of sadness washed over him.

She had busied herself with the teacups, pushing them on to the tray. Out of the silence came the roaring of planes overhead. The heavy sound of bombers passing over.

'You're going to let me help you, aren't you?' she said, her voice firm, businesslike. 'Whatever needs to be done. We can work together. Not at once. I'll let you get home first. We'll sort something out. I'm nothing if not practical these days.' Her voice was lighter: 'Getting someone off the bottle, it can't be worse than juggling with the Voluntary Car Pool.'

He wanted to answer lightly too. But no words came. When at last they did, they were from the Bible, from *Genesis*.

'"I will not let thee go, except thou bless me,"' he said.

II

'I'm always chasing rainbows . . .'

'You'll tire her,' Maria said. 'Or discourage her or something.'

'I could go on all day,' Helen said. 'I don't get tired when I'm singing – ever.'

'It's meant to be fun – not work . . . But he won't stop, won't settle for less than perfection . . . Oh Eddie. Enough.'

She'd heard the sound of the gramophone and both their voices through the open window as she'd lifted the latch of the farmhouse gate. Now when Helen left the room, taking Maria's shopping through to the kitchen, he went back to the same song.

'. . . Why have I always been a failure, What can the reason be?'

She said cruelly, without thinking, 'Why pass your problems on to a child?'

'God's sake. It's only a song, Minnie.'

'Don't call me Minnie.'

'Oh shucks,' he said. 'Anyway, she loves it, you can see that. And I need it. It gives me something to do. Stranded in the back of nowhere . . . The Yorkshire moors. Flamin' Mamie. Worse than down under.'

He had one hand on the electric pick-up, hovering over the record. 'Too slow for her, this one. Perry Como sings it like a dirge. I speed it up a bit and it's just grand . . . It's a good little voice, darling. We've just got to get the squeak out of it. She's a natural otherwise.'

'OK,' Maria said. 'It's just you're too tough with her. You don't treat it like the game it is. You treat it as if it were her career – or part of yours.'

'You don't like to see me happy again –'

'Don't start that.' Her voice was sharp. 'Helen's a child. My child. The child you never gave me.' (Oh, unworthy.)

He said jauntily, lifting the pile of records. 'My child too. I wasn't asked about the adoption but now she's mine too . . . I thought . . . I'll maybe go back to London, after all. There's my

305

piano there. The contacts. Something good might turn up. I don't need a farmhouse holiday any more . . .'

She watched the set of his shoulders in the too wide, slightly garish sports jacket. Desire leaped in her, at first feebly, then when he didn't speak or move – he's going away again, she thought.

'Come upstairs,' she said. (Oh, come on, come in – oh, Eddie.)

'Some fellows make a winnin' sometime, I never even make a gain.'

Nine months together again. (The time of a gestation. The exact time to grow the never-to-be baby. Herself, Maria, doomed for ever to making these comparisons.) He had left Australia two months before the war in Europe ended, but once arrived had had to go to the Isle of Man until June.

Then at last – freedom. An over-excited Eddie, full of plans and hopes, unfulfilled longings. And desire. She had rented, not without difficulty, a small mews cottage in South Kensington. Not too far from Dulcie who was living in Montpelier Square, and enjoying a well-earned rest (though shattered by the news of Jenny's son Jim, shot down in March, only six weeks after leaving Canada). Helen was to join them in July when her convent broke up, and in August they would all go up to Thackton for the remainder of the school holidays. Eddie, rested, would take up his career again in the autumn.

She hoped there would be a career to take up. Either as a result of the internment or just as part of the gradual falling off, (never the same since America), his name and fame had suffered. His records were seldom heard. A generation had grown up to whom his name meant nothing – or nothing they wanted to hear. But perhaps when he appeared in person, it would all be different.

His five years in camp had been in their own way tough. So perhaps she should have been warned. Excitement, happiness, giving him an appearance of wellbeing – if she was deceived so were others. (Women too? Of the missing half decade, she wanted to know nothing – all she'd wanted was to have Eddie in her arms, for Eddie to be inside her again.)

June 1945, in a London almost free of war. They knew no one fighting in the Far East. She had begun to make contacts in the rag trade, to think again. Coupons, rationing, would not be for ever. Uniforms, seen everywhere, had suddenly a temporary look.

And there he was. Fit as a fiddle and ready for love. Eddie of the flicking tongue, warm hands, agile fingers. Strong, gentle, certain. The scent of Eddie's skin, unchanged.

Their first night together again. Such energy, such loving. A man not in his forties but his twenties. 'It was always you, Maria . . . if you knew how often I'd dreamed . . . I'd wake up crying. I was inside you, Maria, and then I'd wake. It was always *you* . . .' Well, yes, perhaps. But how much she'd wanted and needed it to be true, that night of such happiness. At dawn he wept unrestrainedly in her arms.

She might have taken heed then, been warned perhaps. He was so happy. Too happy. But because she was happy too . . . He wanted to go everywhere, be everywhere. Theatres, cinemas. He went to *Perchance to Dream* three times in two weeks, *Gay Rosalinda* four times. He told Maria: 'I could do the lead. I could sing that part . . .'

She'd hired a piano for him. He spent much of the time that he was at home, sitting at it, playing old numbers, trying out new ones.

'Hey, Maria – remember this? *There's a small hotel, with a wishing-well . . .*'

Often he got up very early, and stayed up late as well. He always stayed up late. He bought in, with Maria's money, piles of new records, stacks of sheet music. He no longer had his collection of his own records. He'd been careless with them at the time, then put into store after his internment, they'd been lost in the bombing. He tried to buy more.

'Couldn't you get them?' Maria asked, when he came back empty-handed.

'Not right now. But they're on order. Decca are just about to do a really large pressing of all the '33–'34 ones.'

Another day he said, '*Lilliput* and *Picture Post* are going to do a feature . . . They'll want to come and photograph me at home. I'll give you warning.'

He was out now often all day. 'I've got to look everyone up. Tell them I'm back.' In the evenings he would be so excited that once she accused him of being drunk. He smelled of it.

'Flamin' Mamie. *One* little goddam whisky with old pals. Of course it smells.' But his irritation evaporated as fast as it had come.

'Ambrose is taking me on,' he announced the next evening.

'That's wonderful, Eddie.' But when she pressed for details he drowned her questions with his new record of Guy Lombardo.

'You, you're driving me crazy,' he said.

He bought records, then criticized them. Men, women, alike. He ran down most of them. 'Frank Sinatra – yes, well, too skinny – he's just a craze. Vera Lynn, it's not the real thing, that catch in the voice. Where are the *real* singers? Anne Shelton's good . . . But lots of them, they belong to the war. That's over . . .' If the voice was all right, then the interpretation wasn't.

He was to sing with the Rainbow Club band, for the US troops. 'When you think . . . I guess a lot of people around there remember me from '35 . . . I'll broadcast probably with the AEF Band before they fold up.'

Another day: 'I've got this terrific contract offer with HMV –'

'Before you sign – you are being careful about terms, aren't you? You don't want me to come with you?'

'No, no, not that sort of come. Come to bed. Come to bed *now*, Mariannina.'

She had been his manager so successfully only six years ago. He'd been used to rely on her. Why not now? She wished she'd made preliminary contact around before his return. Now she was too proud, too nervous, to interfere. She was all the same surprised when nobody, no one at all from that world, contacted her. For the sake of Eddie's pride, and at his request ('I don't want you interfering,') she kept quiet.

Two days later: 'Geraldo wants me,' he said in an excited voice. 'We'll go out and celebrate.'

'Look,' she said. 'Geraldo, Lew Stone, Ambrose, you can't sing for them all.'

'Why not?' he asked belligerently. 'Why not? Tell me why not? Why shouldn't I sing for all the big names? *I'm* a big name . . . Flamin' Mamie, isn't it just a matter of establishing myself again? Letting people know I'm back. Once these interviews are out, some broadcasts, new records – they'll be queueing from here to Eros. Autographs, the lot.'

'Bloody Government,' he said another time, 'interning me. But I was singing all the time in Australia. Working hard, organizing concerts. All that practice, it's like exercise. The muscle. I'm in great singing form.' He told her:

'Al Coleman's expecting a spot at the Park Lane. He'll be asking me, for certain – "No one can put a number across the way you do, Eddie." If I've heard that once since I was back . . .'

She asked again if she couldn't come with him, talk to a few of their old contacts. She was known to them all . . . It was only the war had disrupted everything.

'I can get work by myself, thanks. Since when did I need interference? What's wrong with the Sabrini charm? I don't need your Sicilian smiles, and winks, and simpers . . .'

She never thought he might be straying, that he was up to his old tricks again. In spite of his childish tantrums, his irritability, he seemed to have great need of her.

So when in the end everything went spectacularly wrong, the shock was all the greater.

'A movie,' he said, coming home one evening, sheet music piled on a box of records. 'Top secret, though. Korda's behind it. It's a remake of *Showboat*. In Technicolor . . . I can't talk about it. I promised – not a word.'

He wouldn't eat any supper. She had bought him some early raspberries. 'I haven't time,' he said.

'You never have time to eat now –'

'I lost my appetite down under. The food was foul.'

'You haven't lost your appetite for me.' She came up behind him, arms round his neck. 'Come up to bed early, then. I'll stay awake for you.'

He murmured something, then, food left untouched, went into the sitting-room where the hired piano was. The wireless was there too but his presence meant she couldn't listen. She sat in the small dining-room and sewed a sun top for Helen. She would be with them in three days.

'*Over my shoulder goes one care, over my shoulder goes two* . . .' The same number again and again.

Around half past ten she put her head round the door, 'I'm going up.' He ignored her. She stood there a moment but could sense him willing her out.

'*And over my shoulder goes them all* . . .'

She lay awake. Eleven, twelve, one. It was one-thirty in the morning and there'd been hardly a break. She had expected a 'phone call or a knock at the door from their neighbours – a retired admiral and his invalid wife.

'*Five minutes more, give me five minutes more. Only five minutes more in your arms* . . .'

She went down. 'Come on up, darling. You're keeping them all awake –'

'No,' he said. 'I have to get it right. I've only a few hours to get it right . . . And it's good, don't I sound good?'

'Give me land, lots of land under starry skies above, don't fence me in . . .'

By four o'clock she felt desperate. She went down again. He was still at the piano. Sweat poured down his face.

'Eddie, you have to stop –'

'Can't we talk it over, before it's over, before you tell me we're through . . .'

Wild of eye, white-faced. She noticed suddenly how thin in a few short weeks he had become.

The doctor they had had in London before the war was gone, she had no idea where. She had seen a doctor's plate in Ennismore Gardens, round the corner from them. First thing in the morning, she called him out.

By lunch-time Eddie was in hospital. It seemed to her afterwards all a nightmare. Why had she not realized? This excited, now incoherent Eddie, who had wept in her arms.

A manic episode. The shock of returning to his previous life – something he had looked forward to *too* much. The weight of expectations, and excitement. At the hospital they explained to her that they would use the same treatment as for battle exhaustion. Soldiers who had cracked up under strain.

He was drugged for forty-eight hours, so that he slept almost continuously. Then he was given insulin injections. These made him voraciously hungry. He who had barely eaten for weeks put on a white, puffy fat.

She discovered now that he had told everyone in the dance band world that she was in Canada for two years, that she had got a passage there for war work to do with her place on the foundry board. Probably there were other fantasies, but she did not learn of them.

Helen arrived, wanted to meet him, but was not allowed. VJ came and went. Maria did not celebrate. When Helen started day school in September, she was sent to Dulcie's for a fortnight, while Maria took Eddie to the seaside at Torquay. A half-hearted Eddie, excitement replaced by depression. She wondered if perhaps he'd been sedated for life.

He returned slowly, so slowly it was at first scarcely noticeable. At Christmas she took him up to Moorgarth for a month. And then again now, Easter 1946. He was bored, restless, irritable. She persisted in thinking that the fresh air and good food were some kind of healing.

Then she had the idea that he might teach Helen to croon.

She'd often heard her funny little voice singing along to the wireless when she thought no one was listening. And this seemed to amuse him. In other respects they returned to their usual bickering selves.

This is the secret journal of Helen Connors of Moorgarth, Thackton-le-Moors, Nr Whitby, North Riding etc., etc. I received this book for a Christmas present and it has taken me till Easter to write one word in it! It's easier when you have a diary with dates, this just has blank pages so you can start any day, so you don't start at all. The best thing is it has a lock and key, (Maria's idea!) so I can write my secret thoughts.

What are my secret thoughts? It's funny how when you have the fountain pen all filled up and the book open, they all fly away!

This holiday I'm quite busy because we've got School Cert. next term and I'll be doing Matric. I'm the youngest in the class and it's jolly hard work in all the subjects except Maths which is easy-peasy. Botany is BORING!! I like my London school and I like being a day girl, though I'm not sure I wouldn't prefer to live in Thackton all the time again, I can't make up my mind about that. I still miss Uncle Eric terribly.

We are up here mainly because of Eddie who was very ill last summer. It was very tragic after all the time he'd been away, Maria said his brain got quite exhausted, he didn't ever really get over the shock of being arrested and taken so far away when he hadn't been on Mussolini's side anyway.

He's very funny (peculiar not ha-ha), but when he's in a good mood he's super. Because they haven't any children I'm a daughter for him as well as for Maria. The only thing is I don't get treated as grown up enough, after all fourteen is quite old these days. Maria doesn't let me wear make-up but Veronica's mother let's her. Veronica is my best friend since I've been in London. She lives in Baron's Court and her mother is an illustrator, her father was killed at Bir Hakeim. She is fifteen and a half with chestnut hair in a page-boy AND a big bosom (she wears Kestos 38!) She's tall and looks wizard in wedges (that's Alliteration, by the way, Credit in Eng. Lang. coming up next!!) We try on make-up at her house and sometimes her mother helps. Mascara *really* makes a difference to my eyes, and that's the trouble because Maria notices at once, especially the time when I used shoe polish which was JOLLY GOOD.

I don't think I'm very pretty, in fact I know I'm not, I even thought of pasting a photo on one of these pages so I won't forget! Maria says I can be elegant later which is better and that I'm *jolie laide* (Pass in School Cert. French coming up?!) but I must be careful with my skin and not ruin it with Pancake. The trouble is Pancake looks smart and I'm sure I'd FEEL prettier if I could wear it. Anyway what with being small and rather skinny without a proper bosom (Kestos 32 but it wouldn't matter if I didn't), and blonde hair which is wiry really and a funny straw colour, it's all rather difficult. I'd like to wear high heels, but there goes Maria again, 'You'll spoil your insides for having babies if you wear them when you're still growing.' (I wish I was!)

Eddie's really funny. He says things like, when other people say Never Mind, he says, 'Life is just a bowl of cherries, don't make it serious –' or, 'You can't take it with you when you go go go –' He's funny too about teaching me singing, I think he really enjoys it and of course I love it – He even promised that one day, PERHAPS, I could sing with him once in public or even *on a record*!! Veronica was awfully jealous about that. Her mother used to think Eddie was wonderful so I told her he still is really.

I wish he and Maria didn't fight, it's awful when they do, he gets so angry and sometimes she shouts – I stop my ears up because I never never never want to hear anything like that. I know it was silly when I used to think Maria was Our Lady but it's as if a bit of me still thinks she is so I don't want to know about her and Eddie saying bad things to each other.

Whew! No wonder my arm is aching, just look at all I've written, it nearly makes up for all the months not writing anything. PS. I've just been back to the beginning and it says Secret Thoughts, I don't feel I've written any of those somehow. (What about the terrible time when I was a vacky – but I could never write about that. Secret: Sometimes I wish *so* much I had Mam back, though she might not even recognize me, I've changed such a lot and talk posh of course (horrible elocution lessons!)

I nearly forgot! Good news, a long letter from Billy, typed out by Cousin Fred I think, but he really loves New Zealand

and goes swimming every day, and one time I'm to be asked out there.

And so, until another day. Quite a long time I expect, knowing me! Unless a Secret comes along soon of course.

Signed, Helen Marie Connors, Junior Prefect.

The front doorbell of the mews cottage rang, then before Maria was more than half way down, it rang again. Eddie, she thought: that sort of impatience that meant he'd forgotten his keys. But when she opened the door:

'Look who's here,' Jenny said.

'Oh but – whatever? Jenny *darling*!'

Jenny, standing on the doorstep. Smiling, a little uncertain.

'Darling Jenny, come in at once.' Once inside, she was laughing and excited. Nervous. Jenny, twenty-three years older. Neat, white-faced woman in her early forties. The slanting eyes she remembered so well, lightly mascarared now. Practical hands with colourless varnish. Well-cut grey wool suit, a red pillbox hat.

'Tell me, tell me what you're doing here. Is it a holiday, and for how long? Where are you staying? When did you arrive?'

They stood in the little kitchen. Maria putting the kettle on to boil, getting out the china, boiling the kettle, laying out biscuits.

'Last question first. When is yesterday. Courtesy of White Star. And I'm staying – no prizes for guessing – I'm in Montpelier Square. For how long? I'm here for good, Maria.'

'But, that's wonderful. Archie's got something over here?'

'No. Over there.' Her voice had an edge of tears now. 'I've left him, Maria.'

The cups rattled on the tray. She sat down at the kitchen table. She said in a high little voice. 'So English – sitting down to a cup of tea. After dropping that bombshell.'

Maria brought the teapot over. 'Are you going to tell me about it?'

'There's not much to tell. No story really. It's all non-things. Or non-*sense*, as Archie said when I tried to explain. Anyone could have seen it coming, though. We hardly saw each other, and never alone. Separate bedrooms, polite public face, grown up sons . . .'

Her voice grew fevered. 'It could be any couple's tale. Or non-tale . . . I thought: Well, it's not going to be mine.'

313

'So you walked out? How was it taken?'

'Badly. But I'd already managed to book my passage – even though berths are in pretty short supply . . . He wanted to fight with me over every point . . . I said to him, "Jim's gone where he doesn't need us, Gordon's in medical school. And you – you only need me to sit beside you at Rotary Club dinners . . . I came from England – and now I want to go back." "Take a long vacation," he said. "Get around Europe. Go see Eire and Switzerland where they haven't had a war." He said he'd get me journalistic assignments to cover wherever I wanted to go . . . It took him a while for it to sink in. I think it was still sinking in when I left.'

'And Gordon?'

'Fine. Swell. I'd told him the first, you see. He said, "You and Pop haven't had anything good to say to each other for years." And that's about the truth of it.'

Ah, but I remember, Maria thought, noticing the excitable beaded tears. Seeing again the 1923 wedding, Jenny hanging on Archie's arm, looking up adoringly. You are marrying to escape, she had thought.

'Guy,' she said, 'Guy Dennison. Eleanor's adopted – did Dulcie tell you? He's marrying a girl from Naples. Any moment now. They'll be in London in the autumn.'

'Nice for you, Maria – another Italian.'

'Well, hardly.' (I do not care to think of this Laura.) 'No love lost between Neapolitans and Sicilians. My childhood memories of New York. Dreadful.'

She said quickly: 'Tell me more, Jenny. What you're going to do, where you're going to be –'

'I just want to live my own life, to breathe freely.'

'Where, though? With whom?'

'You were always so practical, Maria . . . I'm going to stay on, as long as I want, in Montpelier Square. With Mother.' She said it in an offhand tone, but as if she wanted it noticed.

'With Mother,' she repeated. 'What do you say to that?'

'I heard all right . . . Only I don't understand. I mean, Aunt Maimie –'

'But I'm Aunt Dulcie's child!' It was the voice suddenly in the nursery at Linthorpe Road. '*She's* my mother.'

Secrets, Maria thought, yet more secrets. More than I ever wanted to know. Dulcie, Maimie, Uncle Eric. Dad had not really deceived his wife – rather it had been romantic, a great love.

Subterfuge, heartbreak, misunderstandings. Ah, what we carry round in our hearts. Is it any wonder they break?

'Remember? *I wish Aunt Dulcie was my mother!* . . . And wanting to live in London with her? Well, here I am at forty-two, doing just that . . . And ain't it a grand and glorious feeling?'

'Who told you? Did she?'

'She wrote me. A year ago last April, just after Jim was killed. A ten-page letter. I cried. Oh dear God, how I cried . . . Jim gone – and everything . . . Then I called her transatlantic. I don't know how long we talked. The operator kept saying –'

'You told Archie?'

'It's not his business. Gordon I told – it's his grandma, after all. But all of it, it shook me up. From then out things weren't ever the same. I just planned and planned to quit – all of it, him, the life, everything.'

They sat looking at each other over the table. Maria saying, 'It's going to be very strong tea by now,' pouring some out.

Jenny, trying to make her voice normal. 'Where's the world-famous crooner?'

'Out. He's very hopeful of some recording, some dates this summer. It *must* start up for him again. The illness, the break-down, was ghastly. Really set him back.'

'Oh, and Helen?'

'At school. I'm dying for you to meet Helen. She's helped a lot in his recovery, by the way. He's teaching her to croon.'

'Any good?'

'Squeaky, a bit earnest. But she may have something.'

Gradually the awkwardness passed. Maria asked: 'And Syb, when are we going to see Sybil back?'

Jenny animated, excited: 'We aren't. That's my other great piece of news. Sybil's lost her heart. She's going to be married in the fall. I think she's writing you –'

'Anyone we – you know?'

She picked up a biscuit, let it drop on the table where it broke. 'Garry Mitcheson. She'll have mentioned him, I'm sure. Six foot six at least – anyway, very tall, and handsome but nice with it. Clever, too. He got a seat as a Liberal in the election last year. He's quite crazy about her, *and* young Peter. Can't do enough for them . . . There's a happy ever after for you,' she said, brushing away the crumbs.

But it was her own excitement filled the room. Maria asked her what she was going to do?

'I expect I'll do that famous secretarial course I was always wanting to do . . . *You* did it of course.'

Ah, what I did, Maria thought. And why. What a burden of secrets. It was possible to have kept back so many of them (and always, the worst secret of all. Peter's death). Only geography and perhaps Sybil's companionship had hidden the secret of Guy's birth. One day, I suppose I shall tell her. Or Guy will. *Or Dulcie will.* Who asks permission of whom, to tell which secrets?

'I'm so happy for you,' she said.

12

The pealing, the hammering of bells woke him. All of hell, all of heaven, all of Palermo let loose. A great angry cascade of sound invaded his sleep.

He pulled the pillow about his ears. It made no difference. Laura, in pink silk, lay flat on her back, the sheets turned back a little. She gave little moans in her sleep. He reached out and stroked her breast, cupped it. She opened her eyes.

'I can't go to Mass, it's really not possible.'

'Of course not. Stay here. Rest as much as you can. Dr Crivello said – what did he say?'

'He says I've to take care.'

When he came back from Mass she was sitting up, propped against the lace-edged pillow, round her shoulders a wisp of silk. The nurse, Agata, had brought the child in. She was the old style of nurse, her dress long, her cuffs starched. Baby Silvi struggled in her arms. 'Put her on the bed,' Guy said. She fell at once, spreadeagled in the softness. She made crawling movements, then turned towards Guy.

'She loves her papa,' the nurse said.

'Her mama feels too ill to care,' Laura said. When the child had left, he sat closer to her on the bed, buried his head in her neck. Moist, cool. Scented. 'My hair's a mess,' she said. 'It reflects how I feel.'

'You didn't feel like this for Silvi.'

'Maybe it's because . . . perhaps it's a boy. Old wives' tales, really bad sickness. No use, though, to ask my mother.'

He agreed. No use to ask Signora Varelli, who had given birth to Laura and cried finis – to everything. 'I can scarcely ask *my* mother,' he said.

She gave a half-smile – she understood. But she didn't like Maria, and Maria had not liked her. That was to be the price paid for his happiness and for his reconciliation, his friendship with Maria.

They breakfasted together on the balcony of the apartment,

pots of geraniums at their feet. The morning sun had come up, blazing hot. Laura not dressed yet, in her silk wrap with the swansdown collar. He had bought it in Paris. Everything he had bought on their honeymoon evoked the wonders of Paris, September 1946. Of his happiness.

She yawned all the time as she sat there. She had fresh lemonade in front of her, that she had thought she wanted. But after a sip it was untouched.

She said, 'It's a miracle you don't have any work. A wonder we aren't entertaining some English who don't know what to do with today.'

'Is British Council work as bad as all that?'

She said, 'I don't know how I'm to get through the day, feeling like this. And then an excursion . . . What is she called again, this woman we must go and see – this friend from Mother's girlhood?'

'Tarantino-Falletta. Contessa. You'd looked forward to it – meeting people more interesting than my colleagues. *Exciting* people, you said.'

'When I feel like this? I'm no good before five in the evening.'

'You could sit in the shade somewhere. I can explain your condition –'

'She's English, or half-English, isn't she? She won't have patience with suffering like this. I ought to *grin and bear it*. My governess, I can hear her still . . . Besides, it's a private matter for another month or two. Why should I tell?'

'Can't think why you married me – when English is such a dirty word.'

'You're not English. You may call yourself so when it suits you, but . . . Why don't we talk English at home?'

'I prefer Italian . . .'

For a fleeting second, she looked like her mother. 'I think I'll save myself for tomorrow,' she said.

But he didn't at once recall.

'The Di Benedettos – Virginia, Ruggero. We eat there . . .' She fingered her glass. '*You* go and see this Contessa,' she said. 'It's not as if we'd arranged to take Silvi . . . You go, and I'll rest. Who knows what I mightn't be ready for this evening?' She touched him between his brows, rubbing with her finger: 'No frowning.' She opened her mouth to be kissed.

*

Driving out of Palermo to the Tarantino-Falletta villa it was impossible not to see the evidence of war, the relics of war. Bomb sites, craters. He should have been used to it from his days in Naples but perhaps because the war in Europe was three years ended, it seemed to him worse. And yet poverty, homelessness, and that intricate web (*intrallazzo*, or tangle as they called it) of the black market, a whole economy based on the black market – he knew it from Naples.

Nothing could surprise him after Naples. (Although perhaps England and London especially had surprised him in 1945. So they thought *that* was a black market? The half-pound of butter up from the country, the daring addition of babies' issue orange juice to hardly won gin.) And now to live in Sicily. In Palermo. Laura would have liked to live in Paris. When he had joined the British Council, it had been Paris she had hoped for, while dreading perhaps Portugal or Spain. She had never thought of being, relatively, so near home.

If not Paris, then London (it was an affectation, this rudeness about the English). In 1946 she had drunk in everything about the fashionable parts of London. What seemed to him a shabby post-war Park Lane, an austerity Knightsbridge, had had only glamour for her. Making friends with the newly returned Jenny, she'd done the sights. They made an unlikely pair. Jenny with her eagerness and renewed enthusiasm, Laura with her cool manner masking the excitement of a child in a toyshop. Jenny had teased her, saying, 'Me Colonial, You Wop.'

Paris, although not the place he remembered either from his Grand Tour or his last visit in 1939, had enchanted her – mainly perhaps because it was a honeymoon visit. September 1946. But before that, for the wedding, he had introduced her to a bread-rationed England. Even though the ration was generous and quite sufficient, it had horrified her. Bread was symbolic. 'You can eat all you want of everything, and certainly of bread, when you get to England,' he'd told her back in Naples. It had not been quite so. But in Paris, money had bought the oysters, the steaks, the cream cakes, the chocolates she yearned for. She had seemed like a child. Laura in Wonderland. Laura in the Enchanted City, in the autumn sun.

There was a great rush of English to the continent that summer. ('The sheep who go to Switzerland and the goats who go to France.') Currency was very limited, but he had been able through friends to make arrangements sufficient for their needs. They had done all the accepted things, walking hand in hand along the Seine, leafing through books on the Left Bank, staying in a little hotel in the Rue St Jacob that he remembered from 1939 and which was miraculously, it seemed, under the same management. They sat through a Cocteau play, *Les Parents Terribles* – Josette Day expressing passion in black velvet and very high heels – for which Laura's French was not quite good enough.

And they had made love. He had dreamed of this, from the night of the raid when, dust-covered, they had clung together. Their first night had been in London. Next day they were to take the newly restored Golden Arrow train to Paris. He had joked about a golden arrow, his. She even liked the joke. But the arrow, shot from its bow, had not met its mark. The joking had been easy, the performance not. Simply, he could not penetrate her. His vigorous unsuccessful thrusting frightened him. She took it calmly. 'I've heard of such things,' she said. 'It will be all right.' The second occasion, in Paris this time, it was. With a virgin, he thought, that could be the penalty, the risk perhaps.

But afterwards when they were quiet and content – she smelled as always of frangipani and her own body, cool, delicate – he had thought absurdly and with guilt, of Sheila. Sh sh Sheila (who was over him surely? She had married that summer after a whirlwind courtship, a returned Guards officer – ex-pupil of her schoolmaster father).

Through and successful. A success. It was not difficult to teach Laura . . . 'Show me, show me, and I'll do it.' Within days she was begging for more. As ready as he was. Back in St-Germain-des-Prés after lobster and Montrachet – Laura in the pink satin nightgown sewn for her by Maria.

Successful, and by the next month, pregnant. Silvi, born nine months after marriage. Black-haired, black-eyed, bewitching. Laura had not wanted to feed her, but otherwise everything had been perfect. She had been taken to Naples at Christmas to be admired.

And now, another. A son. Superstitiously, he felt certain. She had not been so sick last time – now from the beginning, she'd felt wretched.

He had been driving half an hour and was well outside Palermo now. He halted the Lancia and looking at his written instructions, saw that he was almost at the villa. The drive up to it was long. Outside, the large wrought-iron gates were opened for him by a porter who might have passed for at least a Barone himself.

'My wife sends her excuses . . .'

The double doors between two of the great rooms had been opened. Luncheon. White-gloved waiters hovered behind his chair. He had not known what to expect of the Contessa. She was small, shrunken almost, with a much-lined face. Dark-haired and possibly wearing a wig. Her dress was pleated silk, her hands gnarled. He judged her to be in her late seventies.

The room they sat in had wall hangings of tapestry from the sixteenth century. The Count was a tiny faded man with wispy white hair and moustache. He had had a stroke four years ago. Now he seemed confused, distrait, ate with difficulty and contributed nothing to the conversation.

The eldest son and heir lived in Rome, where he was in business, Guy learned. He would bring money into the estate if and when he inherited.

Amongst the guests at the table, the only ones anywhere near Guy's age were a young lawyer, Vincenzo Mendola, and his wife. He was earnest, eager, solidly built – speaking a lot about work he hoped to get. Guy suspected him of having an empty engagement book. His wife watched him all the time, whether he was talking or not. When Guy, sitting next to her, spoke, she appeared distracted. 'Excuse me, I didn't catch?' She was plump and exuded aggression.

Also present were a late-middle-aged couple, General Abbate and wife. He spoke only occasionally, his contributions to the conversation being more in the nature of pronouncements. The whole table stopped talking to listen. These pronouncements, or announcements, had a finality which stopped further comment. He pronounced on the forthcoming elections, the state of the economy, and the vagaries of the telephone system.

The last guest was a Dominican in his early forties. Father Clemente. Heavy-jawed, balding, with a charming smile, he came from Sant'Anselmo, a priory a few miles outside Palermo, founded by the Tarantino-Falletta family in the seventeenth century and owned by them ever since.

They ate small grilled songbirds. Early wild strawberries, eaten with cream, were arranged in small baskets, the handles wreathed in yellow rosebuds.

The conversation circled round Guy – it did not touch on him directly. He was asked a little about his work. At one time the priest asked him about his time in the army. 'It's my regret that '15–'18 saw me only a schoolboy. I saw nothing of fighting in a just war. This last one, quite different of course – but if I could have helped stamp out Fascism . . . Aid the allies. The cloth, the habit, prevented me . . . You say you were in Naples?'

Guy was congratulated on his excellent Italian. Hearsay had gone before, that he was adopted of Tuscan parents. He was used to this. (Time enough to decide later whether his children, his *son*, should know the truth. Whether to make Maria a grandmother before the world.)

General Abbate spoke:

'Your experience in Naples, those difficult days, they parallel our difficult times. I am not a lover of things Neapolitan, or indeed of Neapolitans, but some of those same crises – hunger, cold, bombs, homelessness, an ancient city, with problems already, thrown into fresh, unsurmountable confusion – I fear I have seen all this before . . .'

In the silence which always followed one of his pronouncements, Signor Mendola said, 'And Rome, of course. Rome too –' He looked down at the table, his wife's eyes following him. 'The Contessa will feel that. Rome is particularly hers, peculiarly hers.'

'Ah yes, Rome,' Father Clemente said. 'Rome and the Contessa.' Then lightly: 'Tell us the story of the whipped cream, Contessa.'

'Oh but that,' she replied, obviously pleased. 'A nothing. High spirits only. A party that became a little wild. And the old Baron (what was his name, Swedish, Danish I think) and a party so merry that the Count – this very man you see at the table here –' she looked over at him as he toyed with his strawberries '– it was you, *caro*, was it not? The Count in the flush of his youth, wanting to show off to his young wife . . . emptying a whole tureen jug of whipped cream over the Baron's bald head. The Baron was so delighted by the attention, he *asked for coffee to follow*. "Why cream without coffee?" he asked with this great crown of yellow foam sitting on his bald head. And soon the coffee joined the cream and poured down on to his moustaches – he was well whiskered besides the bald head. It was quite a horrible sight but we all laughed, at his pride and pleasure as much as anything. "I am quite the star turn tonight," he said.'

'Ah then, those were the days of plenty,' the priest said. 'Cream to waste, *real* coffee to waste . . . Ah me. And the paper chases, Contessa –'

'For the men only. On bicycles through the old part of the

town. Wild but tolerated. No one thought anything of such lovable eccentricity. My sister and I and many of the other women, we would sit at Latour's eating ices and watching these wonderful men set off. Perhaps a fish supper at Bucci's after . . . A paper chase. I ask you . . . Of course they had no wars to fight then.'

The meal finished, and after coffee she invited Guy to walk with her in the garden. 'We shall talk English,' she said.

Walking past an oleander hedge, then through an avenue of Judas trees, they came to a piece of statuary, a goddess with a broken arm, surrounded by tall cypresses. There was a scent of freesias. They stopped by a fountain, its inside filled with fern and papyrus. Beside it, standing sentry, was a stone lion. Nearby, begonias in urns grew like small trees. The Contessa walked slowly, with small careful steps, using an ebony walking stick. He took her arm as they climbed down to the fountain.

'Thank you, Mr Dennison . . . and now tell me, honestly, what you think of Palermo? Of Sicily? It's very pleasant for me to talk English . . . although your Italian is so excellent . . . Can you make anything of Sicilian?'

'Not very much.'

'Yes, it is difficult. It is after all a language, not a dialect.'

She said, 'It was only my mother who was English, of course. She detested Rome, dreaded my marrying a Roman. Hoped for an English match. She sent me to Princethorpe, a Benedictine convent, for five not very happy years. And then an English Season. But although I received two proposals, I would not . . . Then back in Rome for the winter I met the newly-arrived Count Tarantino-Falletta. A Sicilian, after all that. Oh, so romantic – you have to believe . . . He was very beautiful. That is why it's so sad, what you see now.'

She talked on. In the shade it was cool now. In the distance a bell tolled. He looked at his watch, and saw that it was later than he thought.

'I am sorry we don't meet your wife today, Mr Dennison. Her mother, Amelita – a strange girl. A strange child. Your wife is not like that? Too pretty, Amelita. No strength. This *Varelli* – he fell for the prettiness. And the money, of course.'

They walked back slowly, taking another route past a wall thick with purple bougainvillea. As they came within sight of the villa, she said, turning a little towards him:

'Sicily is a strange country, Mr Dennison. Very strange. Almost

323

sixty years, and I am still a stranger. So as for you, don't think that the Tuscan blood you have in your veins will be of *any* help. It may even hinder, giving you the false idea that perhaps you belong here more than an English person would. Do not fall into that trap.'

He said nothing. As they approached the steps up to the terrace, where the guests sat now over drinks, she spoke to him again.

'I must warn you,' she said. 'There are times, many of them, when it is best to know nothing. Of anything. For most of my life here, I have known nothing. It is best. You understand me?'

'I understand,' he said. *I am my mother's son*, he thought. Remembering suddenly the first shock of that knowledge. Shouting at Maria in the kitchen of Moorgarth. Not wanting to discuss it all, only to shout and curse. His violent sickness after . . . The ghosts of his non-existent Tuscan parents beckoned him – in the light of the Contessa's remarks. How Laura would smile when he told her.

Father Clemente had spent the last four days at the Villa working on family papers in the library. Now it was arranged that Guy, who would pass within half a mile of it, should take him back to Sant'Anselmo.

They spoke Italian. The priest had little or no English. Guy found him pleasant, urbane, relaxed.

'You must visit us, Mr Dennison. As a religious house, it is not large. Only perhaps five of us, and mostly scholars. We lead a quiet, very private life. Preaching, of course. Confessions, spiritual guidance.'

He told Guy:

'I am interested to know what friends you have made since your arrival. You meet people outside your work? But naturally – we have seen you today at the Villa Tarantino-Falletta . . . So sad, the Count. Once a most able man . . . The family history, it is absorbing. I'm very privileged. One of the many old families . . . These are the people closest to God's heart. The old aristocrats – and the peasants.'

'How do you know?' Guy asked. 'Has He told you?' He felt irritated by a tired *aperçu* he had heard many times before.

'Lukewarm,' Father Clemente said blandly, ignoring the annoyance in Guy's voice. 'Aren't most of us *lukewarm*? Sitting in the middle. What did Christ say? That he would vomit us forth

324

from his mouth . . . Whereas the peasants here, with their appalling poverty, their suffering – and the aristocrats with their power, their influence, their potential for evil, and often, their riches.'

He told Guy, 'Of course our island should be separate. What can the mainland, far away Rome, Milan, Turin, do for us? Even if it means turning to America for aid . . . America has been for our poor people the Eldorado, has it not?'

They were almost at the priory now. Guy had a glimpse of a baroque building in grey stone, surrounded by cypresses, juniper trees.

'You won't come in and visit us?'

'No, thank you,' he had told the priest yesterday. 'I must get back to my wife.' And he had found Laura rested, as she'd promised. Tonight, dining at the Di Benedetto apartment, she looked, though pale and fragile, very beautiful. She wore a cream crêpe dress from Rome, bought by him – which soon would be too tight. I shall never tire of her looks, he thought. I shall never tire of her.

Ruggero and Virginia Di Benedetto, new friends. Laura and Virginia seemed to get on well together and he enjoyed Ruggero's company. Their children, Marcello and Natali, at three and a half and nearly two were too old for Silvi – but there would surely be others.

Marcello was running in and out of his mother's arms, Natali laughing and squeaking from behind her father's chair. Guy, who loved children, did not mind. Soon enough their nurse would come for them.

The only other guest was a doctor, a bachelor. Paolo Anello. Guy did not take to him, distrusting for some reason his precise, conventionally good-looking face, disliking his small, very neat white hands. His cutting, slightly high-pitched voice he found unattractive. He was speaking now:

'. . . The whole concert is to be sixteenth-century early baroque,' he was saying. 'Serio has particularly chosen Antonio Il Verso's *Lasciatemi morire*. It's for five voices . . . Il Verso was a native of Palermo . . .'

Guy felt himself distanced, the words floating round him. It was enough that Laura was happy, well, enjoying herself. Then he realized he was being addressed:

'You were at the Villa Tarantino-Falletta yesterday?' Dr

Anello said. 'Patients of mine, of course . . . So sad about the Count. He was a most able man in his day.'

Ruggero said, 'Apparently Mother Church was there also. In the shape of one of the Sant'Anselmo Dominicans.'

'And how well they preach. I believe they're much in demand . . . Excellent scholars too. The Prior is a man of immense learning.'

The conversation drifted on to politics. Then to the elections. And from there, to bandits.

'One wonders if there's a small village or town without them,' Ruggero was saying. 'They're endemic here . . . One born every minute. It happens so easily. Hunger, you steal some food, kill a carabiniere – *carrubi* as they call them – to avoid being apprehended – and what's your future? Nothing for it but to go into hiding.'

Guy asked idly, 'A place called Monteleone – is it anywhere near here?'

Ruggero spread wide his hands. 'Never heard of it.'

Laura looked over at Guy. He thought she half frowned. Did she fear he would give away his origins? (As if I would, he thought. This secret told to so few . . .) Strangely, he had had no desire to visit, and until this moment, no interest whatever in Monteleone. And perhaps it was as well, for Maria had said, telling him the name of her birthplace, 'Yes, you have relatives there. But the break is complete. If some still remain . . . I would rather you did not.' Now, tonight, he did not even know why he had asked.

But yes, Dr Anello was saying, yes, he knew of it. 'Just another hilly village. Massive emigration. It's got nothing to distinguish it from any other . . . Why do you ask?'

'Someone asked *me* about it – in connection with something they'd read.'

'There can scarcely have been much to write.'

That night he dreamed of the stone lion in the garden of the Tarantino-Falletta villa. He was standing talking with Ruggero and Virginia, when he saw it growing suddenly smaller until it had shrunk to almost nothing. 'What's wrong with the lion?' he asked. Both Ruggero and Virginia laughed, but good-naturedly. Then as he began to walk away, he saw that the lion followed him. It had grown again. And was growing. Already it was twice its original size. He began to run. But he could not run fast enough. His legs, growing heavy, rooted themselves to the ground. The lion was coming nearer. He was icy cold with fear. Then suddenly he saw a church in front of him, with a great ornate silver door. It opened for him – and he was safe inside. He began to search for where he could hide.

And then the bells began.

13

'*I cried for you,*' sang Helen, '*Now it's your turn to cry over me* . . . What do I do with my hands – oh, *Eddie* . . .'

'Start again. *Every road has a turning, that's one thing that you're learning.* Pick up at *what a fool I used to be . . .*'

'. . . *I've found a heart just a little bit truer, I cried for you, now it's my turn to cry over you* – I've got the words wrong now –'

'Nothing. You're wonderful. Wonderful. I thought maybe – let's leave that one. I'll sing from the piano with you. Want to try *Two Sleepy People*?'

'. . . *dozy little fellow, drowsy little dame* . . . hey, sparrow, don't worry about your hands, just sing.'

The door opened. 'My God, still at it,' Maria said. 'Outside, you know, it's an English summer. Can't you go in the Park or something? Get out. It's even quite warm.' She took off her hat, shook her hair, then gave Helen one of her loving smiles.

Eddie said, 'I'm not tiring her, it's her wanting to go on, working me to death.'

'And you love it –'

'Of course.' He swung round from the piano, smiled at them both. Flash of the old Eddie. Coaching Helen had given him 'something to get up in the morning for', as Maria called it. And how he needed that. Although there was some work now, long stretches went by when either there was nothing, or it was work so low down on the bill as to be insulting almost. He haunted the agencies. Old friends were kind and put him in the way of what work they could, but since all he wanted was to be the Eddie Sabrini of the nineteen-thirties . . .

Maria explained: 'He was away too long. Once a door has shut like that, it's not so easy to open it again.' Almost to herself, she added: 'And especially, most especially if you've lost the key.' She told Helen:

'We must keep his morale up. He's as good as he ever was. Or – almost. It's the times that are different.'

The one thing Helen didn't like to remark on was his age. The truth was that Eddie was rather old – at least forty-five, and going grey. Maria too, had grey 'wings', but they made her look more smart and distinguished.

They loved each other, of course. She tried to forget that sometimes she heard them quarrelling. (Everybody quarrels. Ronnie's parents do it in public, at the supper table – really angry with rude words.) Once she overheard Maria say: 'I don't care what or who, Eddie, if I don't have to see it . . . I never supposed the leopard had changed its spots. It doesn't matter if they're mature women or silly little girls, *so long as it's kept away from Helen*.' She tried to forget. She remembered how she had thought of the three of them as the Holy Family. Maria, and the absent Eddie who was St Joseph. If there had been a daughter after Christ, then it could be Helen. Maria had once been Our Lady – the sad, serious part of her wanted it still to be so.

She had loved being taught by Eddie two or three years ago. It had been done to help him after his illness, and both she and Maria thought that it had. She let him call them 'crooning lessons', it had a nice funny old-fashioned sound to it.

Several weeks ago they'd started again seriously. Eddie had become really enthusiastic, which made Maria happy (which made Helen happy too . . .)

At first he couldn't decide who to model her on, or what style was best for her. He raved about a singer called Annette Hanshaw. He found some records of her singing, *I'm a dreamer, aren't we all*, and *Six feet of Poppa*.

'She sang around your age, sixteen, seventeen . . . Just listen to the rhythm, that little speech impediment – cute without being cutesy . . .'

It was August 1948 now and she had taken the singing up again because she was rather at a loose end. She had left school in July after taking her Higher Cert. – the results would be out any moment. She didn't expect to do very well – she'd done Maths only as a subsidiary, which was perhaps a mistake. However, Ronnie was going to do a secretarial course and she decided to join her in that. (Maria hadn't thought that a very exciting thing to do. 'But if you can't think of anything else, it's always useful.')

In late July she'd gone with Ronnie and her family to Cornwall for two weeks. Otherwise it would have been London all the summer. When she returned she thought of inviting herself up to Thackton where Uncle Dick might be. Maria didn't want to leave Eddie. Then Aunt Dulcie and Jenny who were to drive around France for a month invited her to join them. She loved them both dearly – but she'd seen herself as the unwanted third: the hanger-on, with her schoolgirl French, sitting on the back seat reading the map wrong, or staying up with them at night, boring them – perhaps being asked out by a boy, and not allowed to go.

Maria was very strict about all that. Eddie was too. Maria had explained. 'We must know who it is, and where you're going. And if we don't know him, then he must come here and meet us first.' So at Christmas she'd brought Tim Aylward (who'd turned out such a heavy-footed dancer that no amount of smooth good looks could make up for it) and at Easter, Bruce Middleton who was a friend of Ronnie's brother, and had kissed her in the kitchen between the smart new refrigerator and the saucepan cupboard. Although it was all quite exciting, it would be much more so when she fell in love, which couldn't be long now. One prayer she made, which Ronnie thought was really mad, crazy, was that it would be someone Maria and Eddie approved of.

But at just seventeen, life was really opening up. She'd been allowed make-up (officially) since Christmas. In fact she'd been really pleased when her Max Factor was still on after Bruce's kiss. She even let Maria give her advice, which puzzled Ronnie. 'I can't understand why you don't get *crosser* with them both, they're awfully strict.' Helen explained that they weren't her real parents so it was somehow different. How different? Veronica asked. 'I don't know,' she said. She couldn't tell Ronnie about the rescue in the sweet shop – she hurried always over those wartime explanations. 'They wanted children but she never had any, so that makes me very special to them. I just don't want to hurt them – either of them.'

Clothes had been a problem in her new grown-up life. They were still on coupons: meanwhile fashion had changed in a dramatic way with the arrival of Dior's New Look last year. Lovely ankle-length full skirts and nipped-in waists filled her with longing after the skimpy short skirts and square shoulders – though she wondered with her lack of height if she might not look swamped. But her waist was so tiny, she yearned to nip it in further still, to swish with layers of petticoats. As ever, Maria came to the rescue.

She enjoyed every minute of her lessons with Eddie. She would make him a snack lunch about one-thirty, then they'd have a cup of coffee and about the time any normal person would be out in the sunshine, they'd begin. The time would run away so that suddenly it would be six or six-thirty, and Maria back home again. They hadn't even stopped for tea.

This evening she rushed out to fetch Maria a drink. 'I'll pour you a sherry, Maria darling' (reminder of how once she'd looked after Uncle Eric), 'then Eddie wants you just to hear this number.'

'I've really put her through the mill with this one.'

'What's it to be?'

'*Button up your overcoat.*'

'Eddie, where do you get them from? Right out of the Ark? Isn't she singing *any* 1948 hits?'

'OK. Sure, some of them. For what they're worth. But she needs standards – to build up a repertoire.'

They went on working together because she loved it (because he loved it), right until she began secretarial college in late September. She and Ronnie went off to Kensington every morning for nine o'clock. They both wore long fawn skirts with petticoats just showing, made up from materials in the July sales, and jumpers they had knitted from Vogue. Ronnie was jealous that Helen's small bust had required less wool. They had used up every coupon in sight.

Helen wasn't at all sure about the college and wished she hadn't committed herself. It didn't help that Maria confessed, she had loathed shorthand and never mastered it.

One afternoon at the end of October, just in from college, she was sitting at the kitchen table eating a currant bun and transcribing a shorthand exercise when the phone rang.

Eddie said, 'Hey, Helen, can you get up to Charing Cross Road *now*? Look, it's really important. Can you do it in half an hour? and hey, Helen, you wear your best outfit – that little ballerina suit.'

She said, her mouth full of currant bun, 'Eddie – what, why?'

But he cut in, full of urgency. 'Look, sparrow, please . . . It's your surprise, you remember I told you about a surprise?'

She thought she would never forget the mixture of fear and excitement and exhilaration. Eddie, in the agent's office, explaining, 'All you've got to do is sing – just like at home. Give it everything you've got . . .'

'*My bones denounce the buckboard bounce, and the cactus hurts my toes . . .*' Her voice shook a little at first. Her hands went all stiff. Then seeing Eddie's encouraging smile. A wink. Suddenly enjoyment took over.

'. . . *And I'm all yours in Buttons and Bows . . .*'

Eddie was singing her praises – literally. Silly Eddie. 'Hey, look at her . . . *just past seventeen . . . she's cute and pert and got that certain – you know the rest . . .*'

'OK,' he was saying. 'Just us two now. We're going to show how we can put a number across. *I got a feelin' I'm fallin'.*'

It was easier to sing with Eddie. She saw he wasn't nervous, just happy as always when he was singing. She did one more by herself. Eddie said, '*Stringalong.* OK?'

'*You may not be an angel, 'cos angels are so few, but until the day that one comes along, I'll string along . . .*'

They took a cab home. When Helen saw Maria's face, she remembered the messy table, the half-eaten bun. She had promised to get the supper ready.

But she had her first professional engagement – with Eddie.

'She's awfully young,' Maria said, over the supper table. 'And what's going to happen to the secretarial course?'

'It's an evening spot, for Chrissake,' Eddie said. 'She can still attend college.'

'And the homework?'

'I'll get that done straight after I'm back,' said Helen. 'It's only for three weeks.' She thought Maria was being a bit dampening.

It wasn't exactly the West End, being fifteen miles out of London, but as Eddie said, it was a beginning. Maria and Jenny came to listen. Ronnie was thrilled for her, and brought her parents in a party.

'*You're getting to be a habit with me,*' sang Eddie. People who remembered him, came up and shook him by the hand. Said, 'Glad to see you back.'

Somehow in those three weeks, something happened to the secretarial course. To her future. Everything altered. She was the same Helen Connors who'd sung squeakily *Someday my prince will come* for Mam. It was the same Helen, but now she was good. It seemed some other engagements might come from this one.

Then they heard they could if they wanted do a week at the Dudley Hippodrome and another at the Nottingham Empire.

She cried the last night in the taxi from the station. 'Mam would be so proud of me,' she said. 'I just wish Mam could have heard me.' Eddie, who she'd noticed wept easily, joined her now. He put his arms round her, hugged her tight. 'You have a family now, you know,' he told her. And 'I know, I know,' she said. 'I love you both so much. And I'm so happy.' She thought afterwards that she'd wept perhaps from happiness too.

She was happy anyway because Maria had said that as far as she was concerned, it was all right to say goodbye to the secretarial college, and begin this singing career. Helen was worried because she knew the fees had been paid in advance but Maria said, 'The young too often have their wings clipped.'

'Were yours?' Helen asked.

'I don't know,' Maria said, 'I never tried to fly.'

A few days later, they were singing together at home, when Maria teased him again about his choice of numbers.

'*Smoke gets in your eyes*,' she said. 'Honestly.'

And he said yet again, 'She'll get nowhere without standards.'

'Nowhere? Where's she going, then?' Maria asked, half laughing.

'Right to the top,' Eddie said. 'And what's more – I'm going with her.'

Helen had sometimes seen film musicals, showing the star's triumphal progress around the world. Trains rushed towards the audience, names flashed on the screen. Cities, theatres, cinemas, names in lights, a storm of applause. Tired emotional smiling hero or heroine, the world at their feet.

Persistent images . . . How different from those star-studded biographies was her and Eddie's life that winter of 1948, spring 1949. Spasmodic engagements. Southport Empire, the Floral Hall, Morecambe, Dundee Palace, the Victoria, Burnley. They played so many palaces that Eddie joked, 'Half our life is spent in palaces.' When they were engaged at the Embassy, Peterborough, 'What's a mere embassy,' he asked, 'to us – used to palaces?' Helen asked, 'What about the Hippodrome – didn't they used to put Christians to the lions there?' They might do so yet, Eddie said.

Travel in dingy third-class slow-stopping trains, cross-country. Bletchley, Crewe. Looking up digs Eddie remembered from perhaps ten or fifteen years back, or if unlucky, trying to get a recommendation from someone else on the variety bill. And then the bill itself: their placing, low down – but first to perform, to a cold house.

In the evenings, out for a hurried early supper. Used to Maria's

333

good, robust cooking, Helen suspected the strong tea, the chips, the Daddy's Favourite Sauce, were doing nothing for her skin. As were the lack of fresh air and exercise. Between engagements, Maria would express her worry. 'I want to do it,' Helen would say obstinately. 'I must do it.'

For her it was all excitement. It was enough just to be doing it. But she could never forget that for Eddie . . . Eddie had once been top of the bill.

And then one evening, he got the bird. She had heard of such things, even seen it on the same film screen which had shown the whistle stop tours. But nothing prepared her for the reality.

A bitter cold day in March. They had a date to do the cabaret at a medical students end of term ball. (She wondered afterwards what had led the committee to choose them – straitened finances perhaps?) She fought all day a sore throat and blocked nose, keeping well away from Eddie so that he didn't catch it. Her voice had been hoarse in the morning. By tea-time it had gone completely.

She, they, weren't too worried. 'Just arrange the numbers without me, Eddie. So what – about the duets and the patter – Sing the songs that made you famous . . . Pretend you're back in the Rainbow Room in 1935.'

It was wrong from the start. They were a lively crowd, their drinking already several hours old when she and Eddie made their appearance. She came on – only to be taken off as soon as the MC had explained her loss of voice. The first number, *Blue Moon*, didn't go too badly except that everyone talked throughout. She felt embarrassed, sitting down in the audience. Then he made a mistake of talking to them. Oh dear God, Eddie, don't. He told them, with tears in his eyes, of the Rainbow Room, of Al Coleman, of the good old days. The readily emotional Eddie.

'Bring on the blonde,' someone called out. Eddie ignored him. Some students at the front struck up their own chorus.

'*Down the lane, down the lane, there's lots of dirty women . . .*'

'The blonde, let's hear the blonde.'

'*Soldiers half a crown, Sailors, half a guinea –*'

'Where's the blonde?'

'*Big fat men two pounds ten . . .*'

Eddie was trying still:

'. . . And now I'd like to sing, *You took advantage of me.*'

'I'll take advantage of her if you won't, chum.'

'Give us the blonde popsy . . .'

'What would you do, chum, what would you do?'

A group in the far corner struck up in unison: *'Why was he born so beautiful . . .'* The chorus was taken up.

The volume of noise increased. Soon it filled the whole room, drowning the band – obliterating completely a gesticulating, ridiculous – yes, ridiculous, weeping Eddie. The MC made ineffectual gestures. Called for order. The rude chorus only surged louder.

'Why was he born so beautiful . . .'

Finally Eddie escaped. Except for a couple of students who made a half-hearted teasing grab at her, Helen slipped out after him unnoticed.

In the corridor outside, he was weeping. She stood behind him. 'I'm here, Eddie.' Her voice scarcely came out. He said angrily, 'Go away. Out. Home to bed. Anywhere . . .' When she didn't move. 'Home – you're *ill*.'

She said: 'Eddie, it doesn't matter, they're only silly boys. They're drunk, Eddie.'

'Get us a cab,' he said harshly. 'Go on. Get us one.'

There was a hospital porter to help. Embarrassed, she bundled a tearful Eddie into the taxi. They sat apart. Tears were still streaming down his face. She felt utterly helpless. She wondered if she should put her arms round him. They hugged for good news, why not for bad?

But she felt hurt and rejected. He was muttering to himself, swearing, as if she weren't there. 'Berks, just a lot of fucking berks. Is this why I bloody sweated it out down under, to get the bird from a lot of berks? Still wet behind the ears when I was packing them in . . . I was making records before they were fucking conceived . . .'

He paid off the taxi, still in this mood. Inside the small hotel they'd extravagantly booked into, he went upstairs noisily, Helen creeping behind. 'Don't tell Maria, that's all I ask,' he said, opening the door of his room. 'Don't you ever tell Maria about this.'

Shivering, feeling now quite ill, she was unable to sleep. She heard Eddie pacing about. Bitter cold outside, bitter cold inside, she was chilled by the realization that perhaps Eddie on his own was not quite enough. That if she'd stood up to sing, it would have been all right. Yet she felt besmirched by it all. When he was mocked, she was mocked too.

If it had happened to her, she knew she would never have managed. One reception like that, and I would be finished. Eddie, she suspected, would be all right tomorrow.

And so it was. The next morning, he was calm, a little sulky.

'I'll expect an apology. They can bloody well send . . . It was an insult to you too. They bloody insulted *you*.'

'Oh, don't worry about me,' she said. 'I'm very tough.'

Her voice came back a few days later, in time for an engagement in Leicester. While there, they stayed with Eddie's little sister Rita who had married a Pole in 1941, and now at the age of thirty-nine had a family of five. Helen felt left out and child-ridden as Eddie and his sister shouted and cried and remembered. Sulked and quarrelled too. Everywhere in the house was a sticky trail of Government orange juice. Her sleeves were gummy with it from the arms of chairs. She sat in it, found it staining her handbag and her gloves, trod in it and wiped it off numerous knife handles.

In the spring clothes came off coupons, and Maria bought her a complete wardrobe. Maria had become friendly with Eleanor Dennison's adopted nephew, Guy. Long letters came from him about his life in Palermo. Maria showed her some (coming as she did from Sicily, they must interest her a lot). Helen remembered the autumn of 1946, and how she had only quite liked his wife, Laura. She suspected Maria of not liking her at all.

Ronnie had finished her course by now and was working for an export firm in Moorgate. So far it wasn't very glamorous. Her boss was married and unattractive.

The summer of 1949, she and Eddie were busy throughout. The sun shone day after day. There were a couple of weeks at Butlins, Filey, and a week in the Belgian resort of Knokke-le-Zoute (her first time out of England). She carried her journal about but never had time to write in it.

Maria worried that she was not having sufficient time off 'to be a girl, to have fun'. By that she meant boyfriends. She herself didn't feel in any hurry. At eighteen she had her life before her, lots of it. When she and Eddie were established, they could take more time off and relax. She knew how easy it all was, if you wanted it. Not just Tim and Bruce, but men and boys who invited her out after performances (remembering Maria's words to Eddie, she wasn't sure what he got up to after they returned to their digs in the evenings. But no hint of anything ever reached her. Maria could be proud, she thought).

336

In October they celebrated a year of working together. By now she wasn't sure how she saw her future – and tried not to think too hard about it, because she could see Eddie didn't want to. For now, she was happy as she was, loving the moment when they came on stage, the band struck up, her cue came, Eddie looked over at her and smiled – and she sang.

'You can throw a silver dollar down upon the ground and it will ro-oh-oll, because it's row-ow-ound . . .'

Twice that summer and autumn she was approached to go solo. And an agent had several times suggested she audition for radio shows. Each time she refused. 'Later,' she said, 'when I've more confidence.' But she knew she was no longer afraid, hardly nervous now at all. Only confident, in love with singing. As Eddie had always been. It felt right. Someone wanted to groom her as a café chanteuse. She didn't care so much for belting out numbers now – her style was growing more intimate. It was suggested someone else take over developing her. 'I could make you into a second Dinah Shore . . . no, even a second Peggy Lee.' Eddie said coldly, crossly, 'Maybe you could, but *this* one's going to be the first Helen Connors.'

She pretended often to Maria that she was in no hurry, that she wasn't ambitious. Knowing that Maria would worry about her in the great world of entertainment without Eddie to watch over her. But the whole truth was that it was Eddie she was afraid for. (If I'm up and coming, he's down and, if not out, going. *That* was the truth.)

They talked sometimes of getting work on one of the liners. Eddie spoke nostalgically of the pre-war days. In 1933 he had gone to South Africa like that. It would be attractive. No digs to find, no meals to worry about, sunshine, sea air, foreign stop-overs, luxury. Well-heeled passengers. 'Who knows, Helen, you might meet a millionaire – marry a millionaire?' As ever, Helen shook her head, explaining that wasn't her ambition. Something Eddie could never understand, with his simple hopes and plans for her. ('You wouldn't actually say no to a Rockefeller, would you?')

They had some work over Christmas, although she had turned down a panto offer because it didn't include Eddie. Then at the end of January, they had a stroke of luck. A couple who were to sing with the resident band at Reid's Hotel in Madeira were involved in a car crash serious enough to put them out of action. Helen and Eddie were offered the job.

It was all a great rush. Except for the week in Belgium she had never been abroad before. She was delirious, sick with excitement. Maria remembered that Sybil's sister Molly had gone to Madeira for her honeymoon in the 'twenties. It was a beautiful island, stopping place of cruise ships, winter sunning place for the rich. Tubercular people settled there (if only Mam had been able to get somewhere like that, Helen thought). Made from a volcano, a jewel off the coast of Africa, as the brochures said. A floating garden in the Atlantic.

The night before they left, she dreamed she was at Moorgarth. Maria was sitting beside her bed, just as she had once used to, a book on her lap. She said, 'You're going to be famous soon, Helen. You won't want me reading to you.' Helen said, 'Read the Golden Lion.' But Maria shook her head. 'I don't want to think about the Lion,' she told Helen, 'the Lion has a heart of stone.' Helen asked, 'Does that mean he's hard-hearted?' She saw to her horror that Maria was crying. 'No, it's you have a heart of stone,' she said. 'You – Helen. Successful Helen.'

She was shaky when she woke. She felt certain, the dream told her so, that she was to be a success, at Eddie's expense. Remembering Maria's tears, that *shan't* be, she thought. We are a team, we are partners, or we are nothing.

They flew out direct, by seaplane, a service which had begun only a few months before. Leaving winter-cold England her excitement grew during the journey. Then her first sight of the harbour, white buildings set on the mountainside beneath a blue sky – which even as they were looking, changed to mist and low-hanging rainy cloud. Then by the time they had been driven up to Reid's, it had changed back. The sea once more lapis-lazuli blue.

The sixty-year-old Reid's Hotel, on the western sea front, had had a new east wing built just before the war. To Helen, after the succession of digs, often in rain, fog or cold, it seemed a dream. Their rooms were at the top. Helen's, on the corner, had a view of the sea. As soon as they'd unpacked, they walked in the terraced gardens. The sun was just going down. The flowers dazzled her – bright red poinsettias, garish bird of paradise flowers, lilac- and rose-coloured bougainvillea tumbling, yellow mimosa, the extravagant red hot pokers.

Inside, guests were sunk deep in armchairs or on sofas, while gloved waiters wheeled tea-trolleys laden with sandwiches, plum cake, madeira cake, iced ginger cake. Everything to make the wartime child's, the austerity adolescent's mouth water. Some were eating on the terrace, where the sparrows fought for crumbs.

She and Eddie ate a light supper in the restaurant just before the guests came down, then went up to change in the hour or so before dancing began. Maria had bought Eddie a new dinner jacket. She had also made Helen a dark green velvet strapless dress which showed off her tiny waist and was kind to her small bust. She had brought with her two favourites – a hyacinth blue taffeta cut down from one of Maria's pre-war frocks, and a red chiffon off the shoulder. She had new make-up, a complete set of Helena Rubinstein, and scent, *Quelques fleurs* of Houbigant, all bought her by Maria.

She tingled with excitement.

'*I let my heart fall into careless hands,*' she sang. '*Careless hands that broke my heart in two.*' She did not once transpose her words. Her hands behaved as if taken over – someone else moved them, perfectly. Open wide, like Eddie's.

'*I'd like to get you on a slow boat to China, all to myself alone.*'

Eddie, smooth, back on form. Eddie singing to an audience not so unlike the audience of his heyday. Tonight wasn't for him 1950, but perhaps 1930.

A woman in black satin, with hennaed hair and a trumpeting voice, asked for his autograph. 'If you knew how I *adored* you as a girl. When you sang *Torn Sails* – I used to weep so frightfully . . .' She introduced her husband, Colonel Maitland, 'who can't dance, poor darling, because of a gammy leg'. There were another couple in the party, and she and Eddie sat with them for a quick drink.

Colonel Maitland remarked, wasn't it quite astounding the sudden rise to popularity of this Donald Peers? Grown women swooning. *By a Babbling Brook.* 'Middle-aged plump Welshman. Odd, eh?'

Before beginning they had given the band their list of numbers. But now there were requests for *Smoke gets in your eyes*, for *Night and Day. The sunny side of the street.*

They sang and sang. She had dancing feet, could hardly keep still as they sang in duet: '*Anything you can do, I can do better . . .*' and '*South America, take it away.*'

Sentimental numbers at the last. Together with requests, they sang half as many again as planned. Perhaps the acoustics were right, perhaps the air was right, perhaps *they* were right.

'*I'm dancing with tears in my eyes, 'cos the girl in my arms isn't you* . . .' Eddie's high note at the end . . .

Up the stairs to bed. Up to the top of the hotel.

Eddie said. 'Leave your worries on the doorstep, just direct your feet . . . They like us.'

'They like us,' she said. 'We're a success.'

'*Gold dust at my feet,*' he said, '*This rover crossed over.*'

She had drunk nothing after the session but felt drunk. 'They *like* us.' (That terrible medical student ball wiped out for ever.) 'Eddie, I'm so happy. Good night, darling Eddie.'

They stood at the door of her room. 'Good night, darling Eddie.' Her arms went round him. His arms round her. Eddie, safe with Eddie.

She could do nothing about the excitement, the certainty of happiness, great happiness. She woke early, and was walking in the terraced gardens before any guests were down for breakfast. Insects were buzzing already amongst the bougainvillea, the unfolding yellow lupins. Eddie, she guessed, would lie in late. He wasn't normally an early riser. So she was surprised to see him join her.

'What are we going to do with today, sparrow?' He was as eager, as excited as she was. Straight after breakfast they walked down into Funchal. The sun shone on them, the lightest of sea breezes blew. They looked at the shops, debated about presents of lace and embroidery, sat in a café and drank coffee and *aguardente* which they regretted. Eddie said, 'The sax player, Jeff, says although the funicular has gone, the thing to do is toboggan down from Monte.' This they did, instead of sleeping in the afternoon. The toboggans were wicker chairs, quite comfortable, on runners, and went at a great crack. The drivers wore white uniforms with straw hats. In spite of travelling and the late night, she did not feel tired.

'I can't believe being here is *work*,' she said.

'More like a vacation . . . *So I shout to everyone, find your place in the sun* . . .'

'I'm so happy, I don't know why –'

'But that's good, sparrow. *Let the whole world sigh and cry, I'll be high* . . . You had a tough time when you were little – you grew up in the war, now you're having *fun*.'

'Are you happy, Eddie?' But she knew that he was.

That evening she wore her red chiffon. If anything, they were more of a success. Colonel Maitland, with a large party this time, clapped loudly at the end of each session. His bad leg was propped on a chair. The hennaed Mrs Maitland danced cheek to cheek with a tall white-haired man. The Colonel didn't seem to mind. She produced a list of Eddie's successes she would like sung during their stay. Could it be arranged with the band?

Eddie read it. Helen saw his eyes light up.

You're driving me crazy. I'm getting sentimental over you. Let's put out the lights and go to sleep . . .

After the dancing was over, they drank with the band. It was well into the small hours before they went up. The sax player, Jeff, said, 'They certainly like you two.' Sam on drums echoed this. 'Atmosphere's quite different. Exciting. Electric. That's got to be good.' Sydney, the leader, hugged Helen to him, rumpling the blonde cap of her hair.

They walked along the corridor to their rooms, Eddie said, 'We haven't music for some of those songs, probably can't get them here. I'll have to sing them – and Sydney and the boys'll make what they can of them.'

'They'll know lots of them,' she said. 'And if we sing even a third, Mrs M will be pleased.'

Outside her door: 'Kiss goodnight?' Eddie said.

'Darling Eddie –' She threw her arms about him. 'Goodnight, darling Eddie.'

His arms tight round her. (Eddie, safe with Eddie.) His jacket was open. His heart beneath the white shirt beat against hers. Darling Eddie.

They stayed clasped together, cheek to cheek. For a second, his lips, his tongue brushed against her ear. His heart, her heart, beat fast, fast, faster.

She wrote her journal sitting down in the lower terrace, beside the coral trees, the tumbling bougainvillea. The book was balanced on her knee.

'Something terrible, and wonderful, has happened. Eddie and I . . .'

She couldn't write any further from happiness, from joy. She had thought she wanted to put it down, secret as it was (and secure, so secure behind its lock and key). But the words for it had flown.

The secret journal of Helen Connors. Volume one. Pages and pages of trivia, pages from six, seven years back. Pages of wondering – what will it be like? Love – and the other thing, what will they be like?

The sun beat down on her bare neck, her bare arms. An elderly couple came down the steps towards her. As they walked past, the man touched the leaf of one of the plants.

'*Hedychium gardnerianum*,' he said.

'No, *Hedychium coronarium*,' she said.

I wondered what it would be like, who I would love, *when*? And then, this. But I never, never thought of this. She wasn't tired at all – would never need any sleep again, unless it was to sleep in Eddie's arms. Eddie inside Helen. My love, Eddie.

So this was what it was all about. Ronnie who'd said, 'It's rather disappointing really and jolly uncomfortable,' knew nothing. Had been wrong, wrong, wrong.

But where the guilt? she thought suddenly, for the first time. Why no guilt? If anyone had told her, had said this would happen she would have hidden her face, blushed in shame – and horror.

There was a sudden clouding over of the sky. A light wind ruffled the sea. She fastened the clasp, took up the journal and went indoors.

'Something terrible, and wonderful, has happened. Eddie and I . . .'

The weeks passed so quickly. There were wonderful outings together, and with members of the band. They became friendly with the Maitlands, who had hired a car. They drove out to the Cabo Girão and gazed down nearly two thousand feet sheer to the Atlantic below. In the village of Camara da Lobos, Mrs Maitland was patronizing and made a scene in a café about the service. Along the road from Seixal their car was washed by a waterfall.

Mrs Maitland told Eddie, 'I never thought I would have the famous Eddie Sabrini to myself. I used to kiss your picture. I had one cut from *Melody Maker*. I kissed it each night. I rated you above Al Bowlly and Sam Browne and Jack Plant . . .'

She was always harking back to old times, old tunes.

'*There's a small hotel, with a wishing-well* . . . I can hear you now . . . And what about, *You didn't know the music, and I didn't know the words*. Such a sad little song . . .'

'. . . My dear,' she said to Helen, 'you'll have to watch your voice if it's to last. Girls these days, they shout their numbers so.'

'Your little stepdaughter,' she told Eddie, 'I think it wonderful the way you've taught her. She's learned the lessons well.'

Oh, the lessons, the lessons I've learned, Helen thought. Not looking at Eddie, not daring, able to look at Eddie. What I have learned *and can never forget.*

It was when she worried about babies that unease, reality would suddenly intrude. It was possible to feel numbed by joy, and then – sudden terror in the sunshine. Standing in the garden of Reid's, smelling the vanilla scent of the heliotrope, she thought suddenly: *But if I have a child.*

'Eddie, you're *sure* it's all right about – babies?'

'Little sparrow. Trust me. Can't you trust me?'

Of course she could. She thought: I'm ignorant, but he, he must know. She didn't want to think . . . She knew what Catholics must and must not do. All that she had pushed aside. *And it doesn't matter.* Above reason, beyond reason – she realized with humility that nothing mattered except Eddie.

Maria. It was as if there were no Maria. They never mentioned her name, unless it was to outsiders.

Every afternoon, every night, every early morning, Eddie told her that he loved her. 'You don't have to worry about anything. You see, you know you're happy, why do you question being happy? People aren't often so happy . . .'

Their last night was almost a cabaret, they sang so many numbers. Mrs Maitland was much in evidence – it was the last night also of her month's stay – asking for request after request. ('Did I put *Fancy Our Meeting* on my list? No? Is there any *possible* teeny-weeny chance . . .')

'And for their last number, their *very* last,' Sydney announced, 'here are *Two Sleepy People* . . . Wake up there, Eddie. Wake up Helen, baby . . .'

'. . . *Two sleepy people, by dawn's early light, And too much in love to say goodnight.*'

Reality was the cold of an English March, damp rain-filled sky, bitter east wind. In the taxi from Victoria, she held his hand. Played with his fingers. His fingers that had played with her. 'Oh, Eddie.'

The bubble of happiness burst. What was to happen tonight, tomorrow, the days and days after? The future that on the island had never been spoken of, because to do so would have been to break the spell. Somehow it will be all right, she told Eddie. (Just as somehow it would be all right – Eddie had promised – about babies.)

She saw that Eddie too, was cold, worried beneath the jaunty air. 'Don't forget, never forget,' he said, 'that we were a success there. It was good . . . and something else was a success, wasn't it? Little sparrow, I love you so much. So much.'

It was mid-afternoon. The sky was lowering. She and Eddie stepping out of the taxi in Rutland Mews, Eddie bringing out a ten-shilling note. The cruel east wind lifting her thin skirt. The austerity look of London, so quickly forgotten.

Jenny was in the house. She was unpacking groceries, putting them away. 'Welcome home.' She kissed Helen, kissed Eddie, exclaimed at how well they looked, invited them to tea the next day.

'Just shopping for Maria – she's really busy *and* has to visit the dentist. I was just leaving . . . Shall I put the kettle on? You've eaten lunch? I expect you're tired.'

'Tired,' Helen said. 'Very tired.'

They drank a cup of tea with Jenny. When she had left, Eddie took the suitcases upstairs. She followed him. On the landing, she stopped and clung to him. She moved towards her room. 'I have to go to bed. I'm so tired.'

'So tired that you can't?'

'No, no. Darling, no, no, of course.' Across the corridor she saw the closed door of Maria and Eddie's bedroom. Not in there. No, never in there. He pushed open the door of her room. 'Darling, darling – what's to become of us?' She fell back against the bedhead. Lying on the bed, knees up. Stroking Eddie's buried head. 'Oh, darling, let's not –'

She lay back, closed her eyes, half sitting, head flung back. 'Oh, darling, darling . . .'

She opened her eyes. The door swung on its hinges, wide.

She looked at Maria. Maria looked at her.

14

The cocaine injection was beginning to wear off. She had one
hand on her jaw, where a stabbing ache jangled every nerve.

'Don't come near me, don't touch me –'

'Hey,' Eddie was saying, 'hey, Maria, look, darling – just let
me talk . . .'

'Talk – you should have your tongue cut out. What you do
with your tongue . . . Get out. Get out of my life . . . No, don't
come near me.'

'You struck me, Maria, you *struck* me, just now. If I can say
something, explain –'

'You can't explain betrayal, since when could betrayal be
explained? Answer me that, *answer me that* –'

She held on to the table. The world was spinning. She sat down
suddenly, falling almost.

'Darling – are you all right? Maria –'

'Don't softsoap me . . . How could you, how could you? Eddie,
how could you? A child – she's a child only . . . what she's been
through in the past. You knew that. A child, and *a daughter* to
you – Isn't it a sin crying out to heaven for vengeance – that
you've betrayed her, us, that – oh God, *Sacru miu Gesù*, all the
years I've thought, known, terrible things of you, but never this.
I never dreamed of *this*.'

'If you shout like that, she'll hear –'

'What if she does, Eddie, what if she does? She can stay up
there till I say she can come down. I don't want to see her, speak
to her. I don't want –'

He had backed against the refrigerator. He moved his head to
and fro as if dodging blows.

'Stop that. I'm not going to hit you. You're not worth it. You
disgust me.'

'You don't believe I can love, you don't believe it's love. I
know it's love . . .'

'You disgust me. What do you know about love? I've heard
love, love, love from you. What is that word worth? Seducing

me in your flat all those years ago – with words of *love*. Worth nothing. It's the word you use when you want an easy lay.' Her mouth grew stiff with pain and distress. The numbness was a pain. 'All those years of saying yes to any woman, getting up skirts, taking down your trousers – and always you use the word *love*. You don't even know what it means . . .'

He was crying. 'I'm trying to tell you, I *love* her.'

She had no tears. His enraged her. She shouted:

'Don't dare say you love her. Don't dare. You get love all right, you ask for love, like a child, you get love – and what do you do with it? I loved you, how I loved you. I would have died for you, Eddie. And now . . . Thirty years, nearly thirty years between you – disgusting. How many people have you betrayed? Idiot, I'm the idiot, the trusting fool, that trusted you with a child like that. Worrying about you overworking her, about the dangers of life on the circuit. And you, *you* were the danger. It was you all the while . . .'

'I loved – we love . . .'

'If she thinks she does – it's childish folly, stupidity, girls who meet you and don't know any better . . . but that it should be her . . . of all people, of all people in the world, Eddie . . . She's ruined – You've ruined her career, everything. What else mayn't you have done – given her a child – can you be sure you haven't done that? If you've done that . . .'

'I haven't given her a child. I wouldn't . . . Maria, I can't give her a child –'

'Don't be deceived by that tiny build. It's all it needs.'

'I can't give her one.' He sobbed and beat his fists dramatically, drumming on the fridge door. 'I can't give any woman a child –'

She stopped. Stunned, she said:

'Any woman? Eddie – what the hell is this?'

'Now you see me humiliated. You wanted to know that, didn't you? You wonder I didn't tell you. A fine Italian boy who can't make babies. A fine thing . . .'

Her voice, icy with pain. 'When did you learn this?'

'Just before we went to the States. '35. I had some tests –'

'And you never told me?'

'Oh God, oh Christ – Maria, let me out of this kitchen. Let me go to Helen. Let me explain . . .'

'Oh, how I hate you,' she said.

15

In the brilliant Sicilian sun, Helen watched the boy at the lemonade stall. He moved so fast that she marvelled. Proud of his skills, slicing in half the huge lemons with their greenish tinge, squeezing them masterfully, powerfully in the hand press. The glass quickly sloshed in a bucket, rattle of ice, stirring of sugar. And all the while he wore a dedicated look, as of one fulfilling his vocation. He had a crowd of customers. A *spremuta*. Tart, refreshing.

She stopped to watch him several times a week, whenever she came past to collect little Marcello from his convent school. Today as she stood there, homesickness, a longing for England, swept over her – a great wave, drowning every other emotion. Here she was in seedy, glamorous Palermo. Governess to the Di Benedetto family. I never wanted to be here. Exciting, dangerous city. I never asked to come.

Small, fair, skinny, her size went unnoticed, but her fairness did not. She did not want to be noticed. She felt wrong. All of her. For ever and ever.

Wouldn't she have been better in Switzerland or Belgium, or Holland perhaps? Here the sun shone all day, the nights were already heavy and warm. People sang and spoke of love. Men eyed her, boldly or amusedly. Sometimes they mocked her, calling behind her back, as she made her way to the school.

I have sun, enough to eat, plenty of lire for pocket money, good and kind employers. She thought of all this before the next wave of misery swept over her.

Homesickness, for what home? What home had she? The house in Rutland Mews: she could not, dare not think of it now. Oh, terrible, shameful memory.

Who was it who had clung to Maria? Sobbing. 'Love me, *don't stop loving me*.' Maria, her head turned away, her strong hands pushing Helen off. Helen, down on her knees. Despair, shame. Like a child, tugging at Maria's woollen skirt. 'Don't stop loving me!'

'Get up, get up – get off me – get *up*!'

'Maria, I'm sorry, Maria, don't stop loving me. You don't have to forgive me.' She choked on the words. 'I'm sorry, I want to make it up to you – can't we make it up, Maria, don't stop loving me. You're *my mother* –'

'Get off me. I'm not your mother. Oh thank God, I'm not your mother . . .'

Maria's words. The disgust in them. Her voice. The rejection. *I have lost Maria.*

Hiding in her bedroom, the door locked. Wanting to walk out of the front door, walk and walk, over the side of some bridge – to cast herself into the Thames. She had looked out of her bedroom window. The leap down was not far enough.

In the end she slept fitfully, lying there waiting till Maria would knock on the door and come in and sit on the bed and say that Yes, in the end, because she was Maria, because she was the Virgin Mary, she could forgive Helen.

She didn't draw the curtains or put on the light. The fantasy persisted. She knew it for what it was – a fantasy. There was no going back now. The Holy Family, desecrated. It never would be again (*never had been*), the Holy Family.

She got up and was sick in the handbasin. She lay quite still in the dark, a dangerous hammering in her head. Her throat felt choked. No sobs, no thoughts. I can't, won't think. Eddie, oh Eddie, where are you, Eddie? The song ran through her head, chiming – sung only last night, in Funchal. *Ain't no sweet man worth the salt of my tears*. But even to think of Eddie was like some dreadful wound.

A motorbike revving up in the street below, beyond the garden. Over and over. I'll go to Moorgarth, she thought. Maybe Uncle Dick would be there. She imagined herself taking refuge. Her own room. The peace, the understanding. I could cook for Uncle Dick. We could go for long walks together. Long walks as once she'd taken Uncle Eric . . .

And then, a sharp knock on the door. Maria's voice. 'Helen.' Leaping up and opening it. Maria, coming in, switching on the light. Her cold voice:

'You haven't unpacked. Good . . . You're to go straight over to Montpelier Square, to Dulcie and Jenny's.'

She said, faintly, 'Moorgarth. I could get an evening train. I –'

'Take your luggage *now*. Straight round to Montpelier Square. I don't want to see you or talk to you.'

348

'But I –'

'You're to stay there till we decide what to do with you.'

'Eddie –'

'Go now. And be quick about it. Just *go*!'

She remembered little about the next few weeks. She knew both Aunt Dulcie and Jenny had been kind to her. She had the feeling Dulcie was puzzled as well as pained. Jenny gave her tasks, simple household ones. She was never out of their sight. The kindest and gentlest of gaolers. But gaolers nevertheless. What did they know? She suspected, everything. She was at once in prison, and in hospital. They treated her with gentleness and care as if she were an invalid. She existed in just such a vacuum, a time warp.

Jenny told her, 'It's better – everyone thinks it's better you never – that you don't see Eddie any more.' But she had not thought she could. As for Yorkshire. How could she have thought she could go to Yorkshire?

Dulcie and Jenny seldom played the radio except for the news morning and evening, and perhaps a play if someone good was acting in it. She heard no dance music. She did not think of herself as a singer any longer.

At the end of the third week, Jenny said, 'Something's been arranged for you, Helen.'

She was told, kindly but firmly, that a temporary post had been found for her as governess to a family in Palermo. Dulcie said, 'I'm sure, like all the young, you want to travel.'

'Isn't that where Guy is?'

'It's Guy who's arranged it. The family are friends of his and Laura's. Maria got in touch with him . . .'

She had not seen Maria again. The preparations for going – she'd perhaps surprised Dulcie and Jenny with her lack of curiosity. She had not asked, *had not cared*, what or who this family was.

A nightmare journey. Raw with fatigue. Jenny and Dulcie dubious, worried a little whether she was fit to travel. (The invalid again.) A journey in which natural beauty seen from the train window only pointed a mocking figure at her desolation. As the mountains, the sparkling lakes and spotless chalets of Switzerland, gave way to Italy, her spirits sank lower and lower.

Guy was there to meet her at Palermo. She had not seen him since the autumn of 1946. She had always liked him, but now she saw him as another of the family, a friend of, ready to criticize, to pass judgment.

'I'm driving you to our apartment first. You can rest there. We'll take you to the Di Benedetto's tomorrow.'

As they drove along, he explained about Ruggero and Virginia. 'Virginia – they told you, she's having a baby in October? The children are fun. Lovely. Easy. You'll be happy. And not too homesick, I hope. There are other English around. British Council people, connections, etcetera. And I've just invited an army friend who was in Naples with me. He comes later this month.'

'How's Maria?' he asked. She imagined that his voice changed tone.

She said: 'Did Maria tell you why I wanted to be a governess?'

'No. She just said you wanted to be one . . . I suppose I seemed an obvious person to ask for help . . . What was the real reason, then? An emotional upset?'

'Sort of. A love-affair that went wrong . . .'

'Want to tell me about it?'

'No, not really. It was enough other people disapproving. I don't want you too.'

'Try me, and see.'

'No, thank you. It's over, that's the main thing. And I'm miles away, forgetting it ever happened.' She said in a small voice, 'He was married, he's married.'

'I see. Subject closed.'

Marcello Di Benedetto, aged five, skipping through the doorway – little blue overall, sandals, white socks, satchel. 'Plis, Miss.' His English, which wasn't coming on at all. He had learned to say 'Mickey Mouse'. And 'Ellen' for Helen.

He skipped always as he walked beside her, satchel swinging from one hand, the other tight in hers. As they turned out of the side street into the busy one, traffic lumbered and whizzed by. It was a twenty-minute walk to the apartment. Sometimes she went with the chauffeur to collect him, but on Tuesdays and Thursdays she came always on foot.

'Miss, miss. Ellen. *Caramella*, plis, Miss.'

'Just one. One only.' He detached his hand, felt in her pocket. One boiled sweet, kept for him. Off with the paper, and into his mouth. Then the trusting hand was back again.

'*Andiamo* to the *Giardino Inglese* this afternoon,' she told him in her halting Italian, mixed with English. They seemed to understand each other.

The secret journal of Helen Connors, Palermo, Sicily, May 1950.

There it is. My last entry:

Something terrible, and wonderful, has happened. Eddie and I . . . Nothing else. I never added to it.

The terrible wonderful thing now is that *it doesn't feel any different*. It's only the guilt – but I can't speak of that. That is *so terrible*. Terrible. It should be about religion and sin but it isn't. It's a *wound*.

It began after I'd been a few weeks here. It must have been buried. Hidden and lying in wait for when I would long and long for home. *Oh, what have I done?* What have I done to *us*? Maria, Eddie, Helen, who once were . . .

What else did I lose besides Maria? My virginity, of course. (But how could I want *that* back . . . after what I've known, what I've learned. And I did love him, I *do* love him – because this is a secret journal I can write it, again and again, I love you, Eddie. Where are you now? One sign from you, one scribbled note, the sound of your voice . . . *anything*. But I didn't, and you didn't. Now I think we never will.)

Friends from before, people like Ronnie – I can't go back, you see. Not for a long time, at any rate. I can't talk to *anybody*. Except Eddie. What could I say about it all – and my hopelessness?

I am frightened here in Palermo. I don't know what (or who) I'm frightened of. But perhaps because I've been sent here as a punishment (or so it seems), it's in some way like a prison. I could run away, but where to? I could earn my living, singing, *if I wanted to*.

Evening. Same day.

I think perhaps I should be brave, and try to write something I can bear to read in years to come. A few ordinary pages – My Life as a Governess in Palermo. That sort of thing. I can try anyway.

Here beginneth.

So far in Palermo, I've seen the Cathedral, the Cappella Palatina, the Norman Palace, the National Museum, four churches, the rather daring fountain in the Piazza Pretoria, and the inside of two hotels – the Hotel des Palmes which used to be the Palazzo Ingham, built by the Marsala king, and the Villa Igiea, which is very art nouveau.

Sometimes I drive out with the family. We've been to Monreale, Bagheria and Cefalù. We've also spent a day at the villa of Laura and Guy's friend, the Contessa Tarantino-Falletta. Both families went out there one Sunday. She speaks English perfectly and was very gracious to me. A Dominican priest who was working in the library there was very kind too and tried to talk to me. But his English was very bad – and my Italian's hardly there . . . Marcello sat on his knee and gabbled excitedly, and he let Silvi play with his rosary and try to pull it up on to her neck. Seeing him, how patient he was, I thought how *sad* it is priests can't have children. I can't imagine religious life at all. For me, that is.

The Contessa talked about the famous bandit Giuliano (he's so famous, he's known in the outside world as well, which I hadn't realized). I gather he's a sort of Robin Hood. His hideout is in the mountains, where journalists come to visit him. But the police are out to get him. So perhaps it is only a matter of time. I would be afraid to be alone in the countryside, though they say he is very chivalrous.

Morning.

I mean to write in this journal every day. I thought maybe it would feel better if I saw everything like a play, with all of us characters in it. Then perhaps I could watch it from outside, and not feel too much.

So here are the *dramatis personae*.

First the Dennisons.

Guy Dennison, 29. British Council lecturer. Already known to me, so I won't put any more. I think he's *probably* as kind as he seems, though you never know. He has been very tactful.

Laura Dennison, 26. His wife. Known to me also (slightly). Guy worships her and doesn't she know it? She always looks as if she's minding her own business, whatever that is. She's nice to me, though I wouldn't trust her with anything that really mattered. Don't know why. She gets ratty sometimes about the Englishness of Guy which you'd think would be the bit that charmed her. ('Another letter from your Aunt Eleanor, or do I say Mrs *McIntosh* – is not that your word for an *impermeabile*?' 'I love Aunt Eleanor,' Guy said. Which I thought was rather nice.)

Silvi and Titì (Caterina) Dennison, 3 and 2. Beauties.

Randall Furness. Age? Joker in the pack. Army friend of Guy's. Out here for a four-week holiday before emigrating to Kenya, to grow coffee. He asked me to show him some of Palermo while Guy's at work in the day, so we've been to – see previous list!

He's very amusing about his and Guy's Naples experiences. He's very loyal but I think might like to be critical of Laura for some things – like not appreciating Guy enough. He knows about the singing – Guy told him about it last year. He wanted me to do some for him, and asked me why ever I'd stopped. Then I said, 'I can't talk about it,' and he was very gentle and nice. Other times he's often what they call, I think, sardonic.

I've let him kiss me a few times. (Where would I get the sort of energy to say no?) I learned only that I perhaps don't like moustaches.

And now, the Di Benedetto family.

Ruggero Di Benedetto. 37 about. Business man. He is very good-looking if you like those sort of looks. And very charming too, if you fall for charm. But he's nice too, I think, and kind. Everyone is kind here. Sometimes he pays me a lot of old-fashioned attention and courtesy. Other times he doesn't notice I'm there. He adores Marcello. Natali too, of course, but he's immensely *proud* of Marcello. He wants the new baby to be another son. Little details – he makes a steeple with his hands, then lowers them in front of his wineglass, tapping the forefingers together while he thinks of what he's going to say. He is quite interested in politics. His wife isn't.

Virginia Di Benedetto. I think she's lovely but I can see that she's not conventionally beautiful. She looks distracted often, far away. Ruggero says she's always like this when she's having a baby – in another world. She has very elegant legs and tiny feet. Her shoes are all made for her – but she has to have special ones now, because her ankles are so swollen (the baby isn't till October but the weather is already very hot).

Marcello Di Benedetto, 5. Adorable. Tries to twist me round his little finger.

Natali Di Benedetto, 3. Adorable. *Can* twist me round her little finger.

The Di Benedetto grandparents. A bent-over granny and an upright grandpa with splendid whiskers. The children's nurse, Rosetta. And a long cast of extras. In the kitchen they all try to feed me up, and make a great fuss of me, though I can't understand a word.

Now SEE how light I've kept the tone! Anyone could open this journal and read to their heart's content, and learn NOTHING.

May 24th. Evening.
Randall proposed to me this morning. I was taken completely by surprise and stammered out something stupid. He said hadn't I guessed anything at all? Of course he wants a wife to take out with him – or at least to join him soon. I don't think he actually came here to look for one, but it's obviously been in his mind all the time. Anyway, I thanked him very much but – no. He took it very easily. The only odd remark he made was, 'You bring out the protective in a man, but I think you're pretty tough.' I told him, yes, I was. He spoke about love, of course. But anyone can *speak* of love. It all made me very sad.

But then I'm sad all the time, aren't I? if I'm to be honest –

It's no good to write this wretched journal. It always ends in tears . . .

Afterthought. I saw in an English paper today, months out of date. A piece about crooners. Just the words . . . 'in the heyday of Al Bowlly, Jack Plant, Eddie Sabrini . . .' Why is just his *name* enough to wake up everything? *Everything.*

Now that she was settled in she went three times a week for Italian lessons, arranged for her by Guy. She went to an elderly widow, Signora di Cara. Together they worked through a grammar printed in 1890 on thin paper with close smudged print. She thought of complaining, but as Guy had not only arranged but was also paying for the lessons, she felt she couldn't – even though he had said, 'Let me know if it doesn't work out.' She suspected he was doing Signora di Cara a kindness.

Sometimes they would read poetry. Or rather, Helen would be required to read – which she did with difficulty. *'Fratelli D'Italia, l'Italia s'è desta, dell'elmo di Scipio, S'è cinto la testa . . .'* while Signora di Cara snored, whistling gently.

The last week in June, Guy had another visitor, the cousin of someone he had been at school with. Adrian Croft-Jenkins, in his second year at Cambridge – and spending the Long Vacation in Italy and France. He would be staying two weeks. Helen was invited over to meet him.

She liked him at once. He was not much taller than her, thin and wiry, with black hair and green mocking eyes. 'Dear heart,' he called her, in a teasing voice. He mocked everything: school, family, his time in the army. 'Dear heart, if you had *seen* the tears I shed. A month's water supply for Catterick. Of course, I should really have been in the *Guards* . . .'

They saw quite a lot of each other. She enjoyed being with him more than she had with Randall. It was more like the brother she had lost (though anyone less like Billy, as she remembered him . . .) He liked to take her into the Hotel des Palmes, which with its high ceilings, and vistas of marble, he felt was an appropriately grand setting for them both to drink in. She sat with him in the bar, sipping Campari, while he talked about Cambridge, and how he shone in the Footlights there.

She told him about her singing career. She had grown used to giving the facts deadpan. She waited for him to mock Eddie – the idea of Eddie, *passé* Eddie. But nothing happened. Perhaps it was beneath his contempt? She said:

'We nearly had an engagement at a Cambridge Ball, in June 1949 –'

'Ah, if you've never been to a May Ball . . . So romantic. What you have missed, dear heart. Next year, *I* shall take you. Wait to hear from me . . .'

In July it became very hot. Some of her mornings were still free, even though school was over now. She spent them often in search of coolness, sitting in cloisters of monasteries. In the afternoons she took the children out.

Early in the month the bandit Giuliano was shot dead. She read that he'd been betrayed by his second-in-command, who was also his cousin. The newspapers and magazines, although she could not understand them, were full of lurid and dramatic photographs. Guy and Ruggero found the circumstances surrounding the death odd. But she understood little of it, wondering only if Adrian had read of it. During his stay he'd been fascinated by the adventures of Giuliano and his band.

Two weeks now since Adrian had left. She had missed him immediately. His departure had brought on a fresh wave of homesickness – just when she had thought it cured.

His teasing voice would come suddenly into her head. She held on to the memory of him, as some kind of reassurance that she came from England and would – some time – return there. Her stay here, which she hadn't chosen, seemed now to have no end in sight. How long would she stay? It hadn't been decided. Her future was as vague as ever – and as alarming.

All this time Guy and Laura were kind to her. She often spent Sunday with them, perhaps going out for a picnic or a drive. Then she would grow wary suddenly, imagining that perhaps Guy knew the real story of why she was out here. That Maria had written to him since. That she was now something faintly disgusting. And she would watch his face for a sign – which she never saw.

She visited churches and museums, monasteries, palaces. No need in Palermo to exhaust the supply. Guidebook in hand, she worked in squares. She even at one stage traced the English connections, the Marsala families of Whitakers and Inghams.

Eating breakfast one morning, thinking about where to go, what to do, Adrian's voice slipped into her memory.

'You *haven't seen* the Capuchin catacombs? Dear heart, I tootled down there at once, before any other of the Musts. It is of course a Must. Quite delightful. Ghost stories and spooky films and grand guignol, all rolled into one. You'll love it.'

So, that's where I shall go this morning . . . She walked out from the city centre, through the Porta Nuova, and along the Corso Calatafimi. A long dusty walk. She stopped at a café and sat half an hour with a *spremuta*.

When she arrived at the monastery, a cab was waiting outside, the lean horse, a nag really, head hanging. At that moment a party of seven or eight people walked out, blinking in the sudden sunlight. A brown-robed monk standing at the entrance said goodbye to them. Out in the road, some children had a puppy on a string and were pulling it, bewildered, in circles.

She said to the monk, in her halting Italian, 'I've come to see the catacombs.'

'Ah yes,' he said, 'But you see this party of people just leaving – they are the last this morning. We close now in ten minutes.' They would open again at three, he said. But this was not an area she could stay in for two or three hours. She must have looked crestfallen at her mistiming, because he said suddenly:

'You have walked here? All right, then. Do please go down . . .'

Down the stairway, and along the first of the corridors. It was all right to begin with. Even though she was alone. (She had thought he would accompany her. But she had had difficulty in making out his accent, could not have heard him right.) In the airy vaulted corridors it was cool, clean, dry. The exhibits well lit. There were arrows pointing – it would be difficult to get lost.

She walked along slowly. The mummified bodies standing upright in niches shaped like coffins had their wrists and feet bound. Burial place for embalmed corpses, it was all much as Adrian had said.

'They desiccate them, dear heart, bathe them in sweet-smelling herbs and roast them in the sun, before stuffing them with straw and dressing them up in their Sunday finery. Some who've lain in a bath of arsenic have their hair and skin. It's all absolutely delicious.'

Here they were in their finery. Silk, satin, lace – tattered. Their expressions sometimes comical, sometimes contorted – as if surprised by death. Some were serene. One man, preserved she supposed by arsenic, had a startlingly brick red face and, after a hundred years, the hair still on his head.

The arrow pointed: a section for men, for women, for lawyers, professors, judges.

There were the children. Babies in lace. Two children standing upright, holding hands. A premature baby. A brother and sister killed by the collapse of a wall.

Little Rosalia Lombardo, dead at two. Her perfectly preserved body lay under glass. Impossible to believe she was not breathing. But the doctor who had achieved this miracle had died suddenly. He had not passed on his discovery. Secret injections – and the secret gone for ever.

Rosalia, dark hair tied with a bow, heavy-lidded eyes, rose-olive complexion – who was she reminded of but Maria? Photographs at Moorgarth of the eleven-year-old Maria, saved from the *Lusitania*.

Oh, Maria. Gone for ever. But to think of Maria was to think of Eddie. Eddie, older than her by almost thirty years. Eddie, one day a grinning skull, *like these* . . .

Suddenly she could no longer bear to be down here. What had seemed interesting, not frightening, as she'd walked peacefully the aseptic corridors was now . . .

I must get out, or I shall go crazy.

Driving me crazy. You, Eddie, you're driving me crazy. *What did I do, what did I do?*

A panic attack. I must get out. Get out, get out. ('Get out,' Maria had said. 'Get out. I never want to see you again.')

357

The skulls, the grinning faces . . . An arrow pointed to The Judges. She began to run in little circles. It was clearly marked, she couldn't be lost. She could not get lost.

She began to sob.

My tears for you, make everything hazy, clouding the skies of blue . . .

I am going crazy. You're driving me crazy.

She leaned against the glass case, waiting for the panic to subside. But she could not stop the sobbing. Or the tune going maddeningly round in her head.

> *You, you're driving me crazy . . .*
> *My tears for you . . . my tears for you . . .*

Oh Eddie, oh Eddie. How I loved you. Breathing in gulps of the cool, clean-smelling dry air, she wept for Eddie, and his touch.

By the exit the monk waited with the key. She made a small donation. 'It was so interesting,' she said in careful Italian.

Half an hour with the dead. What am I doing alive? She walked slowly and tiredly back along the road towards the Porta Nuova.

My tears for you make everything hazy. She was crying again as she walked along. She did not care who saw her. The voice in her head, the song, surely driving her crazy. Oh my darling Eddie.

In the month of August, she travelled with the family across the island to a villa near Agrigento. It belonged to the Di Benedetto grandparents, who travelled with them. The town's name had originally been Girgenti before Mussolini changed it to the more Roman sounding Agrigento. Grandfather called it Girgenti still. 'Ah, my beloved Girgenti,' he said over and over on arrival.

After visiting the beautiful Greek temples she bought a folding picturecard. She wanted to send it to Maria. But she knew that she could not. Yet she longed for news of her. Before leaving for Agrigento she had asked Guy, carefully casual, 'Any news of Maria?'

Guy, equally casually – she was certain he knew nothing – said, 'No. Not lately . . . Why not write to her yourself?'

'We had words,' she said.

Again, the awkward exchange. 'Ah, about the love-affair,' he said.

'Yes, about the love-affair.'

He gave her a talking-to. 'You should write. I'm amazed at her silence. The upset should be over.'

The stay in the villa was good for her. By day they bathed, or picnicked near the temples. In the evening, when the children were back from the beach and were being bathed, she sat in the villa garden – dreaming, watching the view. The sea would be lost in mist, the sky, shades of rose through to pale blue. Swallows wheeled and circled over the rooftops, twittering and calling. In the distance as they flew away they became black dots like insects.

She dated from that place, that time, the beginning of her getting well again. Her cure. (If I am *ever* to be cured.) Sitting in the cool of the evening beside the ornamental palms. Peace in her body. Peace, almost, in her mind.

In September Marcello was back at school. Each morning now she was up early with both the children and the nurse. They breakfasted at seven: cold boiled milk, bread and a little goat's cheese and fruit. Marcello would pick his way through this, leaving the milk always. Then his satchel must be got ready, his books checked, his white socks, his sandals. Usually she went with him in the car. They would arrive: 'Kiss plis Miss?' and then she would see him merge in with all the other blue overalls – crying out a greeting to his friends.

As before, she fetched him on foot, Tuesdays and Thursdays, when Virginia had the car. Otherwise she was free in the mornings. She was still a great museum visitor.

She hadn't heard from Adrian. That's the end of that, she thought. (Perhaps when he goes back to Cambridge for the new term?) She longed sometimes for the ordinariness of a 'boyfriend'. 'Do you have a boyfriend?' people asked. Randall, she had never expected to hear from. She hoped he would marry soon.

Lovely September days. There was talk of how long she could stay. She agreed to stay till Easter when the new baby would be six months. And afterwards? She didn't want to think too hard of the future. Guy suggested she might want to go to university or college. Her maths after all had been very good. But she could not bear this idea, seeing it somehow as a life with great acres of shapeless time, infinitely unattractive. (Students – the word now brought the image, the *sound* always, of Eddie mocked.)

Virginia was very large now. The child was expected in about six weeks. Helen dressed Natali's doll for her and talked to her about the coming baby. She loved the little hands entwined round her neck, the wet kisses.

And above all, she loved the trusting hand clasped in hers as she walked Marcello back from the convent. The leafy plane trees, the wide pavements. Coming out from the convent, she knew the street so well. The little alleys running off that she would never go down, or let Marcello enter. Then turning into the larger busy street: the lemonade stall, the buns and ice-cream, the news stand. Marcello liked to stop everywhere, but it was forbidden. No snacks, no sweets – except the one boiled one she hid in her pocket for him. He tried to get it out. She made him ask.

'*Caramella*, plis, Miss?'

Today he wanted a comic paper. They had to stop at the stall, he pleaded so, to buy his *Topolino*. Then with it tucked in his satchel, he was dancing again beside her, on her inside always, away from the traffic which whizzed and roared past.

A Lancia screeched to a halt just ahead of them. A face leaned out of the back as they came near. A voice called:

'Signorina Connors –'

She stopped, surprised.

'Signorina Connors, *momento* –' Smiling, hand held out.

She moved forward. '*Si, ma . . .*'

Suddenly, the door was flung open. She felt herself grabbed, she was pinched, prodded in the shoulder, a foul-smelling cloth was stuffed in her mouth. A squeak from Marcello, then silence. She felt his body against hers.

The door was slammed. She lay, face downwards. A hand was on the small of her back. Her legs seemed entangled with Marcello's bare ones.

It had all been over in seconds. The car was moving fast, swaying, screeching round corners. Pray God someone had seen, someone was giving chase, the police had been called, the number of the car taken . . .

She struggled to speak, shaking her head to and fro, chewing, gagging on the cloth. The car smelled of sweat and fear. She could hear Marcello whimpering.

The men, she thought there were three, two in the front and one with her and Marcello at the back, talked amongst themselves. Rapid, urgent, often angry-sounding.

One of them said in English, '*You talk – he dies.*'

The car careered wildly. The horn blazing. It seemed an

eternity of jolting and twisting. Half an hour, an hour? The road was bad. Once she thought they were on tramlines.

Three voices. Urgent, bad-tempered. She could understand nothing. She chewed and gagged on the evil-smelling cloth. Her head held down. Rough fingernails through the cotton of her blouse.

Oh my God – she who had not prayed, had scarcely prayed since Eddie – God get us out of this, Jesus save Marcello. Oh, Our Lady, *help*.

The car came to a halt with a suddenness that sent her jerking forward. The gag was pulled roughly from her mouth.

'Marcello,' she cried out.

'*Vasciu!*' shouted the man beside her, harshly. '*Vasciu!*' The car door opened, and she was pushed out roughly on to the roadside. The same man who had smiled and called her name. Dark face, shadowed, pinched nose. ('*You talk – he dies.*')

The car turned with a screeching sound, and drove off down to the right. She could not see Marcello.

She tottered at the roadside. The car was far out of sight now. Only lorries seemed to be passing. She was shaking and sobbing. She began to walk along the dusty road to where it was a little built-up. She came to a small shop. She spoke through bruised lips, but she was crying so much she could not make the owner understand. Telephone? No, they had no telephone. What was the matter, they asked. '*Ma ch'è succeso?*' But she ran off.

She saw tramlines, a familiar name on a tram. She milled in with the crowd, standing on the journey, face pressed against the window. She got off in the Via Roma. She went into the Hotel des Palmes. Running up the steps, across the marble floor, dishevelled, dirty, beginning to sob again. At the reception desk, she said to the startled porter:

'Telephone for me, please. Di Benedetto. At his office. I must speak to him, urgently, privately. *At once . . .*'

'Where were you?' Laura asked. 'I've been trying to get you since about two. You weren't at the Institute . . .'

'They should have known,' Guy said. 'I was over at the University. The lecture course . . . I told you about it.'

'I can't have heard.'

She was sitting near the telephone, a glass of white wine beside her on the small onyx table. The windows were open to the balcony. There was the roar and clang of the evening traffic

361

below. She was dressed in a white skirt with a green belt, and a fawn silk shirt. Cool, elegant. Smoking through her long ivory holder.

The coolness of the room was like a benison. He said:

'Well, what did you want me for?'

She was looking away from him. Her voice quavered.

'Marcello's been kidnapped.'

His first reaction: 'Christ – Why didn't you tell me? The moment I stepped through the door, *why didn't you tell me*? Where is he, *where's Ruggero*?'

'Have a drink or something and try to keep calm.'

'Why, for what reason keep calm?'

He was pacing up and down the room. She remained quite still. He pumped her for information. He learned only that Helen had been involved, that she'd been released and had telephoned Ruggero from the Hotel des Palmes.

'But she's *all right*?'

'As far as I know. Frightened. Shocked. Virginia –'

'Oh my God.' He walked from the drinks cabinet to the bookcase. And back again. Then back again.

He sensed Laura's fear. The air was full of it, like a scent. Not for her the sweats of terror, of agitation. Just a cold calm. Her body, as it had been in Naples, that night of the air raid.

'I was afraid to go over there,' she said.

'We'll go together, Silvi and Titì –'

'I'll speak to Agata,' she said.

On the drive over she was silent, smoking all the while. He knew it was useless to ask her more questions. When he had telephoned Ruggero he had spoken only to the manservant, leaving a message that they were on their way.

Virginia was in bed, under sedation. In the drawing-room, Ruggero sat white-faced. Dr Anello was with him. A bottle of wine and glasses stood untouched. Helen, looking like a bedraggled little bird, was on the far end of the sofa. Her mouth was bruised, the area round the upper lip already blue-black.

He put his arm round her.

'Oh, Guy.'

'Was it terrible?'

She nodded. 'I just want him back. I –'

'We *all* want him back.'

'I just want it to be all right. Poor 'Ginia. There must have been something I did wrong. If I hadn't . . . You see, they knew my name. It was my name they called out . . . Guy, it was very terrible.'

He stroked the top of her head, absently. They had spoken in English. Now Dr Anello said in Italian, 'The little girl – she's pretty shocked. I've given her something . . . And something stronger for bedtime.'

The drawing-room, at this time usually so full of life: Marcello running from sofa to chair, Natali clambering up on Ruggero's lap. The bottle of wine was opened. The wine poured out. Helen refused any. Laura sat beside her, smoking.

The telephone rang twice in the next half-hour. The first time it was Grandfather, about arrangements for a picnic next Sunday. Yes, Ruggero told him, everyone was fine. And of course they looked forward to Sunday, though it was just possible they wouldn't be able to make it. The second call was a crisp business exchange. Each time Ruggero hurried to put the receiver back.

At nine-thirty it rang again. Dr Anello had already left. Guy was opening a second bottle of wine.

Ruggero picked up the receiver. '*Casa Di Benedetto . . . Pronto.*'

In the silence, there was the fussy ticking of an ormolu clock. Ruggero saying nothing. Only listening. '*Si. Si . . . Allora, vediamo.*'

He replaced the receiver. His hand was trembling. There was a fine sweat on his upper lip.

Guy said, 'That was?'

Ruggero nodded.

'I don't want to hear,' Laura said.

Ruggero sent both her and Helen into the dining-room. 'Try both of you to eat something. You'll feel better.'

Helen thrust her hand into Laura's free one. Laura clasped it lightly. When they had gone:

'All right,' said Guy. 'It was, of course?'

'Yes.'

'How much?'

'Twelve million –'

'Good God. Can you do it?'

'Probably not – I think not –' A muscle in his eyelid twitched.

'What sort of conditions?'

'Twelve million, in forty-eight hours. They'll ring back to say where and how.'

'Twelve million – or else?'

'Or else.' He seemed too dry-mouthed to enunciate.

'You can't negotiate?'

'I shall have to – for that sum . . . Dear God, this country. My inclination is to –'

'Helen saw the face – a face, of course. She was afraid even to tell me that. "*You talk – he dies*," they said. At least she didn't run to the police . . .'

Which I would have done, Guy thought. How English I am, with my instinct to rush to the police, to a lawyer – to somebody or something representing law and order. Fair play. Safety. Security.

'Of course she has nothing really to tell. Her description of the car, it's of the vaguest. Black, medium size, that kind of thing. And the men . . . well, they'll only be hired thugs, expendable, anonymous. The one who lured her – they'd have taught him to call out Signorina Connors – probably the only bit of standard Italian he can manage –'

Guy said, 'The worst is, the conclusion from it all – Someone knows your habits. That Helen goes to the convent on Tuesdays and Thursdays –'

'That's not so difficult.'

'Her name too.'

'These matters. If someone is determined. It is quite easy . . .'

'And the voice, what sort of voice? Was anything else said? Or just the demand. The money.'

'The words were –' he spoke with difficulty. Ashen still. 'They were – "I think you wouldn't like a dear little soul to go to Jesus?"'

'Why ever bring religion into it? They have sick minds.'

'Their manner of speaking. It skirts round the dread word. That way, they haven't actually said it.'

Guy quizzed him. If only perhaps to calm him, help him.

'How much can you raise?'

'Eight, even nine. Twelve, no. Someone has an exaggerated notion of the Di Benedetto wealth –'

'The voice – what sort of voice?'

'Oh, very cultured. Soft. Slightly anonymous.'

'And why you, do you think? Apart from this idea of great wealth. There are plenty with fuller coffers –'

'We don't know – maybe some of them too – but it's kept quiet . . . Giovanni Serio – his son was kidnapped in '47, '48 – for stopping contributions to the Separatist movement.' He paused. 'At one time I donated substantially to the Christian Democrats – then stopped, for what seemed to me good reasons. A few months ago I received an anonymous letter – which I ignored. The threats in it were very vague – and solely to do with my business . . .'

The muscle in his eyelid was jerking again.

'My God, this country, this country . . . that we are so afraid, cowardly, corrupt, weak, tyrannized. It could be someone big behind this – or someone very small. Anything can be anything . . . But do you call someone's bluff when it's your son's life?'

He added: 'And this is nothing new – the situation is as old as the hills. It's *when it happens to you . . .*'

Guy said, 'At least, since July, we know it can't be Giuliano's gang . . . He's dead and buried, after all.'

Laura and Helen reappeared. Ruggero asked, would Helen like to go back with Guy? 'Another English person – it might help.'

But Helen didn't want to go with them. She was worried about 'Ginia, she said. And yes, she'd be quite all right.

She wanted to know what had happened. Ruggero promised Guy he would tell her as much as he thought right of the telephone call.

'Ring me up,' Guy told her, 'if you need an ear . . .' Looking at her, he thought: Maria's little waif and stray, contrasting the forlorn, bruised face with the smooth one of Laura. He wished Maria bothered about her more. Disapproval of an adulterous love-affair wasn't really enough.

'I'm frightened,' Laura said. As they lay in bed, her body felt stiff, hard. She clung to him. He thought how their love, hers for him (his for her?) seemed to flourish in the heightened atmosphere of danger.

Early the next morning, Ruggero rang to say that Virginia had given birth to a son. Stillborn. It was the shock, they said – otherwise at eight months, weighing six pounds, it would have had every chance.

Ruggero received two more phone calls. The first one agreed to terms – eight million was accepted and arrangements made for payment. The second call – late at night – said that Marcello would be waiting just after midday the next day, beside the bandstand in the Giardino Inglese. 'Thanks to your good sense and co-operation, it is not after all time for him to go to Jesus.'

He was there. Sitting on a bench, with a bag of *caramelle*, and a *Topolino*. He said very little. Deliberately, he was asked few questions. Guy, who accompanied Ruggero and Helen, saw the father holding the son close.

He had not been ill-treated, after the first shock. He spoke of, 'a little room with white walls. And toys and books.' A man in glasses had read to him. 'They said I could telephone. You can speak to your papa, they said. Tell him we need a lot of money if we are to get you home again.'

Bad men had taken him. Good men had looked after him – and brought him back.

Back, safe and sound. Except, Guy thought, profoundly shaken, disturbed, who now was safe? Who, sound?

❦

16

'. . . And a request now for Mrs Hannah Wilson of Stoke Poges,
Buckinghamshire. She wants me to play "any Eddie Sabrini
record". We don't often get Eddie on Housewives Choice, Mrs
Wilson. Don't know why that is, I remember him as quite a heart
throb. Mrs Wilson says, if I read her handwriting right, "His
voice could make you go all gooey." Hum, Mrs Wilson . . .
Anyway, here *is* Eddie Sabrini, with Al Coleman and his band,
Time on my hands . . .'

Helen snapped off the radio. (Battery-powered transistor in a
green leather case. Very smart. Farewell gift from the family
whose children she had just been looking after.) *Housewives
Choice*. She was hardly a housewife, and now that she lived at
the Bellarmine Club, she hadn't even to make her own bed. One
of the chambermaids did that. Nor did she have to start work till
ten. Flicking a comb through her hair, she looked in the glass to
see if she appeared neater than she felt, and hurried down to the
dining-room. Nine-twenty.

It was warm this June morning, but cool in the basement
dining-room, leading out into the small town garden.

'Just tea and toast, please,' she said to the waitress. In half an
hour's time she would be sitting behind the reception desk in
the hall. Opposite her, a large painting of Cardinal Griffin,
Archbishop of Westminster, and next to it, one of Pope Pius XII,
with the eponymous Cardinal Bellarmine (1542–1621) making a
third. She found the trio's gaze hard to escape.

It was only her second week in this new job. Palermo, left
behind at Christmas, seemed another world now. But she
dreamed still. Her first night here – in the strange bed in the
largish hotel-type bedroom – she woke up at two in the morning,
bathed in sweat, shaking with terror. The dead body of Marcello
grinning in an open grave in the Dominican Priory of Sant'Anselmo (but I only visited there the once, twice at the most). She
had been alone at the grave, till looking round she saw the
face of the kidnapper. 'Signorina Connors, Signorina Connors!'

'Murderer,' she'd called out in her dreams, rigid with terror . . .
(Why him, why there?)

Then she remembered. The last weeks in Palermo. Driving
with Guy and Laura along the approach to Sant'Anselmo – Laura
to go to Confession – she'd noticed a gardener lifting some plants.
As they drove slowly past, he turned his face, for a moment only,
towards the Fiat. Oh, but that's him, she'd wanted to say, that's
him. And then had not. How could she hope he'd be brought to
justice? She'd learned a little, a very little, of what passed for
law and order here in Sicily. How distressed too and embarrassed
the Dominicans would be. And worst of all, the whole terrifying
episode resurrected, would she not have perhaps to go into court
– albeit a mockery? She would have to bear witness. It would
not do. She could not bear it . . . So she had buried the sight –
and the memory of it. Yet not quite, for here it was back again,
in a dream.

At the time, she had seemed to cope. Marcello, too. He had
surprised her at first anyway, by his apparent recovery. Except
that he looked behind him always before turning the corner
anywhere, he seemed the same small boy ('*Caramella*, plis,
Miss.') It all might never have happened. Until the nightmares
began, a fortnight after his return. As if he'd been in shock and
suddenly come to life. Night after night his screams filled the
apartment. Virginia, scarcely recovered from the stillbirth, would
go to sit with him until Helen insisted that, if he'd allow it, she
must stay with him. In the end, he had slept in her room on a
small palliasse, with a nightlight. She read to him, sang to him
. . . Her own terrors and distress put aside. Even Eddie, put
aside.

Attention had to be given to Natali, who had caught some of
the terror, and suffered from jealousy into the bargain. The
nurse, Rosetta, who'd left a little after the kidnapping, had been
replaced by another who was willing to get up in the night but
whose face sent both Marcello and Natali screaming. It wasn't
until the beginning of December when a girl from Agrigento was
taken on, who seemed to have at once a way with them both,
that Helen felt able to escape. The original idea, to stay till
Easter, was not now to be thought of.

With a sigh of relief, she'd packed up to go. To be back in
England, in London, for Christmas (No, I cannot hope to see
Eddie. Cannot hope even to spend the holiday, the season with
Maria). She wrote to say she would be coming back. Maria sent

a short business-like note, telling her that Jenny and Dulcie had invited her to stay, and that she was not to be short of money. Twenty pounds was being paid into Lloyds for her.

Traveller's tales. Strange exotic places, just out of bounds of austerity holidays abroad. She had a lot to say. Jenny and Dulcie and their friends and visitors wanted to hear everything. About the kidnapping she said nothing, except when alone with Jenny and Dulcie, and then very little. She had made it clear she didn't want to speak about it.

Immediately after Christmas she looked in *The Lady* for a post with children. She had to get out of London, away from any chance of seeing Eddie (who it appeared had embarked on a tour of Canada, coming rather low on the bill, she suspected). From what she'd heard, his career was now going nowhere, unless down. In the doldrums. Now when she thought of him something froze in her, as if all the longing and the damage, the hurt, the pain had solidified into some great lump of ice. Since her tears for him had made everything hazy, in the Catacombs, she had not wept for him. Nor indeed for herself.

Out of all the pages of advertisements, there were so many possibles even allowing for her lack of qualifications and her youth, that she felt she might as well prick with a pin. And this she did.

She wrote to Mrs Beverley of Chipping Peverel, a small village near Gloucester (car driver preferred). She was telephoned the next day. Jennifer Beverley, twenty-two, so only a few years older than Helen, had two small children and was expecting a third. She was small and pretty and very harassed. Pregnancy made her nervous of driving the car with the children in it, but she thought if Helen came along too it might be all right. Her husband was working out an Army contract in Libya and she was frightened and lonely.

The village was small, the house, once a vicarage, was old and rambling. The children were sturdy and noisy and demanding, but happy to demand from Helen instead of their mother. 'Oh ask Helen – she'll do it / get it / find it / make it for you . . .' In the evenings, after the children were in bed, she and Helen sat together knitting, occasionally listening to the radio but more often chatting, and often, giggling. They were like two school-girls, or two sisters. Jennifer had left her girls' public school one July and married in October. Her husband had been a returned POW, with nesting fever. 'My cousin brought him to the Tennis

Club the first day of the school holidays, and it just went on from there. And *of course* I don't regret it.'

But after about three months, when Jennifer was nearly six months pregnant, her (very trying) mother who'd been in the habit of ringing up every night and fussing, arrived with her luggage. She was going to stay, she said, and 'look after silly little Jennifer', until the baby was born. No protests would send her away. She gave the children so many treats and presents, undermining all discipline painfully built up, that they clung to her. '*Some* little people love Granny . . .'

She had been against the marriage in the first place. Now the absent husband came under fire. 'I don't know what business Brian had going off and leaving my little darling like that.'

Jennifer, reduced to a frazzle, was no longer Helen's friend and giggling companion. She became offhand and morose. Mummy spoke pointedly of getting 'a good girl in from the village'. When by chance, and not in *The Lady* this time, she saw an advertisement about a Catholic social club opening up in London, with a post as receptionist and/or barmaid offered, she saw it as the perfect let-out.

She didn't know how many were interviewed, but she knew from the first few moments that the job was hers. Mr Palmer was a retired maths master, who had taught with the Jesuits for thirty-five years. She mentioned Eleanor's brother. 'Yes, yes, of course. I know him well.' Guy's name came up. He'd taught Guy. 'Dennison et al., My God, yes . . . When you're next in touch, tell him I was asking after him. *Palermo*, my word . . .'

Perhaps others had these connections and more, but she was never to know because by the end of the conversation he was asking, 'When would you be able to start?'

She shared the work with a middle-aged spinster, who was also on reception but not in the bar. On the whole Helen preferred the bar work.

Geoffrey Palmer wasn't married. His sister Dorothy, once a prep school matron, came to live with him in the flat converted upstairs. She was the housekeeper and often, final arbiter. Because Helen lived in, and they worried that she might be lonely (although she explained she had relations in London), they had already twice invited her upstairs.

Dulcie and Jenny were pleased for her. She heard that Maria was too. She didn't go round to see Maria. Not because she feared meeting Eddie (who, back from Canada, had gone now to Italy for the summer season. Singing with a hotel band, Jenny said), but because it would mean being alone with her. Will the wound never heal? she thought.

Dulcie thought the Bellarmine sounded the sort of place where Maria would have lots of opportunities to meet the right kind of boy. (Oh, ghost of Eddie – never mentioned.) 'I know Catholics are meant to go out with Catholics if possible, which can't be easy in this Protestant country. So you're in a marvellous position . . .'

Helen and the Irish barman, Terry, got on very well together. Terry liked the job but often had trouble turning up on time, so that on three occasions already it had been Helen opening up. The first time he was very repentant. It had not been his fault. 'There's bad clocks about,' he told her.

One Friday evening, the end of her third week, Adrian Croft-Jenkins walked in. She had her back turned, fitting on a measure, when a voice said:

'Well, if it isn't little Helen Connors! Last seen 'neath a Sicilian sky . . . Dear heart, how goes it? Or rather, how *went* it?'

'Not too well, really.' Then she astounded herself by saying in a throwaway voice, 'The son of the house was kidnapped –'

'Never!'

He wanted to know, at once, every painful detail. So did everyone else standing around. She was furious with herself, awkward, almost tearful. She began instead to quiz Adrian, asking him what he'd been doing since Cambridge. Her voice brittle, hectic. She wasn't attending to the drinks, and had to ask for an order of two Guinness and a bitter to be repeated for her. Terry, who'd been all agog when she mentioned kidnapping, now asked her nicely to pay attention to what she was doing.

Adrian had two friends with him, both almost twice his size. All three were drinking gin. They sat up at the bar. The others had moved away, now there was apparently no story forthcoming. Agitated still, she reproached Adrian flirtatiously. 'Well, Adrian Croft-Jenkins, I never got asked to that May Ball.'

'So you didn't!' He seemed genuinely surprised. 'Anyway I was only there as cabaret. I took my sister, as it happened – so that she could have a chance to get off with a chap on my stair at college. She was madly in love with him after only a couple of glimpses . . . It seemed to work. They're getting married this autumn.'

'How romantic,' she said.

'Yes, he swam straight into the net. He's an Hon. as well, so she's getting a little handle to go with it. All most satisfying. If you're not the catch being landed, of course.'

She was busy then for a few moments. When he saw her free again, he asked:

'Dear heart, what's the face that launched a thousand ships *doing* here? Tell me all, I'm wildly curious . . . A barmaid. Well I never.'

It was easy to adopt the same light tone of badinage. She was able to make everything seem to have been chance, and utterly delightful, and rather fun. Everything was 'just for the moment'. Terry, passing her a cloth to dry the glasses, saying, 'Till her Prince Charming comes along – isn't that right now, Helen?' He winked at Adrian, 'Haven't I told her that's me? But she'll not hear a word of it . . . I'm a broken man.'

Helen, busy fitting a measure on to a new vermouth bottle, blushed.

'A simple homespun beer from your fair hands, dear heart,' said Adrian. A square-faced boy standing nearby said, 'Surely you mean home-brewed?'

'Why, has she been making it on the premises?' he asked all innocence. The mood was set for the remainder of that evening's drinking. She did not have to bother about revelations.

It was only towards the end, just before the bar closed, that he referred to her singing. She had forgotten that Guy had told him about it, last year in Palermo. He told everyone at the bar. 'One thing I bet you didn't know . . . Helen's a singer. No, not opera, not RCM. The real thing, a crooner. A real pro. Aren't you, Helen?'

'I *was*,' she said awkwardly, coldly. She was embarrassed. And disturbed by how quickly it was taken up. Terry joined in. 'Wouldn't you sing a little song for us now?'

Several men, and two mixed groups at tables across the room, had pricked up their ears. Silence, while everyone waited for her comments, her answer. Explanations. Excuses?

'I wasn't top of the bill or famous or anything. Lots of the places I sang, they were any old places – anywhere that'd take us. It was all just for fun. I wasn't any good.'

'Let us be the judge of that,' Adrian declared. 'We shall certainly expect to hear . . . Didn't you do it with that 'thirties crooner, *un peu passé*, Buddy Sabrini or something?'

'Eddie Sabrini. He was – is – my stepfather . . .'

'Forgive me, dear heart. We all make gaffes, but Adrian's floaters are the worst . . . Why not take it up again? There're lots of sprightly, slightly absurd tunes about. *Sparrow in the tree-tops*,' he sang in a chirpy voice, '*scared of going home because it's so darned late . . .* Know that one?'

Just before he left he said, leaning forward and clasping her hand, 'I want you to come to supper with me – No, a theatre first, then supper, dear heart.'

She wasn't sure what to expect, or what she wanted to expect. They went to *King's Rhapsody*. She wore her new white piqué dress and bolero – made by herself with a Vogue pattern – of which she was very proud.

After the show, he took her to eat in the King's Road. 'We always come here when we go to flicks at the Classic. They have Kosher margarine with the bread rolls – it's the nearest thing to butter these days . . . Don't you *long* for butter, dear heart?'

It was the first of many outings that summer. He was good for her, even though his remarks would be suddenly piercing, as when he'd looked at her closely once and said, 'Dear heart – yours is broken, isn't it?'

'My heart?' she said. 'Don't make me laugh. My heart's made of rubber.'

'Then it's safe with me,' he said lightly.

Since coming down from Cambridge in June, he'd been working for a small fine arts institute, whose name he seemed to keep hidden, on a project to do with the Festival of Britain. She wasn't sure if he hoped to stay on afterwards.

Once he took her back to his flat, where she met his flatmate, Martin, a sturdily built young man reading agriculture at London University, who'd been an Army middleweight. Adrian identified the family photographs grouped around the sitting-room. 'My mother,' he said, pointing to a dark-haired woman wearing something gauzy, dewy-eyed, with slightly parted lips. A girl, much more robust. 'My sister Jane.'

Helen said, 'The one who trapped the Honourable . . .'

'The very one,' he said. 'And she hasn't even Mother's looks. Ravishing, isn't she, Mother? I have her eyes, perhaps, but not much else.' There was a picture of his brother, Hugh, killed in Normandy in 1944, aged nineteen. 'What even *now* is still called the Flower of English Youth, etcetera.'

Helen said, 'I'm sorry.'

'Oh, we all were, dear heart.' She noticed he had the same flippant tone for everything. How little, she thought, how very little I want to get mixed up there. Yet she felt in his company a heady excitement or sense of danger, none of which was sexual. She described it to herself once, as 'being found out'.

The Proms had started by then. On her free afternoon and evening once he turned up suddenly and said 'They're playing my tune. The *Eroica*. No seats left, though. I perceive the unfortunate need to queueooey . . .' Which they did. But he brought with him a picnic so elaborate, so extravagant, and so unlike the austerity spam sandwiches and bready sausages being eaten around them. From a wicker hamper he brought out champagne, and cold chicken legs, peaches, some Lindt chocolate 'brought back by Mummy from the land of the cuckoo clock'.

They could only get in upstairs in the gallery. He snuggled up to her. Laid his head companionably on her shoulder. 'Don't get ideas,' he said. 'It wouldn't do. I mean . . . I'd be a ghastly disappointment – in *that* department, as well as in others . . .'

She supposed the club was doing well enough. She knew it had been widely advertised in the Catholic press and that the word had gone round in Catholic circles. Those living and working in London, of every age group, were beginning to use it. At the end of her first month a retired Colonel took up residence. She saw him every morning, leaving the dining-room as she came in. She knew he went to Mass every morning in Cadogan Street. In the evening he would come into the bar when they first opened and drink a double whisky. Often he was the only person and if Terry for some reason had not yet arrived, she and he would talk. He often had a book with him. She noticed twice: the Catholic Book Club. He would ask her little questions about the weather and what she had been doing with her free time. 'Dancing,' he said often, 'I'm sure you like dancing. All young girls like dancing . . . Where do you go?' he asked another time. 'I hear the Pheasantry's very pleasant. And the Café de P, has that opened up again yet?'

The arrival of Terry had cut him off. 'Ghastly weather we've been having. And after all that sunshine. Makes you feel winter's just round the corner.'

Another time he was taking afternoon tea in the club sitting-room, and seeing her come in, invited her to join him. It was her afternoon off, she had come in only to collect a cardigan left on a chair – so she agreed.

He was a widower, he told her. They had had one daughter, who had been run over when only a child. 'Of course you don't get over that. One doesn't, you see . . . No, we were never sent another . . .' His eyes had a far-away look. She tried to guess his age. She thought about mid-fifties. He told her then, suddenly, abruptly, that he had wanted to be a priest originally. But the army tradition in the family had been so strong. 'One gets talked out of these things. It's easy to be talked out of something, when you're young.' He talked a lot about the 'young'. Once he said wistfully, thoughtfully, 'Of course it's not too late now, I suppose.'

One evening in early September, Adrian came into the Bellarmine, accompanied by a young man with light red hair, already receding, and glasses, which he took off at once. He had a milky skin, lightly freckled and an open, gentle face.

'Dear heart, may I introduce Dermot Vinney, erstwhile schoolfellow. Just starting in the City as – oh dear, I can't recall. But it's money, filthy lucre – getting or spending or something . . .'

'In fact,' Dermot said quietly, 'it's advertising. In the West End.'

'There I go again, fantasizing – he looks, does he not, dear heart, as if he should have charge of the nation's coffers?'

No, Helen thought, he did not. And even less, someone from the world of advertising.

A man sitting nearby said, 'You aren't handling the Guinness account by any chance? With a name like that –'

Adrian said, 'We met – re-met I should say – after three years out in the world, on the steps of the Oratory. I was just going in to Confession. He was just coming out. His soul looked *very* clean.'

Dermot said Adrian always was impossible.

All that evening, she felt his eyes on her. Adrian said a little later:

'You're not shy about Dermot here knowing you're a real bona fide, paid up, professional singer?'

'Opera?' Dermot asked. 'Oratorio? Lieder?'

'Dance band.'

'Oh,' he said, and smiled. The group sitting round the bar began to tease him:

'Anyway, does the fellow drink Guinness or not?'

'I did at Oxford, but not now.'

'He's so rich – advertising, I mean to say. Is it spirits, Dermot young fellow-me-lad?'

Adrian said, 'Only fifty per cent of him can wear the green. His Da's ever so English.'

'Is that so?'

'Yes, but his sister Bridget's a nun . . . How's that for holiness? And I'm not sure he hasn't an uncle a priest.'

'Can he not speak for himself?'

'He can,' Dermot said. 'Put a sock in it, all of you.'

Two days later he wrote to her. The letter was delivered by hand, and invited her to see *Kiss Me Kate*. She was to let him know which evenings she had free next month, and he would buy the tickets. There was no telephone number, only an address in Baron's Court. She wrote back saying yes (after all, why not?) And waited to hear more.

He didn't come in to the bar again. Nor did Adrian for a while. She was oddly disappointed, wanting to say to him, 'That friend you brought in the other night, he's asked me out.' Then about a week later he appeared in a group of six.

'Dear heart, I haven't been in touch for simply æons. I was in Malta with Mummy. Just look at my suntan. And what have *you* been up to?'

Nothing at all, she told him. She didn't mention the letter from Dermot, although she wasn't sure why. (She didn't think of herself as 'Adrian's girlfriend'. And nor, she supposed, did anyone else . . .)

Then Dermot telephoned while she was on reception. He had the tickets for next week, he said. She must suggest where to eat – 'You know London better than me. Tell me, and I'll book.' She could only think of Gennaro's. 'Gennaro's it shall be.'

It was an odd evening, if only because so often while she was looking somewhere else, she would be aware of his gaze on her. She was uneasy with his mixture of diffidence and anxiety to please, with at the same time a steeliness underneath, at variance with the soft voice and manner.

Over the meal he talked about himself, drawn out by her. He had wanted first to hear all about her, her background, her past. But she never got further, that first date, than telling him about being an evacuee and 'very unhappy'. Uncle Jack and Auntie Hilda was not a tale to be told over the gnocchi and the Valpolicella. Instead she had deflected him on to his childhood.

'It should have been happy, God knows all the ingredients were there. But I wasn't. It wasn't. I only wanted to be grown up. And there was such a long way to go . . .' Yes, well, there had been prep school, and public school and National Service, in the Army. 'In the army I wasn't sure I liked being grown up, after all.' Yes, Oxford had been all right. Not bad at all.

He confessed that he wasn't very used to taking girls out. 'Not one, the whole time at Magdalen. Lady Margaret and Somerville, the women's colleges – too alarming. And then nurses, foreign girls. I never somehow got round to it.' For someone so fearful, the advertising world seemed hardly the place. She would have imagined Adrian more suitable. She said this. He seemed surprised.

'That's quite different . . . It's just ideas, after all. I have the ideas, and they say whether they like them or not . . . Maybe it *is* kill or be killed – but it doesn't feel that way. My family are horrified, of course. It's not a worthwhile occupation at all . . .'

She spoke about the Bellarmine, and her work, but not why she had gone there. She joked about the triumvirate watching over her, about how easily Geoffrey got agitated, and how Dorothy was the calming influence, about the Colonel who read Catholic Book Club books and had even been seen, only yesterday, with a Knox New Testament alongside his double whisky. ('What do you think of this?' he'd asked her, for all the world as if her opinion mattered.)

It was after one o'clock when he brought her back in the taxi. He said rather solemnly, 'We must be careful not to wake up your colonel.' Then just as she reached for her key, he grasped her arm and turned her to him, kissing her very lightly on the lips.

He said, his voice low, 'I hope you don't think that's rather cheek, on a first date . . .'

Surprised, she said easily, with a little laugh, 'Oh no, I think it's rather sweet.'

He didn't appear in the bar again. Several days passed. Adrian, and friends, came again, but no reference was made to Dermot. Adrian, who seemed a bit offhand, distracted, not as cheerful as usual, said, 'You look cheery, dear heart. All the cares of the world are wearing me down. Nothing in particular, you know, but everything in general, which is of course *much* worse. Better by far a named sorrow.'

Later he said, 'You must come and liven me, dear heart. I

shall give a little supper for you. Or what about shaking our livers up at Battersea fun fair?'

The next day Dermot slipped into the Club at lunch-time. She was in the restaurant. Miss Gittings at the desk sent down for her.

'I'm sorry, not 'phoning,' he said, in an urgent semi-whisper, 'I wanted to speak in person. I was too shy – too silly, the other night . . . I have to go away tomorrow. It's a family holiday in Cornwall, we've a house there. We always go. The agency are honouring the holiday even though I'm such a short time there. I'll be away three weeks – it's rather long. I don't know how to say this – but you won't? I mean, if someone else . . .'

'Oh heavens,' she said. 'Yes, I'll still be here when you get back.'

'I never asked, you see, I ought to have done –' his voice went into even more of a whisper, under the watchful eye and listening ear of Miss Gittings. 'Never asked if there was – anyone else? If you've already –'

'No,' she said, 'there's no one else.'

He wrote to her five times from the family's holiday house, near Rock in North Cornwall. The letters were not very interesting. He mentioned a campaign at work for a new margarine. Sitting over a beer of an evening, or driving round the Cornish lanes, faded fuchsia in the hedges – he'd come up with some idea which *might* do. Every English, leafy English, clotted cream, milkmaids, 'even though the wretched stuff won't have been within miles of a cow'. Once or twice the weather had been good enough for surfing. He referred to the family without explaining the names. Including some cousins, there seemed to be at least ten of them.

In his absence she felt oddly lonely. So when the Colonel asked her to join him at his table for dinner, she accepted. The going was heavy. He discussed Thérèse of Lisieux, the Little Flower, moving delicately on to the vow of chastity Thérèse's parents had made when first married, and how in the end it was the wife who had decided to end it. He wanted Helen's opinion. She'd never given such matters thought. (How happily, with what joy, before the guilt, I surrendered myself to Eddie.) She strove to project herself into this other world. She said, 'Well, of course, if they hadn't, there'd have been no Little Flower. Someone has to make the saints, don't they?'

Later he spoke of his wartime experience in the Desert. She tried to remember where Guy had been in Africa, to try and match up. But then to think of Guy was to think of Palermo . . .

Adrian, a little unkempt, collar open, slightly irritable, came and whirled her away to the Classic in the King's Road, and a meal after. Kosher margarine again. She thought of Dermot and his budding margarine campaign. Adrian told her, 'If I seem disconsolate, dear heart, on the very edge of tears, it's problems with my love-life. It's going horribly wrong. And Mother Church is really not helping *at all*.' She asked no questions.

And then Dermot was back. 'You never answered my letters,' he said.

'You put no address,' she said.

'Didn't I? I'm always doing things like that. The family wouldn't be at all surprised.'

She asked about the margarine campaign. 'Quite stuck,' he said. His ideas had got so far and would go no further. Meanwhile someone else was trying to work in piskies. 'I ask you, for God's sake, piskies! The whole thing's been taken out of my hands. We'll lose the account, for certain.' He had been put now on to a coffee advert. 'Kaffee Kup, it's called. That's wrong for a start. Too German – too soon. Of course it's at least one third chicory and quite disgusting. I'll bring you some . . .'

A few weeks later he invited her for the weekend, to meet his family. They lived in Buckinghamshire, in a Tudor house not far from Amersham. In the train going down he prepared her, making sense of some of the names in the letters. 'We're rather a large family on my mother's side. The Teague cousins, over in Ireland – when we visit there, that really is something. Hundreds of them . . . But just at home now, there won't be many.'

There were six children, but only two lived at home: an older brother, recently qualified as a solicitor and now in business in nearby Hemel Hempstead, and Dermot's little sister, Maureen, who was a weekly boarder at a nearby convent. There were almost ten years between Dermot and her. Dermot explained embarrassedly, 'They thought it was safe, you see.'

The absent ones were Michael, the oldest, a married sister, Patricia, and Bridget, the Carmelite nun. Brilliant, Dermot called Michael. A first in Greats in 1939, then straight into the Guards. Fought in France and Greece, decorated twice. Now he was in the Foreign Office, posted to The Hague. 'The sky's the limit for him, in the FO.'

Patricia was known as Cakey. She had called herself that as a child after the Patacake nursery rhyme, and seemed happy to keep the name. She too was brilliant. A First at Cambridge in '41, in History, and then straight into the WRNS. She had not enjoyed her war. 'Such a *frightful* waste of time – when I could have been getting on with being a wife and mother.'

She was certainly that now. On the Sunday she came over for the meal. Her husband farmed twenty miles away but was too busy to come with her. She had met and married in 1945, and had four children already. She was expecting the fifth. 'No we don't mean to stop. I just think it's all absolutely wonderful.' She was dark and vivid and confident: 'Has anyone heard from *Bridget*? We'll have to get our letters in before Advent starts.'

Mr Vinney asked Helen, 'What do you think of our having a Carmelite daughter?'

She wasn't sure what the family made of her. Once or twice she was referred to as 'Dermot's girl', which he didn't deny, but which made him blush furiously. She didn't care for the way they treated Dermot, belittling him continually. She found herself wanting to protect him. They were scathing about his job. 'Sandwich boarding,' they called it. Mrs Vinney made remarks about 'filling in till you find your true vocation, Dermot'.

On the Sunday morning they went for a long country walk together – his idea. On the way back, he turned the conversation towards love, sex, religion. He told her:

'I've never . . . You see, I just feel purity's terribly important. I think if a girl's expected to keep pure herself, then why shouldn't a man? I mean, I don't want you to think I'm not absolutely normal. But I just wanted you to know – because I think I'm falling in love with you. Which makes me very happy. Does it you – a bit?'

'I'm terribly touched . . .' She didn't commit herself. She couldn't. But although she felt wryly amused at the way her purity was taken for granted, she felt sad too.

Back in London, they settled down to regular dates. He would come to the Club to fetch her but never came into the bar. She was secretive about him. She thought of him privately as the rock on which she leaned. Dermot is there, she would say to herself, there's always Dermot. She was not even sure what she meant.

Two weeks before Christmas, he went to Ireland in connection with the promotion not of Guinness but of some sort of cake. While he was gone she had tea with the Colonel. He told her of an audience he had had before the war with the newly enthroned Pius XII. And speaking of Rome, there was a showing of *Open*

City at a small club he knew. Would she possibly consider accompanying him?

After the film, he took her to Wheeler's. 'It's a Friday, of course, and although the ruling doesn't obtain, it's good to be able to keep it whenever possible.' Over a Graves supérieur and Dover sole, he asked her to marry him.

'I feel very apprehensive of asking on such a slight acquaintance. So little time spent together. But I have seen you going about your duties in the Club . . .' The words floated around her. '. . . good Catholic girl. Catholic woman . . . emboldened to make . . . rather surprising request –'

She couldn't answer at all. She twirled the stem of her wineglass. Her toe tapped under the table, almost of its own volition.

'You don't have to answer at once . . . Whether you could ever feel for me what's needed for us to make the rest of our pilgrimage together.' He nervously crumbled his bread roll. 'If I hadn't sensed a natural sympathy between us, I wouldn't have even suggested . . . a gap of twenty years or so is quite considerable. Not to be jumped over lightly –'

'I think it's rather more than twenty years,' she said.

'Surely not?' He hesitated. Tore a little more of the bread roll and crumbled it. 'My forty-eight to your –' He coloured. 'One doesn't ask a lady her age, but twenty-seven, twenty-eight?'

'Twenty,' she said. 'I'm only twenty.'

'How utterly stupid of me. I had thought . . .'

'I was singing professionally at seventeen – perhaps that gave you the wrong idea . . . But didn't you wonder that I had no war history?'

'No, no,' he repeated, covering his embarrassment. 'I have just been unbelievably stupid . . .'

She said gently, 'I can't say how honoured I am . . . but I think, somehow, it wouldn't do.'

'No,' he said, still a bright colour. 'No, no, of course not. How can you forgive me?' He reached agitatedly for the menu and wine list. 'The crème caramel looks awfully good . . . I thought a Barsac with our pudding would be rather nice . . .'

'My colonel proposed to me,' she told Dermot on his return. 'It was rather touching.'

'Did he, by Jove,' Dermot said. He surprised her then by his strong reaction. 'Bloody *cheek*. I mean, for God's sake, an old fogey like that. Must be all of fifty. I hope you gave him the brush-off?'

She surprised herself also. His indignation touched her. Excited her even. She hid her feelings.

'I said a polite no, if that's what you mean . . .'

'Bloody cheek, all the same – poaching on other men's territory –'

'You never thought *you* might be poaching on Adrian's?'

'Well, hardly. His problems never wear skirts. Unless they're Scots, of course.'

'Oh,' she said in a small voice, thinking only how naïve she'd been.

For several nights the Colonel didn't come down to the bar, then one night he reappeared at his usual time. Terry (there were bad clocks about again) hadn't arrived. She was alone, laying out potato crisps in saucers.

'Oh hello,' she said. 'A J and B coming up in a minute.'

He sat down awkwardly. Looked around. He said, 'I just wanted you to know . . . I think your refusal was a sign God wants me after all. Isn't that the most splendid answer to prayer? I prayed that you would say yes. But the answer was no. The answer was – give myself to God. It's wonderful.'

'Wonderful,' she said.

'My colonel is to become a Benedictine,' she told first Adrian and then Dermot. She told Adrian of Dermot's strong reaction.

'But what do you expect, dear heart? You're rather *dense*. He wants you for himself.'

Christmas worried her. She could not go to Maria. The fragility of their reconciliation would not stand living in the same house. She did not know if Eddie would be there. Or where he was at all. Even to think 'I have no news of Eddie,' was to stir up all the heartache. She did not want to go to Dulcie and Jenny again, and was quite prepared to spend it at the Club. 'I don't get on with my adopted mother,' she had told Dermot, and others. 'There was a frightful row, and things haven't been right since. I wouldn't dare to spend the festive season with her.'

'Oh, come to us,' he said at once. Delighted and excited. 'Why not? They'll love it. And we're always one short because of Bridget.'

The Vinneys: belittling Dermot, as ever. Dermot, she thought, my protector, whom *I* must protect – from his family.

This time the brilliant Michael was there, being rude about life in The Hague. He was totally unlike Dermot, dark and dashing with unnaturally bright eyes beneath bushy eyebrows. If he wasn't brilliant, his eyes were. He made a great fuss of Helen, flattering her in a slightly patronizing manner. 'I never thought my little bro would find himself a dazzling blonde.'

The thirteen-year-old Maureen went in for hero worship, following Helen round: 'Can I ask you a worldly question? It's about eyeshadow / mascara / night cream / suspender belts. The girls at St Mary's don't really know, and Cakey couldn't care less about these things . . .'

They went beagling on Boxing Day. The whole family. Helen hated it and had not brought any suitable shoes. She was lent Maureen's spare wellingtons. In their generally jolly way the Vinneys didn't notice she wasn't enjoying it. Only Dermot, who didn't enjoy it either, was sympathetic.

In the train going back to London, he asked her to marry him. 'Can I think about it?' But she knew even as she spoke that she was going to say yes. She couldn't explain her certainty – how could she use the word Love for what she felt, hungry as she was for the days, before Eddie, when she had been good – when she had been loved? She could not imagine her life now, without Dermot. (What else was that but a kind of love?)

They celebrated her saying yes by a visit to the pantomime where one of his cousins was in the chorus.

'I haven't told the family – except I've written to Bridget at once. I hope you don't mind. She's my favourite sister as I expect you've guessed.' Over supper they arranged to go down to Amersham the following weekend to tell them.

He explained that they would have to save money, and that they could not afford to marry for about a year. She had not thought of having to wait. He talked too about birth control – or rather, not being able to use it.

That was something else she had not thought about. With Eddie (why do I always, and only, think of Eddie?) she had not thought at all – and supposed he knew what he was doing. Now it appeared she had been impossibly naïve and ignorant. Dermot, the prudent and knowledgeable. She was to chart her periods from now on. Although they would have a baby straightaway, do nothing to stop one, all the information she gathered would be useful later. Soon there was something new and more reliable coming, with thermometers, he told her.

At Easter, they travelled north to visit an uncle of Dermot's, living in Northumberland. She arranged to come straight from the Bellarmine to meet Dermot at King's Cross. While she was waiting for him, she browsed in the bookstall. There was a glossy gossip magazine, *Bandwagon*. Leafing through its pages, a paragraph caught her eye.

Eddie Sabrini, the crooner, idol of the 'thirties but not much heard of since (he was interned during the war), is an idol once more – in Italy! A record he made of a number called *Perdoniamoci*, for a little-known company, shot to number one over there, where it's stayed for over two months now. Scenes not unlike those that greeted the American Frank Sinatra on his recent visit to the Palladium greeted Eddie at a concert in Turin last week. Screaming and swooning girls, clutching at his garments, crying 'Give us Eddie!' And it's the same story all over Italy. Asked how it felt to be the object of such worship, Eddie (49) said, 'Well, I don't think they see me as a father figure . . .'

'You're very quiet,' Dermot said on the journey.

She thought: I shall never sing again. She felt suddenly such a sense of loss. As if, a singing bird, she had been shut in a cage, the key thrown away.

By next day, the mood was gone. All that remained of it, that overwhelming sense of loss, was a sad, sore feeling. A nugget of unease. (Oh, Dermot, take care of me.)

She had been afraid to tell Maria about their engagement, at the same time relieved to have such news. She put it off until she could do so no longer – telling her only the day before announcements were to go into *The Times* and *Telegraph*.

'That's good,' Maria said. 'That's a happy ending.' She appeared glad, even kissing Helen. To an outsider, there could have been nothing untoward in her reaction. Just the expected joy and congratulations. And yet I know, Helen thought. It is there. A stone, the stone of anger and unforgivingness. Oh Maria, love me again . . .

17

'*Deus, qui proprium est miserere semper . . .*' The clear resonant voice of Father Clemente beseeched God, on behalf of the soul of His Servant Chiara Maria Clementina Agnese Tarantino-Falletta, that she be taken up by His holy angels and borne into Paradise.

Some might think themselves already in Paradise, Guy thought, so dazzling and glittering was the silverwork, the jewels – rubies, emeralds, diamonds winking from the great chalice; the crimson velvet of the altar frontals backing a great burst of silver rays. The Madonna, crowned in sapphires and tourmalines. The crucifix, studded with gems.

And standing in the aisle of the Tarantino-Falletta chapel, the coffin, surrounded by its four tall yellow candles. All that remained of the Contessa.

Beside him knelt Laura. He thought with terror that one day she would die too. (As will I, as will I.) And to the right of her, *their* jewels, Silvi and Titì. This Christmas of 1959, Titì eleven, Silvi almost thirteen. Who is like Laura, who like Maria, who like me? And Grainger blood? He saw in Titì, a young Maria. (Maria, the same age, snatched from the sea by my grandfather. Maria in the photograph albums that first summer of 1915, a bold face, hiding heaven knew what depths of bewilderment and loss.) And in Silvi, when she was anxious, a little competitive perhaps, wasn't there something of Dick? He thought now: I should like to have known Dick better. By the time we were ready to sit down and have a conversation, I was off to the wars. And then geography separated us. Dick, three years dead now. Far too early a death. For all that he conquered his drink problem – and it appears it was quite severe – it had been too late, if not for him, for his body, his liver. His going spelled the end of the foundry as a family concern. All bought up, taken over. Young Peter (*my half-brother*), considers himself Canadian, and plans a brilliant future in the law, aided no doubt by his prominent stepfather. One day perhaps we will take a look at each other. But since I could never speak . . .

But in Silvi, wasn't there also a look sometimes of Tomaso? Her grandfather, who will come to spend Christmas with us, the seedy chain-smoking Tomaso – still absurdly young-looking, still adored by and adoring of Laura. And all right for money – although it was to Laura that the faded Amelita had bequeathed her all.

'. . . *Qui Mariam absolvisti, Et latronem exaudisti, Mihi quoque spem dedisti . . .*'

It didn't seem long since that other funeral. The last remains of Amelita Varelli (who, meeting her in 1943, would have thought she had another sixteen years to live?) and such a collection of never-before-seen relatives, gathered round like vultures. Laura, who had not loved her, pale as ever, in tight-fitting black. And then the Will. To Laura, the family fortune.

So, we are not short of money now. Shall we stay on here? Who would have thought anyway we would stay so long? Laura who had wanted to live in Paris (but never in London), surprising me by her tireless work for charity. Out more often than in. Seemingly reconciled to Palermitan life.

And he himself? He taught at the university now. He had stopped working for the British Council when it had wound up here, with the Institute handed over to an anglophile society. He kept his connections. But otherwise . . .

'*Munda cor meum ac labia mea, omnipotens Deus . . .*'

Titì whispered something, in a loud hiss, to Silvi and was reprimanded by Laura. They were sitting now, listening to the funeral panegyric given by another of the Dominicans, Father Pasquale, pale, podgy, soft-voiced.

The Dominicans were much in evidence. Four of the five were present. Besides the preacher, there were the slight and white-haired Father Cirillo, the large burly prior, Father Alessandro, and of course Father Clemente – first met that visit to the villa when the nausea of pregnancy had kept Laura at home. Occasionally met since, mostly in the days when Laura had taken for a confessor Father Cirillo – a religious phase that had not lasted long (the result, he had thought at the time, of the scare over Marcello). Marcello, fourteen now, never referred to his ordeal, but spoke occasionally of 'Miss', of 'Ellen'. He would visit her, he said, when he travelled through Europe, which would be as soon as he could persuade Ruggero to let him go.

(Helen, married and with a son that very same age Marcello had been when . . .)

Sitting at the front, nearest to the coffin, was the son from Rome. Unmarried. Some way behind Guy could see Dr Anello, Paolo Anello. And Mendola the lawyer whom he had not met for some years now, with his wife. Sitting two benches forward and almost as upright as ten years ago was General Abbate, a widower now. Eighty, perhaps more? The Contessa had been eighty-six and only in the last two years had she been unable to walk, slowly, very slowly, in the garden with him. Sitting on a marble bench by the fountain, talking of this and that. Mostly reminiscences now. And never again as frankly as that first time. The girls were bored by her memories, Laura too, as she harked back more and more often to turn of the century Rome. The happy days. Ices at Latour's. Paper chases on bicycles. The Baron and the whipped cream . . . Silvi and Titì were always a little alarmed by her. Gradually he had seen what they saw: the little wizened face, growing to resemble more and more the mummified bodies in the Capuchin catacombs. Dying perhaps fifty years earlier, she would have had her niche, dressed maybe in the brown silk with ornate lace collars she'd favoured so in her last years.

'. . . Our dear Contessa, who at all times and in all places has supported Mother Church . . . faithful daughter of . . . worldly wealth never corrupted . . .' The smooth voice purred on. 'She married into a family who chose to lavish their riches, not as so many do, on vulgar luxuries – but on a religious foundation. And she was true always to this spirit . . . in the words of St Cyprian, *Habere non potest Deum patrem qui ecclesiam non habet matre* – Our beloved Contessa could not have had God for her father, had she not had the Church for her mother . . .'

He walked a little by himself in the garden, down past the cypresses and the carob trees, to the rose-garden, where the yellow-orange ever-flowering roses were in bloom. Titì ran down after him, saying, 'I want to be with you.' Laura was cross, she said, because she had whispered and giggled with Silvi during the ceremony. 'She says I start it always.' And, 'Well, you do,' he said. But she must have known it was a statement of fact only, not a judgement. (Oh, how I wanted to be naughty, he thought, and how good I was – until St Boniface's. So far there was no fighting Miller in Titì – or Silvi's life . . .)

There was a bird pavilion, standing on thin red brick pillars, wired, and with sheet glass on one side. Inside, the songbirds, safe from the sportsman's gun, fluttered and swooped. Singing always. He and Titì stood a while looking at them. 'They're safe in there, aren't they?' she said. 'No one can shoot them.'

Back in the villa, Laura was talking to Mendola and his wife. They sat all three on a brocade sofa of unbelievable length and depth. Mendola's wife seemed less aggressive, holding out a hand to Titì, and saying, 'But what lovely hair . . .' Vincenzo Mendola talked easily. Guy got the impression he had more work now, that things were less difficult. 'Ah yes,' he told Guy, 'the law, always the law. I sometimes have other ideas, but then find I am not sure of their – advisability.'

Paolo Anello joined the group. Although he looked no older, it seemed to Guy that the eyes had grown more cold, the neat features a little pinched. But the voice was the same as ever. And the hands.

The Prior, Father Alessandro, came over to talk to them. He made a fuss of Silvi, who 'soon will be as beautiful as her mother'. He was pleasant to talk to, if a little self-important. 'Father Pasquale preached well, did he not?' He added, 'And a man of such learning. As am I.' But smiling as he said it. (Guy saw Laura repress a smirk. Boasting did not attract.) He spent as little time in Palermo as possible, he said, although invitations to preach were so numerous they could not be refused. 'What would St Dominic have thought?' But he would rather by far be out of the city. 'I am a man of the countryside. It is in my blood . . . My grandfather came from a mountain village.'

Father Clemente joined them now. The son from Rome, at the far end of the long salotto, could not hear their conversation, so – what did they think, he asked, what changes might be expected from this son? 'It is certain he appreciates the work I have done on the Tarantino-Falletta history. A history full of surprises and interest. 1897 has been reached so far . . . But now we are within living memory it is both of more interest and greater complexity.'

Silvi said, 'I mean to be a scholar,' (Titì pulled a face). 'A wandering one, though. I should like to wander and . . . and . . .' her voice tailed away, her eyes took on a dreamy look as if she were already far away. (Face of Laura, reading Leopardi in the Varelli dining-room . . .)

'What dear little girls they are,' Father Clemente said, a little

388

later. Guy, with whom he'd been discussing not just the son from Rome, but the provenance of some of the earlier manuscripts in the library, warmed to him. Not because of the compliment but because he had always found him pleasant. Forgetting some of the pinpricks of irritation on their first meeting.

'I should like to call on you,' the priest said, as they were leaving.

'And we should like you to call. That would be very pleasant.'

'Perhaps after the Christmas Feast?'

'The situation is as old as the hills. *It's when it happens to you.*'

Guy couldn't make up his mind whether to show Ruggero the letter. Laura, he would not dream of worrying with it. But here was the same sweat and terror he and Ruggero had shared nine years ago. Thank God I have no son, he thought. It was sons who were kidnapped, held to ransom. But the very vagueness of the threats filled him with terror. And he was as little able to run to the police with it as Ruggero had been. To do so might bring about the very thing he feared. His sick terror was worse because it was formless. You can fight the enemy you can see. But this nebulous grey menace, filling the air . . . He thought of sending Laura and the girls to the Di Benedetto villa in Agrigento, even though it was Christmas. The family wouldn't be using it now. But with what excuse? And could not menace and danger travel as easily across the island?

'. . . The situation is as old as the hills,' Ruggero had said, sitting white-faced in the apartment. '*It's when it happens to you.*'

In the end he decided not to show him. And yet how he yearned for someone in whom to confide. My mother. Maria. (Maria who had told him of Minicu . . . lost in the mountains. The overheard conversation. 'A knowledge so terrible, Guy, that it has haunted me all my life – but most of all when something else happened, something so very very much worse, Guy, that I could never speak of it – to anyone.') He had not asked her. Nor would he, ever. Yet in talking of Minicu, she had spoken of another world, one where life was little valued, where an inadvertent witness to an execution which didn't concern him must be silenced. His body, if ever found, picked clean by vultures.

And it was this world with its rank smell, which was closing in on him.

I shall not tell Ruggero.

The letter, now locked in his desk, was typewritten and with no peculiarity except that on close examination the m key was fractionally warped. (Am I to examine all the typewriters in Palermo?)

> This is a warning. Before the year ends you will be asked for a sum of money. Be prepared. It will not be more than you can afford. But it will not be less. Show this letter to no one. The writer, who speaks on behalf of another, wishes you well. But only if you cooperate. If when the time comes you do not, be warned. You may live to regret it. Others will not.

He felt little of the spirit of Christmas, only a week or so away now. The noise, the clatter, the market stalls laden with brightly coloured gifts, the knee-deep litter, the smells of herbs and spices, sizzling oil, the loud calling of wares. The huge and beautiful though often garish cribs, the monotonous wail of the Sicilian bagpipes. All these sights, sounds, smells filled him with terror. They were unreal – it was as if he were watching some play. Simulated festivities: these were players, playing at being merry.

His terror was the worse still for being so vague. The waiting, the not knowing, reminded him . . . When such fear before? Of course . . . waiting with Miller, and Randall, in the assault craft, waiting to go in at Salerno (not knowing the assailant's face, *who* it was would shoot to kill. Jerry lying in wait for us . . .)

But that was only my own death, he thought. Fear for others, fear for *loved ones*, is that not the worst?

Early evening, and he was marking essays in his small study off the drawing-room. Laura had taken the girls to a Christmas party for the San Nicolò orphanage. He could scarcely concentrate. His gloom was such that when the bell rang, he saw it as a welcome interruption.

When he saw his visitor was Father Clemente, he felt a sudden lifting of the spirit. A face he was glad to see. Faint hope. No, not hope, for he could hardly (or could he?) confide in him. But for half an hour, an hour perhaps, to have his mind taken off his worries.

'I promised I would call and lo, I find myself passing near you. I preach at an evening Mass at San Cipriano. Just time for a visit . . .'

'Something to drink? A cognac?'

'Please.' Urbane, smiling, relaxed. Sitting opposite him in the drawing-room, on the green brocade chair with drawn thread antimacassar (elaborately worked many years ago by Amelita).

He asked after Laura and 'your beautiful daughters'.

'I expect to preach a retreat at their convent this Lent . . . Tell me – are you satisfied with their education?'

'For the moment, yes. I expect, I think we may have other plans later –'

'Out of Sicily, perhaps? Of course I envy you your English education. Your private education, it's the best in the world. I speak sincerely. These English Catholic boys' schools – they are a *non pareil*. The standard of the teaching, the care while boys board – we have nothing like that. The boys are with the priests perhaps ten or twelve weeks at a time. What a chance for good influences, for moulding . . . You have no son yet, Mr Dennison, but have you never been tempted to send your daughters abroad for this splendid education?'

'I couldn't spare them,' Guy said. 'I would miss them too much . . . I don't share your high opinion of the system, to be truthful. A child should grow up *with* its parents –'

'Ah, the orphan speaks. You were an orphan, were you not? Something you said once . . . You really knew nothing of your parents?'

Again the Tuscan tale. Aunt Eleanor. Uncle Basil . . .

'What a worthy woman this Miss Dennison must have been.' He twirled his glass in his well-manicured hands, laid it down on the marquetry table. He arranged the folds of his white habit.

'While I am here, there is one matter I should like to discuss. A confidential matter . . . If I may?'

'Of course.'

'Have you recently received – a letter?'

I could not tell Laura, would not tell Laura, he thought. Ruggero, no. But a priest – yes, perhaps? For it would seem obvious, from the way he has phrased it, that others have received them.

He looked at the charming frank smile, the white teeth, wanting to confide. He said:

'Any particular sort of letter? I'm not sure that I follow –'

The priest smiled, spread his hands out.

'A letter with certain – warnings.'

'No.' It was as if the word 'warnings' stirred something in him, akin to panic. How had this dreadful subject come up?

'Think again,' the priest said. 'You are certain?'

Irritated suddenly, he repeated. 'No. No.' He rose. 'Your glass –'

'Not at this moment, thank you . . . Mr Dennison, I am only trying to help. But you must be frank with me.'

'And if I had? What could *you* do?'

'Give advice. Advise you . . .'

'I don't understand.'

'I think you do.'

A sudden feeling of sickness. In the room there was a sweetish smell of stale cigarettes. Reaching for the box, he lit one, busying himself with testing the lighter. He did not offer one to Father Clemente.

'I think you do . . . You have lived here eight, nine years. And are a man of great acuity . . . Mr Dennison, I have been sent here to tell you the terms – It causes me *great* distress – but I am not myself a free person. If I could tell you how I detest being the one who . . .'

'I've told you, *I don't follow* –'

'Come, come. What I am trying to say . . . I think I have made myself clear, that I am only the *messenger*. Of Mammon, alas. Who amongst us would not rather be a messenger of God?'

Fragments of tobacco stuck to Guy's lips. Nervously he flicked them away.

'Certain matters were hinted at, were they not? I must tell you that the figure referred to is –' he spread his hands '– let us say that twenty million would be perfectly acceptable.'

In shock, Guy wanted to say, 'Take it. Take it, then. Take all we have, and go. But leave us in peace.' He felt he was back, dry-mouthed, waiting in the Di Benedetto apartment for the telephone to ring. ('The situation is as old as the hills. *It's when it happens to you.*')

'You must be mad. We don't have that sort of money.'

'No? Perhaps those who decide these matters are wrong? But I do not think so. These figures are not chosen at random. Please, think again. Make it safe for yourself. And for those you love . . . I must explain the terms. I would be wanting in charity if I did not. A time limit, there is a time within which . . . you understand?'

Guy didn't speak.

'Five days after Christmas . . .'

'And if I don't?' (How can I ask such a question, when I dare not *think* it? dare not think – if not.)

Sitting there, trembling inside, he noticed the monk's rosary. The rosary, a special devotion of the Dominicans. The utter incongruity of it all hit him. He heard again the jangling rosaries of the priests of St Boniface's – all the religious he had ever known . . . from the ear-boxing Brother Damian to this smooth, smiling – ah, but how he smiles. (And I liked his smile once, noticed it that first time met at the villa . . .)

In cold fury, he said, 'It might be best, I think, simply to go to the appropriate authorities – if not the Consul here, then our Ambassador in Rome. Or contact the Foreign Office directly . . .' But he knew, even as he said it, that it sounded like the bluster it was. Seeing in a flash the yards of red tape, the murmured evasions, the incredulity, the polite listening ear. And he could not expect action when he wanted it – this evening. ('Yes, yes, of course. We'll arrange with the appropriate authorities for immediate arrest . . .') It would not happen. *And this country doesn't work like that. They are all, the police and the policed, in it together.*

And still the priest smiled. 'Please, Mr Dennison. What folly – saintly folly perhaps, but folly . . .' Without getting up, he turned his gaze towards the wall where a small group of paintings hung.

'What a beautiful Caravaggio reproduction. It almost breathes.'

Guy said coldly, 'A present from Miss Dennison.'

'This English lady who adopted you? So it's a precious possession, if not in money then in sentiment . . .' He paused. 'Your wife and your daughters, so lovely. Are they not even more precious? These are a man's true possessions. Dearer to him than himself . . .' He took up his glass of cognac, sipped it. 'How terrible if one of them, out walking perhaps – were to meet, say, a runaway car. Perhaps a car that is out of control, mounting the pavement? If they were to meet with such a disgraceful, such an unhappy accident –'

He shouted, 'And you call yourself a man of God?'

'Please, Mr Dennison. So loud. Your servant . . .'

'Man of God, you call yourself. You *disgust* me –'

'I call myself nothing. A priest, yes . . . In the exercise of my office as a priest, God speaks through me. But here, you see, here I'm a different person . . . I, and my fellow scholars, we are ourselves victims . . . you would not like to hear.'

Suddenly smiling again, he rose. 'Regretfully, I must leave you. My sermon at San Cipriano. I see already that it is after six . . . To finish this delicate matter. Perhaps you would like to be in touch as to the best method . . . No numbers to be taken of bank notes, of course . . .'

'You are scum – that you wear the cloth only makes it more disgusting. There are other words, stronger words, I could not use them to a priest . . . My upbringing . . .'

'I must thank you for your hospitality – I hope I may call again under happier circumstances. Sit with your wife and daughters . . .'

'Please go.'

Just before he reached the door, Father Clemente stopped. He turned to Guy.

'One piece of advice, Mr Dennison. Lock up your wife.'

Heart drumming, Guy said, 'Is that a threat?' Dear God. Jesus.

'My dear Mr Dennison . . . No, it is simply advice. No more. Let her alter her way of life. It would please Christ. But till then – lock her up.'

As the priest moved forward, Guy stepped in front of him, barring the door.

'Explain yourself.'

The priest smiled. 'Please. Don't act the innocent.'

'Explain yourself, before I lift a hand against you –'

'Come, come. You are a man of the world. Your wife – perhaps you have not realized she is a *woman* of the world?' He paused before adding, 'Count as your friends, Mr Dennison, only those your wife never meets . . . Look about you in the future.'

'It would be beneath me to ask you what you know. I only ask you *how* you know . . . If it's from the confessional –'

He held his hands up as if shocked. 'I can only promise – the seal of the confessional . . . It is not from there I have my information. For the safeguarding of that, a priest would lay down his life –'

'With the sort of stinking morals you have, why should a blasphemous act like that worry you?'

The feet of Father Clemente, white socks under the heavy leather sandals, were almost upon Guy's. 'And now, if you would allow me access. The door . . . Really I must go . . . I wish you all the happiest and holiest of Christmasses. May the Infant Jesus . . .'

'Where are the girls?'

He did not know which was the worst, the revelations, or his fears. He trembled with rage and shock. Could hardly keep his voice steady as he said, 'I don't want them, either of them, to go out by themselves, for anything, at any time. Do you understand?'

'But they never do.'

'The Christmas streets are dangerous.'

'Guy, I'm with them always . . . Someone is –'

'And you too. Not alone. You . . .' His voice, he could hear it cracking. Great breathy cracks. Broken, this is what it is to be broken.

'How many times have you been unfaithful to me?'

Laura. This was Laura. Not even by a flicker betraying anything. (Except me, except me.) Impassive pale face, face on a coin that he had so loved – *that I love so* . . .

'Do you want it in exact figures?'

Taken aback. 'No,' he said. 'Some names will do.'

She lit a cigarette, in the ivory holder. Sitting opposite him, in dull red silk shirt, cream knife-pleated skirt.

'Well – and who has been talking?'

'A visiting priest.'

She sat very still.

'One of the Dominicans. Father Clemente.'

'I told him nothing. If people want to gossip . . . then I wish them good luck.'

Laura. Laura, why, why, why?

'Who. Tell me *who*,' he said.

She shrugged her shoulders. 'Perhaps it would amuse you to guess? You need amusing, the way you are, the mood you're in tonight . . .'

'Who. Tell me who.'

She was silent. He swore at her then. A flood of swearing. Everything he had ever heard in the barrack room. Scarcely one that she would understand. He disgusted himself.

Then more calmly, he repeated: '*Tell me who* –'

She shrugged again. 'Guy, only a fool asks –'

'I *am* a fool. It's you have made a fool of me. *Tell me who* –'

'No one that I – we need be ashamed of. Various . . . Paolo. Paolo Anello . . .'

His churning stomach. A wave of nausea, and pure hate. Seeing those small white hands. Imagining those small white hands . . . He was shaking all over as if he would have a fit.

'Please, control yourself,' she said. 'It's foolish –'

'Who else, who else? I need names –'

'You need nothing . . . Paolo. And after a little while – oh, some time ago . . . Ruggero was one.'

He was silent.

'What do you think I do all day?' she said.

'I know what you do. You give me accounts of your days. And at nights you're with me. You sleep with me, every night.'

'You think that means . . . You cannot be so simple.'

'Yes, I do. I love you, and thought you loved me.'

'Who is talking about love, Guy? I am a good wife to you. I have given you children. This tedious conversation isn't about love.'

'What is it about, then?'

'That is for you to decide. I didn't start it.'

He went on, wading through, thrashing about in this confused sea of pain. '*Laura –*'

She said, 'I don't expect *you* to have been faithful. And you, you have foolish expectations. People in this life should not expect what they cannot reasonably hope for . . . Is it that you see yourself as so devastating, of such overwhelming desirability that no wife need look further –'

'I don't *see* myself, as you say –'

He was shouting. 'Lower your voice,' she said. 'I don't want Silvi or Titì . . . If they should hear . . . Children need protection.'

'Cuckolding me – that's your idea of giving protection, is it? Is it?'

She said almost wearily, 'A few hours ago, everything was all right . . .'

'Two hours ago I didn't know I should be wearing the horns, that probably I'm the laughing-stock of our circle . . . But that's nothing to me. It's you. That *you* . . .'

She was silent, and he began shouting again.

'When did all this start? What did I do? What have I not done? Tell me. Tell me.'

'Guy. But I have always been like this.'

'Always, always – what's always mean?'

396

'Since I knew what it was – how it was done. Some time – during the war some time. Before the invasion –'

'Your parents?' He trembled still.

'Mamma never knew anything of anything. My father . . .' her voice faltered for the first time. 'He loved me. He loved me very much. For him, it was all right. He was my greatest friend. When he came back from the war, he . . . Yes, he knew what I did. It never came between us. It only brought us closer.'

'Why did you never tell me? Why was I never told? It's as if . . . it's like talking to someone I've never met . . . *Why was I never told*?'

'You never asked,' she said. Then after a moment, she added, 'Is that really the sort of thing a young girl confesses before marriage?'

A memory stirred. A puzzled realization.

'In your fantasies, you forget something,' he said. 'You forget, I married a virgin.'

That first night, he thought, remembering, remembering. (And then – oh, but it was I taught you everything, everything.) He was in tears. Everything, he thought, that you now give to others.

'You forget, I married a virgin.'

'Did you?'

When he didn't answer, she said, very calmly, 'I would never have told you this. I tell you now only because you are so . . . because you *trap* me. Yes, I was a virgin, for our marriage. Money bought virginity in those days. I had an – operation. My father insisted on it, not long after he came back. How else could I have hoped for a husband? I was not to know . . . You were indeed a victim, Guy. It was a successful operation, of course. I was sewn up, by this surgeon.'

'Too tightly,' he said. Dear God, yes. Too tightly.

She smiled to herself at the memory. He coloured.

'Well,' she said. 'What are you going to do?'

He wanted then, terribly, to punish her.

'What am I going to do? I am going to tell you about a letter I received five days ago . . .'

As he told her, he saw her go stiff with fear. Her hand, motionless on the long cigarette-holder.

'And what else? I'm going to send you away. You and Silvi and Titì –'

'Where?'

'Paris, London – I don't know – Out of Sicily, out of Italy . . .'

'Paris, please,' she said coolly. 'Not London . . . When? Now? Before Christmas?'

'As soon as possible afterwards.'

Lying beneath his anger was this terrible sadness. Laura, who was not Laura. Laura, mother of his daughters.

'And the demand?' She spoke through stiffened lips. A muscle in her eyelid flickered.

'The demand? I shall pay it. Like Ruggero, I don't wish to dice with death.'

'Do you, shall you go with us – wherever we go?' She sounded almost humble.

'No, I stay here, for the moment.' And when she raised her eyebrows in query: 'I stay here – and expose them.'

18

The children laughed and pulled faces, and from the other side of the Carmelite grille, their Aunt Bridget, alias Sister Joan, wiggled her fingers and grinned obligingly.

'Helen dear, Little Nell, I'm sure you tell them, "We're going to see Aunt at the Zoo."'

Dermot winced. Helen knew he would say after, '. . . just because Bridget's so jolly about it . . . It's a sign of her holiness – She can't possibly think it anything but frightful.'

And Helen would say, 'They're only children. Dermot, they're only babies.'

Benedict at six, was perhaps even more of a baby than he should be. He hadn't four-year-old Daisy's quiet composure. He was shy and easily moved to tears, to hiding behind Helen. Only here, with his aunt, did he seem driven to heights of confidence, jumping up and down and showing off. Doing cartwheels for her. Bridget spoke to him almost, one could say, man to man. Asking him the right questions. Then at some point in the visit, the urge would come on him and he would decide that after all, this was a visit to the Zoo.

'Aunt's a monkey – why can't we feed Aunt? What do aunts – I mean *nuns* – eat?'

'Food,' Dermot said. 'Meals, just like you do.'

'But what meals, what food?'

'Nun food, none food,' Bridget said, giving a great peal of laughter. 'It isn't awfully nice. A bit like boarding-school, really. Very like boarding-school. I didn't come here for the food . . .'

At tea in the convent parlour, Helen wrestled with another wave of sickness. But there were twinges of pain too, a welcome dragging sensation which might mean – (oh please God, a donation to any charity you care to name, fill the Poor Clares' coffers, on my knees at Knock, the trail to Lough Derg, anything, but make it *not* a *child*). Perhaps it was something about the buttercream filling in the sponge, or the strong smell of the fishpaste sandwiches, which Daisy was solemnly squashing and moulding into shapes. The extern sister in frilly headdress poured out tea for them, and milk for the children. Helen thought that orange might have been better. They would be car sick for certain. The jellies were topped with suspiciously synthetic blobs of cream: Benedict stood his spoon up in one and twirled it. Dermot glared at her. Their manners, he seemed to be saying. The vein stood out above his brows that meant annoyance and nervous tension. And it was all her fault.

Back home wasn't a long journey, but it was cross-country. A twisting and turning road. At the back of the Renault the children were edgily quarrelsome. Benedict over-excited, Daisy irritating him by not responding. She was bent over a wooden jigsaw puzzle on a tray.

'I don't think that's a good idea,' Dermot said. 'It'll make her sick.'

Helen said, 'It keeps her occupied. And gives us a bit of peace.'

'You're always talking about peace. Sometimes I think it's the main word in your vocabulary – such as that is . . .'

'I go on about it because it's important to me. I need it –'

'You should have been looking where we've just been. There's true peace. In the Carmel.'

'If that's peace, they can keep it. The peace that passeth all understanding. It passes mine.'

'I don't get . . .'

'With some of them, it's not peace, it's just arrested development.'

'What a foul thing to say – about my sister too.'

'Some, I said. Some of them. Bridget's –'

'I suppose you're an example of maturity? Maturity à la mode –'

'Don't try to be clever at my expense –'

'Anyway,' he said, 'I can see Bridget's happy. It's obvious.'

'You can't possibly tell, just talking about trivia either side of the grille.'

He said, 'You're always running down people, trying to make people like that less holy than they are.'

'I didn't say she wasn't *holy*, or *good*. We were talking about whether she was happy. Fulfilled.'

'Aren't they the same thing?'

She was silent.

Benedict said, 'I wish you wouldn't. Mummy, Daddy, don't

argue.' It was a new word he used a lot. 'I think I'll just go and have an argue now.'

But soon it was he and Daisy fighting in the back. She'd brought modelling dough with them, enough for both. It wasn't supposed to stain or stick, and could be eaten. Benedict's was a lurid pink. Daisy's, green. When she'd moulded the fishpaste sandwiches she had really been wanting this dough. Now they fought over it.

'Can't you control them?' Dermot said.

Daisy was sick. 'Oh poor darling,' Helen said, twisting round, leaning over, using towels.

She could see that Dermot was furious.

'That upholstery's had about as much as it can take. Aren't there tablets or something? Next time, we'll bring Erdmute, even if it means the children squashed up. Then she can take over the squalor.'

'It's only a car,' Helen said. 'A worldly possession.' She wanted to say, 'I *think* I may be pregnant.'

That seemed the history of her life nowadays. Worry on, worry off. Vatican roulette.

Bickering now, with Dermot, on the journey back, she was reminded suddenly of Maria and Eddie. How they had bickered and she had not wanted to know, had stopped up her ears. Our Lady and St Joseph, the Holy Family.

The Vinney family were no substitute. During nearly seven years of marriage, she had felt more and more oppressed by them. Dermot was oppressed too. Something she'd sensed on that very first visit, well before their engagement. It was no less so now. Although he was doing well in his own field of advertising (it was possible even to point to a slogan, and say 'that was Dermot's'), stimulated, animated in a way she didn't often see at home – to his family, it was all still something he did while waiting for better things, or even, as they hinted once, because it was all he actually could do. That the writing of slogans, or contributing of ideas to a campaign might need talent, they couldn't recognize. Lucky Dermot, they said, to be paid for playing around all day. And to show what a ludicrous occupation it was they continued feebly to call it 'Sandwich-boarding'.

She seldom said anything, could not, although she hated to see Dermot put down in that way. Last time they'd been to the Vinney home, Michael (a first secretary in Paris for several years, but soon to be promoted) had said yet again, 'How's the sandwich-boarding, old chap? Still gulling the public?' She had said then:

'But isn't that what *you* do in the FO? I thought that was *your* job?'

Michael had looked at her sideways. 'She talks,' he said. Helen stared back at him. 'So sharp, you'll cut yourself, as Nanny said.' He laughed at her. The others laughed with him.

Dermot looked embarrassed and asked her to please try and not make trouble. 'Don't go for Michael. There's no point. Never has been.'

She really only liked Bridget, imagining her, if the timing had been better, an ally. They had got on well from the first meeting, not long after the engagement. 'Little Nell', she called Helen (she was very large herself), as well as the more sober 'Helen dear'. In those meetings across the grille Helen never criticized other members of the family (Dermot would have been furious), but Bridget occasionally showed that she saw through some of them at least. ('I hear Cakey's expecting again. I wonder if she's aiming for one of those Papal medals? Or a title – how exciting! Papal countess, perhaps, for the largest family in the shortest time . . .')

The most children in the least time. The very same thought which had filled Helen with dread ever since she had said yes to Dermot. In those first earnest discussions he had explained that they must not (were not even required to) have more children than they could reasonably support: the question was how to stop them and still be good. The new temperature method – he was sure that was the answer. Helen was to go to the Catholic Marriage Advisory Bureau. They also bought a book and studied it, although there was no hurry, as Dermot explained. It was easier to have a baby straightaway. 'Then we can do it as often as we want.'

But what was it they did? *He* did? It was a nothing. An act. The act that made babies, that was all.

He had read books about this too, Catholic ones. He'd suggested, shyly enough, that she read them too, but when she declined politely, wasn't put out. He seemed to think it was modesty. 'I'm sure you're right,' he said. 'It's probably better for the woman not to know too much.'

(Oh, what did I know before Eddie? And how quickly I learned. How slowly, if ever, I shall forget . . .)

She tried now never to think of the honeymoon, of those fifteen nights, but especially the first. How to fake virginity? In her misery, for she'd consistently put all thoughts of the wedding night out of mind, she found it easier than she'd thought.

Forget Eddie, forget Eddie – like an incantation, but unplanned, involuntary, as she lay beneath Dermot (carefully taking all his weight on his elbows). A Dermot who was delighted, relieved that after all, it was all so easy – although too soon over. He was very apologetic, 'but the book said, when it's the first time, and if you've been a virgin.' (Cock virgin, she remembered the derisory term.) She had felt only relief, that it was all over. That it had been possible, not to forget Eddie (how could I ever?) but to isolate the memory of him. This inexpert fumbling had nothing to do with the Funchal nights. It had nothing to do with anything, and must be thought of as little as possible.

But then, fatefully, because he'd been reading the books, she had had after a little while to fake pleasure as well.

She did it of course to spare Dermot's feelings, for after all she cared for him, cared enough to have agreed to marriage. But I did it too, she thought, to avoid more fumbling. Or worse – for now he was able to wait longer. Those tedious unbroken thrusts, which in all their lack of variety, their monotonous rhythm, she longer to be over with. So as soon as seemed reasonably possible, there would be her cry of pleasure – (One would do, one deceit. She knew from what he said, that he had not heard of more than one . . .)

Where was her body, her real body, all this while? Not in Eddie's arms. The reality was so removed that no sinful fantasy would have been possible. Occasional flickers of memory, rarely, rarely. (Or even sometimes, a dream – Eddie and I, together again. So that she would wake up crying with happiness, only to realize . . .) In those years after the discovery by Maria, all through the troubled days in Palermo, her terror in the Catacombs, the kidnapping, she had quenched, stamped all that out, as if it had been a fire. It would take more than Dermot's fumbling to rekindle it.

A lifetime of faking lay ahead. And worry too – about conceiving. Benedict born nine months later, a gap of twenty months and then Daisy. Since then, one miscarriage, greeted with relief, shame and heartache all mixed together.

And now here she was worrying again. Dread mornings when her period was late. Usually she had a shorter than normal cycle so that 'late' began earlier than for many other people. Once a month there would be a short-lived freedom from worry (and from Dermot, who thought it disgusting, those who took advantage of the safest time of all), and then back to the early morning temperature-taking.

She lay very still in bed, the thermometer inserted vaginally. She must not move at all. To get a good reading, Dermot thought it better she shouldn't even speak. If the alarm had not woken him, she had to nudge him. By then a child might be in the room. 'Can I get in with you, I want to get in with Mummy, Mummy, *can I get in?*'

And Dermot: 'No, Mummy's busy now.' Then he would get out himself and creep off to wake the au pair. A difficult task, if it was Erdmute.

Ah yes, Erdmute. Latest in a line of au pair girls since just before Daisy's birth. Five of them so far. Two Danes, a Dutch, a French and a Norwegian. And now Erdmute, from Frankfurt-am-Main.

Living in the country as she did, Helen envied friends in London or nearby Cambridge, places where girls would choose to come: where they came in such numbers that if one didn't suit it was easy enough if done tactfully, to dismiss and start again. But in Shalford Pelham, with very little in the way of exciting social life and only the twice weekly language classes in nearby Bishops Stortford to look forward to (and that only after a trying bus journey), it was a different matter. Dermot spoke of getting a second car as an attraction – some of the girls were drivers. Helen herself had not learned, and kept postponing it – putting her reluctance down to first ante-natal, then post-natal fears.

Erdmute – the only girl she had not managed to like at all. She felt sorry for her. Away from home for the first time, spending long stretches of her day with two small children not her own, and because she was sitting the Cambridge Lower this June, much of the remainder studying. Lonely, and fat. She was perhaps one of the largest girls Helen had ever seen. Beside Helen, still tiny, still the sparrow after two babies, she looked even larger. She had been fat on arrival, but now after three months, she seemed to have doubled in weight. Her appetite was monumental and increased as she had more space to fill. The family meals weren't enough (although she was rewarding in that she never spurned any dish, eating everything Helen cooked). In her bedroom she secreted buns, cakes, sausage rolls, chocolates, toffees, Polo mints for which she had a passion, and biscuits. Any and every kind of biscuit. As she went about, dusting, hoovering, washing up, she would keep a packet of ginger nuts or chocolate digestive in the pocket of her flowered overall. Her bedroom – she was an untidy girl – was a mess of half-eaten packets, mixed in with copies of *Stern* from home, gramophone records lying out of their plastic sleeves, and paper bags with stale Chelsea buns. 'We'll get mice,' Helen warned her.

Loud music came from her room in her time off. They had put in there for her an old radiogram from the Vinney household. She bought records in Bishops Stortford when she went to language classes. Bobby Vee, Buddy Holly, Pat Boone. Black Dyke Mills Band, which seemed to stir her. An eclectic mixture. Helen, who never mentioned her past, dreaded sometimes that Dermot might.

Erdmute had no friends, except for two Danish girls, Vibeke and Karen, joint au pairs in the house of acquaintances a few miles away at Patmore Cross. These two, who had the use of a car, befriended her, but it did not seem to work very well. She trailed an unhappy third.

Once only she had been to a Young Farmers Dance, and for a week or two afterwards, a middle-aged red-faced man who gave his name only as Fred, called to see her. Each time she rushed to her room, banging the door shut.

It seemed to Helen the only time she did shut it. Otherwise she seemed incapable of doing so. When she was asked, it was always, '*Ja*, Mrs Finney, *ja*.' But an hour later it would be open again. Although the children would not turn the knob for themselves, passing the door ajar was too much. Dermot had fastened a little bolt high up. ('If Erdmute could just slide it when she goes out . . .') But because the room was on the ground floor and next to their playroom, they went in, and ate the biscuits. There were scissors too, an open penknife, bottles of pills lying about. Hazards for a six- and a four-year-old.

Erdmute wore a striped woollen wraparound skirt, with a checked shirt, all covered by a large shapeless beige sweater or black cardigan. On top, in the daytime, one of six flowery overalls Mutti had sewn for her. Doing the housework, she was accident prone. She had broken six Hoover fan-belts already. She would drive the machine savagely over the children's plastic toys, then: 'Mrs Finney, Mrs Finney, the hoofer is once more *kaput*.'

'At least she doesn't smoke,' Dermot said.

'Perhaps if she did, she'd eat a little less.'

But Erdmute was good with the children. They loved her, partly perhaps because she let them steal biscuits from her pocket, and also because she would rather sit with them than do the housework.

My children, Helen thought, what to say of my children? Benedict, whose birth brought me closer to Maria again. (Herself, sitting up in bed at Queen Charlotte's, Benedict in her arms. Maria walking in, her eyes filling at once with tears, then suddenly throwing her arms about both of them.) Before, Helen had thought Maria, who had had no child herself, might be jealous – but it had not been so. If they were ever to be truly reconciled (and perhaps they had gone as far in that direction as they ever would), then it would seem to be her children who would be the instruments of it.

Maria did not seem to care much for Dermot (and in fairness, nor he for her), but this did not matter too much. Maria, if not Our Lady these days, was still, as in the litany, a refuge. When she was up at Thackton, which she was increasingly now, ever since Uncle Dick had left her Moorgarth in his will, then Helen liked to take the children up there for a week or two at a time – not minding the long train journey.

By tacit agreement, they spoke rarely of Eddie. There were never any signs of him in the house. 'He's still a great success with the Italians,' was the most Maria said. Sometimes in conversation she would speak of 'When I was married . . .' The past. Maria's past. A great sadness would envelop Helen then.

Maria loved both the children. There was never a hint of favouritism. Whereas I, Helen thought, I . . . It would be wrong to love Daisy the best – and of course, she did not. But she *liked* her more.

Benedict. Ah yes, Benedict. Her heart bled for him. He favoured the Connors family: with his small wiry body, his peaky, often querulous face, she was reminded again and again of Billy as a child. (The adult Billy, known only from photographs and infrequent letters, ran a successful garage in Dunedin. He was married himself now, and planning to visit England in the next year or two.) The Vinney family remarked on it, saying that except for his eyes, which were Dermot's blue, he was very much Helen's son. They said that especially because he whinged. He seemed always to have whinged. He was a mother's baby, Mrs Vinney said. Clinging to Helen, at the sight of anything new, any strange person. At other times he would be over-bold, cheeking and defying, or rushing around as this afternoon, trying to use up limitless supplies of manic energy. He irritated Dermot, who felt Helen should be able to deal with all this. (And if we should have another, she thought again – willing and willing the twinges of pain to become a period.)

She didn't care for his name. Dermot, through his family, had chosen it. It had been his grandfather's, and Cakey so far had not used it. So it would be appreciated if . . .

'You let them decide everything,' she had said angrily, but weakly. So soon after the baby and with early feeding difficulties – oh, what the hell, she thought. Now, the name seemed to suit well enough. And she had grown to like it. She was not allowed to call him Ben.

But when twenty months later, they had a daughter, she felt it was her turn to choose a name. Looking at the serene expression (unlike Benedict, she seemed glad to have arrived), the smooth red cheeks, the feathering of reddish gold hair she'd thought for no reason – Daisy. The Vinneys, as soon as they heard, told Dermot, no – it was foolishly quaint, Cakey pointing out that it wasn't a saint's name, so wouldn't do anyway.

Helen said Daisy was often a diminutive of Margaret, or at least Marguerite. She could be baptized Margaret, but she must be known as Daisy. 'Whose daughter is she anyway?' she asked, forgetting for the moment that Dermot didn't like the name.

How different was Daisy from Benedict. In many ways, a Vinney. Yet oddly, disliking the Vinneys, Helen could see only beauty and good things in Daisy. Daisy with the solemn, grave face, the composed expression, the sweet easy nature. Thick straight red-gold hair, milky white skin dusted with freckles. And some of the same air of vulnerability which had first drawn her to Dermot. But there perhaps the likeness ended. In childhood photographs, while physically resembling Daisy, he had looked anxious, striving, as if already faintly disapproved of. Daisy's face wore an expression of almost adult gravity. She loved order. She loved to tidy things. Newly arrived post would be stacked in a neat pile, shopping would be unpacked and the packets and tins arranged in an orderly pattern. 'Daisy tidied,' she would announce. On the sallies into Erdmute's room, while Benedict stuffed himself with Polo mints, she would be found arranging Erdmute's shoes in a neat row, or lining up her gramophone records.

In this devotion, this desire to help Helen, and others, Helen saw, though it was so different, some of herself and Mam all those years ago. (Wanting to make Mam happy – and all right and well again. And not being able to.)

A wet February afternoon. The children's half term. She was carrying in the washing, now even wetter, when the telephone rang.

'Helen, dear heart, is that you?'

'Adrian –'

'I didn't recognize your voice – so mature. Have you taken up smoking? Look, I'm staying not far away. In Spellbury. I've come to value some paintings . . .'

'Can we see you?'

'The thing is, I've only tonight – then off at crack of dawn. Dinner here tonight, I *have* to attend . . . But I've wangled you both an invitation – can you get over? What about the sprogs? Can you leave them?'

She said, 'Dermot's away, Adrian. It's some sort of Scottish campaign. He's in Glasgow.'

She asked where the dinner was? Yes, she said, she had an au pair she could leave the children with, and of course she wanted to come, but she had no car – and couldn't drive anyway.

Adrian said he'd arrange something. 'Leave it to me, dear heart.' He called back half an hour later to say that Colin Gilchrist who lived in Westmill Green and was absolutely charming ('you'll love him') would have to pass through Shalford.

'He'll bring you, and take you back . . . How little I've changed, dear heart. Not only clever, but kindly and efficient too . . .'

A slightly sulky Erdmute who for once had an invitation of her own. She had arranged to go to the cinema with Vibeke and Karen. She gave in with bad grace. Helen felt selfish.

Colin Gilchrist, who came for her at seven, was very tall and gangling with short curly hair. He drove a small MG into which he only just seemed to fit.

'Hallo, I'm your escort for the evening.'

They were talking soon. They talked the fifteen miles of the journey, or rather he asked the questions and she answered them. He asked her all about herself. Past, present, future. She told him of Benedict and Daisy, Dermot, the Bellarmine Club, a little of Palermo, and then, passing over them quickly, her dance band days.

She said without thinking, 'But that's what I really liked doing. I was never so happy –'

'Well, it's a funny thing,' he said quietly, 'I was sure I'd seen you before. And now it fits. Did you – was it you –?' When he mentioned the medical ball of 1949, she felt sick again with the memory.

Eddie getting the bird. (All that ribaldry, shouting, singing.) Eddie in tears. Fucking berks . . .

'Yes, it was me,' she said.

'I'm really ashamed. I was at the time. Can I apologize for us now? We got disciplined, you know, banned this and that. All sorts of upsets.'

'It got forgotten pretty quickly,' she said. 'None of that's anything to a real trouper. There are worse places to have died. And anyway the next round of applause cured it.'

'As you'll have gathered, I left medicine anyway. I wasn't really cut out for it, and the family business was in need of young blood. So . . . But most of my companions then, they're pretty reformed characters now. There was a reunion at a wedding lately. I took my fiancée along and she was most disappointed. Hell wasn't raised at all.' He said, 'So you were a success then? I was really sorry at the time not to hear you sing. Eddie Sabrini, wasn't it? I'll never forget. And what were you called then?'

'Helen Connors.'

'You should never have been brought on, little Miss Connors. You were too tantalizing, that was the problem. A glimpse and then whisked away . . . But you were obviously quite a success later. What fun. Though I suppose marriage put a stop to it all?'

'Yes,' she said, 'marriage put a stop to it.'

The house where they were to dine was large, and full of art treasures. A gold cherub stood in the hall, and paintings seemed to cover every inch of wall. Their host was loud-voiced and dictatorial, his voice booming the length of the dining table.

Adrian had not changed. Happy to see her, teasing, proprietorial. He was determined, he said, not to monopolize her but he *must* hear everything.

'You haven't told me, dear heart – how you fare in the wilderness? The rural depths. And scarcely to have been in touch . . . I thought I was going to be *godfather*. Fearful disappointment. Next time?'

She could say nothing, remembering now, angrily, Dermot's decision. 'We can't . . . Benedict wouldn't want a queer for a godparent –' And when she had asked indignantly, why ever not? he had said, 'By the time he gets to know him, he'll be an old queen. It could be embarrassing. And then of course, it's not really in the *spirit* of the exercise.' Against such a brick wall, which she suspected of being a Vinney one, she could only murmur, 'Well, he did introduce us . . .'

Also at the dinner table tonight were an old mother with a wandering deaf aid, for whom everything had to be repeated (the origin perhaps of her son's loud voice?), and two daughters of about thirteen and fifteen, who found anything done or said by Adrian absolutely killing – dissolving into breathy giggles. Neither of their parents noticed.

Helen felt unhappy, uneasy, the feelings of sickness making her certain there was to be another baby. Before leaving yesterday, Dermot had said, 'You should look at your chart again – perhaps you've miscalculated the days?' But she had not.

Pudding was being served, a crème brûlée, with a jug of fresh cream. A dish she would normally have enjoyed. Indeed she would have enjoyed the whole meal, but she felt now only acute nausea.

Talking went on around her, over her. Suddenly she realized that she was the subject.

'Did the face that launched tell you about her singing career? Quite the thing, she was. Gave it all up to *receive* at the Bellarmine Club. I mean to say . . .'

Then Colin, explaining about the medical ball.

'But what a dreadful thing. Helen, dear heart, you never told me . . . Nothing of course to her life in *Palermo*. Didn't she speak of that?'

Please God no, she thought. For a moment, as she looked down the table, the faces, the figures, seemed as if cut-outs. Faces: kind like Colin's, hearty like her host's, despairing like the old mother's, a little wicked like Adrian's – but none of them real.

'She never told you about the kidnapping? My dear, it was quite frightful – she was all but abducted herself. The little boy, you see . . .'

The faces blurred for a moment, then as they reappeared they had a fuzzy edge, or halo around them. For a second she wondered where she was. Then, sharply, back again. Adrian's voice:

'. . . *flung* into a motor-car, which sped off into the night . . .

no, I think it was *afternoon*. Helen, dear heart, it's your tale –'

She became sweaty with sudden fright. As she looked down the table, the eager listening faces of the two young girls blurred and vanished. For a split second she saw, heard, a Lancia screech to a halt. A voice, 'Signorina Connors, *momento* . . .' A foul-smelling cloth stuffed in her mouth, Marcello's body against hers. Terror.

And then suddenly Marcello's face turned into Benedict's. It was Benedict now, screaming and struggling. She tasted the foul gag, felt the rough hands that snatched at her. There was a crawling sensation at her hair roots – then clammy faintness. She had to stop herself crying out, 'Benedict!'

'Hey there, are you all right?'

'I think I'm – not very well.' Everything blacked as she slumped forward, hand clutching at the table.

Immediate concern. An ivory fan waved in front of her face. Cold water to sip. 'No stays to loosen?' Adrian asked, his voice concerned beneath the flippancy.

'No, all right really. All right in a moment . . . The wine, perhaps. Overdoing things. I'm . . .'

She lay down on a leather sofa in the library. All she wanted to do was to get home. To undo the premonition. See that Benedict was all right. Tucked up. Asleep. *Safe*. The younger daughter, Annabel, came out to sit with her. 'Mummy said it's best I stay, in case you fall off or down, or get worse.' They were going to send for the doctor.

A few moments later Colin came out to her, saying that he was taking her home.

'But you haven't finished your meal. Cheese. Port.'

'I can come here any time. The important thing is to get you back home and into bed.'

In the car going back, she said, 'I'm terribly sorry. I never do this sort of thing. Am never ill. I don't know what it was. I had this horrible sort of . . . because of talking about the kidnapping, perhaps, a horrible premonition, vision. My son. That something's happened to him.'

'You'll find – it won't be anything.'

'So clear. So terrible. So horrible.'

He said, 'I don't think you'll find there are too many Sicilians breaking into Shalford Pelham houses, abducting little boys . . . You've been overdoing it maybe?'

'Yes,' she said. 'I'm worried too. It could be that.'

'About what?'

She amazed herself by saying (I feel I have known him all my life): 'Worried I might be having another baby. I feel I couldn't cope. I know two's not many. But somehow . . . And now, you see, I should have had a period five days ago . . . So . . .'

He said, 'It's an unlikely bit of information for an ex-medic student, only I think I picked it up there – but just before a period – I'm sure I remember, it can make you very heightened, not psychic, but sensitive. Christine, my fiancée, she dreams, the most fantastic . . . Horror movies, you know. It could be just that.'

'It could be,' she said.

He said then, 'You're not – forgive my asking, but you're not very happy, are you?'

'No,' she said, 'I'm not.'

He said no more. She said no more. By now, though, she was sweating, trembling with anxiety. As they entered the village, she became at once more and more certain of disaster.

But 'See,' he said, as they drew up outside the house. 'It looks peaceful enough . . . I'll come inside with you, though, just so you can see everything's all right. Which it will be.'

It was a little after half past ten. The lights were off in the hall. She could see the low watt bulb up on the landing. 'I'll hurry upstairs,' she said. She was on the third step when the phone went.

'I'll answer it,' Colin said.

'Dermot,' he said. 'Your husband, I think. Dermot.'

Dermot's voice, against crackle and cackle. He spoke from some crowded room.

'Look, Helen, I'm downstairs in the hotel. *Where were you?* I rang at nine and Erdmute was as vague as ever. Quite incomprehensible. A man came, she said.'

'Yes, well. You see, Adrian –'

'It wasn't Adrian answered just now. I know Adrian's voice –'

'Dermot, don't shout.'

'*Who have you brought back* from wherever you've been? Go on, tell me. Two nights away and you –'

'I didn't. I got a lift. He, Colin – he's just come in for a moment –'

In the hall now, Erdmute, pale-faced, wrapped in blue fluffy dressing-gown, her hair clinging greasily to her broad scalp: 'Mrs Finney, all is gut. Benedict, Daisy, they sleep gut.'

'Thank you,' she turned back to the phone. 'That was Erdmute. Everything's fine . . .'

His voice was still angry, raised. She tried to ask him about the presentation today. 'Do you think you'll get the account?' But he seemed scarcely to hear. If she didn't know his habits she would have thought he'd drunk too much.

She cut through his protests. 'I'll see you tomorrow. Back around seven? I've Gillian and Rachel coming to tea. The Pitman children. Susie has to go to the dentist.'

'I'm sorry,' she said to Colin, as she put the phone down. 'My husband got himself a bit worked up. He's always like that when he's away from home. He worries about us.'

Colin said, 'But all's well upstairs. You're relieved, at peace?'

'Thank you. Can I offer you a drink? What about a whisky, or the port you missed? Some coffee?'

'No, really. You need to get to bed.'

Suddenly she felt enormously, frighteningly, dizzily tired. She could hardly stand up.

On the doorstep, Colin said, 'Now I know where you live, we must meet again. Christine and I – we get married in June. Why don't you sing at our wedding?'

It was raining next morning when she woke. She felt sick still, and hangoverish, although she'd drunk only one glass of white wine at the dinner. Almost at once the memory of last night came to her in a confused replay. She had behaved badly, made a fool of herself. She pushed it all to the back of her mind, together with a fit of anger against Dermot. Queasy, still sleepy, she told herself to be reasonable, and forgiving. It was only his insecurity made him behave like that. There but for the grace of God . . . Events in her own early life made *her* difficult, Dermot said. Reminding her sometimes, 'You're bound to be disturbed, after that dreadful couple.' (And oh my dear, if I should ever tell you of Eddie . . .)

The church clock struck seven. No sound from the children. She thought of getting out to wake Erdmute, as Dermot did so dutifully each morning, but decided against it. She dreaded going into that cluttered room, with its biscuit crumbs, its dregs of hot chocolate dried in cups, and the mound that was Erdmute under the *Federbett*.

Then she remembered the thermometer. Before you get out of bed, always . . . From habit she reached for it. Then as a wave of sickness came over her, she thought: It doesn't matter, it's not needed now. She dreaded having to tell Dermot tomorrow evening. 'No, nothing. It must be almost certain.' Dreaded even more his easy acceptance. 'It would probably be rather nice. As Cakey said, two's hardly a family . . .'

Last time he'd made this comment, she had said snappily, 'Two point four is. It's the national average . . . perhaps we need to produce some sort of monster now, three-fifths missing?'

'What horrifying bad taste,' he'd, rightly, said. (Oh Dermot, I will not do. I really will not do.)

She had thought that when the two little girls came, they might all go for a walk in the woods ten minutes' walk away. Although it was still only February, several afternoons lately had been mild and sunny. But by the time she and Erdmute had given the children breakfast it had begun to rain.

Daisy spent the morning with plasticine, her favourite toy at the moment. Her concentration and her dedication were that of a child twice her age. Pressed on to the tin tray were long delicate shapes, chains and coils, and roundish heads, with smiles. She put the smile in with a teaspoon handle. Although there was nothing there really to make him so, Benedict was jealous. It wasn't the skills or the results but perhaps the dedication he coveted. His own ongoing Lego tray and box was the victim of his moods: constructive today, destructive tomorrow. A morning spent pulling apart what Erdmute had perhaps patiently fitted together. He had a fleet of Dinky cars and lorries which ran between Daisy's legs, or in front of her as she went by. 'Get away from my lorry, you stupid girl.'

It rained solidly all morning and looked set in for the day. Erdmute broke the Hoover fan-belt again. Benedict's Lego was to blame, she said, sighing at the hopelessness of it all: the wet weather, the Lego, the pieces of broken plastic which lay in wait for her daily. She had a class this afternoon. Helen suspected her of wanting to hurry because some of the prep had not been done. She went to her room for an hour before lunch, Frank Ifield and Bobby Vee came through the closed door.

She appeared when the meal was ready, grudgingly apologetic that she hadn't helped. 'Soon they give us examen. I must, you understand?' She ate three helpings of egg and potato pie and two bananas, and disappeared to catch the bus.

In the early afternoon after *Watch with Mother* on television – today was *Tales of the River Bank* – the children rested always for an hour. Helen usually wrote letters then, or tried to read quietly. Today she wanted only to sleep.

At half past three Susie Pitman arrived with Gillian and Rachel. Susie, wife of a hospital consultant, headscarfed and wellington-booted, with a breathy, enthusiastic, warm manner. Standing on the door step, she spoke non-stop.

'Here they are, Gillian's been talking about it all morning. You'll see she's dressed as a nurse – didn't know they made the outfits that small . . . See you fiveish, I'm not expecting too lengthy a session with the tooth-yanker . . . Erdmute still eating you out of house and home? Our new one arrives next week. A Great Dane again, they're the best.'

Both Gillian and Rachel were well-mannered, self-assured little girls. Gillian at almost six was Benedict's contemporary, but he would seldom play with her for long – losing his temper, lashing out at her, or running to Helen. Rachel, as placid as Daisy, was a sleepy child, heavy-eyed. The family called her 'Dormouse' from her habit of falling asleep, any time, anywhere. Susie said delightedly that even after the longest of afternoon rests she was still never difficult to put to bed in the evenings.

For a while they were all in the playroom, while the rain splattered against the french windows. Gillian announced she wanted to go out. 'I have to visit my patients, in hospital.' Helen said no. She gave in gracefully. A running-about game between the playroom and the hall began. Daisy asked for the plasticine tray to be put up out of reach. Benedict for no reason had planted a determined thumb in one of the smiling heads.

Helen went through into the untidy morning-room where she kept her desk and papers. In there was a sagging sofa with a very loose wrinkled cover – a cast-off of the Vinneys. Rachel had found her way in there and was asleep already, curled up, thumb in mouth. 'Sh . . .' Helen said to Benedict who had followed her in. He began to cry and cling to her.

'What is it?' she asked.

'Gillian's took my ambulance truck.'

She sat down, next to Rachel. He climbed on her knee and snuggled up.

Gillian and Daisy were playing with the toy xylophone. Gillian's voice, 'That's not a proper tune – give it *me*.' From Daisy, no protest.

Benedict (poor, poor Benedict, how is he to get through life?) burrowing into her, not minding that she was as bony as ever (the sparrow that Eddie had loved). He wept. 'Don't,' she said, knowing it was about nothing – unless about being Benedict.

She called out, 'All right, Gillian?' Rachel didn't stir. 'Yes, please, Mrs Vinney,' called Gillian.

Benedict had fallen asleep. Her own eyes drooped together. In the peacefulness, Gillian and Daisy could be heard singing. There were shrieks of laughter from the direction of the playroom.

'Mrs Vinney, Mrs *Vinney*.' She opened her eyes suddenly. Gillian was standing in the doorway. 'Come quick,' she said, 'Daisy's got a funny face. She went to sleep. Come and *see*.'

Helen, shaking off Benedict, stood up at once. She rushed out, Gillian's hand in hers. But it wasn't to the playroom she was led.

Erdmute's door stood wide open. Biscuits scrunched beneath her feet as she rushed across the room. Daisy was lying, half sitting up on the bed. A plastic record sleeve covered her head and shoulders entirely.

'Daisy's my patient, she went asleep, asleep . . .'

Benedict, hurrying behind. He began to whimper at once, as Helen, leaning over, tore at the plastic. Shaking Daisy, breathing over her. Her solemn little face, blue. And quite still.

Gillian was crying noisily, hiccuping. Benedict wailing.

Oh my God, oh dear God. Both children were clinging to her as, trembling, her legs buckling, she dialled nine-nine-nine.

19

The telephone rang in Guy's apartment, making him jump. The bell was not a loud one but he jumped easily these days. He did not answer it at once. Getting up from where he'd been lying on the sofa, he placed a paperweight on his pile of papers. A light breeze blew in from the open balcony.

He crossed over to the phone.

'Mr Dennison?' A young, slightly nasal voice. Unknown to him. Hesitant, pleasant. 'I have heard, from certain persons, that there are – informations you require?'

'That would depend,' Guy said carefully. 'Who do you speak for?'

'Oh, for myself only . . . My interests, though, are I think the same as yours. I would like to see . . . Perhaps I can say I would also like to see justice done. I think from what I have heard that we may be able to help each other. I have the information. You plan the downfall of certain persons. Do I interest you?'

'You could do.'

'I can assure you, our aims are the same. When it reached my ears that you wanted to know certain things, I thought at once we should meet.'

'Yes,' Guy said warily.

'If the prison gates are to close behind certain persons . . . I think you are interested in proof which could lead to some arrests. Perhaps I can supply this –'

'How can I trust you?'

'Mr Dennison, you must trust someone. I am your friend. Those that have done you a wrong, have wronged me also. Is that not sufficient?'

'*If* we meet – where would it be?'

'You will receive a letter. I must tell you that for physical reasons, it is difficult for me to come to you –' There was a click, and the line went dead. Guy pressed the rest once or twice, said 'hallo, hallo.' But there was nothing.

Alone now again in the apartment. Teresa who cooked and

cleaned for him had left an hour ago. His papers were all as he had left them when the telephone rang, under the *presse papier*, waiting to be worked on. But he could settle to nothing. He poured himself a Campari and crossed to the sofa, picked up an *Oggi*, and flicked through its pages. Some film star he had scarcely heard of had revealed the existence of an eighteen-year-old daughter. ('Yesterday for my image I hid her, today I am proud . . .'), some students were interviewed about one of their group who had gone berserk, killing his parents, aunt, and two of his sisters ('He was always the gentle one amongst us – Guido, we used to say, you must stand up for yourself . . .'), a mother was photographed in the doorway of her raped and murdered daughter's bedroom ('Only yesterday, I said, tidy this room or else . . .')

The pages blurred. He closed the balcony windows. Inside the room, cooler now, he could smell the bitter, tangy scent of lemons – the bowl on the low table, near the magazines and journals.

I walk with fear, he thought. No, more than that, I get up with it, eat, drink with it, *go to bed with it*.

He slept alone. Laura and the girls had been in Paris for over four months now, Tomaso joining them for the first two. They rented an apartment. The girls were at school with the Canonesses of St Augustine. Whether he had a marriage, he was not certain. Probably yes. There had been a reconciliation of sorts, a calming down (on his part, she had never been anything else), a coming together, united by danger. Laura afraid, was to him . . . There was nothing he could do, in the face of her fear. He felt a terrified deep sadness that all their moments of greatest happiness should have been the result of fear. I am only the one who protects (an air raid in Naples, the kidnapping of Marcello . . .)

He remembered suddenly himself as a child – soon after Aunt Eleanor had given him the beloved Leo. Had he not thought *himself* the Golden Lion? Prowling around the garden at Park Villa, and then up again at Moorgarth, showing off to the seven-year-old Betty. 'I am the Golden Lion. Betty, there are wicked men coming after you, but *I can rescue you*.' (Then he had spoilt it all by playing also the part of the bad man – there had been no one else around to do it – until plump Betty had stood up to him, turning round and hitting him hard – not needing rescuing after all.)

How he missed Laura. How he loved her. He missed Silvi and

Titì, who had just begun to be friends as well as daughters. They wrote to him. They asked, 'Papa, when are you coming to Paris?' They were tired of all the special French tuition they needed to keep up with their classes. They missed their friends. They understood nothing, really. He wished sometimes they would say, 'Mamma cries for you,' or even 'Mamma talks of you all the time.' But that he could not imagine. That would not be Laura (even were she to feel it, that would not be Laura).

Five long months, and what had he accomplished? It had been a life almost without friends. Acquaintances, colleagues, yes. But friendship . . . He thought it might be natural if, betrayed by Ruggero, he called him out. A straight fight. Or visited Paolo – and cut off at the wrist those small white hands, silenced for ever that voice. *I am as bad as any of them*, he thought. At the same time, I can do nothing . . . Would do nothing. What others were there whose names he hadn't learned? Betrayed by my closest friend. He could never speak of it – unless it was to confront him. *And that I cannot do.*

It seemed to him that after all these years, he had no idea who he really was. A Grainger, a Verzotto? Even perhaps by symbiosis, a Dennison?

And that great will to live? Remembered now as vividly as if it were yesterday. Running for cover on the beach at Salerno, the 8 mm shells screaming overhead. Resting behind the lines in that apple orchard, knowing he had *survived* – so far. Fighting up through to Naples. Miller going, Fletcher going.

Now, he thought, I resemble more that soldier, just risen from his sickbed, coughing and breathless, walking up to Moorgarth – to harangue Maria. ('I hope I die. I hope I'm killed – soon.')

And that, he thought, is what may well happen. *And I do not care.*

Sometimes he could think rationally that this was just a depression. Occasionally, he would stand outside himself and see for a moment: cuckolded man, family recently held to ransom, now living alone and attempting in some sure fashion to expose and bring to justice the authors of all this terror (and I do not forget the terror of Ruggero, who should be my enemy). But most of the time, he did not think like this. He felt more often than he thought. Fear.

He had been appalled too at the news from Maria of the death of Helen's child. He had written to Helen at once. But what did one say? What could one say? He wrote from the heart, trying to send her a strength which he did not feel himself. For he could think only of Silvi or Titì – stretched out, eyes shut.

Walking back now from the balcony, he sliced some lemon, placed it in his glass and poured out more Campari. He thought that probably he should eat something. Food had been left ready for him. Teresa always sat with an old uncle on Thursday evenings. But he could not face the effort, the heaviness of sitting down and pushing the food in. He had lost weight recently. But then having a build which could easily run to fat, and without the height to carry it – maybe it was better, even a good thing.

He planned to finish his university post at the end of the year, in June. He had decided to stay for that. Then he would leave for Paris. (What he would do in Paris, he had no idea. Would they stay there? Where would they go? He had promised Laura Paris for the time being . . .)

His main aim – the downfall of the Dominicans – seemed to him some days amazingly simple, at other times a hopeless venture – and one better left alone. I don't know what I'm doing, he would think, and that is the cause of my fear. It was fear always of the unknown.

Get out, said all his instincts. They had said it even more clearly last week with the death of Vincenzo Mendola.

Until two months ago there had been no one to speak to. Then he had struck up a surprising, sudden, unlikely friendship with Vincenzo Mendola, to whom he'd gone over a small legal anomaly: difficulty about the lease of the apartment and liability for the joint guttering work. It was only then that he'd discovered, somewhere during the roundabout, courtesy-laden conversation, that here was a potential ally. And an ally he had proved. He burned with the need for justice. He had friends, connections in *L'Ora*, in *Il Giornale di Sicilia*, better still a friend who was starting up a new journal. 'Better that you should not meet him. But exposure – with enough evidence, in something like this. You have your letter still?'

Of course he had. His inclination at the time had been not to keep it, but good sense had suggested he did.

Vincenzo confirmed for him how Palermo was divided up and shared, north, south, west, east, in quite a wide radius. If these priests worked on their own, then protection for their victims could be secured. But if they were themselves part of a wider circle, then to go in deep was to lay oneself open to worse evils. Fear ruled indeed.

'You know how Sicily works? You know how she has worked for centuries? And now that we are in the second half of the twentieth century it is not so very different . . .'

'I have some news for you,' he had told Guy one morning by telephone. 'What time are you back from the university? . . . Good, then I am with you at seven o'clock. We talk and go out to eat. My wife and the children are at her mother's villa at Cefalù.'

There was no Vincenzo at seven. Nor at eight or nine. It took Guy until midday the next day to discover that he had been involved in a car accident, that between his apartment and Guy's he had been knocked down by an Alfa Romeo whose brakes, it appeared, had failed . . . Guy drove over at once to Cefalù. The plump wife who once had been so aggressive wept in his arms. He could say nothing.

Now he would like to have asked him: 'If after all I receive the promised instructions, do I go? Will I be followed? Who knows? Is the other person in danger? What am I about to be told? Am I really about to be told all I need to know?'

I shall go, he thought. The fear of setting out, the fear on the journey and the fear there, it could not be worse than this fear alone here – wishing for an end to it all.

It was a week before he heard. The letter in a plain blue envelope was neatly block printed. It was not long. The writer hoped Guy was still interested in 'certain matters', he himself was as eager as ever to help. 'I cannot travel far from my home. As I said, I must ask you to visit me. Please come on the afternoon of the 24th, about five. There are petrol pumps at the entrance to the village. Tell the one you see there, that you are the visitor for Aspanu. He will bring you to me. Come by car. Come alone.'

Enclosed was a small map, cut out from a larger one, showing the outskirts of Palermo and the route from there up to the village of Monteleone – marked with an X.

He could not work, could not sleep (but he had not been sleeping before). All these years that I have not been curious . . . Maria's birthplace. And the home surely of who knows how many of my kin? *And I can say nothing.* He knew that even had Maria not asked he would not have wished to. But there seemed to him some terrible irony that what looked like perhaps a break-through, the means to his clearing up everything, should take place there, in *that* village.

Once I have been and come back again, it will be a closed chapter. I shall have seen Monteleone – and it will be seen to be an ordinary village like any other. Small square, fountain, cobblestones, alleyways running off, brightly coloured washing strung from window to window, tables outside the houses where old men sit in the sun and women sit shelling beans, or making tomato paste. A small café perhaps with a few tables. Ah, and the petrol pumps, modern addition . . .

He took with him the original letter, and his briefcase. Although he would almost certainly commit everything to memory, he might wish after to make notes. He took also a revolver.

It was a quiet time of day, mid-afternoon, with little traffic on the road, and the journey took him much less time than he expected. Also his Fiat was fast. With only a few miles to go, he saw he was some twenty minutes too early.

The early summer sun was high, remorseless. The fresh shirt he had put on before leaving was drenched already – heat, sweat, and fear.

Of what am I afraid?

Standing outside the Fiat, he stretched his arms, mopped his brow, looked up at the sky. Kites wheeled overhead. Nearby a flock of lean, long-necked sheep grazed in a group of olives, the bells round their necks chiming as they moved. A profusion of wild flowers grew by the wayside – the crimson poppies standing out. Long narrow bees buzzed amongst the rosemary and the thyme. Aromatic. The air heavy with it. And everywhere the tall thistles, blue, purple, yellow, as tall sometimes as a man. To his left and further down, the railway line passed. Standing there, he heard the high-pitched hoot of a train.

He did not want to arrive in Monteleone. Everything was too much. I should not have to cope with my present fears – *and* something deeper, darker, my heritage. My inheritance.

But there they were, the two petrol pumps at the entrance to the village. A ramshackle building behind them. He stopped the Fiat. Almost at once, a young man, not very tall, with a low brow and eyebrows close together, came towards him. Guy said, 'I am the visitor for Aspanu.'

'I am Rosariu. You leave your car here. It will be safe.'

They walked the few yards up to the square. Then on down another street, and past the church. A church quite large for a

422

small village, and with interesting silverwork on the door. They stopped at a house standing apart from the others. Rosariu rang the bell.

To the servant, he said, 'The visitor.'

The room was cool and smelled of wax polish and lemons. On the table was a little dish of macaroons, and some small coffee-cups.

He saw why his host had not been eager to make the journey to him. Crutches lay beside his chair. He rose with difficulty. He was in his late twenties perhaps, with thick black hair lying flat. Heavy lips in a bow. A curiously sweet smile. In the room, full of heavy dark furniture, the blinds were half drawn.

'We sit here a little, and drink some coffee. Then as the sun becomes less, we may perhaps sit in the garden.'

Polite conversation – oh, the customs of this country, Guy thought. Whether it is something bad, something good, always this formal, ritual dance around the subject.

In the end it was he who broached it.

'I think you have something for me?'

'Please – ask me any questions. I am here only to help, so that justice should be done.'

And then a wealth of detail:

'You see, Mr Dennison, I was once a Dominican. Not a priest. I never progressed beyond the novitiate. But before my illness – you see, I am a victim of infantile paralysis – I was sent to study with these fathers. For perhaps a year or more. I learned there things I would never wish to have known . . . The story is particularly disgusting. Whited sepulchres . . . For a young man to learn such things.'

'Yes,' Guy said. 'Extortion. I know of that. I wish I did not.' He asked, 'How did you hear of me?'

'I am in a position to know . . . I know, for instance, it has been told me what has happened to your colleague, your friend. You have a friend, Vincenzo Mendola?'

'I *had* a friend . . .'

'Exactly.' He sipped his coffee.

'Where to begin, if I am to tell you of all their iniquities? Boccaccio would delight in them. And yet such things are possible anywhere where the religious life is entered for reasons other than the love of God . . . Do not think, Mr Dennison, that it stops at extortion. If that were all. That and yes, kidnapping. Ransom. Not many. It is too risky, I think. But they have no trouble of course in finding persons to carry out their work. A servant, a farm worker, gardener. Someone who will do the unpleasant part.

'Alongside the preaching, the giving of spiritual advice (they are very lavish with that), is an elaborate and exceedingly pleasant way of life. I wonder sometimes the Tarantino-Falletta do not turn uneasily in their tombs, to think what has become of their foundation . . .

'If it stopped at extortion. They are no strangers to the business world. Property dealing . . . Their bank accounts – in their own names, of course – would surprise you by their size. There is little they cannot afford, if they wish it. Extortion can be very profitable when added to other successful ventures.

'It is not even a life without women. These vows of chastity, poverty, obedience. They obey no one. They are not poor. And they are not chaste. Certainly, in my time there – and it is one of my most shameful memories – women were frequent visitors. Night visitors. Smuggled in. Often in the disguise of nuns with, say, their Reverend Mother, of the Dominican order – visiting of course for the most acceptable of reasons.

'The fruit farming – there is little to say about that. But the pigs . . . pigs are not only profitable, their presence can be very useful. A pig is good to eat but also not very discriminating in what it eats. And there is this excellent machine they have for grinding and making palatable food from all kinds of unlikely ingredients. I need say no more? You understand me? I hope you are as filled with disgust as I was. As I *am*.

'And now,' he said, 'shall we go outside, sit outside a little while? The garden is very pleasant. Secluded. A terrace, it looks down on the world below.'

It was very hot still outside. In the garden a lizard chased its tail. The benches they sat on had an intricate pattern of vine leaves and bunched grapes. They were not very comfortable. The few flowerbeds were edged with majolica tiles.

Beneath them, a bus could be seen trundling up the winding road. Aspanu commented:

'How altered things are. A village once so totally isolated, with Palermo as distant as 'Merica is now. See, we have petrol, a reasonable mechanic manning the pumps, a bus that calls three times a week. It will be bringing back –' he took out his watch '– several who went to market this morning. It will return with many empty seats.

'Show me the letter,' he said, a little later. When he saw it, 'Yes,' he said, 'there are some distinctive . . . the type. I think you will find –' He brought out a piece of paper. 'See this, typed three years ago. When I made out certain lists for them. I think you – or those you inform, will find the typewriter in the cell of Father Cirillo. I can describe it exactly.'

Drinks were brought out to them where they sat. Guy commented on how pleasant it was.

'This house I live in – the family house . . . My great-grandfather was a person of some importance here. His name was Don Cataldo. He was also known as the Lion. He was a man of honour and much respected. People are very different nowadays. Nowadays there is not the same respect . . .'

Time to go.

'You told no one you were coming here? You told no one of our meeting?'

'Of course not.'

'Here you are safe. In my own village.'

He got up slowly, reaching for his crutches.

'I shall walk with you to your car.'

'No, please not. I am all right.'

'I insist. If you have the patience to wait for me. We walk slowly.'

As they came through the square he saw the bus standing waiting. Very slowly they made their way down, to where the Fiat was parked.

He did not notice at first. It was Aspanu who remarked, 'You have some damage . . .'

The nearside front tyre had been crudely slashed. Ribbons of rubber hung loose.

'What can I say? When you are our guest . . . I shall have to settle this matter.'

He spoke to a small boy, sharply, 'Fetch Rosariu.' He said to Guy, 'Your spare wheel is in order? Give Rosariu your keys. He changes it for you. Speedily. You and I can drink in the café.'

There were three tables outside. They sat in view of the square. The café owner, a heavy man with drooping moustaches, came out to wipe the table. He brought with him a small bowl of roasted chick peas. Aspanu ordered wine.

'So unfortunate,' he said. 'You won't be late for any appointment?'

'No, no. Nothing.'

As they sat there the bus lumbered past on its downward journey, rattling over the cobbles. It looked half empty.

His head spun. With the heat, with fatigue, with all he had heard, with weeks and weeks of emotion and loneliness. He wanted suddenly to ask . . . felt even that the unfortunate slashing of the tyre had been so that he would have time to ask.

'Verzotto,' he said. 'Does the name mean anything? Someone of that name – someone I met, who mentioned Monteleone . . .'

Aspanu looked blank. 'It is not a name known to me . . . but then, there has been so much emigration. So much change . . . Perhaps it was a long time ago? Perhaps there are relations but by another name? Who knows?'

He turned his head. 'Look – Rosariu.'

And there was Rosariu, with the car keys, and the news that the tyre was fitted.

They said their farewells there at the café. Aspanu said: 'I do you this favour. Some day perhaps you will do me a favour? You have been most welcome in our village . . . You are sure you have not been made late? I must apologize for Monteleone, that such things happen . . .'

Leaving, Guy looked back at the village. Everywhere, old men in black sat in groups, on chairs, talking. Women, young and old, outside their houses. Almost all in black. Children running about. He thought of Maria. 1960, he said to himself. Transpose the last two figures and it was as it had been when she left. How little had changed really since 1906. Some progress had come, of course – in the shape of petrol pumps, and a visiting bus.

Once outside, he drove fast. Before long, he had overtaken the bus. The road wound on down. In the valley below, a man was leading his donkey to drink.

Then there was a sudden pounding, difficulty with the steering – and oh Christ, the inevitability of a puncture. Something on the road perhaps? or a faulty spare tyre, his spare tyre not in good order.

He brought the car quickly to a halt. He got out, and looked. Yes, it was. He swore. Then swore again. This was sod's law: when the spare tyre is in use, you will have a puncture.

Near where he had stopped, there was a wayside drinking fountain. Water gushed invitingly out of the mouth of a stone lion. Suddenly, sharply thirsty – perhaps it had been the chick peas, he leaned forward and drank. Then he washed his face, splashing it, splashing his hair.

As he lifted his head, he saw the bus, caught up with him, come rattling round the corner. Why ever not, what the hell, he thought, angry about the tyre. Why hang around? He locked the car hastily (madness perhaps to leave it, but how else am I to get home?)

He flagged down the bus. As it set off again, the driver, taking his money, shrugged his shoulders at Guy's tale, half smiled. The bus was almost empty. An old woman, a cloth bundle on her lap. Two boys, sitting close together whispering and laughing. Right at the back, an old man.

It was as they were rounding the second bend that the explosion happened.

He was already looking vaguely in the direction of his car. Now he turned fully. He jumped as if he'd been shot.

'Did you hear that? That noise? An explosion. My God.'

The old woman stared straight down, fumbling with the bundle on her lap. The two boys looked embarrassed, as if he had said something indecent. He appealed to the driver.

The driver said, 'I heard nothing. I was watching the road ahead.'

The man at the back spoke up. 'They're dynamiting the rocks again. We're to have a smart new road. They have said so in Rome . . .'

As the bus rattled and twisted and turned throughout what seemed the longest journey of his life, Guy shook. Some of the time, dizzy, he had to clutch at the seat so as not to slip. The water drunk from the lion's mouth was only a memory. He felt a raging thirst, licking his dried sore lips continually.

Within two hours of reaching Palermo, he had boarded an express for Rome. By late the next afternoon, he was in Paris.

20

Carmel, 7th October 1960, Feast of the Most Holy Rosary.
Dearest Little Nell,

This is not an easy letter to write, and I hope you will forgive my addressing it to you, rather than to Dermot. But over the last eight years I have come to feel closer to you than to most of my family. When you wrote to me after the tragedy, although it was only through prayer I could offer to help, I was very moved that it should have been me in whom you wished to confide all your fears and sorrows.

Now I am confiding in you. For the last few years I have been experiencing great unrest – an unrest that has not yielded to any of the traditional remedies. Neither fasting nor prayer has resolved it. I have been questioning more and more often, the whole of my past life, my decision to enter here, my place in the community, my whole vocation.

Perhaps it is enough to say that after much prayer and searching, I have come to a decision. I am leaving the Carmel. You, with your understanding heart, will know something, dear, of what this means. It is not just the emotional upheaval, the complete negation of all I thought I stood for – there is also the practical aspect. I am thirty-nine, and trained for nothing. I am also completely out of touch (more perhaps even than I realize) with the world of today. When I entered in January 1940 – the feast of the Epiphany! – the war had scarcely begun to make its changes (and what at just eighteen did I *know* of that world anyway?)

Everything has of course taken time. There have been tiresome procedures to go through. And naturally, with the best of motives, there have been those who sought to dissuade me, although at all times I have received nothing but the greatest kindness and understanding from my Superior, and from my Sisters in Christ.

I am going to ask two very tremendous favours of you, dear.

So unused am I to having 'wants' or desires of any sort, that it is very difficult for me to write this. But firstly, could you tell Dermot for me? (I am writing to the rest of the family today.) I know, dear, that you will do it well. The other request is, when I come out, in about four weeks' time, may I come to you? For a while at least. I don't know what you want to tell Benedict? I shall of course be dressed as an aunt, not a nun . . .

'Well,' Dermot said, 'what you wanted has come about. Weren't you always saying she was unfulfilled? Now she's coming out in search of fulfilment –'

'How you twist my words. Some idle remark ages ago. That time in the car, when we'd visited – wasn't that when? Daisy was sick all the way back and you –'

He snapped, 'Don't. Don't talk about her in that casual way. As if she were still here. It's unnatural.'

'No, natural,' she said sadly. 'No, it's natural. It's you that . . .'

Perhaps that was the worst, now. That in the eight months since Daisy's death she had scarcely been allowed to speak of her. She could see his suffering, but could do nothing to help, was not allowed to help.

And she suffered too. Naturally. There had been friends to lean on. Sympathy had flooded in. Letters and more letters. Guy wrote from Sicily. Bridget's Carmel had sent three Masses. Jenny, bereaved herself soon after – Dulcie died in a cold spell early that March – wrote at length.

And Maria. Perhaps now the reconciliation was as complete as it would ever be. But enough, enough for her. Maria, in Thackton all the time now, invited her up with Benedict. She had gone there for three weeks, before joining Cakey and her family of eight in the Cornish house. A miserable time. Cakey, pointedly it seemed, calling out as the surf crashed on Polzeath beach, 'Watch out for the children. Supervise them every moment!' Saying to Helen, 'Is it all right to leave the children with you? You will watch them, all the time?'

They blamed her, of course. She had been responsible, through her carelessness, for Daisy's death. Dermot blamed her. To sit dozing, even five minutes.

Erdmute had been sent home at once. He could not bear her in the house. She had gone over to sleep at Vibeke and Karen's, then left for Frankfurt two days later.

Those nightmare days after. Dermot referring obliquely to the possible new baby, and then, the day after the funeral, a period so heavy she wondered sometimes if it hadn't been an early miscarriage. And the recriminations. 'Didn't you know where they were – what they were doing? *Why weren't you with them?*' Only Dermot and his family had been like that. Susie had not been. Susie was devastated, knowing that although Daisy had put the record sleeve on herself, Gillian had not known to pull it off. But she did not blame. 'No one can be in two places . . . the children had the run of the house after all. *No one is blaming you*. It could have been me.' And the coroner, at the inquest: nothing but sympathy, the sympathy of the court. (A comment about the dangers of plastic bags, a recommendation that manufacturers write a warning. This new hazard of modern life, the minus side of modern inventions.)

But perhaps because Dermot couldn't express his grief any other way, couldn't speak to her of it, *couldn't even speak Daisy's name* – he continued to blame her. '*Why weren't you with them?*'

So she had written to Bridget, pouring out her heart, her sorrow, her guilt. Above all her guilt. (She who with Eddie had felt none.) And Bridget had written back, a letter that surprised her with its insight, its understanding. (And now it was for her to help Bridget. For them to help Bridget.)

The visit to Maria had been an escape from this blame. Oh, the benison of those few weeks at Moorgarth. The sitting-room, with its log fire on summer cold days. The happy ghost of Uncle Eric (making wartime cakes for him, walking the moors and the bluebell woods, holding the nails for him as he hammered the broody hen coop). Watching Maria with Benedict.

She learned then that Guy was in Paris. There was a letter from him while she was there. 'It doesn't tell me very much,' Maria said. But she had been invited out to see them, and would be going straight after Helen's stay. She was as ever open in her dislike of Laura. Her own news, which she said Helen might find strange was that Jenny and she, after joking one day about the ancient right to graze seven sheep at Moorgarth, had suddenly found themselves talking seriously of farming the place again.

'Mainly sheep, I think. Maybe a cow or two in the barn. Hens again, of course . . . It may seem odd. But then Jenny and I are good friends. We are comfortable in each other's company.' This farming, it had suddenly come to them, was what *both* of them would like. 'And Uncle Eric would like it so,' she said. 'I think he'd be more than a little pleased . . .'

But the blame was still there on their return. And perhaps more so, after the dreadful Cornish holiday. Blame: the background to, the excuse for, Dermot and she not getting on. 'We aren't getting on very well.' That trite phrase. How truly it expressed Dermot and Helen this autumn of 1960.

Oddly, it was singing (that once she had vowed never to do again) which brought her back to life, a little. In September, friends of Colin and Christine's, jazz aficionados, opened up a small club two evenings a week. It was Colin's idea she should sing there. Dermot was not keen. 'I want to,' she had said. 'I must have something of my own.'

'You have,' he said, 'you have a child.'

She didn't argue with Dermot in that mood – but she went to the club just the same. She was almost happy while she was there. As if a great curtain came down, protecting her from her loss. It would not be raised till she was on the way home, and facing Dermot's disapproval. He rarely came to hear her.

The club was in Furneux Green, ten miles away, and about twenty-five from Colin and Christine's. It was just possible one way by bus. The return journey around two in the morning would have to be done otherwise. The first few times Dermot drove her there, although he would not come in. (Babysitting had to be arranged. They had no au pair now.) But it seemed obvious she should accept Colin's offer for them to collect and return her. They came only a little out of their way to do so.

Dermot did not like the arrangement. He did not like either Colin or Christine (whom Helen had taken to at once, so small and plump to Colin's gangling height, so warm, bubbling with life, and lately, so excited and so tactful about their baby, expected in the spring of 1961.) He had never got over his unreasoning jealousy of Colin, who had so kindly driven her back from a dinner party and come inside to see the children were all right.

She might never have stopped, the singing came back so easily. A change of style. A more mature voice. New, different people to work with. A small resident group.

She sang standards. She sang as she had sung with Eddie. So many of their old numbers. And it *did not hurt.*

Some of her old troubles came back. But only if she was nervous. Transposing her words, worrying about her hands. She

431

was nervous the night Dermot brought her and agreed to stay. He had with him an advertising colleague who was staying the night with them, and wanted to hear her.

Transposing her words: ('Pass it off,' Eddie had said, 'we all do it, don't notice it.')

'*A hard man is good to find,*' she sang. It didn't go unnoticed. Someone clapped. Someone else cheered.

Dermot was furious. Embarrassed too. 'How could you be so vulgar,' he said, when they were back home again. 'How could you be so coarse?'

'I didn't do it on purpose.'

'Really? I got the impression it was thought the smart thing to do. In that sort of world.'

'What sort of world?'

'You know . . . Your sort of world.'

'Anyway,' she said lightly, annoyed, upset, the tears not far away, 'a hard man *is* good to find.'

'If anything is meant by that –'

Perhaps her remark had been deliberately cruel. Better not to think of, much less speak of that side of life. She had scarcely been able to bear it since the death. As if death were here in the bed with them.

The advice of friends did not help. 'Make another baby. Make another baby as quickly as possible.' But the idea filled her with dread. When she heard the well-meant advice for the third time she felt only a dumb anger. A new child would not be Daisy. Might it not be, worse still, a reminder? She could not explain her morbid fear of this intruder, for intruder it would be, who would sleep in Daisy's cot, sit in the high chair, play with her toys . . .

Dermot felt differently. Although never mentioning Daisy by name, he spoke of Benedict's loneliness. Giving her twinges of conscience. He worded it always, 'Darling, you want us to be a family again, don't you?'

And so for his sake she put aside the thermometer. And worried. But when after two unguarded months, no child had appeared, she made other arrangements. She could not make a moral issue of it. I must survive, she told herself. And this is how. It would be no good to have a cap fitted – the likelihood of discovery was too great. Finally in early June, on the pretext of buying an outfit for Colin and Christine's wedding, she had gone up to London for the day and had a ring fitted.

She had felt ashamed not only of her deceit, but of her reluctance to be touched. The feeling had grown worse over the months since the death. Shame, self-disgust, pity for Dermot (it is I the bad one), all warred within her. How long too before her fertility would be questioned? Fortunately, in late September, in one of his gentler moods, he suggested they wait a little after all. 'Until you feel more able to cope, until you're ready,' he said. And so it was back to the (pretence now) of the thermometer.

Benedict – what of Benedict? He had become very withdrawn after Daisy's death. For several days after, it seemed, Helen and he had clung together. He asked her over and over why Daisy had gone to Heaven. 'What's the hurry?' he said. Using an expression which was often used to him. ('Don't rush so, Benedict, what's the hurry?')

'Why's Daisy had to go? *What's the hurry?*' he asked Helen, again and again.

Perhaps she needed to be of help to someone, perhaps it was at that moment just the right thing for her. But Bridget's arrival, tired and a little emotional but calming down remarkably quickly, was good for them all.

In the twenty-odd years since she had entered the Carmel, Bridget had not walked down a country road, let alone a busy street. Even a small town like Shalford Pelham was full of strange sights and sounds. Her third day she was almost run over by a bright red Heinkel three-wheeler – a novelty to Benedict, but to her an amazement – stepping out of the way only just in time.

Some of the changes were less than might be imagined. Clothes after all she had seen worn by visitors. There had been family photographs. But a visit to a London theatre to see *Fings ain't wot they used to be* had her bubbling over with excitement and animation: on the Underground back to Liverpool Street, feet tapping, half-whistling. She wanted, like a child, to do everything she hadn't done for years. At first clothes didn't bother her much. She had not been interested before, she said. She went out dutifully with Helen and was kitted out with winter coat, skirts, jumpers, nylon stockings. Then looking at shoes, she became intrigued. Even ones with medium heels were strange – she practised at home with them, asking for Benedict to take her arm, 'in case I take a header'. Soon after she bought a pair of very high stilettos, of two-tone leather with a strap for support.

Her feet were rather large. At the same time she decided on impulse to change her spectacles, ordering blue plastic frames in a swept-up style which didn't really suit her.

It had been agreed she spend at least three months and preferably six with them, while she thought about her future. She of course visited her family. But since they were amazed and critical that she hadn't gone there in the first place, the visit was not a success.

Food – there was a small delicatessen in Shalford Pelham – she wanted to try everything. And after the first few weeks to cook it herself. 'I'll cook for you all,' she would announce. 'Tonight is *Spanish* night.'

Helen had thought Dermot might be shocked or upset by some of this. That Bridget should leave at all he had found disturbing. The whole point of the Carmel brought into question. (Helen's being the first to hear had shattered him. 'Why a letter to *you*, who are always so critical?') Helen had pointed out that nothing was altered. The Carmel was the same, neither better nor worse – it was just that Bridget was not suited to it, and had found out before too late. 'It's still the powerhouse of prayer it was yesterday,' she said, remembering a convenient phrase.

But after the first few difficult weeks, he seemed to be coping well, sometimes even entering into the spirit of the fun. Watching the two of them together one day, struck suddenly by a fleeting family resemblance – she thought: *If only I loved him.* A thought that filled her with such sadness that it overrode for the moment the death of Daisy and all the accumulated gloom of a dark November afternoon.

Bridget was learning to drive. She allowed Dermot to teach her – then changed her mind. He was too anxious, she said. 'As soon as I've passed a test, dear, I could take Dermot to the station, and then we'd have the car for the day. I could drive you to your jazz club too.'

She came and listened to Helen three times in those first few months. She was amazed. 'How do you do it? How do you stand up there and sing alone? And Scat, those lovely meaningless noises you make, I love them.' To an ear attuned to plainchant only, the rhythms must have seemed amazing, but Bridget took it, like everything, it seemed, in her stride. (Although Dermot had said about the stiletto heels, 'I think you're taking *too much* in your stride . . .')

She and Bridget talked a lot. Just as Bridget confided in her the history of her spiritual turmoil, her hopes and fears for the future, so Helen felt she could speak to Bridget, about everything. Confidences about thermometers and Dermot, contraception, the ring. 'Ah well,' Bridget had said, 'it has to be between you and God, doesn't it? Only *you* know, dear, what you can cope with.'

But perhaps the greatest benefit of her stay with them was the improvement in Benedict. Every excitement, novelty, they must do together. And there was so much he could show her. Not least, of course, television. Sitting him on her knee to watch *Bootsy and Snudge* ('Did you get that joke, Aunt? I'll explain later'), she brought him back to life in a way Helen could not. (Perhaps he and she were too alike, too united in their grief?)

And yet, oddly, she would feel sometimes that it was she, not Bridget, who was waiting. Waiting to decide.

She found that she needed now to get away at regular intervals. Going away helped. If she could get away everything fell into perspective, became on her return a little more bearable.

Just before Christmas she spent three days with Jenny. She did not take Benedict, who was still attending school – she would be back in time to see him as the surly innkeeper, saying 'No room at the inn,' in the school nativity play. Jenny, who still missed Dulcie fearfully, told her all about the farming ideas, project. They planned to begin in the spring.

Christmas was a difficult time. How not? When she had to lay out not two stockings, but one – when *everything* was a reminder. When toys and presents, and excited children seemed everywhere.

There was an expedition of the four of them to see *Oliver*, since Bridget had so enjoyed the earlier Lionel Bart show. On Boxing Day they went to *Peter Pan* and Bridget held Benedict's hand while he squeaked with pleasurable fear at Captain Hook. Home again, he woke in the middle of the night, screaming about crocodiles. Bridget arrived first on the scene. Helen, pulling on her wrap, found Benedict's head already buried in her ample bosom. She waited to feel jealousy, but none came.

'*Ain't no sweet man that's worth the salt of my tears*,' she sang. Bridget had come to listen and led the clapping in an embarrassingly enthusiastic manner. Dermot was there unwillingly. She knew he was jealous of her singing (the only thing I have, she

435

thought – *my* singing), but that he would never admit it. He sniped in the car going back. So much so that Bridget said, 'Oh, you two . . .'

Somehow the quarrelsome uneasy mood followed them home and upstairs into the bedroom. She was tired yet over-stimulated, as always after these evenings. He said:

'I suppose you're waiting for me to say you sang well. For those who like that sort of thing, that's the sort of thing they like . . . I'm sure you're very good at it – but now that Bridget . . . It's a nuisance Bridget wanting to come along. Making Benedict-sitting problems –'

She said, 'He could have come too.'

'A child. Into an atmosphere like that. You must be mad –'

She said, 'Anyway, if Bridget hadn't happened to leave the convent, we'd have needed a sitter tonight.'

'Hardly. I wouldn't have come.'

'At least,' he said a few moments later, 'those problems will be over when he goes off to prep school –'

'That's not for quite a while.'

'Next September.'

'So little – *Seven*, Dermot. Does he have to?'

'It did me no harm. He's down for it, so he'd better go. He's too clinging anyway. First it was you, and now it's Bridget.'

He said next, 'Unless of course a baby comes.'

'Unless a baby comes.'

'You *are* going to get over this – feeling, about replacing . . . about conceiving again?'

'Oh yes,' she said tiredly. 'Eventually.' She said then, meaning it. 'I'm sorry.'

For what was she sorry? For everything. She wanted to apologize just for being Helen. She said it several times, 'I'm sorry. I'm sorry.'

In the end he said, 'I don't know what about. Come to bed. I'm sorry too – if it's something I said. Or didn't say.' He sounded gentle, but exasperated too.

She was standing over by the bow-fronted chest of drawers, where there was a bowl of blue hyacinths. In winter Maria grew these in pots all about the kitchen and sitting-room at Moorgarth. The sweet and almost cloying smell evoked the farmhouse. Suddenly she wanted desperately to be there.

Thackton, Moorgarth. Maria – who had said she would always be welcome.

She said to Dermot, 'I thought of spending a few days up with Maria, now that school's started again. Benedict –'

'Bridget will look after him.'

Of course Bridget would look after him. And in the morning when it was suggested, she was only too glad. Benedict, eating cornflakes, thought it a good idea.

Five days, a week, ten days, Helen thought. If I could just be away, at peace. She thought more and more often now of *peace*.

She would leave the next morning. That evening when the cheap rate came on, she tried to ring. But the operator told her the number was engaged. She tried again later. And then didn't bother. In the morning before she left, it would be too early to call anyone. I shall be a surprise, she thought. Imagining Maria's welcoming arms.

It was already after four when the small train pulled into Thackton. The January light, poor all day, had gone completely. Electric lights had come on in the rows of cottages backing on to the station. (Oh, dark station of my wartime childhood.)

Carrying her bag, she began the long walk up. The wall glistened with frost. There was a bite in the air, a smell perhaps of snow – the air which smelled so different from Shalford. The cold set her teeth on edge.

Turning into the village (sudden twinge as I see the sweet shop, lighted, the chime of the doorbell as someone goes in), walking up past Park Villa. Then at last, the welcome sight of Moorgarth.

The sitting-room light was on, and as she came into the courtyard, she saw the kitchen light through the half-drawn curtains. If the door is unlocked, I could walk in and surprise her . . .

She decided to ring. The door opened. Guy stood there.

'What a lovely surprise,' he said. He was in shirtsleeves. The warmth of the kitchen came to her like a blessing. 'Maria never said. I'd have met you at the station.'

'She doesn't know. It was an impulse, I came on an impulse.'

'Let me take your bag . . . I'm afraid,' he said, smiling, 'you've travelled in the wrong direction. Maria's in Montpelier Square. They're sorting out some legal matters before Jenny winds everything up there.'

'I never thought. I tried to telephone –'

'She's back tomorrow evening. Want to wait?'

It wasn't so much disappointment she felt as a sort of shocked surprise. The order of things was wrong. There came over her a sudden unexpected – and quickly checked – proprietary feeling about the kitchen, about the whole of Moorgarth. Maria and I, we kept it going as a home all through the war. We looked after and loved Uncle Eric . . .

He had hung up her coat. She took off her hat, shook out her hair.

'Do you want to go upstairs first? There are two bedrooms to choose from. They're both made up. One's always ready for Jenny.'

When she came downstairs:

'Could you give me a hand tomorrow? I've got a brace of partridge for Maria. Hung just right. I want to have a meal for her but I'm pretty inept at cooking. And the Aga – but you'll remember – it has to be wooed. I don't seem to know the way to its heart.'

'But of course. Of course.'

She was sitting at the kitchen table. He was making her a cup of tea. She asked:

'Are you in England for long? You haven't told me what you're doing, or anything –'

'Running away, I suppose.'

'Oh,' she said. 'That makes two of us.'

He was busy over by the dresser, getting cups and saucers.

'Tell me,' he said.

'Oh well, it's nothing. Just everything . . .'

He said slowly. 'I was terribly sorry – about Daisy. I wrote, I know, at the time, but one can't – in a letter. It's . . . Not that anything I can say now would be any better. But, well – you are talking to the father of daughters.'

She bit her lip. To hide the flood of feeling. The desire to rest her head now on the table and weep for dead Daisy.

'Thank you. I know – and thank you. Thank you, Guy.' Absentmindedly, she stirred her sugarless tea.

'How are they, Silvi and Titì?'

'Well. Beautiful. And very fluent in French now.'

'It's not them you're running away from?'

'Dear God, no.'

'Who then, what then?' She said, 'It's not fair to say "*Tell me*," when you never say anything about you.'

'My marriage is over. That's all.' He said it quickly, sadly.

'Tell me.'

'To put it in the simplest terms, it's Laura. Laura needs other

438

men. She needs to be unfaithful. It's a pattern, apparently. Not unfaithful occasionally. But constantly. Regularly. It doesn't worry her. And when I knew nothing – it didn't worry me. It was all right – until I discovered. And then . . . You knew about my – our – getting out of Sicily in a hurry? I got into deep water –'

'Maria didn't say much. Just that you were in Paris, and that Laura and the girls had gone ahead.'

'She wouldn't have wanted to awaken your memories of Marcello. Nor of course do I –'

'No, please tell me. Please go on.'

'. . . I got into deep water. Laura and the girls were already in Paris for safety. When I joined them there in May, I thought at first . . . I wanted to give it six months or so, to see if everything would be all right. *Could* perhaps be all right . . . And at first there was my gratitude just to be alive, to be with them all again.

'But it was if anything worse than before. Because I knew – I knew and felt a fool for knowing. Just as I'd felt one for *not* knowing, before. I found it impossible not to be suspicious. Not to be always wondering. And I was right. Alas, I was too damn right . . .' He paused. 'And simply – I cannot live like that.'

'What are you going to do? What shall you do?'

'I arrived here three days ago – after spending six weeks alone in Paris, staying away from the apartment. I need time to think. Here, with Maria, it's a good place for thinking . . . But yes, it's all over. For certain.'

'I'm sorry,' she said. 'What else can one say?' What else could she say? She remembered Laura, not seen for over ten years now. Beautiful, impassive Laura. Strange Laura.

She asked him now to tell her something of what had happened to him. Why exactly he had left so quickly.

'You don't mind that you'll be reminded of Marcello and all that? I'd hoped that was buried for you. Forgotten.'

'It isn't,' she said.

He explained about the extortion. Of the danger to Laura and the girls. And later, to himself.

'Those Dominicans. One of them you met out at the Tarantino-Falletta villa. Five of them. Quite on their own. No one else powerful behind them, whatever they hinted. You can imagine the horror of the Chapter in Rome, who knew nothing of all this. To the outside world, the five of them had the appearance of such sanctity. Such learning. On official visits from their superiors they dissembled wonderfully . . . A positive factory of evil. Flourishing far in excess of the green bay tree – to the tune of millions of lire. I was trapped. Foolishly thinking I was being given information by one of their enemies. I was simply being set up by them. The Prior's *nephew* of all people. Coming from a long line of experienced villains, I should say. And I believed every word . . . But I'm here to tell the tale. God must have something worthwhile in mind for me – I certainly wasn't *meant* to be still around . . . The time fuse in the engine or whatever went off within minutes of my leaving the car. I must be one of the few men alive who thinks of a puncture with gratitude and affection . . .'

'And they're still at large?'

'They've in fact been arrested. All five of them. And the Monteleone nephew. Plus some others. There's to be a trial – but not for many months. Maybe years. I hold out no hope whatsoever of a satisfactory, fair or just conclusion . . .

'But there, well,' he said. 'That's enough of all that. Now you're going to let me cook you a meal . . . And by the way, we've got field mice – rather a lot of them. It's the intense cold. We were expecting to be snowed in.'

Guy asked her, 'What do you think of their farming ambitions – Jenny and Maria? I think it rather splendid. Maria's been spending weeks at a time living over at what used to be Reeves's farm. The sons were all killed in the First War, but the daughter married someone who took over. Now their son farms it. Maria's been staying with them and learning. She said it's the best way of all. She gave me a wonderful account of some ram sales. She has the language perfectly already . . .'

The fire in the sitting-room. Log fire. The same fire she'd made up so often. Baking cakes for Uncle Eric, eating tea together. Honey from Eleanor's bees. 'What's the news from Tunisia?' Worrying about Guy. Turning on the wireless for six o'clock. (And there stood the wireless still, in its walnut casing, to the right of the fireplace, on the table with the shelf underneath for the *Radio Times* in its Florentine leather cover.) And here were blue hyacinths standing over by the window, and on the centre table, just as she had pictured.

Guy said, 'Let me pour you some more claret. It masks the rather odd flavour of my sauce. You don't have to be polite. I should have let you cook – except it's hardly a break for you . . .'

'Oh, but it tasted *good* . . . Of course I don't cook always now. Bridget does a lot of it.'

'Tell me about Bridget. Since you won't tell me about yourself –'

She began the tale of the Carmel. Bridget's letter. The Carmel itself. The Vinneys. And then back, and back and back. It was good, very, very good, just to talk. To tell.

'So,' she said, ending up, 'things aren't right. Not really right.'

'No, they don't sound it. But perhaps they can be made so?'

'Perhaps.'

'Well,' he said, 'for someone who wouldn't tell, you've told quite a lot.'

She said suddenly, 'Do you remember when you came to meet me at Palermo that time in 1950? When I was so dreadfully unhappy. You said then, "Tell me," and I wouldn't.'

'I remember,' he said.

'The married man was – Eddie.'

She didn't look at him when she'd said it. She felt shock waves of late guilt. (Why did I speak? Why have I told him?)

'Well, yes – I knew that.'

'Did Maria? I thought . . . You see, it was all pretty hidden, pretty disgraceful.'

'She told me a few years ago. No, I didn't think anything terrible –'

'No, no. Well, if she'd told you. That's all right, I mean. You obviously talk a lot together.'

'Nowadays, yes. One of the reasons, perhaps, why . . . why we are so close. I'm Maria's child, you see. Maria is my mother –'

She wanted to say, 'She's my mother too.' But then she took in what he'd said.

'I'm Maria's child,' he said. 'It's a long story. But perhaps if we're exchanging secrets . . .'

'Exchanging secrets,' he'd said. At the end, and they'd been talking it seemed for hours, she didn't know what to think of anything.

She said when he'd finished, 'Maria wept when she first saw Benedict.'

'Does that surprise you?'

'Not now.'

She began to clear the table.

'No, leave that, please . . . Look what I found yesterday.' He was over by the cupboard to the left of the fireplace. 'Remember this? I'm sure you do.'

Pale crimson cloth-covered book with gold title. He laid it, open, in front of her – where she had just cleared a place. He stood behind her.

'There he is, the Golden Lion. Remember him?'

'Of course –'

'A much loved fragment of my childhood. And yours –'

'And Dick's,' she said. 'Dick coloured it in.'

As he stood behind her, looking over at the book, his hands rested lightly on her shoulders.

She turned the page and there was the colouring in. The place where Dick's yellow crayon had missed the line.

'I should have borrowed it for Benedict and Daisy. I still could –'

'I was the Lion once,' he said. 'I was going to be so brave. Rescue princesses. Save lives.'

His hands remained on her shoulders. She sat very still. Knowing that she could not move, would not move. She felt suddenly very cold. Warm only where his hands rested. She trembled.

There was silence. Only the sound of the logs splitting, spitting in the fireplace.

'I thought,' she said, her voice not very sure, 'I wondered about doing more singing. If I could fit it in with being a good mother. I mean, if Dermot – if Benedict . . .'

She spoke very fast. Then faster. On and on.

Guy continued to stand there, behind her, his hands never moving.

21

'First she takes your husband,' Jenny said, 'and then your son
. . . And yet you love her still.'

'Yes,' Maria said. 'I love her . . . very much. I don't see how
anyone who saw her in that sweet shop could do otherwise.'

'But that business of Eddie –'

'Oh, but I've forgiven her, I forgave her long ago. Over the
years, gradually . . . With Eddie, my anger just burned out, the
flame leapt so high it burned out. But with her . . . a stone. It
melted. And yes, I loved her again. She became my child again.'

'And now, what's to become of her? Of them?'

'I knew,' Maria said, 'I knew at once. I walked in here, and as
soon as I saw them, I knew . . . What's to become of them? I
should frown on it – but I can't. I'm just terribly, unreasonably
happy – and concerned, anxious for them . . . I don't know . . .
I took *my* happiness. I defied both religion and, to begin with,
convention, for Eddie. And have never I suppose regretted it –
through all the suffering. But here there are all sorts of difficulties
. . . Children. The children mustn't be made to suffer –'

'How not in this case,' Jenny said, 'how not? Oh,' she said,
exasperated, 'why can't people get it right in the first place?'

'Who are we to talk?'

'Some people have it right,' Jenny said lightly. 'Prime examples
of connubial bliss are darling Eleanor and her doctor. Late
seventies, both of them, and last heard of walking in the Dolo-
mites. It'll be skiing next . . .'

Then she said, 'If we're thinking about partnerships, aren't *we*
a funny, unlikely pair – starting out on new careers just a few
years before we claim our pensions?'

Maria said, 'Fred Emsley, at Reeves's farm, told me I had
good hands for lambing. Small and strong. How's that for a
compliment?'

'You think it's going to be all right?'

'Oh, I'm not worried about our making a success of it. I feel
sometimes as if . . . in my bones . . . Are they so very different

– purple hills and grey skies of Yorkshire, scorching Sicilian sun and barren mountains? Aren't the aims the same, to wrest a living from the soil? We have more in common than ever I realized.'

'Perhaps we should restore the silk mill here? We may do that yet . . . Unless one of us goes off and gets married.'

'I don't think of myself as *not* married. Even though it's over. The woman, that Baronessa Eddie lives with – she sounds to be very adoring, whatever he's up to on the side. They've been together nearly eight years now. I imagine he rather enjoys the Baronessa bit . . . And after all, though he's not so big in Italy any more, he's still a draw. I *think* he's happy.'

'You could still meet someone . . .'

'I don't think – for me. You see, I never wanted anyone but Eddie.'

Snow lay powdered on the flagstones of the yard. A slate-grey sky, heavy with it, lowered above the Rigg.

Jenny said, 'Did you know you sleepwalked again last night?'

'No.'

'If only I weren't so nervous . . . Noises. I think always – drunks, burglars, madmen . . . Ghosts even. But I came down and you were there in the kitchen. Just in your nightdress. You seemed to be searching. "Where's Dick?" you said, "where's Dick?" You sat down at the kitchen table. "O lovely princess, if you only knew what I have gone through to find you . . . Heart of stone," you said. "No, heart of gold . . ." Were you dreaming? It didn't seem to mean anything. Do you know what it meant?'

'Ah yes,' Maria said, 'I know. I know.'

Winston Graham

'One of the best half-dozen novelists in this country.' *Books and Bookmen*.

'Winston Graham excels in making his characters come vividly alive.' *Daily Mirror*.

'A born novelist.' *Sunday Times*.

The Poldark Saga, his famous story of eighteenth-century Cornwall

ROSS POLDARK
DEMELZA
JEREMY POLDARK
WARLEGGAN
THE BLACK MOON
THE FOUR SWANS
THE ANGRY TIDE
THE STRANGER FROM THE SEA
THE MILLER'S DANCE
THE LOVING CUP

His immensely popular suspense novels include

THE WALKING STICK
MARNIE
THE SLEEPING PARTNER

Historical novel

THE FORGOTTEN STORY

FONTANA PAPERBACKS

Susannah Kells

The superb, dramatic chronicles of the Lazender dynasty, set against a brilliant picture of England through the centuries. Susannah Kells is a major new British talent, writing in the great storytelling tradition of Daphne du Maurier.

A Crowning Mercy

Four intricately wrought seals – each owned by a stranger, each holding a secret within. These are Campion Slythe's key to the inheritance from her unknown father – her chance to escape from the worthy marriage which awaits her. But to claim her inheritance, and to find again the love she discovered on one golden summer afternoon, Campion must follow the course her father's legacy charts for her. And it is a road full of both peril and enchantment.

The Fallen Angels

Secure beneath the prosperous English sun, the 'little kingdom' of Lazen is unaware it is a house under siege. From the heart of Revolutionary France, the Fallen Angels - the most dangerous men in Europe – spin their web of intrigue, seeking the fall and the fortune of the Lazender family. Only the beautiful Lady Campion Lazender can save the great estate. But one man stands between Campion and disaster – Gitan, the mysterious gypsy – a man who could as easily be her enemy as her lover . . .

'Excellently done . . . Susannah Kells is a natural story-teller' *Catherine Gaskin*

FONTANA PAPERBACKS

Fontana Paperbacks: Fiction

Fontana is a leading paperback publisher of both non-fiction, popular and academic, and fiction. Below are some recent fiction titles.

- ☐ THE ROSE STONE Teresa Crane £2.95
- ☐ THE DANCING MEN Duncan Kyle £2.50
- ☐ AN EXCESS OF LOVE Cathy Cash Spellman £3.50
- ☐ THE ANVIL CHORUS Shane Stevens £2.95
- ☐ A SONG TWICE OVER Brenda Jagger £3.50
- ☐ SHELL GAME Douglas Terman £2.95
- ☐ FAMILY TRUTHS Syrell Leahy £2.95
- ☐ ROUGH JUSTICE Jerry Oster £2.50
- ☐ ANOTHER DOOR OPENS Lee Mackenzie £2.25
- ☐ THE MONEY STONES Ian St James £2.95
- ☐ THE BAD AND THE BEAUTIFUL Vera Cowie £2.95
- ☐ RAMAGE'S CHALLENGE Dudley Pope £2.95
- ☐ THE ROAD TO UNDERFALL Mike Jefferies £2.95

You can buy Fontana paperbacks at your local bookshop or newsagent. Or you can order them from Fontana Paperbacks, Cash Sales Department, Box 29, Douglas, Isle of Man. Please send a cheque, postal or money order (not currency) worth the purchase price plus 22p per book for postage (maximum postage required is £3.00 for orders within the UK).

NAME (Block letters) _____

ADDRESS _____

_____

_____

While every effort is made to keep prices low, it is sometimes necessary to increase them at short notice. Fontana Paperbacks reserve the right to show new retail prices on covers which may differ from those previously advertised in the text or elsewhere.